D1223559

Russia and China Their Diplomatic Relations to 1728

Harvard East Asian Series 61

The East Asian Research Center at Harvard University administers research projects designed to further scholarly understanding of China, Korea, Japan, and adjacent areas.

Russia and China Their Diplomatic Relations to 1728

by Mark Mancall

Harvard University Press Cambridge, Massachusetts, 1971

Distributed in Great Britain by Oxford University Press, London
Library of Congress Catalog Card Number 74-85077
SBN 674-78115-5
Printed in the United States of America

Preparation of this volume was aided by a grant from the Ford Foundation.

To my parents

And now what shall become of us without any barbarians?
Those people were a kind of solution.

—C. P. Cavafy

Foreword

The Sino-Soviet confrontation along the world's longest border is beyond the bounds of our observation but not of our concern. To understand the national aspirations of these two great peoples in Inner Asia today, and the strategic traditions of the two empires from which they have emerged, is an exacting task worthy of a whole team of scholars with a broad command of languages and of the disciplines necessary for the study of cultural, economic, and political interaction. As the triangular Sino-Soviet-American relationship develops, what could be more important for our future?

Mark Mancall, a one-man team, developed his linguistic skills and acquired his cultural insights in successive years spent as a graduate student in Helsinki (studying Mongolian documents), Taipei, Leningrad, and Tokyo. His gift for languages went along with his gift for finding friends in the local communities. His cultural insights were aided by a wide-ranging interest in the disciplines, particularly social anthropology and latter-day developments from it. The result was a multicultural capacity for the international life of modern scholarship such as many seek but few attain.

This volume focuses on the problem of Russian contact faced by the Manchu conquerors of China in the seventeenth and early eighteen centuries, a problem complicated by many factors: the Manchu dependence on their Mongol allies and therefore on control of Mongolia as well as of Manchuria, their long preoccupation with the subjugation of China, the arrival of Russian pioneers as border marauders, and the gradual Manchu recognition of the Russian empire as a potential rival in Inner Asia. The complexities of the story are not simplified by our general ignorance of them in the West. Today they lie in the substrata of China's national consciousness.

But the Chinese nation under Mao Tse-tung has now expanded to fill the confines of the old Ch'ing empire of the Manchus, and Mr. Mancall's analysis has both intrinsic and practical interest for us.

East Asian Research Center
November 1970

Acknowledgments

During and after my years of graduate study and research in the Department of History and Far Eastern Languages and at the East Asian Research Center, Harvard University, while this book was taking shape, I received constant kindness and endless encouragement from teachers and friends. Teachers extended me their friendship and friends their teaching, so much so that it is now difficult for me to distinguish between them.

John King Fairbank's counsel, wisdom, and imagination have had an incalculable influence on me, as they have on more than one generation of students of China both in the United States and abroad. The example of his exacting standards of excellence and the profundity of his friendship both as a teacher in the fullest sense of that word and as a human being place me in his debt in more ways than can find expression here.

Benjamin I. Schwartz and Richard Pipes, both of Harvard, and Raymond H. Fisher of the University of California read the manuscript rigorously, and I am indebted to them for numerous improvements. Dorothy Borg of Columbia University and Virginia Briggs at Harvard devoted themselves to assisting me over the rough spots. Harold L. Kahn of Stanford University and Maurice Meisner of the University of Wisconsin provided the humor and judgment to keep my work and myself in perspective. A special debt of gratitude is owed to the late John M. H. Lindbeck.

As a participant in the first year of the U.S.-U.S.S.R. student exchange program, I owe a special debt to Geronty Valentinovich Efimov and his colleagues in the Department of History of the Countries of the East (Kafedra Istory Stran Vostoka), Leningrad

University, for their comradeship in the search for knowledge and for the many lively hours spent in debate with them, during which disagreement was no bar to respect or affection. They will find much in this book with which to take issue, and that is as it should be. I also wish to remember my many friends and colleagues in what was then known as the Institute of Oriental Studies (Institut Vostokovedeniya) of the Academy of Sciences of the U.S.S.R., Leningrad. The dim light in the institute's library in no way diminished the glow of their friendship nor the brilliance of their scholarship.

Many individuals in Finland, Taiwan, and Japan facilitated my work. The specialists and keepers of the records at the Library of the University of Helsinki and the Library of the Suomalais-Ugrilainen Seura, at Academia Sinica in Taiwan, and at Tōyō Bunko in Tokyo, never stinted of their time or efforts on my behalf. At the latter institution I wish to mention particularly Chūzo Ichiko and Masataka Banno. A special note of affection and gratitude is owed to Jean and T. T. Tuan of Taipei, who raised Chinese studies for me from the academic to the human level.

I am grateful to Harcourt Brace Jovanovich and The Hogarth Press for permission to include as a motto a passage from "Expecting the Barbarians" in *The Complete Poems of Cavafy,* translated by Rae Dalven.

M. M.

Contents

Maps

Russia and China Their Diplomatic Relations to 1728

Introduction

The ideological component in international conflict is not new to the twentieth century. Historically, it was an important element in China's relations with the West, even as it is today. Europe and the Far East met territorially only along the frontier between Siberia and the Manchu Empire. Whereas other European states met China in their trading vessels, factories, and colonies, Russia and China shared an extensive common frontier, where they fought and traded much like any other nations in geographical proximity. But with a difference. Russia represented the Christian (albeit Orthodox) West, with its special view of the international order. Sovereigns were moral and legal equals, and commerce was by the middle of the seventeenth century a legitimate and even praiseworthy activity, which enriched the state and reflected an individual's moral character. China, however, represented the Confucian Far East, with its hierarchical view of the international order and its rejection of commerce as a socially esteemed activity. The Russian and Manchu empires had to develop institutions that would permit them to coexist despite the inadequacy of their shared assumptions.

In the nineteenth century the West, especially Great Britain, tried to resolve its ideological conflict with Peking by imposing on the Confucian bureaucracy, through force of superior arms, its own assumptions about interstate relations and economy.[1] The Opium Wars epitomized the fundamental conflict between Western concepts of free trade, the "rule of law," and individualism, and Confucian concepts of an imperially ordered, hierarchical society. In the 1840's certain Chinese bureaucrats realized that the Manchu Empire, to survive, would have to adopt some aspects of Western material civilization, particularly in the field of armaments. Later, Peking had to adopt Western institutions as well. For instance, after their disastrous defeat at the hands of the Anglo-French allies in 1860 the Ch'ing were forced to establish a primitive foreign office, the Tsungli Yamen, which translated a standard textbook on international law and began to use Western legal principles to defend the Ch'ing Empire against the West. Other elements in the West, such as the missionaries, favored and encouraged the process of change. Yet the Ch'ing court and the Confucian bureaucracy continued to fear that the forced opening of Chinese society would lead to the undermining of traditional institutions and the disintegration of traditional assumptions. The climax of this struggle was the Communist revolution, marking China's final acceptance of Western concepts of history and society while at the same time constituting a devastating criticism of the West, symbolic of China's rejection of Western institutional tutelage. In contrast, during the eighteenth century the Manchu and Russian empires had managed to postpone just such a break. They had achieved a modus vivendi by creating a treaty system that institutionally shunned the political and intellectual problems associated with their ideological conflict. The creation of that Sino-Russian treaty system is the subject of this study.

Much has been written about relations between Moscow and Peking after October 1, 1949, and even after November 7, 1917. But Sino-Russian relations were not born on either date. Russia and China had known of each other at least as early as the Mongol Empire, when their subjects met at Karakorum, then the world capital; and they have been in active bilateral contact ever since the early decades of the seventeenth century, when Russia's first diplomatic and commercial caravans wended their long and dangerous way to Peking. This book traces the development of Russia's diplomatic campaign to establish commercial relations with Peking from the middle of the 1600's to 1727, when the Sino-Russian treaty system took final form. It also traces the Manchu response to the Russian initiative. The Manchus, having fallen heir to Confucian tradition as they incorporated China into their empire, did not accept the Russian contention that international society was composed of discrete and legally equal states. They lived in another reality, in which international society was organized on different principles.

The Tribute System

The institutional expression of the Chinese view of the world order inherited by the Manchus is known as the "tribute system." Any attempt to describe this system encounters certain intellectual problems. First, it cannot be explained in terms of Western usage and practice. It would be misleading to look for modern Western equivalents of traditional Chinese institutions or concepts: they might resemble each other in structure or function, but they would have quite different significance when examined within the contexts of traditional Confucian and modern Western societies. The tribute system must rather be understood, in all its ramifications, in terms of the vocabulary and institutions of traditional China.

Second, the analyst must constantly bear in mind that the concept of the tribute system is a Western invention for descriptive purposes. The Confucian scholar-bureaucrat did not conceive of a "tribute system" as an institutional complex complete within itself or distinct from the other institutions of Confucian society. There is not even any word for the system in Chinese. Nor did he conceive of a peculiarly "Chinese" civilization. There were only civilization and barbarism, which were conceptually related in that they defined each other—what was not civilized was barbaric. Civilization was, to use Vadime Elisseeff's apt phrase, an empire without neighbors.[2] Thus, the Chinese state was not a state at all in the conventional meaning of the word, but rather the administration of civilized society *in toto*. The emperor, far from being the ruler of one state among many, was unique. He was the mediator between heaven and earth, the cardinal point in the universal continuum. In other words, the emperor was not a temporal political ruler but a figure of cosmic dimensions. In the annual fertility rite, for instance, he plowed the sacred furrow not so that Chinese crops could grow but so that crops per se could grow. The rituals he performed, or those performed about him, were not particular but universal.

The emperor was possessed of two distinct but related personalities. As a key point in the cosmos, he was the embodiment of virtue, whose task it was to carry out the rites required for the continuing harmony of the universe, in both its natural and its social aspects. This personality was identified by his title *t'ien-tzu,* "son of heaven," a son not in a biological but in a holistic sense. His second personality was that of a human being, the man at the apex of organized civilization. In this personality, styled *huang-ti* or "emperor," he could stray from the path of true virtue, betray his role as Son of Heaven, and cause disharmony in the universe. The first *huang-ti* had been the first emperor of the Ch'in dynasty.

Entrance into the Chinese world order was accomplished through correct observance of the ceremonies, forms, and practices appropriate to contact with the emperor in his personality as Son of Heaven.[3] During the Ming dynasty prior to 1644, tributary relations were supervised by the Board of Rites' Reception Department.[4] The Board of Rites itself was charged with the correct performance of Confucian rituals. Relations with certain tribes of aborigines along China's cultural frontiers (which were not necessarily coterminous with the area of the emperor's effective political or military power) were managed by a department of the Board of War. Although for purposes of description the Ming Statutes made a clear geographical distinction between, for instance, "northern barbarians" and others, it did not distinguish between them in the organization of its formal tributary mechanisms.

The Manchus modified and refined the Ming tributary system even before their conquest of China proper in 1644. An office was created to handle Manchu relations with the Mongols, probably before the official establishment of the Manchu Ch'ing dynasty at Mukden in 1636, and in 1638 this "Mongolian Office" became the Li-fan yuan, usually translated as the Mongolian Superintendency or the Court of Colonial Affairs, but perhaps more properly translated, in view of the exact meaning of the title and the nature of the institution, as the Barbarian Control Office. After the Manchu entrance into China in 1644 and the transfer of the dynastic capital to Peking, the Li-fan yuan became an integral part of the tribute system, using the rites and forms of the traditional Confucian Chinese system to conduct relations with the "barbarians." With the expansion of the Manchu dominions, the Li-fan yuan took over relations with Tibet and Sinkiang as well as with Mongolia.[5]

The Mongols were the Ch'ing dynasty's first allies and vassals. Like the Manchus, they were a frontier people, essentially peripheral to the center of East Asian civilization, whence they wished to draw luxury goods and political emoluments by raid or by trade. As an auxiliary military force, they participated in the Manchu conquest of China. The Mongols were Lamaists, looking toward Tibet as their spiritual center, not Confucians facing the emperor's throne. The Manchu alphabet derived from the Mongolian, and the Manchu language contained many borrowings from Mongolian as the result of long contact. Once the Manchus had conquered China, it was to their advantage to continue the Li-fan yuan, which had already served them well in their relations with the Mongols, as the instrument for handling their problems in Central Asia. Those problems, common to all continentally oriented dynasties in the North China plain, were control of the Central Asian peoples through techniques of divide-and-rule, and prevention of attacks along China's frontiers. Such problems did not confront the Manchus as directly along their other frontiers.

The existence during the Ch'ing of two tribute offices—the Board of Rites and the Li-fan yuan—which did not overlap in geographical responsibilities though they shared ritual procedures, is an indication that the Manchu image of the East Asian world differed from the earlier Ming. Under the Ming, the world had been divided into two distinct parts: China and non-China. In a conservative Confucian Chinese reaction to barbarian domination under the Mongol Yuan dynasty (1260-1368), the Ming had raised high and largely undifferentiated barriers between itself and the outside world, regardless of the nature of that world. The Ch'ing, however, lived in a perceptually more complex environment. The Manchus themselves came from an economy based originally on a mixture of hunting, fishing, and animal husbandry, technologically far different from the sedentary grain-growing economy of China. That the Manchus clearly recognized a difference between themselves and the Chinese was apparent throughout their dominion in China, during which strict regulations prohibited marriage to Chinese, and Manchus did not become peasants but remained rigidly within the structure of their own martial society. The court went so far as to attempt to preserve the difference by means of ritual hunts recalling the Manchus' original way of life.

Mongolia, Sinkiang, and Tibet, forming a crescent astride China's northern and western frontiers, shared certain fundamental characteristics. With the exception of parts of Sinkiang and certain Tibetan valleys, where there was a precarious, oasis-based agriculture, these regions were suited more to extensive nomadic animal-husbandry economies than to intensive agriculture. Where cities existed at all, as at Urga in Mongolia or Lhasa in Tibet, they were not based primarily on control of the agricultural hinterland, as in China, but on their particular religious and commercial functions, from which they derived their livelihood. Thus, the societies of the northwestern crescent more resembled the Manchu homeland in Manchuria than they did China proper. This resemblance was emphasized by Manchu prohibitions on Chinese emigration to any of these areas. None of these regions, including most of Manchuria before 1636, had accepted Confucianism and other aspects of Chinese culture as the organizing principles of their own societies.

The regions to the east, southeast, and south of China sharply differed from the northwestern crescent. Extending from Japan and Korea through Southeast Asia to Burma, they were presumed to be dominated, like China, by sedentary, grain-growing economies. They were thought to have adopted Confucian principles for the organization of government. They used the Chinese calendar and the Chinese language when addressing the emperor. Indeed, in Korea, Annam (Vietnam), and Liu-ch'iu they used Chinese even within their own governments. Their rulers were understood to be traditional Confucian monarch-vassals of the emperor of China. Japan, Korea, Liu-ch'iu, and Annam may at times have fit this supposed pattern fairly closely; and if Siam and Burma did not as agricultural economies, they nevertheless somewhat resembled China. All the organized states in the southeastern crescent thus shared with China similarities in environment, grain-producing technology, and intensive land-use and settlement.

As a result of the northeast-southwest regional differences, the world as viewed by the Manchu conquerors of China was also divided into two, but not along the China–non-China axis of the Ming. China proper, most of East Asia, and Southeast Asia appeared to belong to one ecological system; the northwestern crescent of societies, which exhibited different environmental characteristics, belonged to another. Beyond China and its two surrounding crescents lay wasteland, deserts, high mountains, impenetrable forests, or water—all of which contributed to the unity of East Asia and made it an almost closed "international" socio-economic system.

The organization of the tribute system reflected the Manchus' dual perception of their empire's environment. The societies of East and Southeast Asia were included within the jurisdiction of the Board of Rites, which was itself charged with the performance of the broad spectrum of rites transmitting Confucian culture inside China itself. Ritually, these regions were an extension of China proper beyond the immediately effective control of the emperor. The societies of the northwest crescent, however, were under the jurisdiction of a quite separate body, the Li-fan yuan, whose sole function was the conduct of intercourse between them and the Ch'ing.

This distinction was required for the maintenance of good relations between China and nomadic Asia, on the one hand, and between China and agricultural Asia, on the other. Economic similarity between communities may well give rise to disunion; that is, social cohesion depends on economically or ecologically necessary exchanges, not merely on the exchange of marginal luxuries. For instance, trade between China and Southeast Asia may have been economically convenient for Peking because transportation costs on Siamese rice brought to the China coast by sea were less than on rice transported to the coast from interior Chinese provinces. However, despite higher costs, rice was available in the interior of China, and the state could survive fairly well without the transportation of rice from Southeast Asia. In contrast, China and the societies of the northwest crescent were engaged in exchanges that were considered necessary for the stability of Chinese society. The imperial power in China required horses and other products of Central Asia's animal-husbandry economy that were not adequately produced in China. The Central Asians, for their part, needed Chinese tea, grain, and other products of China's sedentary agriculture and her cottage industry. The exchange was one of necessity more than convenience.

This, then, was the world into which the Russians wandered, both by chance and by design, during the seventeenth century. One cannot say simply that the tribute system was a reflection of Confucian ideas on the international scene. In fact, the tribute system per se did not exist except as a complex of many institutions interacting with one another. Had the particular nature of those institutions not resulted in important or unexpected increments, both physical and political, the system would have been changed or abandoned. It existed not because Confucianism dictated its existence but because it provided mechanisms for dealing with the universe on the basis of prior, detailed observation. This book concerns the development of a working compromise between the tribute system and the new ideas introduced in the traditional East Asian world by the Russians. When later the English, in the nineteenth century, were unprepared to effect such a compromise, worlds came into conflict, and China is still adjusting to her defeat.

Chapter I The First Sino-Russian Conflict

Yermak the Cossack raided into western Siberia between 1579 and 1584, captured Sibir, the capital of Kuchum, the Tatar khan, and formally opened Siberia to Russian exploration and settlement. Advancing quickly along the Ob, Enisei, Lena, and Amur river systems, Russians reached the Pacific Ocean at the Sea of Okhotsk in 1639. In just sixty years the basis had been laid for Russia's emergence as an Asian and Pacific power. Early in the eighteenth century Bering voyaged out into the North Pacific, discovered the strait that bears his name, sailed along the American coast, and began the fur trade in Alaska. Within a few years Russian trading posts and settlements had been established on Unalaska, Kodiak, and other Aleutian islands; by the middle of the century there were rumors in New Spain of Russian intentions to move southward into California.

Historians often compare the Russian advance across Siberia and the American Westward expansion, and indeed there are strong resemblances.[1] Russians and Americans both sought new sources of fur in the wilderness. Settlers followed the fur hunters, who themselves had often followed outlaws. Settlements were built as stockades, whose inhabitants warred with and subjugated the indigenous population, proselytized, colonized, and extended their political and cultural influence to the Pacific. But there was one important difference. America reached across the continent to the Pacific at a time when Spain's power in the South and Britain's power in the North were weak and waning. With the exception of Texas, Americans encountered comparatively little opposition to the fulfillment of their "manifest destiny." Russia, however, having arrived earlier on the North Pacific scene, encountered on both sides of that vast ocean virile and vital imperial powers, blocking her expansion southward along the coasts of the Pacific.

In East Asia the young and robust Ch'ing dynasty of the Manchus was conquering China at the very moment that the Russians entered the Amur River valley at their rear. The Russian confrontation with the Manchu outposts deflected Moscow's exploration and colonization activities to the North Pacific, the inhospitable Arctic, and eventually North America, where they came up against the northwestern reaches of the Spanish Empire in New Spain. The Portolá expedition and the Spanish occupation of Alta California in 1769 were a direct response to the threat of Russian incursions into that territory.[2] Thus, between the middle of the seventeenth and the eighteenth centuries, both the Manchus in East Asia and the Spanish in western America, finding Russia at their back doors, moved successfully to resist her further advances and contain her on the shores of the North Pacific. By 1867, with the American purchase of Alaska, Russia had retreated to continental Asia.

From the very beginning of Russia's advance into Asia, her power had been primarily continental rather than maritime and transoceanic. It thus confronted all along its Central and East Asian frontiers the only other significant power in the area, the Manchus' Ch'ing Empire. This empire was multinational and continentally oriented. In addition to the Manchu rulers, it included such diverse ethnic groups as Chinese, Mongols, and Tibetans, as well as numerous minorities. The Russians, in the course of their movement across Siberia (which in the seventeenth century was still a politically undifferentiated part of the Asian continent), came into contact with peoples who were themselves under Manchu suzerainty or were affiliated with tribes within the Manchu Empire. In their efforts to conquer or at the very least subdue and economically exploit these peoples, the Russians came into conflict with Manchu power in areas that the Manchus felt were a part of their own homeland. The earliest arena for Russo-Manchu confrontation was the Amur River valley. The appearance of the Russians there in the 1640's was a logical development in the rapid expansion of Russian power across northern Asia. It posed the problem of Russia's relation to the Ch'ing tribute system. The result was determined partly by the aims and methods of Russia's eastward expansion.

Russia's Siberian Expansion and Commercial Policies

Muscovite Russia expanded into world empire through the conquest of Siberia in search of fur. Previously significant in the commerce of Kiev and Novgorod, fur played a highly developed and sophisticated role in the Russian economy in the sixteenth, seventeenth, and eighteenth centuries. It was an important element in the annual state income, fluctuating between 3.75 percent of the state's revenue in 1589 to 11 percent in 1605 and 10 percent in 1644.[3] As long as new fur-bearing lands remained to be opened, the position of fur in Moscow's income retained its relative importance. But by the beginning of the eighteenth century Siberia's fur resources were becoming exhausted, and after Peter the Great developed new sources of state revenue to satisfy his quickly growing needs, fur fell to only 2 percent of the total state income, although throughout the eighteenth century fur continued to occupy a paramount position in the economy of the Siberian colony.

During the sixteenth and seventeenth centuries Moscow used fur for many purposes. Large quantities were sold on the domestic market or exchanged for necessary commodities and services by the state. Development of the Siberian fur trade depended primarily on exports, since most Russian furs were sent abroad to satisfy the increasing European and Asian demand for quality pelts. In the second half of the seventeenth century, however, competition from North American beavers and foxes lowered prices on the European market and resulted in a large accumulation of stock in Moscow, where the flow of fur from Siberia had continued unabated. The value of fur depreciated seriously. Increasing North American competition prevented the situation from correcting itself, so that Russia had by the end of the seventeenth century lost her dominant position on the European fur market. A solution to the problem of disposing of the growing stock of fur pelts was sought in trade with Asia, especially China.

Russia's export commerce by land with Asia was dominated by the state, in contrast to Russia's European trade, which was largely in the hands of private merchants. The state's attempts to monopolize the Asian trade was brought about not by the nature of the fur trade but rather by the importation of silk. During the late sixteenth and early seventeenth centuries silk was perhaps the most important single Asian export to Europe. Russia, astride Asia's land frontiers, was in a particularly favorable position to participate in the silk trade. The tsars sought profit through the creation of a Russian state monopoly on silk, which in turn required a monopoly on those items exported in exchange for silk, primarily sables and other expensive Siberian furs. The monopoly on exports to Asia did not derive from any particular set of decrees, nor did it totally exclude private participation in the Asian trade. In fact, at the end of the seventeenth century, when Russo-Asian trade had reached its highest development, the state monopolized only certain specific kinds of fur.[4]

Monopoly was already a feature of Russian commerce by the sixteenth century. Foreign merchants traveling to Moscow for trade were not allowed to conduct business en route. State officials required that merchants arriving in Moscow present themselves first at the treasury, where the goods the state desired to purchase were chosen and payment made in money or other goods, usually fur. Only then could the merchants trade on the open market. The same procedure was employed for foreign merchants going to trade in towns other than Moscow. In this fashion the state retained for itself the right of first choice of foreign goods. In the course of the seventeenth century further restrictions were added in order to limit contact between Russian and Asian merchants.[5]

Moscow often dispatched caravans with pelts and other commodities to Asia, particularly to Persia, Khiva, and Bukhara. During the sixteenth century private merchants were strictly forbidden to participate in this caravan trade, but in the seventeenth century a few privileged Russian merchants were allowed to accompany the state caravans, provided that they did not deal in forbidden or restricted goods. Only the "treasury merchants" were exempted from this rule, in payment for their commercial services to the state. Restrictions on the private export of furs to the rest of Asia from Siberia were much greater than those on private exports to Europe from Russia itself. Sables and black foxes, which commanded the best markets and highest exchange values, were almost completely monopolized by the state. At the same time, Persian, Turkish, Greek, Bukharan, and Indian merchants all participated in Russia's commerce with Asia; some even settled inside the empire itself. For instance, a specially privileged group appeared in Siberia, generically known as "Bukharans." Despite their group appellation, they appear to have come from many places besides Bukhara, forming "a sort of free masonry of Central Asian merchants" who traded as far south as India and as far east as China, as well as among the various Siberian cities and settlements. Some maintained their headquarters and residences in Tobolsk.[6]

While the most important function of the fur supply was its use by the state treasury in international and domestic trade for the benefit of the tsar's court, it also played vital roles in other aspects of Moscow's economy. Government agencies used pelts to obtain necessary commodities or to pay the expenses of their emissaries both at home and abroad. Fur was used as a medium of exchange because the Russian economy did not yet produce sufficient quantities of gold and silver to support a monetary system. Fur also played an important role in diplomacy: pelts were often sent as gifts to foreign rulers and dignitaries or used as subsidies in international politics.

The continuing importance of fur in the Russian economy, together with the progressive depletion of fur resources through predatory hunting techniques, led Russians into the unexplored lands to the east in search of new supplies. Russian expansion through Siberia, like the earlier spread of settlement in European Russia itself, usually followed river systems. Political and commercial power came from the control of key points on or between the various rivers, and certain well-defined steps were repeated over and over until the Russians finally reached the Amur and the outposts of the Manchu Empire.

The first step was to bring a river system under the political and commercial control of a population center by military conquest or, in previously unexplored regions, through exploration by bands of men in search of fur. In the second step military control of a riverine system was strengthened by the construction of blockhouses or "ostrogs" at strategic points, usually at the portage between one river and the next. The ostrogs provided a means of controlling transportation and commerce along the rivers: through domination of portages one could facilitate or hinder the trade that was so vital to the Russian cities and settlements. The ostrogs also provided a base for defense, since attackers were often forced to pass through the portages.

The establishment of ostrogs and other settlements led to a third step in the process of colonial expansion: officials and merchants fanned out into the surrounding countryside, subjugating and exploiting the indigenous population. The expansion cycle then repeated itself as expeditions set out from the ostrogs into still more distant and unexplored territories, which were brought under control through the same process. The Ob, Enisei, and Lena river systems were all conquered in this fashion, one after another.

The successful exploitation of Siberia required a government that could satisfy two essential requirements. First, it had to control the population, both Russian and native; second, it had to protect the interests of the state, which were paramount in the Siberian fur trade. The structure of Siberia's civil and military administration developed out of the way in which the land was opened.[7] The groups of men who ventured into new territories were quasi-military in organization. They were led by an official known as a *voevoda,* who commanded the troops, supervised the construction and defense of the new towns and blockhouses, and administered both civil and military affairs. The voevoda's power derived from his role as commandant in the centers of population that served as foci for the collection of tribute furs, as markets for the fur trade, and as bases for further expansion. The perquisites of office and the opportunity for corruption in remote Siberia, particularly in the fur trade, made the voevoda's position much sought after. Appointment was for a specific period of years, rarely renewed. As civil officials, the voevodas were aided by a staff of clerks and assistants organized on the principle that wide authority was not to be conferred on any single man. As the chief military officer on the local scene, the voevoda was served by "boyar sons," men of the petty nobility, who were often appointed to command the smaller blockhouses and special winter quarters. Cossacks were the most important and numerous group in the colony's military organization. They were divided into two groups. One, the military Cossacks, were on active service and received a salary. The other, the village Cossacks, were agricultural, free-holding colonists who received the use of land, exempt from taxes, in lieu of salary.

The voevodas, together with their assistants, were also the chief financial officials in Siberia. As Moscow's business managers in the colony, they were charged with watching over and increasing the sovereign's profits. The financial administration included a group of officials recruited from the local petty merchant class and called "tselovalniks," or sworn men who had kissed the cross and Bible while taking the oath of office. The tselovalniks, who received no salary, participated in the collection of taxes and duties, the distillation of alcoholic beverages, and the management of public houses. Whereas most of the customs collectors were chosen from the Siberian communities, the customs heads were drawn from Russian towns north of Moscow. They occupied an especially important position in Siberia, since the customs houses, located on the frontier between Siberia and Russia, Siberia and China, and at various places within Siberia itself, were a major source of state income. The voevodas were not unnaturally jealous of the power of the customs heads, inasmuch as the customs provided a lucrative source of income. A system of checks and balances was meant to ensure that neither the customs heads nor the voevodas took too great an advantage of their position as collectors of the state's income.

The state took many other measures to control and benefit from the financial administration of Siberia. It specified routes for the transport of merchants and merchandise and created an elaborate passport system, which registered a merchant's goods as well as his person. The state collected as customs 10 percent of the value of all private goods placed on the market and severely punished the sale of private goods in unauthorized places. To further increase its control over the private sector of the economy, the state built a special *gostinny dvor* or merchants' compound in every major town; the merchants were required to transact their business there or in the town market place under official supervision. The state also had monopolies over such things as rhubarb, tobacco, salt, and alcoholic beverages.

The state's Siberian fur trade was managed by whichever agency controlled Siberian affairs at the moment. Originally under the direction of the Department of Ambassadors (Posolsky prikaz), Siberia by 1637 had come under a special department created to meet its needs, the Siberian Department (Sibirsky prikaz). This department appointed the voevodas and was responsible for the fur trade.

The state utilized three basic methods to obtain the pelts it needed; *yasak* (tribute) from the Siberian natives; a tithe imposed on the private Russian merchants and traders in Siberia; and purchase on the open market under highly circumscribed conditions. The word *yasak* was Old-Turkish in origin. It had several meanings, but in Siberia in the late sixteenth and early seventeenth centuries it signified the compulsory tax imposed on the natives by the Russian government, as opposed to "voluntary gifts," which were known as *pominki*.[8] Traditionally yasak had been a tribute paid to a victor by the vanquished, and it continued to have this significance in the relations between the Russians and the conquered Siberian natives. As an institution, yasak had been found before the Siberian conquest among the Ostyaks, Buryats, Kirghiz, and Tungus tribes. A similar institution, the *dan,* had also been in use in Kiev, Novgorod, and Moscow. With certain modifications, therefore, the use of tribute as a means of acquiring furs and subjugating natives was not a new experience in either Siberia or Russia.

The yasak paid by the natives to the Russian state was almost always in the form of fur, chiefly sables, though cheaper furs, and occasionally entirely different commodities, were accepted. The collection of the yasak was the voevoda's chief responsibility. Either by military force or by promising protection against their enemies, he induced the natives to agree to pay the yasak to the state at stipulated intervals. Payment was assured by the detention of hostages in the Russian blockhouses. The natives either brought their yasak to the towns or blockhouses themselves, or the voevodas sent out collectors to the native areas. The rate of payment was often fixed at so many pelts per head of population, with certain exceptions, such as the aged and children. The collection of yasak tended to be well organized and regular when the Russians were dealing with settled tribes, irregular when dealing with nomads. At times it was even necessary for the Russians to offer gifts (*podarki*) to the natives to encourage them to bring the yasak to the state. Throughout this period the Moscow government, aware that the yasak was one of its chief sources of fur income, took measures to ensure the protection and well-being of the indigenous population. If the people were too deeply disturbed, they would be unable to deliver the yasak. Forced baptism, mistreatment by local officials, and excessive demands on the natives' resources were all discountenanced in Moscow's policy of preserving the stability of native society.

The participation of private enterprise in the exploitation of the fur wealth of Siberia forced the state to develop institutions whereby it could secure for itself the best pelts exported by private trappers and merchants. A tax or tithe resulted.[9] The state took one-tenth of all the furs that private individuals of whatever rank brought out of the forests. The tithe was collected in the form of every tenth pelt from each kind of fur-bearing animal. It was originally collected by the voevodas and their assistants, but the opportunities for corruption were so great that eventually the customs heads and tselovalniks took over the task. Although the voevodas did not participate directly in the new system, they served as checks upon the honesty of the customs officials through their regular examination of customs receipts and collected furs. The tithe was collected in various places, eventually including Nerchinsk.

Although the yasak and the tithe accounted for most of the pelts acquired by the state, a third major and several minor methods existed whereby the state tried to secure its control over the fur resources. The purchase method was the major one applied to both private Russians and Siberian natives. Representatives of the state purchased furs from "serving men" who had acquired them as gifts, through permitted hunting, or as extraordinary exactions from natives during yasak collection expeditions. In addition, fur might be confiscated under certain circumstances or used as payment for state-manufactured alcoholic beverages in the state-owned liquor stores. All the pelts, by whatever means collected, were sent annually to the Siberian Department in Moscow after appriasal at local Siberian prices. The difference between the local appraised price and the appraisal in Moscow at Moscow prices represented, according to the contemporary accounting system, the profits that accrued to the state if the furs were sold on the market (transportation costs do not appear to have figured in the establishment of a "price"). The profit averaged around 20 percent, though at times it may have reached as high as 100 percent, or occasionally even 500 percent.[10]

Many of the institutions of Moscow's Siberian, and even its European, economy were of a redistributive character; that is, they functioned to collect and dispose of products on the basis of principles other than those of a market economy. This was particularly true of the mechanisms used for the collection and disposition of fur. The yasak and the tithe were both functionally redistributive because the choice of furs was essentially the state's. The purchase method was also re-distributional, rather than functioning as a market-price mechanism, since the state set the prices at which the furs were purchased, chose them itself, and then disposed of them through channels other than Siberia's officialdom. The entire Siberian economy was considered the tsar's private property, and the tithe and purchase systems were mechanisms for licensing participants in that economy.

Despite the rapid growth of Moscow's fur trade, the state's fiscal policy in the time of crisis during the late sixteenth and early seventeenth centuries handicapped the growth of general commerce by restricting trade activities to certain localities in order to facilitate the collection of taxes on commercial transactions. Stratification among burghers in the second half of the sixteenth century also slowed the development of commerce. Although the state's commercial and tax representatives received no remuneration for their services, they were exempt from taxes, and under the existing taxation system their share devolved upon less well-to-do burghers. The position of burghers engaged in local commerce was further aggravated by the influx into the cities of tax-exempt groups who competed advantageously with them. The hard-pressed burghers often left the cities, state income declined as the desertion of taxpayers grew, and the burden of the remaining urban taxpayers grew ever heavier as they were forced to make good the payments of those who had fled. The clamor for relief grew louder, until the need for a solution finally found expression in the code of 1649, which forbade changes of residence and gave townspeople a monopoly on industrial and commercial occupations.

The New Commercial Statute (Novotorgovy ustav) of 1667 sought to provide relief for merchants engaged in foreign trade. By the middle of the seventeenth century Moscow had not yet developed a strict system for the regulation of commercial intercourse with foreigners, such as characterized the economies of Kiev and Novgorod. Dutchmen, Swedes, Germans, and Englishmen had their own commercial premises and organizations in major Russian towns; in Moscow they occupied a whole suburb. Russian merchants, however, severely complained against the role of foreigners in internal commerce and presented a series of petitions requesting the interdiction of foreign competition on the internal market.

The New Commercial Statute, which was an answer to these petitions, reflected the transition from a primarily redistributional, import-centered economy to export-centered, mercantilist, and particularly bullionist economic concepts. Its monetary policies directly influenced the growth of Manchu-Russian trade. The statute sought to protect the Russian merchant class by liquidating the privileges of foreign merchants, who were permitted to trade only at ports and frontier cities. All goods imported or exported by foreigners were subjected to a 5 percent duty on weighable goods and 4 percent on all others. Foreigners were permitted to trade in internal Russian cities on the payment of a 6 percent sales tax and a 10 percent transport duty. Since these duties did not apply to Russian merchants, they were an effective blow at foreign commercial activities inside the country. The middleman role was secured for Russian merchants by forbidding foreigners to engage in retail trade with Russians. Foreigners were also forbidden to trade among each other. Any infraction of these regulations resulted in the confiscation of all the offending merchant's goods in favor of the tsar.[11]

While many of these measures appeared to conform to the characteristics of a redistributional economy, other important provisions of the New Commercial Statute were strictly mercantilist, seeking to increase the inflow of precious metals and inhibit the export of coinage. Foreigners had to pay duties in alberthalers, and purchases made inside Russia were duty-free if payment was made in gold or alberthalers. Other efforts were made to improve Russia's bullion position by diminishing the import of luxury items. Foreign wines, for instance, paid extremely high duties. The state's bullionist policies were strongly reflected in the various ambassadors' instructions concerning trade with China, in which they were repeatedly urged to bring back gold, silver, and precious stones.

The Thrust into Amuria

In 1628 the Russians invaded the territory inhabited by the Buryats, a Mongol people living west of Lake Baikal. A series of expeditions established blockhouses and collected yasak from the natives, while other expeditions were drawn further into eastern Siberia, beyond the lake, by rumors of fur, gold, and silver. Fur was in fact quite plentiful in eastern Siberia, and gold and silver could be had from Mongolia in exchange for pelts, but climatically the area was inhospitable, and the Russians were sorely pressed for food.

The colonists received their first definite information about Amuria (the Amur watershed) after the establishment of Yakutsk in 1632. Using the new settlement as a base of operations, hunters followed the Lena River to its mountainous source and at the same time discovered the Shilka and the Zeya, two streams lying beyond the mountains and outside the Lena River system. On the banks of these rivers they met natives who told of fertile grain fields along the Amur to the south. Maxim Perofiliev, an early expedition leader, made one of the first such reports to Yakutsk in 1641. He had met a Tungus, a member of an eastern Siberian mongoloid people related to the Manchus, who had visited the country of the Amur, observed its population, and noted its agricultural and mineral resources.[12] The voevoda of Yakutsk dispatched twenty men to check the information. Arriving that same year on the Angara River, they collected more information among the Tungus and purchased articles of silver as well as blue paint, all of which, according to the Tungus, came from the Amur. A year later one Ivan Moskvitin claimed that while voyaging down the Uda River to the Pacific, he met a Tungus who reported grain fields along the Shilka River. The Yakuts, a Turkish tribe in northeastern Siberia, obtained similar information from travelers to and from the Amur region, which they reported to the Russians. But no one reported that the inhabitants of this distant, unknown region had already been drawn within the power penumbra of the Manchu international order in East Asia.

The first attempt to collect direct information about the rumored riches of the Amur was made in 1643. Enalei Bakhteyarov, a secretary, was appointed leader of an expedition of seventy men, who were to follow the Aldan or the Olekma rivers to check on the grain field rumors. Bakhteyarov proved to be incompetent, however, and the expedition came to nought.[13]

The voevoda of Yakutsk, Peter Golovin, determined to explore the matter further, since Yakutsk was in perpetual need of outside grain supplies. He appointed Vasily Poyarkov leader of a new expedition.[14] Little is known of Poyarkov except that he was literate and militarily skillful. The choice of a literate man to lead the expedition testifies to the seriousness with which Golovin regarded the affair. Men who could read and write were few and far between in seventeenth-century Siberia, but if the Amur proved as rich as rumors had it, the voevoda would require written reports. Poyarkov's expedition included 112 cossacks, 15 hunters, two tselovalniks, two interpreters, a guide, and a blacksmith. Guns were provided for each man, and a cannon with ammunition was taken along as added protection against hostile nations. According to Poyarkov's instructions, he was to proceed up the Lena, the Aldan, and one of its branches, whence he would cross the mountains to the source of the Zeya and sail down it to the Shilka.

The tselovalniks were included in the party because on the way he was to demand tribute from the natives, in small quantities so as not to alienate them, but sufficient to pay the expenses of the expedition. He was also to inquire into the relations between the natives and China, determining whether and for what purpose Chinese officials visited the region.

Poyarkov's expedition left Yakutsk on June 15, 1643. The journey up the Aldan was particularly arduous, and when by the first of November ice began to form in the river, he had not yet reached its headwaters. Winter quarters were built, at which forty-three men together with the heavier supplies were left. Poyarkov himself led the rest of his group across the mountains, reaching the Brynda, a tributary of the Zeya, by the end of November. Making camp on the Umlekan about December 13, Poyarkov learned from the local populace that buckwheat, oats, millet, peas, and hemp grew along the Shilka, but that copper, silver, lead and blue paint were obtained from China through trade. Since food was not abundant near the camp, the Russians foraged to survive, which brought on their first open conflict with the local population. A group of some seventy men attacked a nearby village, captured two natives, and tried to force entry into the village itself. They were repulsed and fled under cover of night. Poyarkov, perhaps because rations were so short, did not permit all of the attackers to return to camp, and those left outside were forced to live by foraging and, eventually, consuming captured natives or Russians who had died of starvation or been killed by Poyarkov. Poyarkov's behavior, both then and later, set the tone for the future relationship between the Amur natives and the Russians—a relationship that eventually favored Manchu policy in the region.

With the arrival of spring Poyarkov was joined by the men he had left on the other side of the mountains, and the reunited group sailed down the Zeya. News of Poyarkov and his band must have traveled downstream ahead of the expedition, because the natives continued to impede the group's progress. On one occasion a party of twenty-seven Russians was attacked, of which only two survived. The entire expedition wintered in 1644-1645 at the mouth of the Amur, where the Russians captured three

Giliak hostages to ensure native deliveries of supplies and tribute. In the spring of 1645 ships were built and the expedition proceeded north along the shores of the Sea of Okhotsk to the mouth of the Ulya River, where they wintered in 1645-1646. They returned to Yakutsk overland on June 22, 1646, just three years after their departure.

The Poyarkov expedition was significant in several respects. First, it provided the first Russian eye-witness information about the Amur and its resources. Second, it alienated the local inhabitants along the Amur and warned the Manchus of the Russian approach, enabling the Manchus to take steps to stop the barbarian invasion. Third, the expedition demonstrated that the Aldan-Zeya route was not suitable for mass Russian immigration to, or grain transportation from, the Amur region. If the resources of the area were to be exploited, the problem of geographical access had to be solved. In 1647 a hunter who had camped on the Tugir, a branch of the Olekma, visited Yakutsk and described a route that might prove more convenient than the Aldan-Zeya system. A quick exploratory probe proved him correct, and the new route along the Olekma became Yakutsk's major road of access to the Amur.[15]

The second important attempt to conquer the Amur was made by Erofei Pavlovich Khabarov.[16] Khabarov, like Yermak, was one of those remarkable men who stand out in the history of the Siberian conquest more for their audacity than for their culture. On March 6, 1649, he petitioned the new Yakutsk voevoda, Frantsbekov, for permission to raise at his own expense 150 volunteers to collect tribute along the Amur. The petition itself was probably a mere formality, for within a month the group was on its way. Following the Olekma route, Khabarov reached the Amur with little difficulty. The country through which he passed was depopulated, undoubtedly as a result of former Russian depredations and the fear of new ones. At one point the Russians met three mounted warriors, who conversed with them from a distance. Khabarov followed the warriors for about three days, passing through deserted villages. In one he found an old woman, who gave him false information.

Khabarov's report, made on his return to Yakutsk on May 26, 1650, underscored the value of the Amur and the role it could play in eastern Siberia's economy. He claimed that grain had been found in large pits in the deserted villages, which testified to the agricultural potential of Amuria. He concluded that only two weeks would be required to transport sufficient grain to Yakutsk to satisfy its annual hunger, and that only six thousand men would be needed to conquer the Amur basin.

By the summer of 1650 Khabarov had equipped a new expedition and returned to the Amur. At the Daur village of Albazin a group of natives gave him battle until forced to flee by the power of the Russian firearms. Khabarov pursued the fugitives and captured 117 head of cattle. The Russians now fortified Albazin and left it in charge of a small garrison, while Khabarov, with the majority of his party, started on November 24 to pursue the natives. Ten days later he fought another battle and won, thanks to the superiority of his modern weapons over the bows and arrows of the local inhabitants. In his report for the year Khabarov once again valued the Amur highly, claiming that at Albazin alone there was sufficient grain in storage to supply Yakutsk for five years; enough could be extracted from the natives to feed twenty-thousand men or more.

After wintering at Albazin, Khabarov started out again on June 2, 1651, with over two hundred men and three cannon. In order to increase his mobility and thus acquire an added advantage over the natives, he built light boats for advance parties and heavier boats for his main force, the cannon, and the horses. For four days the expedition passed through destroyed or deserted settlements, until at sunset of the fourth day they reached a village named Guigudar. Here, evidently for the first time, Khabarov encountered several Manchus, who refused to fight, claiming that they were under strict orders to avoid conflict with the Russians. Khabarov's account of his victory in the ensuing battle with the rest of the natives is exulting: "With God's help . . . we cut them all down, head by head . . . big and little we killed six hundred and sixty-one."[17]

Khabarov remained at Guigudar for six or seven weeks, sending throughout the countryside a demand for tribute and promising destruction if it were not forthcoming. His men reported a deserted country; those few natives who fell into Russian hands claimed that they had just paid tribute to the Manchus and could not afford to pay it a second time. Russian plans to winter at the mouth of the Zeya were thus dealt a severe blow. On September 7, Khabarov boarded his boats and sailed out of the country of the pastoral Duchers and Dahurs, who were vassals of the Manchus, past the mouth of the Sungari River, and into the country of the Achans, a fishing tribe, where he wintered at a site not far from the modern city bearing his name, Khabarovsk. Although the Achans at first appeared friendly, a combined Achan-Ducher force numbering between eight hundred and one thousand men attacked the Russians on the night of October 8. Superior arms gave the Russians the victory. But repeated successes in their conflicts with the natives must have lulled the invaders into a sense of security, for the arrival of a Manchu army took the Cossacks completely unawares.

As a result of Khabarov's 1650 and 1651 campaigns, the Dahurs and the Duchers had dispatched requests to the Manchus either for protection or, failing that, permission to accept Russian suzerainty. These petitions were forwarded to Peking, where orders were given that an army be sent to find Khabarov and drive him from the Amur. The leader of the Manchu expedition was Hai-se, general of the Ninguta garrison in Manchuria. The Manchu forces moved against the Russians at Wu-cha-la (Achansk) in the spring of 1652.[18] The Manchus apparently understood neither the nature of their enemy nor the fact that the campaign was not simply a raid on their territory but the forerunner of a concerted Russian colonization attempt. Just as their bombardment of the Cossack encampment was succeeding, Hai-se ordered his troops not to kill the Cossacks but to try to take them alive. No army can be forbidden to return the fire of its opponents and still keep the field. In the path of their retreat the Manchus left behind seventeen muskets, two cannon, eight flags, 830 horses, and a large quantity of provisions. Khabarov himself reported that his men had killed 676 Manchus; he lost only ten Cossacks killed and seventy-eight wounded, although his figures were perhaps exaggerated.

The battle at Wu-cha-la was only the first step in the development of a Manchu military response to Russian incursions into the Amur River basin. The initiation of an active Manchu policy materially changed the situation in Amuria, forcing the Russians to develop new tactics and concentrate on a concerted approach to actual settlement. Reports to voevodas began to state that the presence of Manchu troops in a given region prevented the Cossacks from venturing far into hostile territory. The effects of the withdrawal of the Manchu forces before achieving victory were mitigated, it would seem, by the restrictions that the new situation placed on Cossack movements.

Khabarov's victory by default over the Manchus was the last important achievement of his career on the Amur River. On April 22 he left his winter camp to sail up the river. On the way he met a group of 117 Cossacks, who were supplied with lead, powder, cannon, and other necessities that had been dispatched to Khabarov from Yakutsk the year before. Khabarov, however, had lost not only his spirit but his control over his men, for on August 1, 136 members of his band mutinied, deserted, and took a considerable amount of the plunder and tribute collected during their sojourn on the Amur. With his force reduced to 212 men, Khabarov was unable to make the deserters return to the fold. At the end of the summer of 1653 Dmitry Ivanovich Zinoviev, a Moscow official, arrived in the Amur basin with reinforcements, supplies, and pay for the members of Khabarov's Cossack group, which by then had grown to 320. Zinoviev took Khabarov back to Moscow, having appointed Onufry Stepanov in his place.[19]

Khabarov's career on the Amur in many ways recapitulated the earlier history of the conquest of Siberia. Essentially it was a raid sent out for the collection of tribute and plunder, of the kind upon which the Russian administration of Siberia thrived and for which it had been established. Khabarov's departure marked the end of the period of raids on the Amur and the beginning of a period of attempts at permanent settlement, based on the realization that only thus would the Amur be incorporated into Russia's territories. But the situation in Amuria in the forties and fifties of the seventeenth century was significantly different from the situation in Siberia fifty or sixty years earlier. The defeat of the khanate of Sibir between 1579 and 1584 had eliminated any element capable of opposing the spread of Russian power from the Urals to the Pacific Coast of northeastern Siberia. In the Amur

Valley the situation was more complex. To the south of the river was the Manchu Empire, just reaching the height of its power, whose domains included, even if only nominally, those areas occupied by the natives of the Amur basin. The tactics employed by Poyarkov and Khabarov, which had earlier worked so well in Siberia, could only rouse the Manchus to further action to protect their subjects and their interests.

The Cossack band was at the mouth of the Zeya when control passed from Khabarov to Stepanov. Food was scarce because the Manchus had instructed the Dahurs to abandon their fields and move to the valley of the Sungari River. Stepanov was forced to sail back down the Amur into the lands of the Duchers. Here he wintered, obtaining grain from the natives. In the spring of 1654 he returned upstream to the Sungari's mouth, where a party of 50 Cossacks increased the size of his band to 370 men.[20]

Stepanov's actions once again led to direct conflict with the Manchus. On May 20, 1654, he entered the Sungari River and sailed upstream three days. A Manchu force in the area, under the command of Ming-an-ta-li, soundly defeated the Cossacks and forced them to retreat.[21] Although on returning to the Amur, Stepanov's forces were further augmented by more than thirty men from the Baikal region, he had lost confidence. He abandoned his plans to build permanent blockhouses on the Zeya and, under pressure to find winter quarters, built a blockhouse called Kumarsk on a bluff overlooking the Kumar River, making great efforts to secure the site from Manchu attack. The Manchus, who had been slowly following the Cossacks, came upon Kumarsk on March 13, 1655, and laid siege to it until April 4, without forcing its surrender. As a result of their policy of removing natives from an area infested with Russians, the Manchus' own food supplies began to run short, and after destroying the Russians' boats along the river outside the fort, they withdrew. Once more the Russians were encouraged by a victory by default over the Manchus, and toward the end of the summer Stepanov again descended the Amur and sailed up the Sungari, where he wintered among the Giliaks, living off the grain he had gathered during the autumn.

The Manchus now made further preparations to push the

Russians from the Amur. In order to starve out the enemy, Peking ordered the Duchers who lived at the mouth of the Sungari, a tributary of the Amur, to burn their homes and move to the streams of the interior, out of reach of the Cossacks. The departure of these grain-growing natives increased the difficulties encountered by Stepanov's Cossacks in the collection of grain and provisions: they were soon forced to confine their operations to the lower Sungari, where they supported themselves by fishing and plundering. The increase in the number of Siberian outlaws who controlled the upper reaches of the rivers and preyed on Russians as well as on natives also forced Stepanov during 1656-57 to stay on the lower reaches of the waterways.[22]

Peking's preparations for the struggle continued apace, and on June 30, 1658, a conflict took place on the Amur just below the mouth of the Sungari. The Manchu victory was apparently due largely to their use of water forces and the evacuation of the natives, which increased the supply difficulties of the Russians at Kumarsk. Forced to descend the Sungari in search of food in the spring, the Cossacks met a Manchu fleet of 45 to 47 boats on June 30, which surrounded them. Stepanov and 270 of his men disappeared in the battle; of the 222 who escaped, 180 finally deserted to roving outlaw bands. The outlaws lived in the vicinity of the Zeya, collecting tribute from the Tungus villages, until they were almost wiped out by the Manchus in 1660.[23]

The Manchu victory of 1658 cleared the Amur of official Cossack bands as far as Nerchinsk. This defeat, combined with the permanent shortage of men and supplies in Siberia, forced the Russian government to halt its penetration of the area. Further Russian incursions were undertaken not by officials but by outlaws, who refused to accept the dictates of Moscow's government or were escaping Moscow's laws. Official Russian activities were limited to the three blockhouses of Nerchinsk, Irgen, and Telenge. Nerchinsk, the most important of the three, had been founded in 1653 by Afanasy Pashkov, the first voevoda in the region. His instructions to Stepanov to return to Nerchinsk had not been delivered in time to avoid the catastrophe of defeat.

Sarhuda, the commanding general at Ninguta who had won the victory over Stepanov, died in 1659, to be succeeded by his son Bahai, who was placed in command of the Ch'ing forces in the area of contact with the Russians. In 1660 Bahai won a victory over some Cossack outlaw bands in the neighborhood of Ku-fa-t'an village. The Manchus killed more than sixty men, in addition to those who drowned in the river, and captured forty-seven women, as well as firearms, shields, and armor. As a result of this engagement, with its demonstration of Manchu power, many of the Cossack outlaws on the Amur returned to Yakutsk or to the new colony at Nerchinsk. By not pursuing them to Nerchinsk, the Manchus left their Russian problem unresolved.[24]

Nerchinsk also had its difficulties. Early in 1664 thirty-six men in the three ostrogs deserted, and the forty who remained were besieged by Mongols. Under these favorable circumstances local Tungus tribes approached the settlements and stole the Russians' horses. At the same time, while the Russians were restricted to the Nerchinsk region, the Manchus expanded their activities along the lower reaches of the Amur. According to Russian reports, on one occasion nine "Chinese" junks traveled as far north as the Tugursk Gulf in the Sea of Okhotsk to spy on Russian activities, and more than seventy boats were rumored to be stationed at the mouth of the Amur.[25]

The Russians were at first reluctant to return to the area from which they had been expelled, and their inactivity in Amuria encouraged the Manchus to sink back into inaction. Thus, a favorable situation was created for the return of the Russians in greater force with ideas of a more permanent settlement. By the end of 1664, 124 Russians lived in the neighborhood of Nerchinsk, and the number grew with each passing year. The influx of outlaws further strengthened the Russian hand. The most significant outlaw group was established in Albazin by Nikifor Chernigovsky. In the early sixties, or perhaps as late as 1665, Chernigovsky, a Polish exile in Siberia, and some Cossacks from the Ilimsk area killed their voevoda. It was rumored that the voevoda had taken a fancy to the wife (or sister) of Chernigovsky, who had committed this crime in revenge. To avoid punishment, the Pole crossed the mountains to the basin of the Amur. With eighty-four men he reached Albazin, the former capital of Albazi, a native prince tributary to Peking. There they built an ostrog, which soon had a population of three-hundred.[26]

Albazin was built in the form of a square: each side was 120 paces long, with one side facing the Amur. The settlement prospered as a gathering place for Russian adventurers and outlaws. Chernigovsky, undoubtedly a capable leader, dispatched successive expeditions to rebuild ostrogs that had been destroyed in previous battles with the Manchus, as well as to collect yasak from the natives. Because the outlaws had no hope of returning home, their settlement acquired a degree of permanency that was lacking in earlier colonization attempts. Ultimately some 2,700 acres of land were brought under cultivation in the neighborhood of Albazin.

Despite the establishment of a permanent Russian settlement in the heart of Amuria, there are few indications of contact or conflict between Manchus and Russians in the decade after 1660. There is a Manchu report of 1668-1669 (K'ang-hsi 7), probably referring to the Russians, that a people called Lao-ch'iang from the Lo-ch'ê country invaded Heilungchiang to plunder sable skins. The men were described as having high noses, deep green eyes, red hair and fierce temperaments. Their forces were said to be strong and expert in the use of firearms. They had a cannon, called by the Manchus the *hsi-kua-p'ao* or watermelon cannon, which "could measure the distance of the enemy . . . one touched by the explosion would be mortally wounded. The Manchus were all afraid of this cannon." A year later new reports of Russian incursions reached the court, but the emperor canceled an expedition against the invaders "on the grounds that it would disturb the people."[27]

During this first period of conflict in the Amur, the Manchus won four of the five engagements and almost, if not quite, controlled the situation. Although Russian accounts tend to glorify the heroism of the Cossacks and explain their defeat by reason of overwhelming odds, such was not the case. The Russians claimed that 2,000 Manchu troops were employed in the battle at Achansk in 1652 and 10,000 in the siege of Kumarsk in 1655, but the garrison of Ninguta, which had jurisdiction over the Amur, had at its disposal only about 2,000 men altogether. Not all of these, moreover, were engaged against the Russians. An estimate of a total Manchu army of 1,400 plus boat crews and servants, as against

500 well-armed Russians in the battle on the Sungari in 1658, is probably a more accurate approximation of the strength of opposing forces during the fifties.[28]

Despite their initial success, the Manchu inability to carry their campaign through to its logical conclusion—complete destruction of the Russian presence in the region, including Nerchinsk—enabled the Russian government to reestablish its authority in the Amur. Albazin continued to develop. Chernigovsky, fearing a Manchu attack at Albazin, finally asked for the protection of the Nerchinsk voevoda. At the same time he offered his submission to the tsar. The offer was accepted, and in 1671 Ivan Olukhov was sent from Nerchinsk to take command at Albazin. In 1672 Chernigovsky was pardoned for his crimes, and he and his companions received a reward of two-thousand rubles for their services in Amuria. This reassertion of official Russian control over the Cossacks in the Amur, and the use of Albazin as a base for exploration and expansion in the Ussuri and Sungari regions, made further conflict between Russians and Manchus inevitable.

The Manchu withdrawal after the battle of 1660, their failure to garrison the Amur, and their reluctance to push for total victory in the mid-sixties were the results of lack of proper preparation and consequently a shortage of supplies. Chang Yü-shu, a famous scholar of the K'ang-hsi period, recorded in his *Wai-kuo-chi:* "In the reign of the Shun-chih emperor, the court considered the launching of an expedition to punish the tribes of O-lo-ssu and considered ordering Korea to furnish provisions. However, the emperor sympathized with Korea, a tiny nation which could not provide provisions for our great army; therefore, the expedition was cancelled."[29] Furthermore, the depopulation of the Amur by court order, which was intended to limit the supplies of food available to the Cossacks, also limited the supplies available to Peking's own armies. Finally, the Manchu logistic failure in the Amur was a direct consequence of the Ch'ing dynasty's natural preoccupation with the problems of consolidating its position in the newly conquered empire. The Manchus faced a serious manpower shortage. According to contemporary reports, for instance, in 1668-1669 (K'ang-hsi 7) all adult Manchu males at Ninguta were conscripted to fight inside China proper.[30] The Manchus were therefore unable to take advantage of the basic weaknesses of Russia's position in the Amur. By the time they once again turned their attention to the problem of Russian incursions along their northern frontier, they found themselves facing not outlaw bands of Cossacks but permanent settlements officially integrated into Russia's Siberian colony.

Chapter II **The Beginnings of Sino-Russian Diplomacy**

Russia's eastward expansion in search of fur and her resultant conquest of eastern Siberia and settlement of Amuria in the seventeenth century were not the only attempt on her part to search out and exploit the wealth of East Asia. Parallel to the conquest, and simultaneously with it, the Russian state sought access to the fabled market of China through diplomatic contacts for the encouragement of commerce. The collection of intelligence among Central Asian nomads who were in contact with China's Ming dynasty led to the dispatch of successive missions to China. Caravans, missions, and embassies added to Moscow's store of knowledge and lore concerning China and, in a tentative fashion, demonstrated the economic benefits that might accrue to the tsar's government and court if trade with China were established on a legal and organized footing. As it was to be for England in the nineteenth century, the China market was an almost irresistible attraction for Russian state and private commercial interests in the seventeenth and eighteenth centuries.

Moscow's early efforts to establish a regularized and regulated commerce with China failed, however, for several reasons. The first contacts with Peking were made in the years when the Ming were in sharp decline, facing internal rebellion and external attack. While the Ming may have been interested in some form of eventual commercial relationship with Moscow, the dynasty's time and power were waning fast. In the early years of the Ch'ing dynasty the Manchus were too preoccupied with establishing their power and legitimacy to undertake a diplomatic or commercial *détente* with Russia. Their conquest of China had to be legitimized in terms of Chinese concepts of society, international as well as domestic, if the relatively few Manchus were to rule China's vast population. Consequently, almost from the beginning of the Ch'ing dynasty, an extraordinarily conservative and rigid Confucian traditionalism commingled with and placed restrictions on the Manchus' "barbarian" pragmatism. Although Confucian orthodoxy did not engulf and smother the Manchus until almost a century after the conquest, they clearly recognized from their earliest days in China that the dynasty's power rested on the consent of the upper ranks of the bureaucracy and the gentry. The conquerors were forced to conform to Chinese etiquette and the Confucian *Weltanschauung* in the strictest fashion wherever and whenever possible. Later, in 1689 and 1727 after the Manchus had successfully subjugated China, they proved themselves quite capable of casting aside conformity to the Confucian tradition when self-interest, or the necessity of adjusting pragmatically to the realities of international politics and commerce, dictated. But before the end of the 1680's, when Russia was first probing Peking's diplomatic front, the Manchus could ill afford to transgress the norms of Chinese behavior patterns, nor did the Russians present them with sufficient cause to do so. Russian ignorance of Chinese court ceremonial, therefore, inhibited the growth of a Sino-Russian relationship before 1689. Ceremonial was the outward expression of the Confucian world order, and the Russians simply didn't know the drill.

Russia's inability to present Peking with sufficient cause to cast aside traditional Chinese forms of behavior was compounded by the fact that the Manchus evidently failed to identify the Cossacks along the Amur with the missions from Moscow until 1670. Manchu concepts of world geography were hazy at best, just as were the Chinese, and they believed that the land whence the Cossacks came was "located beyond the great ocean, 10,000 *li* eastward from us."[1] The Manchus, so conscious of the difference between continental and maritime power, must have been led to believe that the Cossacks' country was beyond the sea by the prominence of water transport as a means of Russian travel in Siberia: the Russians crossed Siberia and arrived in Amuria principally by water. Whereas the Cossacks must be from a maritime power, the missions from Moscow, which came overland, must be continental in origin; there was no reason for Peking to identify the two as related in any way. Consequently, before 1670 the Manchus were intellectually in no position to use diplomatic pressure on Moscow's embassies to achieve a settlement in Amuria. At the same time, the Russians themselves, not yet confronted with the necessity of finding new markets for their fur pelts in the face of North American competition on the European market, were not as vigorous in pursuit of their commercial aims in East Asia as they would become at the end of the seventeenth and beginning of the eighteenth centuries.

The history of Russo-Manchu intercourse before the Second Opium War (1856-1860), which ended with the revision of China's diplomatic institutions and fractured the Confucian world order, can be divided into three fairly distinct, if totally unequal, periods. The first, lasting up through the curious Milovanov mission of 1670, was characterized by the almost purely economic motives of Russia's missions to Peking. The second period of diplomatic contact, from 1670 to 1689, included only one mission, the remarkable embassy under Nikolay Gavrilovich Milescu. At that time both sides recognized that the establishment of commerical relations and a solution to the Amur problem were intimately related, but the embassy failed, and Russia and the Manchu Empire went to war in Amuria. This period ended with negotiations at Nerchinsk and the conclusion of a peace treaty in 1689, which created a Sino-Russian treaty system for the conduct of trade and the settlement of disputes. The third period, from 1689 to 1858, ending with the Treaty of Aigun, Russia's first imperialist treaty with the Manchus, saw the development of a stable relationship between the two empires within the framework of the treaty system created at Nerchinsk and renegotiated at Kyakhta in 1727. Throughout these three periods, with two notable exceptions, the diplomatic initiative lay almost entirely with Moscow.

Early Contacts

Although the most favorable combination of circumstances for an attempt to communicate directly with Peking did not develop until the first half of the seventeenth century, Russians had experienced contacts with Chinese, often by chance, at least as early as the Mongol Empire, when both Russia and China were subjected to the Chinggiside House of Mongol rulers. Concrete evidence is sparse, however, and these contacts have left only indistinct echoes. There were, for instance, Russian goldsmiths and warriors at the court of the Great Khan in Karakorum.[2] It is probable that they were prisoners, taken into Mongolia in the imperial service. The Mongol emperor was said to have had a detachment of Russian soldiers at his court, who were assigned to guard the capital and to participate in expeditions against rebellious princes.[3] Russian princes were at times forced to journey to Karakorum to make their submission to the khans and to receive their symbols of office. Yaroslav, the Grand Duke of Vladimir, and his son, Alexander Nevsky, are both supposed to have visited the Mongol capital for this purpose. Later, the Portuguese Mendez Pinto, who claimed to have traveled in China between 1537 and 1558, said that he met Russian prisoners or servants of the Mongols in China's Shansi Province.[4]

The Mongol rulers of that vast empire which extended from the Pacific Ocean to the shores of the Black Sea and even beyond did not prohibit trade or intercourse among their various subject peoples. The passage of Marco Polo and others along the inner Asian trade routes between Europe and Asia testifies to the relative ease and safety with which such journeys could be made. Karakorum was a cosmopolitan city, visited by Chinese, some of whom made it their permanent residence as servants of the Mongol khans. It would not be presumptuous to assume that Russians met Chinese in Karakorum and learned about China's wealth. Information must have gone in the other direction as well. Pallady Kafarov, one of Russia's earliest and greatest sinologists, discovered a manuscript map in Peking, probably made in the fourteenth century, whereon a country called "A-lo-so" was located in the northwestern part of the Mongol empire. "A-lo-so" is very probably an attempt at transliterating "Rus'."[5]

The disruption of the Mongol Empire in the fourteenth century closed the convenient land route from Europe to China. Nevertheless, indirect contact between Russia and China continued, based on the extended Central Asian trade routes. Chinese goods were sold in the markets of the Golden Horde, but whether they were passed along the silk routes or were brought by Chinese merchants themselves is not known. Russians visited Samarkand in 1404, where they were "recognized as on a level with the merchants of India and China; consequently, their trade was quite respectable."[6] In 1466 the famous Tver merchant Afanasy Nikitin left on a trip to India. When he returned to Russia in 1472, he recorded in a book the information he had collected about India, Persia, and China, though he himself did not visit China.[7]

At the same time that European explorers began to visit the coasts of India in the late fifteenth and early sixteenth centuries, finally reaching Canton in 1514, European merchants made parallel efforts to develop a land route to China. Foreign diplomats and merchants visited Russia seeking information and permission to pass through the tsar's domains to the trade routes. As early as 1520 the Genoese Paolo Centurione visited Moscow for this purpose. In 1557 Ivan the Terrible gave an Englishman, Anthony Jenkinson, permission to cross Russia to Bukhara, where Chinese goods were said to be available, so that he could trade and gather information concerning a trans-Asian route to China. Unfortunately, by the time of Jenkinson's arrival in Bukhara, Chinese caravans had ceased visiting that Central Asian city.[8]

Moscow's own efforts to establish direct contact with the Chinese were motivated only in part by the growth of European interest in a land route to the Far East. Internal conditions were equally, if not more, important. The sixteenth century was an era of almost unending warfare for the Moscow state, climaxed by the Time of Troubles at the beginning of the seventeenth century. The election of the Romanov family to the Russian throne by the Zemsky Sobor of 1613 was only the first step in the reorganization and reorientation of Russian society, which was to accelerate under Peter the Great. Since the state treasury's resources had been severely strained by the chaotic conditions, the state sought ways to convert its newly acquired Siberian fur wealth into gold, silver, and precious stones, with which most states in the mercantilist era attempted to fill their coffers. China presented an attractive and convenient market, closer to Siberia than western Europe. Thus, the same forces that impelled Portuguese, English, and Dutch mariners to seek sea routes to China also impelled European and Russian merchants to look for land-based commerce in China.

Through his interest in the fur trade, the tsar was Russia's first and greatest merchant. The state, as an extension of the tsar's household, initiated Russian efforts to trade with China. As early as 1582 Moscow decided to send a mission to investigate the opening of a route to China. Foreigners were permitted to assist the undertaking. In 1587, for instance, Tsar Fedor Ivanovich guaranteed Lithuanian and Polish merchants free transit through Russian territories to China and the Orient.[9]

The Time of Troubles inhibited any definite plans the Moscow tsar may have had for opening direct trade with China. However, perhaps as a result of the chaos in European Russia, the voevodas of Siberia were at that time granted the right and "power to send embassies to neighboring states and lands." The conduct of certain limited foreign relations by provincial officials is not unknown in situations of political instability or in areas where geography makes transportation difficult. Consequently, energetic and imaginative voevodas played a significant role in the initiation of relations with China.

The western Siberian ostrogs were the centers for diplomatic and commercial relations with the steppe nomads, through whom Moscow obtained its first concrete information about China and made its first efforts to establish contact with Peking. The first attempt to reach China was based on information brought to Tomsk by two Kirghiz princelings, who excited the Russians' imagination by stressing China's wealth and telling them that the Chinese wore golden robes and the emperor received "all kinds of precious stone and other things" from many lands. The Tomsk voevoda, V. V. Volynsky, equipped and dispatched a trading expedition in 1608. The caravan was to travel as a commercial embassy to China through the lands of the Altyn-khan, a Central Asian nomadic magnate, whose aid was required if the venture were to succeed.[10] While the caravan was en route to the Altyn-khan's headquarters, it was learned that he had been driven away by the Jungars. Unable to find him, the Russians returned to Tomsk in March 1609.

More information about China was obtained in 1616 through

Tomilko Petrov, a Lithuanian prisoner of war who, according to the prevailing custom, was sent to a frontier post for military duty. The voevoda of Tobolsk, Prince I. S. Kurakin, sent Petrov and Ivan Kunitsin, a "mounted Astrakhan Cossack," to obtain the nomadic Kalmuks' recognition of Russian suzerainty, as part of the process of incorporating Siberia's indigenous population into the yasak system. Petrov and Kunitsin eventually found themselves in Moscow, probably in 1617, where they made a deposition concerning their mission. They claimed to have met Chinese officials who had gone among the Kalmuks "for the *yasak*," and from whom their information on China probably came. They described, by hearsay, the size and style of Chinese cities, the customs of the Lamaist Church (which was primary in the Kalmuk community), and the suzerain-vassal relationship between Peking and the nomads. China was "a city built of brick," through which flowed "a great river, the name of which they could not say." Large and small vessels came to China to trade, and "corn grows plentifully."[11]

These first two Siberian attempts to contact China demonstrated that Russian access to the Central Asian trade routes was tenuous at best. Until the tide of Russian expansion swept beyond Lake Baikal in the 1630's, the Altyn-khans controlled the Russian road to China. Moscow had already recognized this, and on June 29, 1615, even before the Petrov-Kunitsin mission became known in the capital, the Kazan Department, which was then in charge of Siberian affairs, had ordered one Ivan Petrov and Vasily Tyumenets to go to the Altyn-khan's headquarters "on State affairs." Kurakin was instructed to aid their mission in every way possible. Petrov and Tyumenets left Tobolsk on May 10, 1616. If Tomilko Petrov's status as the voevoda's own envoy is fairly clear, the rank and status of Ivan Petrov and Vasily Tyumenets is confused. In addition to outfitting their expedition, Kurakin gave the envoys written instructions to appear as his, not the tsar's, ambassadors.[12] Later Petrov and Tyumenets followed their Moscow, not their Tobolsk, instructions. The former were oral, and the transcriber of their deposition remarked that "nor could they tell for what reason Prince Ivan Kurakin gave them that Instruction, since neither of them could read or write." This confusion over jurisdiction in foreign relations arose from the independence that characterized the activities of the Siberian voevodas and that was to plague Russia's relations with China for over a century.

The Petrov-Tyumenets mission had the specific objective of establishing relations with China. Through the Altyn-khan's good offices the envoys were to obtain as much detailed information as possible and to propose to the emperor of China that he "send in return for our envoys, his own great envoys, with those serving people [Tyumenets and Petrov]." The Russians did not meet any Chinese at the Altyn-khan's court, however, for in their deposition they indicated that their information concerning China came from "people belonging to the Altyn Tsar and . . . others."[13]

A picture of China as a land of power and wealth emerges from the Petrov-Tyumenets deposition. Peking was a city built of brick and "so huge that it took ten days to ride around it on horseback." China was rich in satins, velvets, silks, gold, silver, wheat, barley, oats, and millet—all goods that would appeal strongly to Russians. The two envoys from the Altyn-khan who returned to Moscow with the mission emphasized China's strength to their Russian hosts.[14]

Intrigued by the second-hand picture of China that was beginning to emerge, Moscow launched a bold policy aimed at the collection of direct information from Peking. Tsar Mikhail Fedorovich wrote Kurakin in 1617 that Moscow had decided categorically not to establish official relations with either the Altyn-khan or China for the moment. Instead, he sought detailed first-hand information. To that end the tsar instructed Kurakin to send Cossacks "or other people" to visit China "not as envoys and not as from yourselves, but making some pretense for their visit." These agents were to reside in the Middle Kingdom, collect information, and report to Moscow. This was one of the first attempts by Moscow to curb the independence of the voevodas in foreign relations. The tsar's specific injunction against sending envoys per se is doubtless indicative not of a policy opposed to the establishment of relations with Peking but of an attempt by the tsar to reserve for himself the right to send embassies and to receive any commercial profits accruing from them.[15]

The Petlin Mission: First Direct Contact

The immediate reason for the Petlin mission lay in the tsar's letter to Kurakin, but in fact its beginnings lay much deeper, in English interest in the Ob as a possible route to India and China.[16] As a result of the publication in England in 1555 of a book entitled *Of the Northeast Frostie Seas and the Kingdoms Lying that Way, etc.*, the Englishman Stephen Borrough was sent in the next year to find and explore the Ob.[17] Mericke, the English representative of London's Moscow Company during the second decade of the seventeenth century, became interested in the Ob as early as 1611, and when he found himself in special favor at the Russian court as a result of his aid in concluding a peace treaty with the Swedish in 1617, he decided to use the opportunity to advance his interest. He requested, in addition to general privileges for English merchants in Russia, specific permission for Englishmen to travel to Persia through the Volga and to seek a route to China and India through the Ob. The Russians refused him but offered to ask the Siberian voevodas to obtain information concerning the Ob. Since Mericke had been urging the matter at the Russian court for several years prior to his formal request, the overt English interest was undoubtedly what prompted the tsar at this moment to send a mission directly to Peking. The instructions to Petlin specifically mentioned the Ob as one possible route.[18]

The organization of the expedition was traditional, and Kurakin took great pains over it. It was outfitted by the local Tobolsk and Tomsk voevodas on direct order from the tsar, and its expenses came from the state fur treasury. On April 6, 1617, Kurakin wrote the voevodas of Tomsk that in addition to Maksim Trupcheninov, the intended leader, and Ivashko Petlin, interpreter, the group included seven servingmen from Tobolsk; Tomsk was to appoint four Cossacks as messengers. Ths mission was to be equipped with the furs left over after the Petrov-Tyumenets mission to the Altyn-khan. At the last moment Trupcheninov was unable to make the journey, so Petlin, who had been appointed specifically "for writing," became leader.[19] Petlin's original position on the staff as a scribe and translator was in the Siberian tradition, since voevodas were always assisted by literate clerks. At this early date neither the tsar nor the Moscow government participated directly in the organization process, but later, when the possibility of reaching Peking became a reality, Moscow took on itself the closer supervision of the organization of embassies and the choice of personnel.

The Petlin mission was conducted in accordance with the traditions of Central Asian diplomacy. The exchange of envoys in the steppe was difficult because of the lack of proper transportation and defense along the trade routes. Consequently, for protection and ease of movement, visits of official delegations were returned by envoys who accompanied the delegations back to their court. The obvious need for envoys to return to their own courts provided a continuous occasion for the exchange of diplomatic representatives. Petlin's expedition followed this pattern by beginning its journey in the company of Ondrushka Mundov of Tobolsk, who was appointed to accompany envoys from the Altyn-khan on their return trip. These envoys were probably those who had accompanied Petrov and Tyumenets back from the Altyn-khan's court. The mission left Tobolsk in 1618.[20]

Ivashko Petlin left a detailed account of his journey and his impressions of China in his *stateyny spisok* or deposition, written in 1619, the first Russian eyewitness account of China. He was struck, above all, by the size and grandeur of the walls and cities he passed. The expedition followed the Great Wall for ten days, during which it met no one, passed through a gate guarded by giant cannon with balls as big as a man's head, and visited a city that was "good, a fine affair, and the towers are as high as those of Moscow." Peking impressed him most of all. He reported that it was a very great city, white as snow, around which it took four days to travel. Great towers, high and white, stood along the city wall, which was also "high and white as snow picked out with different colored paint." The entire city was "beautified with all sorts of wondrous things."[21]

More important was Petlin's description of his activities in Peking and of the diplomatic and court ceremonial he observed. Although he had been given no political tasks and was merely to travel and observe, he appears to have been received by the Chinese as a tribute-bearing mission. This supposition is supported by the fact that he was lodged in the "Great Embassy Courtyard," and that the question of tribute was raised in his discussion with various Ming officials, whom he failed to identify.[22] Four days after his arrival at Peking the court approached him as to the purpose of his visit. He claimed that he had been sent to China by the tsar "to make enquiry as to the kingdom of China and to see the tsar [the Chinese emperor]."[23] Since his statement was unsupported by his written instructions, which he had certainly read, being a literate man, one can only suppose that it was curiosity, not policy, that prompted his request for an audience with the emperor. Nevertheless, his inability to present "gifts" from the tsar to the emperor prevented his admission to an imperial audience. The lack of "gifts" or tribute goods can be explained in two ways. First, although he had received furs enough for wages for two years and supplies enough for one, he may not have been given sufficient furs for use as gifts since his nondiplomatic status did not require them. Second, as an interpreter along the frontier, Petlin was undoubtedly acquainted with Central Asian diplomatic usage and the tribute system. Yasak was, after all, a form of tribute, which governed Russia's relations with the Siberian tribes and nomads in the steppe. Aware of the significance of such gifts, Petlin may have refrained on his own volition from presenting any to the Chinese court.

Although charged with no diplomatic tasks and excluded from imperial audiences, Petlin's mission had one curious political byproduct: receipt of an invitation to the tsar to trade with China, written in the form of a letter allegedly by the Ming emperor Wan-li, but more likely penned by a minor official in the emperor's name. Although Petlin brought the letter to Moscow, the Russians were unable to find anyone to translate it until 1675; in the meantime its contents remained totally unknown.[24] Had the letter been translated immediately, it might well have led to the pursuit of commercial relations at once. Be that as it may, the letter itself, despite the cleverness of the 1675 translation (the original is lost) which sought to mask any Chinese pretentions insulting to the Russians, was an indication of Ming attitudes toward the Russian strangers. It was a clear expression of the tributary relationship. The author of the letter, for instance, used the words "up and down" to describe the exchange of communications between Russia and China. The expression meant "the exalted station of the Chinese emperor and the inferior one of the tsar." The translation obscured the full intent of the original, since in Moscow "to carry up" meant to bring to the tsar, while if the letter were originally composed in Chinese, it would have necessarily placed the Chinese emperor on a higher level than the Russian tsar. Whereas the opening phrases of the letter referred directly to trade, the writer continued, "bring the best you have, and I in return, will make you presents of good silk stuffs." These comments, together with remarks concerning China's custom of never sending ambassadors abroad and the inability of her merchants to travel to foreign markets, gave a close description of the tribute system, which reached a high point of development in the late Ming. Peking would have reasonably expected the Russians to participate in it.

The Petlin mission in 1618 was Russia's first direct contact with China and its last until 1653, though Moscow continued to gather information about the Celestial Empire. In Russia, available energies and capital were more and more involved in difficulties with the West and in the rapid expansion to the Pacific shores. In China, the Ming dynasty was beset by the problems of decline, while to the north the Manchus grew in strength. In between, the Central Asian turmoil, which often accompanied the decline of a dynasty in China, disrupted the trade routes. Conditions in neither empire could support the establishment of commercial relations with the other. The Altyn-khan remarked plaintively to two Russian envoys in the mid-1630's: "My country is poor and contains no articles of value; it is long since we have been able to visit either China or 'the Land of Tangut' on account of the wars of the Chakhar tsar, Duchin."[25]

The First Ambassador: Fedor Isakovich Baykov

The information obtained by Russia about China in the years after Petlin's mission was undoubtedly meager. Yet the most important single event in East Asia—the Manchu conquest of the Ming empire—was clearly known in Moscow. The consequent upheavals in Central Asia were also probably noticed by Russian envoys, who throughout this period continued to visit nomad chiefs. By the 1640's the Russians had made contact with the Buryat Mongols and, further south, with the Khalkhas. Since the Khalkhas, together with the Chahar Mongols, supported the Manchu conquest of China, it is not unlikely that Moscow learned of the conquest through them.[26] In any event, before the departure of the Russian embassy to Peking in 1653 Moscow certainly knew of the Manchu conquest, because the embassy's documents were addressed to the "Bogdykhan Tsar," an appellation used by the Russians only in connection with the emperors of the Ch'ing, or Manchu, dynasty.[27]

The 1653 embassy was the first one, in the true meaning of the word, sent from Russia to China. Led by Fedor Isakovich Baykov, it lasted until 1657. In addition to collecting the usual intelligence requested by Moscow, it was charged with conscious diplomatic and commercial goals dictated by Russia's internal and international problems. In 1648 the Russian government had faced a serious rebellion, which by 1651-1652 engulfed such trade and industrial centers as Moscow and Pskov. The Black Death made serious inroads into the city and village population. Relations with Poland over the Cossacks in the Ukraine were strained. In 1648 the state had been forced by Russian merchant interests to inhibit Russia's foreign commerce by depriving foreign merchants of the greater part of their privileges in the country. The English, for instance, lost free trade privileges, and their retail trade inside Russia was seriously restricted. Foreign merchants in general could visit only the Arkhangelsk region in the north. Russian fur exports to Europe, already declining because of North American competition, were further decreased by the Anglo-Dutch war, beginning in 1652. The English conducted a naval campaign against Holland to keep Dutch ships from entering foreign ports; they went so far as to attack Arkhangelsk at the end of July and the beginning of August, 1654. In the south, too, there was a trade decline. A Swedish merchant in Russia reported in 1653 that trade with Persia had almost come to a standstill.

At precisely this moment Baykov was sent as ambassador to

China. The Moscow state, badly in need of income from trade, sought to exploit its Siberian fur resources wherever possible. The embassy's staff included tselovalniks or sworn men, emphasizing its commercial aims.[28] If Baykov's embassy was fundamentally commercial, it was nonetheless unrelated to the developing Amur situation. Baykov's instructions made no mention of the Amur. The omission was not the result of a conscious policy of avoidance on Moscow's part but merely indicated that in the minds of Russia's rulers, as in the minds of the Manchu court, the two problems of trade with Peking and the Amur conflict were not yet related.

The Baykov embassy began as a trading caravan, similar to those sent at about the same time into Persia and Central Asia. The "Great Treasury" in Moscow sent Baykov first to Tobolsk, "for matters connected with His Majesty's trade and commerce." There Baykov was to study the problem of trade with China, paying particular attention to the types of goods to be exchanged, trade routes, and estimates of expected profits. As a frontier community in constant contact with Central Asia, Tobolsk was a logical place for such an investigation. Baykov was also given fifty-thousand rubles, to be spent in Moscow and elsewhere for the purchase of goods for trade in Siberia and China, where he was to obtain in exchange silk or, preferably, silver, gold, pearls, and precious stones.[29] Sometime before the end of 1653 or about the beginning of 1654, however, Moscow decided to turn the original trading venture into a full-scale diplomatic mission to negotiate trade with China on a firm and permanent foundation. A letter dated February 11, 1654, and addressed to the Manchu emperor was sent to Baykov in Tobolsk. It contained a proposal for the establishment of diplomatic relations and recounted in detail the tsar's descent from Caesar Augustus and the Grand Prince Rurik. It explained that, because the tsar had not previously corresponded with the Chinese emperor or exchanged ambassadors, he could not know the Bogdykhan's correct titles. If, however, the Bogdykhan would write the tsar through Baykov, or send his own envoys, the Russian government would thereafter use his titles in proper style. The letter concluded with a statement that the tsar wished to live with the Bogdykhan in "loving intercourse" and a request that Baykov not be detained in Peking but allowed to begin his homeward journey without delay.[30]

Baykov himself received instructions, in five paragraphs, prescribing in considerable detail the behavior expected of him in Peking. It was Moscow's first attempt to deal with the problems raised by the nature and meaning of Chinese court ceremonial and diplomatic usage. Baykov was instructed to negotiate with the emperor alone and to avoid all entanglements and dealings with frontier officials or the emperor's ministers in Peking. He was not to bow down to anyone or anything but the emperor's own person, explaining that his faith prevented his bowing to stones, such as palaces and thresholds. He was not to kiss the emperor's foot, though if called to do so, he might kiss his hand. While delivering his credentials and the tsar's letter to the emperor, Baykov was to make a speech, outlined in the instructions, declaring the tsar's intention to live "forever in friendship and love" with the emperor. He was to promise that if Chinese merchants or envoys came to Russia, they would be received with honor, conducted to Moscow, and allowed to trade duty-free.

In addition to these diplomatic instructions, Baykov was given a detailed list of subjects about which to gather information. Besides "enquiring secretly" into the emperor's present attitudes and future intentions toward Moscow, Baykov was expected to make a commercial survey of China, covering such matters as goods available on the Chinese market, whether Chinese or foreign, trade routes, tariff conditions, and the ability of the Chinese market to absorb Russian goods. One item mentioned specifically was vegetables, perhaps because of eastern Siberia's economic inhospitality. Moreover, the embassy was to collect data on Peking's court ceremonial, religion, and the strength of China, under such headings as people, treasure, armies, cities, and current military engagements.[31]

The commercial importance attached by Moscow to the Baykov embassy was further indicated in a letter, dated February 16, 1654, addressed to the voevoda of Verkhoturie, in which he was instructed to extend all possible aid to the ambassador and his suite "so that they may hasten on to the Chinese state this very summer." Any losses incurred by delay would be the responsibility of the voevoda. The letter demonstrated the direct commercial interest of the tsar in establishing trade with China. Trade was to be carried on with state goods, and profits were to return to the state. The state's bureaucracy in Siberia was responsible for aiding the successful conclusion of the mission, diplomatically as well as commercially. There are indications that the tsar decided to increase his original 50,000-ruble investment by supplying specific state goods, mostly pelts, in addition to those Baykov had already purchased.[32]

Shortly after receiving his instructions and the tsar's letter to the emperor, Baykov dispatched Setkul Ablin, a Bukharan resident of Tobolsk, to announce the Russian embassy to Peking.[33] Curiously enough, the Ch'ing court mistook Ablin for the ambassador himself, come to China to present tribute. The misunderstanding is obvious from the edict with which Ablin was dismissed from Peking after fulfilling his mission. Addressing the tsar through Ablin, the Manchus declared that although no Russian ambassador had visited China before, Russia had now "sincerely turned toward civilization" and sent an envoy to present local products—that is, tribute. Consequently, the emperor bestowed special gifts on the tsar, which he declared "clearly manifests our sublime intention of entertaining strangers with hospitality." The tsar was instructed to receive the gifts respectfully and to devote his "loyalty and obedience to us forever in order to respond to our grace."[34] The wording of the edict supports the assumption that Ablin fulfilled all the ceremonial requirements of the Ch'ing court, including the kowtow. The Manchu conclusion that Ablin was actually the ambassador may have been due to bad interpretation or conscious misrepresentation.

Despite Moscow's careful preparations, Baykov's embassy was for several reasons a total diplomatic failure. The overriding reason was the Manchus' need to conform to the strictest Confucian orthodox behavior, but other adverse factors influenced the outcome even before Baykov had entered Peking. The precedent set by Ablin had reinforced the Ch'ing court's expectations of compliance with its ceremonial demands, whereas Baykov's own instructions, and his concepts of behavior befitting an ambassador, prevented compromise. Furthermore, since the Manchus assumed that the Russian embassy had already arrived and departed Peking under Ablin, no preparations were made for Baykov's arrival, either at the frontier or at Kalgan, the first important city inside the Manchu Empire. In his stateyny spisok the ambassador complained repeatedly and bitterly that no transport or provisions had been prepared for him. His reception upon arrival at Peking was equally frustrating. He claimed that there "were sent only ten men or so, to half a verst beyond Kanbalik [Peking]," among whom only two were officials, "of whom one sits in the Mongol Office [the Li-fan yuan], the other in the Chinese office [the Li-pu?]."[35]

Baykov and his Manchu opposite numbers, whom he failed to identify, never succeeded in solving the ceremonial problem, and it was on this rock that the embassy finally wrecked. Arguments began at the entry to Peking itself, when Baykov, in accordance with instructions, refused to kowtow at the capital gates. Further complications developed over the drinking of a ceremonial cup of tea. Upon being presented with a cup of tea boiled with butter and milk, Baykov refused to drink on the grounds that the day was a Christian fast. His refusal was doubly insulting to the Manchus as the tea had been sent by the emperor himself. A compromise was reached when Baykov accepted the cup but did not drink from it.

After their entry into the capital, Baykov and his embassy were provided with all the perquisites of a tribute mission. They were lodged, for instance, in a "courtyard," which was probably the Li-fan yuan's customary residence for tribute bearers from Central Asia, where they were supplied with food and drink according to rank.[36] But the ambassador's unwillingness to fulfill the expected tribute ceremonies perplexed, confounded, and finally angered the Manchu officials. Two major problems emerged. The first was the manner of presentation of the tsar's gifts. The second was the Manchu insistence that Baykov deliver his instructions and the letter to the emperor before an audience could take place. Both problems, insisted the Manchus, had to be solved within the context of the tribute tradition.

According to Baykov, on the embassy's second day in Peking, Manchu officials came to collect the "gifts" sent to the emperor by the tsar. Baykov refused to hand them over, insisting that he himself would present the gifts, together with his credentials, to the emperor. He reported the Manchu reply: "That is your master's way: not ours: and one Tsar does not dictate to another." The issue was joined. The Manchus pleaded, cajoled, offered to compromise, and threatened that they were authorized to take the gifts by force if necessary; but Baykov persistently refused any compromise. In his deposition he laconically described the denouement: "But those Privy Councillors protested: 'We do not take the royal treasure from you as robbers: we take from you the royal gracious gifts, by sovereign command, because they were sent by your great Lord to ours.' So they took those gracious royal presents from the Ambassador by force on the 4th of March . . . And the government officials, having taken the Tsar's gifts, packed them in a bundle; but whither they carried them is not certainly known."[37]

Two days later, Baykov was ordered to appear at the Li-fan yuan with his letters of credence. What transpired between then and August 12, when the demand was repeated, Baykov does not make clear. That pressure may have been brought to bear is indicated by his removal to a different place of residence on April 1, but he does not describe his new quarters in detail.[38] On August 12 he was threatened with death if he did not hand over the documents. Because of his continued refusal, the tsar's gifts were returned and Baykov was dismissed from the capital. As the Manchu officials explained, "you have failed altogether to obey [the emperor's] commands; you have not come to the Ministry, to the State officials, bringing the letter of credence, nor have you bowed down *in our fashion* [italics added], falling on your knees."[39] The ambassador's refusal to conform to the tribute system tradition released the Manchus from any necessity to aid his departure. His final dismissal from Peking on September 4 took place, Baykov himself commented, "by no means politely." He was furnished with neither transport nor provisions, as would have been customary.

The departure from Peking was not the conclusion of the embassy. Baykov evidently felt that he had to make one last effort to see the emperor. Accordingly, one day before reaching Kalgan on the homeward journey, he sent a messenger to the Li-fan yuan, offering to fulfill the demands of the court if he were allowed to return to Peking. Although the offer did not mean that he either understood or accepted the strictures of the tribute system, as his next actions demonstrated, the Manchus evidently believed that the Russian ambassador had finally "turned toward civilization," for they sent an official from Peking to examine Baykov's sincerity and take a deposition from him with his new promises.[40] The official found that after dispatching his first offer, Baykov had moved his embassy to Kalgan, still further from the capital. The move was interpreted, correctly within the context of the tribute tradition, as a sign of disrespect for the emperor and personal insincerity. Thus, on September 25 couriers arrived from Peking to refuse the Russian's offer. His last effort to reach an accommodation with custom having come to nought, Baykov returned to Russia, arriving at Tobolsk on July 31, 1658, with Chinese goods valued at 1,668 rubles.[41]

If Fedor Baykov was not a masterful diplomat, he was a keen observer who turned his attention to various aspects of Chinese society, including its history, customs, economics, and architecture.[42] Peking impressed him deeply, and he conveyed home a vivid description of it. The main streets, he reported, were paved with natural granite. On each side were dug great ditches, leading to small canals and lanes, "so that there is no mud in the streets"—which must have deeply impressed a Russian. His description of Peking's houses sounds almost like a Russian fairytale. During his six months' residence in Peking, Baykov had ample opportunity to study the local inhabitants, whom he described in some detail, making careful distinctions between Chinese and Manchu women, for instance. The Chinese were "well-grown and clean," but their women had little feet "like those of children"; he had heard that they "squeeze them" on purpose. Their dresses were short, with slits on the sides and wide sleeves. The Manchu women, in contrast, had "full-sized feet" and wore long dresses so that their feet could not be seen.

While in Peking, Baykov did not become a devotee of the Chinese cuisine. Having probably been raised on stout black bread, he remarked with evident distaste that the inhabitants of the capital "eat all sorts of abominable food . . . they eat dogs, and sell boiled dog-meat in the shops, and they eat all sorts of things that have died." To compound the injury, "all food is dear."

Since the Manchu occupation of Peking was barely thirteen years old when Baykov visited the city, he could observe some of the social consequences of the conquest. He distinguished between the Manchus and the "old Chinese," who were still holding out in the south. The Manchus in Peking constituted no more than a tenth of the population, he observed, "but of Chinese there are vast numbers." Local control was military. Whereas Manchu officials "go about on horseback . . . with swords and bows and arrows," the Chinese traveled on foot or horseback, always unarmed. "And in the government offices there are no Chinese, except labourers and traders and craftsmen."

The ambassador's recitation of goods available on the Peking market reads like a merchant's litany: apples, pears, cherries, plums, melons, watermelons, grapes, cucumbers, walnuts, hazelnuts, and "other unknown kinds" of fruit; onions, garlic, radishes, and turnips that ripen toward the Great Fast; honey, wax, and loaf sugar; ginger, pepper, cloves, cinnamon, but "whether or not there are any other spices is not known for certain, nor where they grow, whether in Kanbali or not." He also noted the easy availability of silks, pile or smooth velvets, damask, gold, silver, precious stones, and pearls. However, he reported that although gold, silver, and precious stones were plentiful, they were expensive or impure. The goods he purchased in shops "were bought at a great price compared to the Russian." The silver coins were mixed with copper and lead to more than fifty percent of their weight, as were the silver vessels. Pearls were twice as expensive as Russian pearls, and he did not find any precious stones he wanted to purchase. The high prices and impure coinage made Baykov less than sanguine about the possibilities for the development of Russian trade with Peking. The only Russian goods for which he found a demand were ermine and arctic fox pelts, while sables, beavers, and red fox skins were already plentiful on the market.

In terms of intelligence, therefore, Baykov's embassy must be judged a success, though a diplomatic failure. The ambassador provided Moscow with more detailed information about Peking and China than it could have obtained through its contacts with

Central Asian nomads, who simply did not have the kind of data Baykov collected or Moscow needed.

Setkul Ablin and the First Commercial Caravan

Setkul Ablin, Baykov's Bukharan messenger to Peking, returned to Russia by a different route from the embassy's, missing it completely. He first learned of the Russian failure in Peking while wintering among the Central Asian nomads en route to Russia. This news launched him on a career that was to make him Russia's first "old China hand," so to speak.

Ablin reported the rumors of Baykov's failure to the tsar in Moscow and, thinking Baykov was still in China, requested permission to return to meet him and bring back the state's fur treasure. At this point Moscow, probably well in advance of Peking, began to perceive dimly a connection between the Russian-Manchu conflict on the Amur and its own efforts to establish commercial relations with Peking. In a letter that the tsar ordered the Ambassadorial Department to prepare for Ablin to carry to Peking, the Russians mentioned a rumor that Baykov had been detained in Peking "in consequence of Russian troops having entered the Amur region to chastise the insolence of the local inhabitants, not knowing that they were Chinese subjects." The tsar promised that in the future he would refrain from sending troops to the Amur and would instruct his subjects to live in peace and friendship with their neighbors. On the strength of this promise he requested the emperor to send instructions to the natives along the Amur to avoid quarrels with the Russians. He also expressed hope that Baykov would be allowed to leave Peking without delay and that Chinese merchants would be allowed to visit Russia.[43] Baykov was not in fact delayed in Peking because of the Amur situation, but Moscow could not know it. However, the letter was never delivered, because Ablin's departure was canceled when news of Baykov's safety reached Tobolsk and Moscow.

The tsar, recognizing that Baykov's failure might close the door to the development of ties with Peking and that the embassy had been commercially inconclusive, planned a new mission with two apparent objectives. First, the mission was to keep open the tenuous lines of communication between Moscow and Peking that Petlin had established and that Baykov had damaged. Second, the tsar wanted to test the real value of Russian-Chinese trade for Moscow. Toward these ends he decided in February 1658 to send two messengers to Peking. Ablin and Ivan Perfiliev, a boyar son from the town of Tara, were given gifts and a letter for the emperor, together with cash for commercial purposes.[44]

The tsar's new letter to the emperor differed from Baykov's in one important respect: it contained Russia's first specific commercial proposals for Peking. The tsar, rather grandly, offered to send the emperor and China any desired goods or commodities. He also requested permission for Chinese merchants to visit Russia with "all kinds of goods," in return for which Russia would permit the Chinese to export, duty-free, whatever they purchased. In short, the tsar proposed an exchange of trade missions and free trade. The Amur question was mentioned neither in the letter nor in any accounts of the mission written upon its return.[45]

Moscow took precautions lest the new mission encounter the same difficulties that had ruined Baykov's. Ablin and Perfiliev were instructed to proceed quickly to Peking, where they were to hand the tsar's letter to the emperor directly. Forewarned by Baykov's failure, however, their instructions included a specific provision that the messengers could, if necessary, hand the letter to the emperor's "nearest people" rather than directly into his hands. This amendment to the usually anticipated procedures was doubtless made in the interests of commerce, but it also resulted logically from the gradual accumulation of Russian experience in dealing with Peking. The two messengers—they were not envoys—were also instructed to purchase gifts for the emperor to the value of two hundred rubles. For this sum they obtained "forty sables, thirteen black fox pelts, four lengths of good cloth, ermine coats, and some mirrors." The Great Treasury gave them five hundred rubles and additional pelts, with specific instructions concerning the cash and barter purchases to be made in Peking.[46]

Despite Moscow's precautionary measures, when the Russian messengers reached Peking in June 1660, the Manchu court found the tsar's letter offensive. The Russians still failed to understand the tribute tradition: for instance, the letter should have been dated according to the Chinese calendar. The emperor's advisors evidently proposed to dismiss the messengers summarily, but the emperor, in an edict remarkably temperate and conciliatory in tone, outlined a new Manchu policy toward Moscow: "Although the memorial of the Ch'a-han han [the tsar] is boastful, proud, and impolite, nevertheless as with foreign states which turn toward our civilization, we should forgive them in order to demonstrate [our principle of] hospitality to strangers. Since he has sent envoys to bring a memorial, this shows his sentiment of longing for justice. Let the Board of Rites treat the envoys with dinners and receive a part of their tribute. Meanwhile, we shall bestow some special gifts on the Ch'a-han han and his envoys, but we need not send him an envoy nor return him a letter. Your office should instruct his envoys as to the reasons why we decline them an audience, because his memorial is proud, boastful, and disobedient.[47] This was, if anything, meant as an encouragement to Moscow, couched in the only terms possible for the Ch'ing court at the time.

The emperor's gifts to the tsar included twenty-five pieces of damask, three beaver skins, three leopard skins, three pieces of velvet, three sealskins, and ten puds of tea. Ablin sold some of the damask and "all of the tea" in Peking and purchased 352 precious stones.[48] En route back to Moscow the expedition was plundered by Mongols, but despite this mishap it succeeded in reaching Moscow on November 1, 1662, with goods valued at 1,969 rubles.[49] The mission proved the feasibility of trading profitably with Peking. Although it had no diplomatic accomplishments to its credit, a handsome return on an investment of something less than 1,000 rubles was its most important achievement.

This initial Russian commercial venture was significant beyond purely commercial profit. It was the first conscious, albeit tentative, Russian effort to find the level of institutional intercourse with China that would best facilitate the growth of trade. Baykov's inability to deliver the tsar's letter to the emperor demonstrated the need for a different approach to the establishment of relations with Peking. Moscow's willingness to modify customary diplomatic procedure to accommodate the Ch'ing court, as shown by permitting delivery of the tsar's letter to court officials rather than to the emperor's own person, was met by the Manchu willingness to moderate China's position. This compromise foreshadowed an institutional arrangement for communication between subordinates rather than between tsar and emperor. As the emperor's decree indicates, Ablin and Perfiliev succeeded in delivering the tsar's letter, though it was accepted as a memorial. The fact that the two men were messengers rather than envoys facilitated communication.

Ablin's Second Mission

Drawing on past experience, Moscow moved another step forward in the refinement and articulation of its China policy when in 1668, six years after Ablin's return to Russia, it sent him on a second commercial mission to Peking. Impressed with the commercial success of Ablin's first caravan, the tsar as early as 1664 had ordered him to prepare a second. He instructed the Bukharan to purchase goods in Moscow, Yaroslavl, and other Russian cities at the treasury's expense, which were suitable for sale in China. Ablin was also to obtain yasak furs in Siberia through the state treasury.[50]

In the tsar's original plan Ablin was to act as the state's agent in the preparation of the second caravan but was not to make the Peking journey himself. Instead, the government intended to send the goods prepared by Ablin with a Tobolsk nobleman, accompanied by merchants and "Tatars," who would carry a letter to Peking similar to the one first taken by Ablin. On reconsideration, however, the state recognized that the dispatch of a new letter might complicate rather than facilitate commercial operations. Moscow had finally begun to distinguish between trade and diplomacy, evidently hoping to succeed in commerce by strict separation of the two activities. This understanding was stated clearly in an edict sent by the tsar to Tobolsk in December 1667, in which he decreed that the state's goods should be sent to China as the private goods of private merchants. He designated

Setkul Ablin and certain other Russian traders "private merchants." Ablin, as caravan head, received an official passport and hired twenty-six guards. At the voevoda's command the Russian merchants in Tobolsk elected three tselovalniks and the Bukharan merchants elected one. These men were responsible for the state's investment. Ablin arranged for the departure of the caravan in the company of some Kalmuk envoys returning home, hoping in this way to avoid difficulties with the nomads.

The tsar's letter of December 1667 gave the value of the goods to be exported to China at 4,500 rubles. Ablin was "to sell and barter these goods for local Chinese commodities, which would be suitable for the Muscovite State, and in all to seek profits for the Great Sovereign." The goods were remarkably varied: 1,082 yards of broadcloth of various qualities, valued at a bit over 1,991 rubles; 20 pounds of red oranges at 369 rubles; 4 mirrors at 12 rubles; 397 Russian red leather skins at 457 rubles; watches at 15 rubles; 60 gilded skins at 50 rubles; 2 pieces of coarse broadcloth at a little over 8 rubles. The bulk of the merchandise, however, consisted of furs: 3,574 ermines, 1,719 white fox skins, 163 otter pelts, 1,500 squirrel skins, 788 gray and red foxskins, 2 wolf skins, and 80 hare skins, as well as 2 pure red foxskins.[51] This was the first time that fur played a predominant role in Sino-Russian trade, and it kept that position for almost a century and a half.

Ablin left Tobolsk on July 13, 1668, arriving at Peking in June 1669 after a journey lasting forty-eight weeks and three days. Outside Peking the caravan was met by "a Chinese official" who conducted it into the capital and lodged the staff at the "embassy court" of the Li-fan yuan. Ablin, remembered for his willingness to conform to traditional court ceremonial, was with five of his staff presented to the young K'ang-hsi, who had ascended the throne since the Russian's last visit. Throughout his life K'ang-hsi demonstrated a broad curiosity and great vitality in his contacts with foreigners. At this informal audience in the emperor's garden Ablin handed the tsar's gifts to the emperor's officials, including 380 rubles worth of fur and broadcloth. At a later date he had another personal audience with the emperor, who sent the tsar a silver mug, velvet, silk, and tea, all valued in Moscow at 1,055 rubles.

The Russians remained in Peking less than a month, during which time Ablin "with all the people of his caravan" was invited three times to dine in the emperor's garden, together with Bukharan and Kalmuk envoys and merchants. The emperor himself, however, did not attend the dinners. The Russians traded freely in Peking, aided by an interpreter and by two important and ten minor officials and merchants appointed by the emperor to assist and record the results of their trade in detail. This assistance demonstrated the emperor's direct interest in commerce, even if his court did not actually participate.

Shortly before departing from Peking, Ablin was invited to the Li-fan yuan for an interview. The emperor, he was told, had received the tsar's gifts "with honor" and hoped to receive Russian envoys and merchants in China in the future. They would always receive "sustenance and all kinds of considerations." At the same time the Li-fan yuan lodged a complaint concerning some 170 tribute payers who had switched allegiance to Russia. This was the first of such complaints, which were to become chronic in later years. The caravan was then dismissed from Peking with provisions for two months and a convoy as far as the Great Wall.

Central Asian disturbances delayed the caravan's homeward progress, so that Ablin reached Tobolsk only on October 11, 1672, four years after his departure. Arriving in Moscow in January the next year, he made a full report to the Siberian Department. Exporting 4,500 rubles' worth of goods, he sold 3,484 rubles' worth in Peking for 11,507 liang (he equated the liang, or ounce of silver, with the ruble's purchasing power). With this he purchased 2,334 large, medium, and small pieces of silk, which alone were valued in Moscow at slightly over 11,119 rubles; 2,532 precious stones, 144 yards of velvet, 33,000 yards of nankeen, 5 puds of raw silk, and various miscellaneous items. The Chinese goods were valued in all at 18,715 rubles—a not inconsiderable profit on an initial investment of only 4,500 rubles. Ablin was rewarded for his success with a silver ladle, fifty rubles cash, and several lengths of broadcloth and silk.[52]

Ablin's first caravan demonstrated to Moscow that trade was its own reward. As an end in itself or as a means toward a commercial end, diplomacy would only complicate the pursuit of trade; it introduced a new factor, which within the context of the Chinese institutions inherited by the Manchus required a noncommercial response, the tribute ceremonial, in addition to trade. The principle of separating trade and diplomacy was applied with remarkable results to Setkul Ablin's second caravan. His status as a private trader allowed him to perform whatever ceremonies were necessary to the completion of his commercial duties without thought to political consequences. The Ch'ing court, for its part, was free to record his arrival in Peking under whatever rubric it wished, choosing in this case the rubric of tribute: "The Ch'a-han han of O-lo-ssu [Russia] sent envoys to present tribute. Then dinners and gifts were bestowed upon them according to regulations."[53] A convenient modus vivendi was thus worked out, which permitted each side to handle the problems of its relations with the other as it saw fit, without transgressing its own principles, customs, or assumptions. The results were great profits for the Moscow treasury and presumably for the Ch'ing court as well.

This caravan also showed Moscow the great value of Russian fur on the Peking market. The state now knew that it had an exceedingly profitable monopoly if it chose to develop it. Faced with declining fur markets in Europe and attracted by this new source of profit, Moscow began to explore methods for placing its China trade on a more permanent basis. The Siberian Department organized a detailed examination of all those who had participated in the caravan, in order to determine what goods should be sent to and brought from China in the future. The investigators concluded that it would be most profitable to export expensive broadcloth in bright colors but small quantities because of Peking's warm climate. They also decided with little difficulty that cheap fur in general, but expensive sables in particular, would be the most important Russian exports. The survey indicated that it would be cheapest and most profitable to import pearls, gold, precious stones, raw silk, dyed silk threads, and silk cloth from China. The Siberian Department also tried to estimate the possible future value of the China trade. In a report prepared for the tsar before the dispatch of the next embassy to Peking, the Siberian Department suggested that there was sufficient fur available in Siberian collection depots to send 10,163 rubles' worth to China. On the basis of Ablin's experience it estimated a profit of slightly over 34,593 rubles.[54] The China market was obviously worth pursuing.

Precisely at this moment, however, when fifty years of seeking trade with China appeared about to be crowned with success, events in the Amur basin began to intrude on Russia's policy of developing relations with Peking. Just as Moscow succeeded in discovering a nonpolitical basis for Sino-Russian trade, the basic political problems raised by the Russo-Manchu confrontation along the Amur could no longer be avoided or dealt with only locally. Henceforth, the Amur problem and the establishment of relations with Peking became inextricably joined.

The Recognition of Identity: Milovanov's Mission

Two closely related problems forced the Ch'ing court to develop an integrated response to the heretofore apparently unrelated challenges of Russian colonial expansion in the Amur Valley and Moscow's diplomatic approach to Peking. The first problem was the continued and now increasing pressure of Russian settlement in the area of the Amur, which created the second, the fact that the Russian presence there allowed the local inhabitants an alternative object of allegiance. In other words, natives wishing to escape payment of tribute to Peking could switch allegiance to the Russians, who in return for payment of the yasak (which at first was usually less than Peking's exactions) would extend their protection against the Manchus. The issue of "fugitives," those natives who switched their allegiance and tribute payments, remained the single most pressing problem in Sino-Russian relations down to the end of the eighteenth century.

The first important instance of an Amur native switching allegiance from Peking to Moscow was provided by Gantimur, a Solun chieftain who had taken part in the Manchu attack on Kumarsk in 1655.[55] Gantimur set in motion a train of events that was to result in the Milovanov mission and in Peking's final recognition of a common identity between the Amur Cossacks and the diplomatic missions from Moscow. With his relatives and some forty men of his tribe, Gantimur went over to the Russians sometime between 1667 and 1670. In 1684 he was baptized and given a rank in the Russian nobility with the title and name of Prince Peter Gantimurov. Moscow placed him in charge of the Tungus and Mongol tribes in Amuria, and he made his permanent residence at Nerchinsk. The disposition of his person remained a serious issue until his death at the end of the century.

The Ch'ing court, disturbed by Gantimur's defection, began to reconnoiter Russian positions along the Amur by sending agents disguised as merchants and hunters into the area. It hoped these disguises would attract little attention.[56] In 1669 four scouts disguised as merchants were sent into Nerchinsk, where after being entertained by the unsuspecting voevoda, Danilo Arshinsky, they were sent home well provisioned. In April 1670 one Sharanda, a local representative of Manchu authority, delivered a letter, allegedly from the emperor, to Arshinsky at Nerchinsk. Reporting this to the tsar almost a year later, in February 1671, the voevoda stated that he had had the emperor's letter "translated into the Tangut language; but whether the translation is correct or not he, Danilo Arshinsky, cannot say; for in Nerchinsk there are no interpreters."[57] How, or why, the letter was translated into Tangut, which is Tibetan, is not clear, but Arshinsky had to act promptly, whether or not he understood its contents, because Manchu forces were stationed only two days away from Nerchinsk. Obviously unable to obtain instructions from Moscow in time, the voevoda followed the tradition that allowed a large degree of independence to the Siberian bureaucracy in the field of foreign relations. He sent the Cossack Ignaty Milovanov and two companions to Peking on April 19, 1670, with a letter for the emperor. This mission returned on August 11, 1670, with what again purported to be a letter from the emperor to the tsar.[58]

If the Milovanov mission were of interest for no other reason, the contents of Arshinsky's letter to the emperor would alone make it noteworthy. The exchange of letters between frontier authorities, or between a voevoda and certain officials in Peking, was well within the tradition of both Russian and Manchu empires. What was not in accord with tradition, either Russian,

Manchu, or Chinese, was Arshinsky's demand that the emperor of China become tributary to the tsar of Russia![59] Arshinsky also informed the emperor that the Milovanov mission and its letter were sent at the order of the tsar, which was of course untrue. When Moscow heard of his action, the hapless voevoda was dismissed. Curiously enough, the Ch'ing court, far from reacting unfavorably to Arshinsky's suggestion that it submit to Moscow, accepted the letter as a *piao,* a tributary memorial signifying Moscow's submission to Peking. The court, however, did not learn of the actual contents of the letter until at least six years later, during the Milescu embassy. While Milovanov was at Peking, the letter probably remained untranslated, or at least translated inoffensively, as is indicated by an entry in Chang Yü-shu's *Chao-tai ts'ung-shu*: "In the fourth month of the ninth year [of K'ang-hsi's reign] Russia sent an envoy to present his piao as a sign of submission, but the text of it was incomprehensible; the script went from bottom to top, like Taoists' charm seals. Therefore, their envoy was summoned to translate the document in order to present it [to the emperor]."[60] Since Milovanov himself was illiterate, he could not have given a translation of the document. Nor is it likely that any translator, Russian or Chinese, would have been willing to give offense to delicate Manchu sensibilities.[61]

Gantimur's flight to Nerchinsk and his recognition there of the tsar as his sovereign must have brought home to Peking the fact that Nerchinsk was the seat of Russian state power and authority. This was further supported by the Manchu reconnoitering of Russian positions along the Amur and by the Milovanov mission. Since Milovanov carried a letter from the tsar, or so the Manchus were given to understand, they could now identify the "Lo-ch'a" of their frontier with the "O-lo-ssu" whence came Petlin, Baykov, and Ablin. Within this context the entire episode of Sharanda's visit to Nerchinsk and the Milovanov mission can be understood as the first effort on Peking's part to determine the relationship between Albazin (the Cossacks) and Nerchinsk, on the one hand, and Nerchinsk and Moscow, on the other.[62] Regardless of what they had been before, the unruly "Lo-ch'a" now had to be regarded as an extension of Moscow's power into the Amur. Milovanov brought a letter back from Peking indicating that while the identification had not been made before, it was now clear.[63] The letter stated explicitly that Manchu hunters and trappers had reported Albazin Cossack raids against the indigenous population of the Amur, who were tributary to Peking. The emperor had considered sending a punitive expedition against Albazin, "but he was told that they were subjects of the Great Tsar" and refrained from doing so. Instead, he sent his representative to Nerchinsk and received the envoy Milovanov. Now the emperor "had learnt for certain that in Nerchinsk fort dwelt a *voevoda* and a military people, subjects of the Great Lord." The letter included a request that the tsar exert sufficient control over his people on the Amur that disputes might not again break the peace.

The recognition of the relationship between Moscow and the Amur resulted in a distinct shift in Manchu policy. The Manchu military response to the Amur problem and their diplomatic response to Russia's commercial efforts coalesced into a new, unified approach. The nexus of the new policy was to be the exchange of commercial privileges for an Amur settlement. The new policy line began to emerge while Milovanov was still in Peking. Despite the fact that he was only a messenger, and a mere frontier official at that, he was admitted to an imperial audience, where he kowtowed, and was entertained grandly during his stay in the capital. Nor did the Manchus forget to impress him with their military might and wealth. But most striking was the persistence with which the Ch'ing officials impressed Milovanov with the commercial advantages of the Peking market. Milovanov's description of his conversations on this subject indicate that the Manchus were making tentative proposals. "And the Chinese," he reported, "asked for young sables and summer-killed black ones, and sable bellies, and ermines, and squirrels, and white arctic foxes." The Manchus also assured him that all manner of products, including gold, silver, copper, tin, lead, powder, silks, velvets, nankeens, and satins, were produced inside China and could be exported, with the exception of weapons such as bows, iron arrowheads, sabers, plate-armor, and helmets.[64]

To ensure Moscow's understanding that trade was now dependent on peace along the Amur and Russian withdrawal from the region, the official who accompanied Milovanov back to Nerchinsk presented the tsar, through Arshinsky, with gifts including "a hat and embroidered coat of brocade, a silk belted gown with knife, six pieces of silk, two of velvet, two of satin, and a saddle and bridle." At the same time he "begged call the Great Lord's attention to the fact that Nikiforko Chernigoff and his men from Albazin kept attacking their frontier people, the Dahurs and Djuchers." The new policy was given even clearer expression in the letter Milovanov brought back from Peking, in which the hope that "people should go quite freely, and continually, for trade purposes" was balanced against the threat to Manchu security in the Amur basin.[65] The policy had its first trial when Nikolay Gavrilovich Milescu arrived as ambassador in Peking in the mid-1670's.

Chapter III Milescu and Mala

Nikolay Gavrilovich Milescu's embassy to Peking climaxed Moscow's campaign to establish permanent diplomatic relations with the Manchu Empire on the basis of accepted European practice. It occasioned nothing less than a direct confrontation between European and East Asian diplomatic systems, in which the protagonists were superb representatives of essentially incompatible views of the world. Milescu, a well-educated European intellectual and diplomat, was haughty in the knowledge of his own theological and secular tradition, together with his experience at the grandest of Europe's courts. Mala, his Manchu counterpart, was one of the Ch'ing court's leading "barbarian experts," who reflected accurately the Chinese tradition to which the Manchus clung so tenaciously in the initial years of their conquest of China. Moscow, east of West but very much in the mainstream of a European tradition that had not yet been universalized through imperialism and colonialism, insisted on the equality of nation-states and sovereigns, while the Manchus presided over a system that recognized the existence of only one civilization, one human society, universalistic in its pretentions. Mutual accommodation was achieved only when each side, after military conflict, had eschewed the imposition of its own assumptions on the other and cooperated in the development of a network of culturally neutral institutions for political and commercial intercourse.

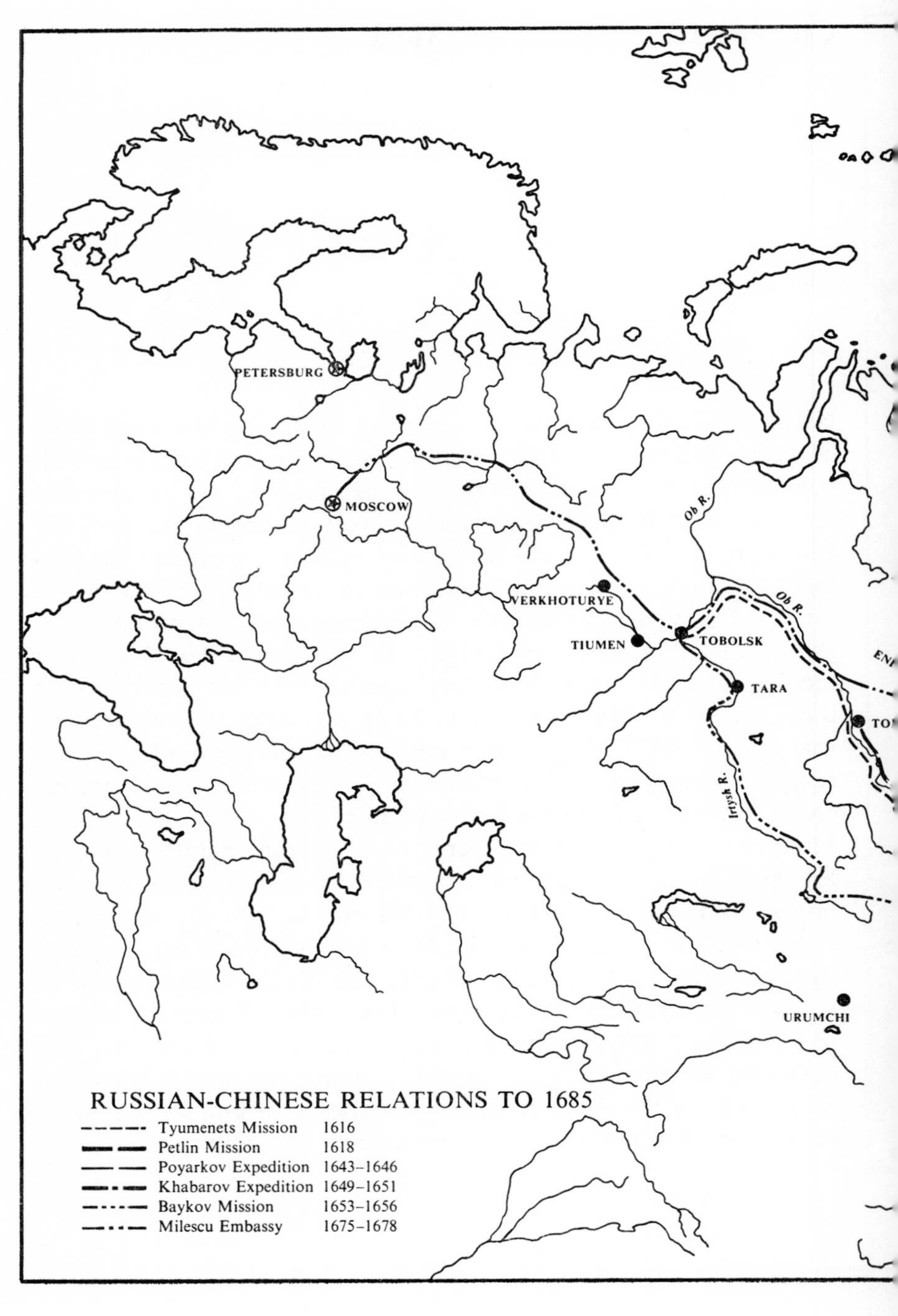
PETERSBURG
MOSCOW
Ob R.
VERKHOTURYE
TIUMEN
TOBOLSK
TARA
Irtysh R.
URUMCHI
RUSSIAN-CHINESE RELATIONS TO 1685
Tyumenets Mission 1616
Petlin Mission 1618
Poyarkov Expedition 1643–1646
Khabarov Expedition 1649–1651
Baykov Mission 1653–1656
Milescu Embassy 1675–1678

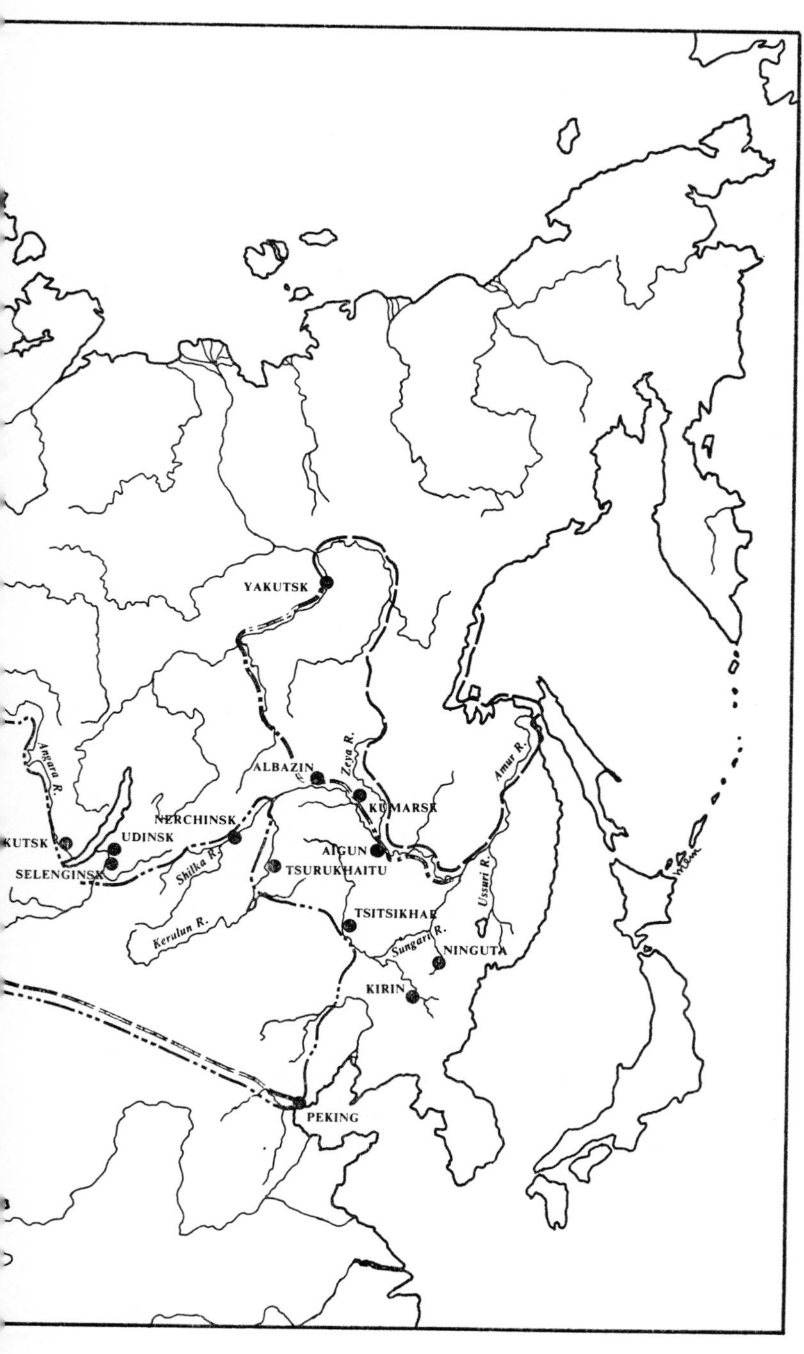
YAKUTSK
ALBAZIN
Zeya R.
KUMARSK
Amur R.
Angara R.
NERCHINSK
UDINSK
KUTSK
SELENGINSK
Shilka R.
TSURUKHAITU
AIGUN
Ussuri R.
Kerulun R.
TSITSIKHAR
Sungari R.
NINGUTA
KIRIN
PEKING

Chapter III Milescu and Mala

Origins of the Embassy

Milescu's embassy to Peking can be considered from two points of view. On the one hand, it was a further, more intensive move in the process whereby Russia sought permanent and profitable relations with China. On the other hand, the embassy was only one aspect of a larger effort by Moscow to develop relations with the East in general. The same economic factors that impelled Moscow to make a new move in China's direction also gave rise to a similar and almost simultaneous attempt to develop commerce with India.[1]

A continuing series of internal and external crises dictated Russia's search for commercial profit in the East during the 1670's. Internally, the revolt led by Stenka Razin was put down in 1671 only with the greatest difficulty. Since both the revolt and the conflicts with Russia's neighbors to the West had required large state expenditures, the state sought to refill its coffers through commerce. The political situation in western Europe, however, impeded the development of Russian trade in that direction. Three Anglo-Dutch wars were fought for supremacy of the seas, the third of which (1672-1674) found Holland confronted by a coalition of England, France, and Sweden. Although the English withdrew from the struggle in 1674, the French continued to fight until the conclusion of the Peace of Nijmegen on August 10, 1678. This western European conflict resulted, *inter alia,* in a distinct decline in the quantity of Indian goods available at Arkhangelsk—goods that previously had been brought to that far northern Russian port on Dutch and English bottoms. At the same time difficulties in the south with the Turks kept Near Eastern trade routes closed to the Russians.

Increasing European interest in opening a land route to China provided the immediate impetus behind Milescu's mission. Intellectual as well as commercial circles (particularly German intellectuals) were interested in the project. Leibniz, for instance, quite early in his career argued for the opening of such a land route, and in 1672 he memorialized Louis XIV on the possibilities of direct trade between Europe and Egypt, India, and China.[2]

Whereas the Turks blocked the southern routes, Russia, Orthodox but Christian, provided direct land access to the East.

A German doctor in Moscow named Lorenz Rinhuber propounded these ideas in Russia, where German influence was strong in the second half of the seventeenth century. Many Germans and other Europeans worked in Moscow, where the Nemetskaya Sloboda or German Quarter was the center of their colony. Rinhuber was directly interested in the development of communications between Europe and China through Russia. By 1672 he had come to the attention of several highly placed persons in Moscow, including Artemon Matveev, the uncle of Natalia Naryshkin, who had just married the tsar, and the tsar himself, Alexis Mikhailovich. Rinhuber, who conceived of his native Saxony as the tutor to a europeanizing Russia, interpreted the proposed European-Asian relations as including a Sino-Russian rapprochement and a Russo-Abyssinian entente against the Turks. The doctor emphasized Russia's favorable geographical position for the role of mediator between Europe and Asia; he also pointed out that trade would bring Russia (and doubtless Saxony, too) greater profits than, for instance, the opening of mines.[3]

Although Rinhuber had no appointment either as Saxon or Russian diplomatic agent, he accompanied the Russian envoy Semen Mikhailovich Protopopov to Altenburg in Saxony in the summer of 1674. Protopopov's mission, undoubtedly inspired in large part by Rinhuber's ideas, was to discuss with Ernst, the elector of Saxony, such problems as establishment of a general European coalition against the Sublime Porte, a Russo-Abyssinian entente to attack Turkey from the rear, and means to develop Russo-Chinese commercial relations. Ernst, however, was ill, and his son Friedrich, who ruled in his stead, was not particularly interested in Rinhuber's distant projects. The mission came to nought. Since Rinhuber did not return to Russia until August 1675, he arrived too late to participate in Moscow's embassy to Peking, although he had certainly influenced Moscow's decision to dispatch a full embassy. Milescu had in fact been appointed ambassador to China on July 13, 1674, just before Protopopov's mission, so that Moscow had evidently made the decision to send an embassy to

Peking before discussions with the Elector of Saxony, and Protopopov's mission was merely an effort to use every possible avenue to explore the development of relations with the East.[4]

Nikolay Gavrilovich Milescu

In Milescu, Moscow had one of the most widely educated and experienced diplomats of the age. Although he is chiefly remembered for his journey to China, Milescu was also one of the important contributors to the Greek Orthodox renaissance of the seventeenth century. Through Padua-educated Greeks from islands under Venetian domination, Italian influence was particularly strong in Constantinople, reenforcing Hellenism and Orthodoxy in the East. The Orthodox Church was the only possible manifestation of Hellenic culture in the Turkish empire. It became the center of the renaissance, which was at once a revival of the church and a vain effort to achieve Greek political independence. The paramount animator, organizer, and leader of this cultural-political movement in the second half of the seventeenth century was Dositheos, the Patriarch of Jerusalem, who was resident in Constantinople. Milescu was a student, friend, and confidant of Dositheos.[5] The school of the Patriarch of Constantinople, one of the chief academies of the Greek renaissance, also enjoyed its period of greatest expansion and influence at about the same time.

Nikolay, son of Gavril Milescu, was probably born in 1636, the scion of a noble Moldavian family with property in Vaslui.[6] Greek Peloponnesian in origin, the family had left its homeland sometime in the sixteenth century to seek its fortune in Romania. Nikolay studied under Basil Blassios at the Patriarch's school in Constantinople. Under its rector, the theologian and amateur historian John Kariophyl, this Western-oriented school had become a great intellectual center, where the students studied Latin and humanism.[7] Milescu's knowledge of Latin was to stand him in good stead in Peking, where he had extensive and important contacts with the Jesuits.

After completing his studies, Milescu returned to Moldavia, where he was appointed secretary to the Moldavian hospodar (or prince) Stefan Georgits.[8] This position suited him well, requiring a wide knowledge of languages, particularly Latin. After Stefan Georgits was deposed by the Turks in 1658 for attempting a rapprochement with Russia, Milescu continued to serve under his successor, George Ghika. Ghika appointed Milescu a *spathar,* the court functionary who sometimes served as a bodyguard, and by this title he has been incorrectly known in history.[9] As a spathar, Milescu commanded a detachment of a thousand soldiers sent by Ghika to Transylvania to support the Turks against Prince George Rakoczy, who had rebelled against the Porte. In late 1659 or early 1660 Ghika was transferred by the Turks to another Romanian principality, where Milescu accompanied him as grand spathar, remaining in his service until September 1660, when the prince was deposed by Constantinople. Milescu then returned to Moldavia, where he became the favorite of the hospodar Stefanitsa, one of his fellow students in Constantinople. Stefanitsa, however, was deposed in 1661, and Milescu left Moldavia for Wallachia, where Gregory, the son of George Ghika, now reigned. Gregory appointed Milescu *kapoukehaia* or diplomatic agent in Constantinople, where he continued to serve until the Turks deposed Gregory in 1664 for supporting the Austrians in a war against the Porte.[10]

During this early period of his life, Milescu engaged in literary as well as political activities. His most ambitious work was a Romanian translation of the complete text of the Bible. Though not published, it served as the basis for a translation by the Wallachian prince Servan Cantacuzene, printed in Bucharest in 1688.[11]

Unable to return to the Danubian provinces after Gregory Ghika's deposition in 1664, Milescu began a journey through western Europe, visiting the court of Elector Friedrich Wilhelm in Berlin and proceeding to Stettin, which was under Swedish rule.[12] There he found his first master, Stefan Georgits, who was living in exile on a small Swedish pension. Georgits sent Milescu to Stockholm in October 1666 with a request for an increased pension and with letters for the Swedish king and queen and the French ambassador at the Swedish court, Simon Arnauld, Marquis de Pomponne. Pomponne, who later became minister to Louis XIV, became Milescu's close friend and wrote of him to Paris, "I was surprised to find a man living so close to Tartary, also instructed in languages, and with a general knowledge of all things."[13] It was probably Pomponne who suggested that Stefan Georgits send Milescu to Paris in connection with a proposal for an anti-Turkish crusade. Milescu arrived at the French capital in July 1667, bearing letters to Louis XIV from his own prince and from Charles XI of Sweden. Louis promised to intercede with the Porte on behalf of Georgits' throne, but to no avail. The prince died in exile on January 27, 1668, and Milescu decided to return to Moldavia, where he took service with the reigning prince, Ilias Alexandru. By this time Milescu was "one of the most cultivated men of the nobility of his nation, having experience in political and diplomatic questions" and, above all, maintaining close relations with Constantinople, particularly with Nikusia Panagiot, the Porte's influential grand dragoman.[14]

Milescu's arrogance and conceit, inspired by his wide travels, high connections, and broad intellectual attainments, led him to attempt to seize the throne from his new master. Prince Ilias, a stranger in his country, had inspired considerable popular discontent during his reign. Hoping to capitalize on the situation, Milescu conspired against the prince, convinced Constantinople that Ilias was in treasonous league with Poland, which was then at war with Turkey, and tried to depose him. He failed, however, and before he could flee, was arrested by Ilias, who as punishment had him mutilated by cutting the cartilage separating his nostrils. This mutilation, derived from Byzantine custom, disgraced the criminal forever: he could never hope to occupy the throne in his own right. Milescu left the country, physically marked as a traitor.[15]

Milescu's service under the Moscow tsars and, eventually, his journey to Peking originated in his close connections with Constantinople's Orthodox clergy. He maintained contact with three important Greek leaders: Blassios, his former teacher at Constantinople, Dositheos, Patriarch of Jerusalem, and Nikusia Panagiot, the Porte's grand dragoman. These men were united by a common belief in the "Great Idea," one of the earliest expressions of the doctrine of the political and religious unity of Orthodox Christians: the liberation of Orthodoxy from the Turkish yoke. The Orthodox clergy, led by the patriarch, tried in every way to promote this "idea" by means of a political rapprochement between Russia and her co-religionists in eastern Europe. As early as 1654, for instance, Blassios negotiated with Moscow on behalf of Stefan Georgits, looking toward Moldavia's recognition of Russian suzerainty.[16] Dositheos was the leader of the movement, and Panagiot was one of the great supporters of Orthodoxy and an opponent of Jesuit penetration of the Romanian province. In his opinion the Jesuits were more to be feared than the Turks. Both men were known in Moscow as trusted agents of the tsars, and Russian envoys to Constantinople were habitually instructed to contact Dositheos on their arrival.[17]

Milescu was in Constantinople in Dositheos' train in January 1671 when the patriarch received a request from the tsar for "a person knowledgeable in foreign languages for translating religious works and for service as a diplomatic translator." Dositheos recommended the disgraced Milescu, giving him a personal letter of introduction to the tsar. En route, Milescu visited Panagiot in Adrianople, where he was charged with a secret mission in connection with the grand dragoman's efforts to arrange a Polish-Russian peace. He visited Michael Wisznowiecki, the Polish king, sometime early in 1671 and on May 23 passed through Smolensk into Russia.[18] He reached Moscow in June, where he delivered his letters and Dositheos' recommendation.[19]

During his first period of service in Russia, Milescu remained a minor bureaucrat. Although his interest in Balkan politics continued, only after his return from Peking did he become the Moscow representative of the Orthodox Christians living under Turkish rule. Before the journey Milescu was little more than a refugee seeking asylum and protection from the consequences of his treason. He was appointed to the Ambassadorial Department on December 14, 1671, "for eternity," with an annual salary of one hundred rubles, a handsome income for a man in his position.[20] The chief of the Ambassadorial Department and Milescu's immediate superior was Artemon Matveev, one of the most important figures in Russia at the time.[21] Under Matveev's leadership the Ambassadorial Department became a center of Western influence, and Milescu, as a learned man widely traveled in the West, rapidly gained Matveev's favor. Matveev became the Romanian's personal protector, giving him the freedom of his house, the center of Moscow's intellectual life. The spathar was appointed tutor to Matveev's six-year-old son, Andrei, whom he taught both Greek and Latin.[22]

At the Ambassadorial Department Milescu's chief occupation was translating diplomatic documents, historical and theological works, and making compilations. The most important were copied out in particularly fine illuminated editions for presentation to the tsar. As author or editor of almost the entire output of the Ambassadorial Department at that time, Milescu came to the tsar's attention and was given an audience. His salary was increased to 132 rubles per annum, and he was given a new assignment: translating the court's secret diplomatic correspondence.[23]

As the tsar's new favorite, Milescu found his star rising rapidly in Moscow. At the end of 1672 or the beginning of 1673 on the tsar's order he took possession of the apartments, library, and manuscripts of a former favorite, the Greek bishop Paissios Ligarides. Milescu replaced the bishop in the scholarly and political, though not the ecclesiastical, aspects of his role as representative of the Greeks in Russia.[24] At the same time he served as interpreter for various foreign embassies, for example, the Danish embassy in 1674. By the time the tsar selected him as ambassador to Peking, Milescu had become an important figure in Moscow's diplomatic and intellectual circles.

Preparations

Milescu's instructions were not completed until the end of February 1675, more than seven months after his appointment, because Moscow evidently wanted to await the results of Protopopov's conversations and inquiries in Saxony. When completed, the instructions contained a preamble and fourteen distinct and numbered paragraphs, the whole constituting a summary of Moscow's "China policy."[25] The tsar's overwhelming interest in establishing regularized commercial relations with Peking was demonstrated by the fact that fully half of the instructions directly concerned commercial matters. Four points dealt with diplomatic relations, which it was hoped would facilitate the commercial aims of Russia's China policy.

The development of a bilateral trade system remained Russia's sole commercial objective in China. Milescu was instructed to arrange for the merchants of each empire to travel freely to the other. However, Moscow was by now clearly aware that while she might be allowed to trade in China, it was another matter for Chinese merchants to come to Russia. If Russia alone played an active role in the trade, the entire burden of transportation costs would lie on her shoulders. Three articles (V, VI, and IX) dealt specifically with this problem. The ambassador was to demand the dispatch of an envoy to Moscow, who was to come "with a declaration of friendship and love." Even more important, he was to bring gifts of precious stones, velvets, satins, and other valuable goods. Moscow specified that she wanted from one to three or more thousand puds of silver which, together with the precious stones and colored silks, could be exchanged at the state treasury for whatever goods the Manchu envoys might select. In other words, Moscow sought a diplomatic solution to the commercial problem of equalizing the costs of transportation. At the same time she still wanted to develop private trade, to which end Milescu (evidently outside official channels) was to persuade "all kinds of Chinese merchants" to make the journey to Russia, where they would receive the royal favor.

Recognizing that commerce depended on the development of short, safe trade routes, the tsar devoted three articles to the opening of new routes. Four rivers were to be explored as possible roads to China: the Ob, Enisei, Selenga, and Irtysh. Astrakhan was to be explored as a possible Sino-Russian entrepot, and the ambassador was to send two men from Peking to Astrakhan to scout the route. Milescu himself was to return to Moscow by the shortest possible route, hopefully by sea and river.

Since the regularization of commerce depended in large part on the establishment of accepted modes for political contact, four articles in the instructions dealt with this problem. An agreement was to be reached concerning the language and form in which the emperor or his ministers would correspond with the tsar. Latin or Turkish was preferred. That Moscow had not yet perceived the quality of the traditional East Asian international order, in which China's tributary rulers held their titles from the emperor, was demonstrated in the Russian insistence that Milescu guard against the emperor's appropriating to himself the titles of "other Great Lords around him." The same article suggested that Milescu and the Manchu ministers exchange lists of their respective masters' titles. Moscow's rigidity in this matter was shown in the requirement that the emperor was to use exactly those titles in addressing the tsar that the tsar used to name himself in his official letters. Within the context of these diplomatic and commercial instructions, the ambassador was to convince the Manchus that his master wished only to live in love and friendship with China.

The Milescu instructions also indicate that Moscow did not yet fully appreciate the nature of the frontier problem. The only article dealing with it concerned the results, not the causes, of the conflict: the ambassador was to determine whether Russian prisoners were held in China and, if ransom was demanded, to offer no more than thirty rubles a head. Questions of translation and technology also merited only one point each.

Finally, the instructions included articles dealing with two miscellaneous topics. Milescu was to obtain for the tsar the services of Chinese masons for the construction of Chinese-style bridges inside Russia. To complete the unfinished business of previous embassies, he was also to carry to Peking four letters received from China "in ancient times" and ask the Jesuits to translate them into Latin, "for in them there may have been demands from the Chinese court, which are unknown till now to the Russian tsar."

The tsar's *gramota,* or official letter, to the emperor exhibited the same lack of comprehension of the Confucian world order as did the instructions. The letter opened with a recitation of the tsar's titles, claiming his descent from Caesar Augustus and asserting his sovereignty over all parts of Russian Siberia, Bulgaria, and the Caucasus. In contrast, the address and title used for the emperor were modest indeed: "To the most noble Bogdykhan of the city of Kanbulak [sic] and of all the Chinese Kingdom Ruler." The tsar then based his case for the establishment of relations with China on the fact that he corresponded to mutual advantage with the various Christian and Moslem rulers on his frontiers. Regretting the lack of communications with China in the past, the tsar declared that he wished only peace, friendship, and uninterrupted contact. In an obvious effort to overcome foreseen difficulties over titles, the tsar begged the emperor's forgiveness if he addressed him incorrectly.[26]

In addition to the instructions and the gramota, the ambassador received gifts for presentation to the emperor in Peking and to the various Mongol princes he might meet en route. The emperor was sent 800 rubles' worth of sables, black foxes, broadcloth, mirrors, amber, watches, and other "curious or valuable" items. Milescu was given an additional 1,000 rubles' worth of sable pelts for the purchase of Chinese goods and 500 rubles' worth to pay duties if the Manchus so required. Two hundred rubles of sable pelts and ten puds of tobacco were provided "for distribution to various commissions," that is, for bribery. Six gerfalcons and ermine pelts, valued at 100 rubles, were given to the ambassador for miscellaneous gifts and expenditures.[27]

Accompanied by his suite, goods, and gifts, Milescu left Moscow on February 25, 1675, and arrived at Tobolsk on March 30, carrying a special edict to the voevoda of Tobolsk concerning supplies for the convoy and selection of the shortest and safest route to Peking. He remained in Tobolsk until May 2, when the river opened for navigation. During this time he collected information in preparation for his tasks in Peking.

Milescu in Siberia

When the embassy arrived at Tobolsk, the local voevoda, Peter Saltykov, immediately called a meeting of local boyar sons, merchants, and Cossacks to advise the ambassador on the choice of routes to China. An outbreak of fighting had cut off the route used by Baykov and Ablin, and Milescu chose to travel to Peking through Nerchinsk and the Amur River Valley.[28] Tobolsk's chief importance or Milescu, however, was the presence of Yury Krizhanich, a Roman Catholic slavophile monk of Serbian nationality who had been exiled to Siberia by Alexis. Krizhanich was one of the first exponents of the rudimentary doctrines of Pan-Slavism, which were so closely related to the "Great Idea" of Dositheos, Panagiot, and Blassios.[29] The ambassador and the monk undoubtedly had much in common intellectually, for Krizhanich wrote that the Romanian contacted him immediately upon arrival in Tobolsk and dined with him twice daily until his departure.[30]

Milescu was particularly interested in the information on Siberia collected by Krizhanich during his years of exile at Tobolsk. The monk had written a book, *Description of Siberia,* to which he allegedly appended a smaller work entitled *About the Chinese Trade,* which he sent to Moscow, perhaps before 1675.[31] (This work on Sino-Russian trade has been lost, but it is highly unlikely that it arrived in Moscow in time to influence the decision to send Milescu to Peking.) The monk translated for the ambassador "one great book printed in the Dutch language, about an embassy which they sent eight years before from Holland to China." The work was probably *Gedenkvaerdig Bedryff,* the account of Peter van Hoorn's embassy of 1666-1668.[32] Krizhanich also allowed Milescu to copy his own books and data on China. He firmly believed that Russia would profit greatly from trade with China, and he envisaged the use of those profits to support Russia's role as protector of the Orthodox Christians in the Turkish empire. He thus reenforced Rinhuber's ideas from a different vantage point—one more closely related to Milescu's own Balkan ambitions and interests.[33]

In addition to information, Milescu collected in Tobolsk the major portion of his suite. With the assistance of the voevoda he selected six boyar sons, six falconers, and six assistant falconers, together with forty guards of convoy (twenty Litvins, sixteen Cossacks, and four newly baptized natives). He also added specialized personnel to his staff. One Grigory Kobyakov, a Cossack who had visited Peking for Danilo Arshinsky, voevoda of Nerchinsk, was taken on for his knowledge of the route. Spiridonka Bezryadov, a dragoman, was chosen "for interpreting the Kalmuk and Tartar tongues." All these men were given two years' wages in advance and a third year's wages in merchandise, "in accordance with what was done formerly in the cases of Fedor Baykov and Setkul Ablin."[34]

Milescu's preparations for his negotiations at Peking entered a new phase when he arrived at Eniseisk on July 9. While at Tobolsk, he had collected general information on Siberia and China; now he began to pay particular attention to conditions along the frontier and the political situation inside the Manchu Empire. As he received information concerning the Manchu-Russian confrontation along the Amur, the ambassador began to develop the lines of argument that he would later use in Peking. He informed the tsar, for instance, that he had heard a rumor that the Albazin Cossacks, numbering some three hundred, had "of their own accord made war on Chinese subjects" who farmed along the banks of the Argun, about five days march from Albazin. While admitting the fact, Milescu denied its significance. Far from attacking the "Chinese," he suggested, the Cossacks had been invited to visit them so that they could shift their allegiance from emperor to tsar.[35]

Milescu also received information about China's internal politics throwing light on China's failure to retaliate against Albazin, which must also have contributed to a stiffening of his own already unbending attitudes and policies. In a letter to the tsar dated July 18, 1675, Milescu relayed information brought by Gavril Romanov, an agent of the merchant Evstafy Filatiev, who had been in China for trade.[36] Romanov reported that the Manchus, fearful that his caravan was the advance party of a Russian invasion, had delayed him at Kalgan for three weeks while they searched the steppes, permitting him to proceed to Peking only when they found nothing suspicious. Trade at Peking, he added, was worse than it had been in previous years. Milescu explained these events to the tsar in terms of a war that had recently broken out between the Manchus in North China and the Nikans, or Chinese, in the south, and he concluded that the war was going badly for the Manchus.

Against this background of an anti-Manchu rebellion in China and Peking's failure to retaliate against Albazin, Milescu began to exaggerate what he considered to be the essential weakness of the Ch'ing position in China. Romanov had told him that "Russian deserters" in Peking believed that two thousand Russian troops would suffice to conquer not only the Amur but all of North China to the Great Wall, "the Bogdykhan being at present extremely weak, mightily afraid of the cossacks, and greatly upset by the war [with the Chinese]." This opinion was supported by Mongol envoys on their way to Moscow, who visited Milescu at Eniseisk and told him that the Manchus had been defeated several times by the Chinese, "so that in the end the latter [the Manchus] will perish and the old Chinese conquer them as before."[37] Consequently, the ambassador wrote Matveev that "the present would be a favorable time to gain honor," since the Manchus "are the worst sort of people and not warlike." Suggesting a Russian attack on China, he promised to reconnoiter the frontier and report on its terrain, populace, and armaments—"the latter, I hear, very poor." Milescu approached the Chinese frontier with a deep conviction of the Ch'ing dynasty's weaknesses added to his own arrogance and conceit.

On July 18 the ambassadorial caravan left Eniseisk for Nerchinsk. Passing through Selenginsk on October 2, Milescu was impressed with the role that a settlement could play as an emporium in the trade he hoped to establish with Peking. He reached Nerchinsk on December 5, and on December 19 he wrote the tsar a long letter reporting on the conditions of unrest and even revolt he had found among the natives along the frontier. The continuous and piecemeal expansion of Russian-occupied territory in southern Siberia, in which the natives were hard pressed by the Cossacks, had created such a situation that Milescu had difficulty finding sufficient transport and provisions for his large embassy. "But by God's mercy and under Your Majesty's happy auspices, I reached Nerchinsk safely."[38] As he approached the frontier, the ambassador's position on several problems hardened further. At Irkutsk Milescu met Gantimur, who expressed fear that the tsar might order his return to Peking. Milescu promised that Moscow would never surrender the aged Tungus chieftain, thereby adopting a position from which he would be unable to retreat during his negotiations with the Manchus.[39]

On December 30, just as the embassy crossed the Argun River, an incident occurred that further rigidified Milescu's position on the frontier question. Coming to a place where horses and cattle were seen in the distance across the steppe, the ambassador sent a group to investigate while the embassy made camp on a small island in the river. The natives fled as the Russians approached, and the one man who was captured, though he said he was a Russian subject, refused to provide the pack animals Milescu required. Instead, he informed the ambassador that the nearby Namiasin Tungus paid tribute to no one and possessed plenty of cattle. Since the Namiasins distrusted the Russians and were well armed, their chief agreed to visit Milescu only on condition that two Cossacks be left in their village as hostages. Eventually the embassy secured some twenty horses from them, by barter or purchase, but were refused any camels.[40]

Outraged at his inability to acquire sufficient transport for his embassy in the frontier region, Milescu yet understood frontier politics sufficiently well to explain to the leaders of the independent Namiasin Tungus the vulnerable position in which they were placed. The Tungus chieftains explained that they were willing to pay tribute to the tsar at Nerchinsk but feared attacks from the Kontaisha, a Mongol prince who himself demanded tribute payments. This was a basic complaint of the indigenous tribes along the Sino-Russian or Mongol-Russian frontiers: they could not pay tribute to two masters. Milescu's reply, as he reported it, was a straightforward statement of the aggressive policies he favored for Russia. Native refusal to pay tribute to Moscow, he declared, would result in punishment not only against the Tungus but against the Mongols as well. Russian expansion in Buryat country demonstrated the tsar's ability to enforce his will. Nor was it possible, he concluded, for the Namiasins "to remain independent on the borderland of the tsar's and the Chinese emperor's dominions, where the way must be made clear."[41] Nevertheless, the Namiasins were adamant, and despite promises to the contrary, they fled in the night.

By the time Milescu reached the frontier, he had not only established policy positions on subjects not touched upon in his instructions, but his self-assumed attitudes left almost no leeway for maneuver in the forthcoming negotiations. The inherent rigidity in Milescu's policies was reenforced by the peculiarities of his temperament and personality. "In his dealings with Turks and Greeks," writes one of his biographers, "he had developed a character at once haughty and cunning, a love of intrigue and an absence of scruple which were to weigh on him all his life." He crossed the frontier on January 13, 1676.[42]

Milescu and the Manchus: A Conflict of Assumptions

From the first contact between the Russian embassy and the representatives of the Ch'ing court right down to the ambassador's departure from Peking, Milescu's negotiations with the Manchus were characterized by an inability to agree on basic assumptions or procedures. The Manchus at first adopted a "wait-and-see" attitude. Unable to elicit information from Milovanov, whom Milescu had sent ahead to announce his arrival, the court proceeded to discuss the manner in which the embassy should be received. On January 20, 1676, the president of the Li-fan yuan submitted a secret memorial to the throne offering specific suggestions about the immediate steps to be taken with regard to Milescu. The president assumed that the embassy had come in reply to the letter sent with Milovanov in 1670; Milovanov's appearance to herald the embassy's arrival must have supported this supposition.[43] The president also assumed, at Milovanov's suggestion, that the hazards of winter travel would prevent the embassy's arrival before spring, which left considerable time before officials need be sent to meet the Russian ambassador. He concluded that the wisest policy would be to send Milovanov back to Albazin in the spring along with two representatives of the Li-fan yuan, who would await Milescu's arrival and, if transport was insufficient, requisition animals from the Soluns. Milescu was to be examined at the frontier, but whether or not his documents were in proper tributary form, he should be brought immediately to the capital. In other words, the Li-fan yuan recommended a policy of accommodation and caution, which the emperor adopted on January 26.

Meanwhile, back on the frontier the Manchu authorities in the settlements along the Nun-chiang, apprised of Milescu's arrival but lacking orders from Peking, met the ambassador on January 23, three days before Ch'ing policy was formulated at the capital. Unable to allow the embassy to proceed further without court instructions, the local authorities dispatched a Russian messenger under Manchu guard to inform Peking of the ambassador's arrival. The court reacted immediately, and a courier arrived on the Nun-chiang on February 16 to announce the approach of an official party. The Manchu delegation, led by Mala, arrived on February 26.[44]

During the next fifty days Mala, in accordance with Peking's instructions, held up the embassy at the Nun-chiang and ceaselessly conversed, argued, and negotiated with Milescu, attempting to discover the embassy's objectives, to formulate procedures to be followed upon its arrival at Peking, and to examine the specific issues the Russians wished to raise at the capital. The two men discussed the entire range of problems at issue between their two empires, and each had an opportunity to explore the personality and test the resolve of the other. They locked horns in a mighty combat.

If Milescu was very much the product of a Byzantine education tempered by extensive travel and contact with western European political and intellectual circles, Mala was a typical representative of the middle-to-upper echelons of the Manchu bureaucracy. Born into the Manchu White Banner, one of the administrative divisions of the Manchu population, Mala was a nephew of Nikan, who throughout his service under the early Ch'ing emperors Nurhaci and Abahai had been principally concerned with the problems of Manchu-Mongol relations. In 1636 Nikan was appointed director of the Li-fan yuan, which at that time was concerned mostly with Mongol affairs. In 1647, three years after the Manchus entered Peking, he became president of the Li-fan yuan. He retired in 1653 and died in 1660 without a male heir. Mala, with his uncle and two younger brothers, inherited Nikan's titles, Mala himself becoming a *ch'ing-ch'e-tu-yü,* third class (one rank below a *nan* or baron).[45]

Mala's own career reflected his uncle's interest in barbarian affairs. His first official appointment was as a clerk (*pi-t'ieh-shih*) in the Li-fan yuan. Sometime in 1648-1649 (Shun-chih 5) he was sent to assist in the suppression of an anti-Manchu rebellion at Ta-t'ung, Shansi,[46] where he led a troop of Mongol soldiers in the siege of the city. In 1650-1651 (Shun-chih 7), Mala was appointed an assistant administrator (*fu-li-shih-kuan*) in the Board of Finance (Hu-pu), and shortly thereafter he was promoted to the position of departmental director (*lang-chung*) in the Li-fan yuan. Although his activities between 1650 and 1676 are unknown, he presumably continued to serve in the central administration of the Ch'ing dynasty. In 1675-1676 (K'ang-hsi 14, which ended February 13, 1676), a Chahar Mongol prince rebelled.[47] Mala offered his services to the throne in a military capacity, claiming that he, being well acquainted with Mongol affairs, could play a useful role in the suppression campaign. His memorial suggests a man who was either ambitious or out of favor, but zealous in pursuit of the dynasty's policies. He was ordered to collect troops from various other Mongol banners and join the attack against the rebels. After the inevitable Manchu victory, Mala was elevated to the office of commissioner of the Transmission Office (T'ung-cheng-shih). On February 17, 1676, he was appointed junior vice-president (*yu-shih-lang*) of the Board of Rites (Li-pu) and sent to meet Milescu on the Nun-chiang.[48]

Mala was very much a traditional Ch'ing bureaucrat. If his career departed at all from the norm, it was in his specialization in barbarian affairs when other Ch'ing officials tended toward generalized service. As a barbarian expert, he must have felt keenly the tensions that characterized the dynasty's early years. The Manchus were themselves a comparatively small barbarian tribe, engaged in bringing to a close their conquest of the vast Ming Empire. In order to win and maintain the loyalty of the Chinese gentry and bureaucracy, without whom they could not rule their new empire, the Manchus were forced to enter the rigid mold of Confucian orthodoxy, particularly in the area of external relations. Confucian orthodoxy on the international scene meant the acceptance of China's central and superior position, which the Manchus defended wherever possible. Mala, by virtue of his position as representative of the Ch'ing court in negotiations with Milescu, had to play the role of defender of Confucian orthodoxy in the eyes of both the Chinese bureaucracy and the Russian embassy.

The Russian ambassador and the vice-president of the Board of Rites grappled with two distinct sets of problems during their fifty days on the Nun-chiang. The first related to matters of form, including precedence, etiquette, and ceremonial: in symbol-oriented traditional societies these matters held paramount importance since the distinction between symbol and reality was very vague. The second set of problems related to matters of substance, mainly the Ch'ing complaints against Russian intrusions into the Amur Valley and the closely related question of fugitives switching allegiance from Peking to Moscow.

The differences in diplomatic assumptions and style were so fundamental that the two envoys encountered their first difficulties in arranging the initial meeting.[49] Mala sought to use the occasion to impress the "barbarian" Milescu with Ch'ing paramountcy. Upon his arrival Mala took up residence in the same village where the Russian embassy was quartered. He sent an intermediary to instruct the Russian ambassador in the etiquette of Confucian civilization, having him suggest, as if on his own, that Milescu make the first move and visit Mala at his residence. Intent on the form rather than the content of the symbolic gesture, Mala justified the request by explaining that en route to the Nun-chiang he had fallen from his horse while chasing hares and had injured his leg. Milescu had indeed observed Mala's arrival in a cart, but while admitting the possibility of such an injury, he adamantly refused to do anything that would admit Mala's higher rank. Being acquainted with the use of sedan chairs, he insisted that Mala "could very well visit me in this way, since it was not far to come." Each side was willing to compromise on the details of the action but not on the action's symbolic meaning. Mala then suggested setting up an "office" in a building halfway between the two camps, where Milescu could visit him. Milescu claimed that, "as was customary with all nations," it would be improper to visit the office of a Manchu official before the presentation of his credentials to the emperor. Mala agreed to visit the ambassador if the latter would set up his tent "in an empty space." Milescu replied that if Mala could visit him in an empty tent, he could as well visit him in the Russian embassy's compound. The ambassador countered with a suggestion that both parties start by separate routes for Peking, meet on the road, and carry on discussions while traveling. Mala obviously had to reject this proposal, since his instructions specifically stated that he was to examine the Russians before allowing them to proceed to the capital.

A compromise in the form of the first meeting was finally reached on March 2, through a combination of Manchu threats and of pressures from within Milescu's own embassy. Mala evidently recognized that the only solution to the impasse lay in an avoidance of symbolic meaning. He recommended that the two men ride to a distant village and meet in a building "with wide doors." The encounter would then take on the character of a chance meeting, outside of protocol, and the wide doors would allow the two men to enter simultaneously, thus dissolving Milescu's objections to appearing as the inferior. Mala supported his proposition with a threat to withdraw from the scene and communicate Milescu's obstinacy to the emperor. In the meantime, the ambassador's staff had become restive over the long and seemingly pointless delay. Their impatience with Milescu's unyielding policies forced him to compromise, as it would time and again in his future dealings with the Manchus. Having decided to remove the entire issue from the necessity of following Confucian protocol, Mala could agree to Milescu's counter-suggestion that the Russian embassy set up a tent in a distant field where the two could meet, the ambassador entering first. He even agreed to give Milescu written guarantees that Manchu envoys visiting Moscow would follow Russian court behavior: he knew that China was unlikely to send any envoys to Moscow. The first problem was solved, therefore, on the basis of a specific rather than a general compromise. The entire issue of precedence and ceremonial was merely postponed until the Russian embassy's arrival at Peking.

The second procedural problem arose from the Manchu requirement that Mala examine the Russians' documents before they proceeded to the capital.[50] At their very first meeting Mala informed Milescu that he had strict orders "to take from me [Milescu] Your Majesty's letter and open it and read it, to see what, in fact, it contained." Milescu refused with two arguments: (1) the emperor had the power to treat an ambassador in any way he saw fit, but Mala had no such delegated powers; (2) it was international custom for any official delegated to meet a foreign ambassador to have official credentials identifying him as his master's representative. Mala had no such credentials. Milescu assumed a further position wholly unacceptable to the Manchu delegate: placing the tsar's honor and power on a level with the emperor's, he threatened to use the Cossacks to "defend to the death His Majesty's letter." In this issue of the tsar's letter, as in the matter of arranging the first meeting of the two envoys, the argument over procedure represented a basic conflict between two different systems for the conduct of international relations and, indeed, two international societies. Both men were now well aware of this. Milescu based his argument on Western diplomatic usage. *"All sovereigns,"* he stated, "were in the habit of receiving ambassadors, especially from their neighbors and friends."[51] Mala insisted on the primacy of Chinese diplomatic usage, because there was no other correct form. All tributary documents had to be submitted to the proper government offices, through whom they were presented to the emperor. The incongruity between two independently developed diplomatic systems could not be resolved on the basis of common assumptions or a general agreement on ceremonies. Chinese practice was a ceremonial representation of East Asia's hierarchical international order. In the Confucian tradition, ceremony was itself reality, or at the very least a means of controlling reality. Milescu's refusal to compromise was not diplomatically dangerous; it threatened the very fabric of Confucian society.

Mala's procedural demands were closely related to the two substantive issues raised in the Nun-chiang conversations—the fugitive problem, with special reference to Gantimur, and the Russian raids across the frontier to collect yasak from native tribes. The assumption in Peking that Milescu's embassy was in the nature of a reply to the letters about these matters sent to Danilo Arshinsky in 1670 had led to the original demand that Mala examine the contents of the tsar's letter, since that document should have contained replies to the Manchu demands of 1670.[52]

Mala raised the issue of the return of Gantimur to Manchu jurisdiction in his first meeting with the Russian ambassador. Milescu, who already had committed himself to Gantimur in Siberia, successively used three contradictory arguments to defend the Tungus chieftain's position as a Russian subject. First, neither the tsar nor the ambassador had any knowledge of the Gantimur affair, since the letter of 1670 had remained untranslated. Mala destroyed this argument by pointing out that Milovanov had been explicitly informed of the issue during his 1670 visit to Peking; moreover, Mangutei, who evidently had a rudimentary knowledge of Russian and accompanied Milovanov back to Nerchinsk, had translated the emperor's letter for Arshinsky. "I got out of that difficulty," Milescu later informed the tsar in a rare moment of candor, "by saying I quite believed the cossacks had been told to speak of Gantimur to the tsar, but in fact they had not done so." Milescu's second argument was that Gantimur was only one of some one hundred thousand Russian subjects in Siberia; the central administration could not take cognizance of each of them. Finally, he claimed that Gantimur had never been a Manchu subject, was now a Russian subject, and that possession was, in the final analysis, its own justification.

In connection with the other substantive issue—the Russian raids across the frontier—Mala made several complaints to Milescu. The Cossacks at Albazin, for instance, had "not many days since" collected tribute from a certain Tungus chieftain. Milescu likened the case to the Gantimur affair, claiming that the chieftain, whom he called Petrushka, was a Russian subject born on the Lena River. Having committed crimes against other Russian subjects, he was merely being punished by the Cossacks. A second Albazin raid by Albazinian Cossacks was a particularly complicated affair.[53] Milescu reported to the tsar that a certain chieftain of a village in Manchu territory had petitioned the Albazin Cossacks to come and, appearing to use force, take his people back to the Russian settlements, where they would accept the tsar's sovereignty. The Tungus betrayed the Cossacks, however, by sacking their own village and retreating further into Manchu territory. The Cossacks returned to Albazin causing harm to no one. The ambassador further claimed that the local Manchu representatives had been embarrassed by the incident, may have profited from it, and sent messengers to the Cossack settlement requesting that the affair be kept quiet. Mala's version was completely different. The Cossacks had come as marauders, the terrified natives promised to accompany the Russians peacefully back to Albazin, but they slipped away to the Nun-chiang and Manchu protection. The Manchu delegate also linked Cossack raids with unfair Russian trading practices. The Cossacks would invite Manchu subjects to a feast where, after binding them tightly and forceably dispossessing them of their sable pelts, they would beat them, crying, "Give us the rest you have hidden!" Mala commented: "That is the nice sort of person your cossack is! There is no one like him on this earth."

Milescu made a dual response to the Manchu complaints. While he would not admit the validity of the charges, he was prepared to promise the appointment of officials who would maintain order along the frontier and prevent the future occurrence of raids. He was sufficiently aware of the dangers involved in a continuation of the old policy of uncontrolled frontier populations to take action while still on the Nun-chiang. Informed on April 15 that the Albazin Cossacks were prepared to send a tribute-collecting expedition down the Amur, Milescu immediately forbade such a venture, though more from fear for his own safety, perhaps, than realization of the possible international consequences.[54] He was not, after all, convinced of Manchu military power.

Mala reported the substance of his conversations with Milescu to the emperor in a memorial from the Nun-chiang dated March 19, 1676.[55] Convinced that Milescu was telling lies and that he could not believe his statement that the tsar's letter contained only expressions of good will and friendship, Mala asked for instructions. The emperor asked for the opinion of his court on April 3, and three days later "the wangs, beiles, and nobles gathered together" submitted a memorial outlining a new policy.[56] Balancing Milescu's claim that no one in Russia could understand Peking's letters against the obvious fact that the ambassador had arrived as a tribute envoy "to present local products" and ask after the emperor's health, the court concluded that Mala should conduct the embassy to Peking in order to show the Russians "the high intentions of our emperor, caressing distant states." Upon Milescu's arrival the court would question him closely and submit another memorial. The emperor approved these suggestions the next day, April 7, in effect deferring all policy decisions on both procedural and substantive matters until the embassy arrived in Peking.

The emperor's decision to allow Milescu to come to Peking despite Mala's memorial may have been inspired in part by fear of Russian military intervention in Manchuria in the midst of the Manchu struggle with Wu San-kuei in the South. At the end of March, for instance, Mala had been deeply disturbed by rumors spread by one of Milescu's interpreters, "a Chinaman by birth," to the effect that one-hundred thousand Russian soldiers were located "in certain uninhabited places, who only await a sign . . . to rush in and slaughter and pillage." A fortnight later, on April 8, one of Mala's retinue approached Milescu to inquire whether the ambassador expected the arrival of any persons from Russia. Milescu replied that he only expected a courier whom he had sent on an errand to Yakutsk. On April 10 in an obvious state of alarm, Mala sent repeatedly to Milescu "to ask what Russians were coming after me, for his people were greatly alarmed, fearing it meant war." On April 12 a courier arrived with a box of medicines for the ambassador; the next day, in the course of a conversation with Mala, Milescu flung open the box and cried, "Behold our troops that you have so continually asked about."[57]

Mala and Milescu failed in their efforts to reach a plateau of common assumptions in their first round of negotiations. But the Manchu, lacking authority to conclude agreements with the ambassador, who would not in any event have been willing to enter definitive negotiations before his arrival at Peking and reception by the emperor, had used a wide variety of techniques to elicit information. Wine and presents flowed liberally, and on one occasion Mala invited Milescu to go fishing. Mala was particularly skilled in the use of psychological approaches. He tried, for instance, to wear Milescu down through tedium and exhaustion born of repetition; the ambassador complained frequently about the "going to and fro," the discussions "and so on, with much iteration." Despite the failures, the fifty-day meeting on the Nun-chiang was also the most important episode of the entire embassy. Although only specific compromises were made and no precedents set, each side used the talks to explore thoroughly the policies and arguments of the other. The positions adopted by each were to remain unchanged. Milescu, with no previous experience in China, went to Peking having actually learned little from his contact with Mala, whom he persisted in regarding as a minor obstructive official. His European experience allowed him to believe that in Peking he would see the emperor, who would set everything right. Mala, however, returned to Peking with deep-seated suspicions concerning Milescu's character. His only hope was that in the capital greater pressures could be brought to bear on the barbarians.

On April 17, an auspicious day for beginning a journey, according to Manchu belief, the embassy left for Peking in 100 two-wheeled carts, accompanied by 156 men. The trip took twenty-nine days, during which the debate on procedural matters continued. The common disagreement was amplified by numerous incidents en route. On May 11, for instance, Mala informed Milescu that a high official was coming toward them along the same road. Because the official carried the emperor's own letter to the Mongols, the ambassador would have to dismount and kowtow to the document. Milescu refused. He was only willing to dismount, he declared, if the official came expressly to greet him, "but were he bound on other of His Majesty's affairs, then it were no business of the Ambassador's to greet him." The dispute was sharp, but in the end Milescu turned his embassy off the main road until the emperor's letter had been carried past. Immediately upon arrival in the capital the embassy was conducted to a compound "not far from the city wall," where according to Milescu "the Hollanders, who were there in Baikoff's time," were lodged. It was apparently the compound reserved by the Board of Rites for tributary envoys. The courtyard, he reported, was spacious, but many of the buildings were old and in ruins. "There are no gardens or wild growth of any kind, and the whole is most gloomy—like a prison." As soon as the embassy was inside, the Manchus posted a strong guard at the gate.[58]

The arguments begun on the Nun-chiang were continued in Peking. Principally, the court demanded that Milescu take the tsar's letter to the Board of Rites for translation and presentation to the emperor before he was granted an imperial audience. Milescu used six different arguments, all based on European practice, to support his own demand that he present the tsar's letter, unopened, directly to the emperor. The first argument was Russia's power and importance. Mala argued in reply that the Dalai Lama, the Kalmuks, Mongols, Bukharans, Dutch, and Portuguese all followed established procedures for the presentation of credentials; the Russians could be treated no differently. The ambassador turned his statement into a threat, reminding Mala that he was "well aware that you have enemies as well as friends." Next, Milescu argued that if, as Mala insisted, the embassy was a response to the emperor's letter of 1670, the emperor must accept the credentials in person. Third, Milescu argued on the basis of custom and law that the Dutch and Portuguese followed the incorrect Manchu forms because they were only "petty potentates." The correct models were the Caesar of Rome, meaning the Pope, the sultan of Turkey, or the Persian shah, all of whom received the tsar's letters directly from the hands of ambassadors. The tsar was "not asking the Bogdykhan to introduce something new, but only to apply what has been in vogue since the world began." Furthermore, it was customary for ambassadors to follow their own customs in foreign courts. Milescu cited the use of hats as an example. In Russia, a subject of the tsar never bowed to the monarch with his hat on, whereas Turks and Persians kept their hats securely on their heads in the presence of their sovereigns. Milescu also pointed to the distinction between faith and custom. Faith, he declared, was immutable, but custom changed with time as advantage dictated. Court ceremonials were a matter of custom, not faith. This was of course a European, not a Confucian, distinction. The ambassador's last three arguments referred to the equality of monarchs, the greater importance of a monarch's letter over the person of his ambassador, and personal orders and loyalty.

Mala countered the Russian ambassador's arguments with his own, in defense of Chinese-Ch'ing custom. First, custom was ancient and immutable. Second, it grew out of necessity and practice. Once made, custom could not be altered, even by the emperor. "As when the hair on a man's head growns thin and grey," Milescu wrote the tsar, "nothing can alter it, so with their customs, which could not be changed just to please the tsar." Mala went so far as to admit that if the emperor broke with custom in order to accommodate the Russians, "it would be said that he had altered the custom not out of friendship for the tsar but from fear of him." Consideration for the opinions of the Chinese bureaucracy was undoubtedly the prime factor in Mala's insistence upon the preservation of correct ceremonial forms.[59]

Despite numerous attempts at compromise on both sides, the court rejected all Milescu's demands on June 2. Faced with the choice of surrendering or returning home in failure, the ambassador surrendered. The way was now opened for an imperial audience, which in turn raised new questions. Milescu was ordered to practice the kowtow so that he would be perfect in its performance. He was also informed by Mala that the tsar's gifts would not be presented with the credentials, because "it is not our custom to mix them up with the letters." Milescu agreed, with reservations. While he did not refuse to perform the kowtow, he wanted to wait until the conclusion of the ceremony of presentation of the tsar's letter. He also insisted that the presents and letters be presented together, and that the presents not be called tribute. "Both on the road and here in Peking we have heard your people call the presents—tribute!" he exclaimed. "That we repudiate; for our sovereign Lord and Master takes tribute, indeed from many countries, but renders it to none." These reservations were tantamount to total surrender, which the Manchus recognized. Mala informed the ambassador that he ought not to worry about tribute terminology. The common people, he said, spoke in ignorance of the facts, and it was unnecessary to pay any attention to their words.

On June 5 Milescu presented the tsar's letters and gifts at a gate of the palace in the presence of the grand secretaries but not the emperor. He placed them on a table covered with yellow silk, and during the ceremony neither side spoke a word.[60] The official entry in the *Shih-lu* for this date shows clearly that from the court's point of view the presentation of Milescu's documents took place entirely within the framework of the tribute system.[61] The entry reads: "The Ch'a-han Han of O-lo-ssu [the tsar] sent his minister Ni-kuo-lai [Nikolay] . . . to present local products. He memorialized that O-lo-ssu was located at a great distance, that it had never communicated with China and could not understand the Chinese language, and did not know the proper form for memorials. Now, the Ch'a-han Han has turned toward Civilization and has sent a tributary embassy. The emperor decreed that 'since O-lo-ssu, located at a remote distance, has now sincerely turned toward Civilization and especially sent her minister to present local products, she indeed deserves encouragement. In regard to what is memorialized, let the princes and ministers deliberate and memorialize.' "

The Manchus interpreted the ceremonies performed by Milescu in terms of their own hierarchical view of international relations. While Milescu was undoubtedly aware of the specific implications of his actions, he did not perceive that the Manchu insistence on customary procedures did not refer solely to Russia. His insistence that Russia was a greater empire than the petty kingdoms of Portugal and Holland was entirely comprehensible to Mala. What was incomprehensible was that Milescu insisted on the equality of Russia and China in a world in which equality was unknown.

The man who had once aspired to the throne of his native land was finally received in audience by the Ch'ing emperor on June 15. Despite last-minute objections, he kowtowed, bowing three times and prostrating himself nine times. Attempting to maintain his own dignity at the court's expense, Milescu allowed the audience ceremony to take on the appearance of a race between himself and the master of ceremonies: "And the crier, seeing that the Ambassador bowed quickly, began to call out in haste. However, the Ambassador and his people did the kowtow in that way, bending neither low nor slowly."[62]

The Uses of Pressure and Commerce

Milescu had little contact in Peking with Manchu officials other than Mala, who used several forms of pressure to force the ambassador's compliance with Manchu demands, both before and after the compromise on ceremonial. Three methods predominated: restriction of the Russians' freedom of movement in Peking, direct or veiled threats of action against Russia proper, and restrictions on commerce. Milescu had to spend his time combatting minor irritations while the Ch'ing government leisurely formulated policies in answer to the questions raised by Moscow in its instructions to the ambassador.

The embassy's lodgings in a special court enabled the Manchus to restrict its freedom of movement merely by placing guards at the gate and preventing Russian egress. Since these guards speculated in the sale of provisions to the embassy, Milescu on more than one occasion begged Mala to allow his followers to go out of the court to purchase necessities. The summer was hot, the situation became unbearable, and many fell ill. As bad as conditions were, the ambassador was galled primarily by the fact that other foreigners and Russian common merchants were allowed comparative freedom of movement. The restrictions were so tight that even Verbiest, one of the Jesuits resident in Peking in the service of the Manchu dynasty, was refused permission to send fresh fruits and vegetables to the Russians. Russian skill at swimming and diving resulted in one peculiar exception to the general confinement. On July 16 representatives of the court approached Milescu to inquire if he had in his suite any men who could swim and dive. Milescu haughtily replied that "with us every man could swim." Mala had evidently observed Russian aquatic sports while he was on the Nun-chiang and reported them to the emperor. Consequently, on July 20 four Cossacks were released to put on an exhibition for the emperor. Upon their return they reported to the ambassador that the Manchus had "brought two men of their own," who could not compete with the Russians in swimming or diving. A second exhibition was arranged on August 7, shortly before the embassy's departure.

Mala claimed that the emperor himself had ordered the isolation of the Russians. He also justified their virtual incarceration on the grounds of chronic Russian misbehavior. The guards were placed at the gate ostensibly to prevent quarrels between the Russians and the local populace. On the few occasions when the Cossacks were allowed out on the streets, in groups of five or six, and only after strenuous arguments on Milescu's part, incidents took place, and the emperor's own authority had to be invoked to demand that the ambassador keep his men in check. On July 28, for instance, Mala complained that some Cossacks had beaten the Manchu guards and wandered at will near the city walls "for pleasure, not for business."[63]

Threats were another form of pressure. Mala began threatening Milescu almost immediately after their arrival at the capital. Before reaching the ceremonial compromise, he informed Milescu that while they were still on the Nun-chiang he had received instructions to march against Albazin and Nerchinsk if the tsar's letters contained threats or insults.[64] At another point he told Milescu that the emperor could keep the embassy in Peking or dismiss it at his pleasure, and that it would have to remain until Milescu surrendered his documents.

Commerce, the embassy's major concern, was the area where it encountered the greatest difficulties. Mala prevented the opening of trade until the day after Milescu was received by the emperor, when the ambassador was informed that the emperor had given orders for the gates of the compound to be opened for trade. Lists were prepared of all available goods, which were divided into groups according to whether they belonged to the state treasury or were the private possessions of members of the embassy staff. By June 17 many merchants had entered to inspect the goods but none had made any purchases. It was soon apparent that strict control was being exercised over the merchants, who were inspected by clerks and soldiers at the gate upon both arrival and departure, "under their armpits, in their trousers, and down their boots," to see if any goods were being carried away. A month later public and free trade had yet to begin, and Mala suggested that if the Russians wanted to trade on the open market, they should come as merchants and not as ambassadors.[65]

It is apparent from Milescu's own stateyny spisok that controlled access to the market was not the only cause of the embassy's commercial difficulties, nor was official cupidity the only reason for strict controls. Strict prohibitions existed on the sale of specific items to foreigners. These items included, for instance, articles made of iron or copper (kettles and swords), as well as military goods like bows, arrows, knives, stirrups, and gunpowder. Milescu admitted quite baldly that the Russians contravened these regulations whenever possible. "The cossacks bought such things secretly," he conceded, but the Manchus were scrupulous in returning the purchase price when the articles in question were discovered and confiscated.[66]

Another impediment to the development of trade was the poor quality of the Russian goods. Milescu himself recognized this while camping along the Nun-chiang. He had exchanged the treasury furs brought as gifts for the emperor for the pelts brought by private merchants for trade. The treasury furs, he pointed out, were of such poor quality that "none were sold . . . and seeing the good ones, the buyers would not have them [the treasury furs]." Black foxskins were particularly difficult to dispose of, despite Milescu's offer to accept goods in exchange, rather than the preferred silver.[67]

Above and beyond the specific commercial difficulties of the embassy, Milescu discussed with Mala the more general problem of Russian-Chinese trade. He used two main approaches. First, he suggested that China needed Russian goods, and if the market conditions did not improve, Moscow would cut off trade. Russia, on the contrary, did not need Chinese goods. Russian silks, gold thread, velvets, taffetas, clothing, horses, and armaments were all better than similar Chinese products. Milescu's second approach was an appeal to the relationship between trade and international friendship. The tsar had instructed him, he told Mala, to speak of trade "in its proper sense, i.e., for the benefit of both sides, that it might serve as a tie of friendship." "Every ruler," he concluded, "naturally desired to enrich his people, and if there was to be no going from us to them, either of merchants or envoys, how could there be any friendship?"[68]

The unfamiliar surroundings in which he found himself in Peking, as well as the strange institutions through which he had to deal with the Manchus, encouraged feelings of persecution in Milescu, which can be discerned in his stateyny spisok. Yet the problems he faced in trying to organize and conduct both his embassy's trade and Sino-Russian trade in general were perhaps broader than apparent to him. The ambassador had a highly personal view of the course of events, in which his opponents were viewed merely as individuals or at times the entire Chinese bureaucracy, but not the Chinese system of assumptions and institutions. Furthermore, the Chinese—Mala in particular—were as interested in their own welfare as the ambassador was in his. Whereas Milescu sought to maximize the profits of his embassy through high prices based on the scarcity of Russian furs in Peking, the Manchus, who were as aware of the laws of supply and demand as were the Russians, sought to use institutional controls to keep prices as low as possible. Limitation of access was one method. Since it would have been highly uneconomical for the embassy to return to Siberia with its goods unsold, the Cossacks and private merchants in the embassy's train were thus forced to sell at prices lower than they wished. Milescu suggested at one point that duties be collected by the Ch'ing court on a free and public trade, but the court found that a controlled duty-free trade was more profitable. Moreover, duties would have gone into the state treasury, whereas the profits from a controlled trade accrued to the bureaucracy itself. Although Milescu railed against Manchu commercial policies, the Russians themselves eventually organized their China trade on similar monopoly principles.

The Jesuit Betrayal

The Jesuits resident in Peking and serving the Manchu court aided Milescu throughout his trials and tribulations at the capital.[69] The fact of their assistance is particularly ironic considering that Milescu, as one of the leading Greek Orthodox intellectuals, had often entered into polemics with Rome. Nevertheless, an examination of his stateyny spisok shows that the Jesuits time and again betrayed the interests of the Manchu court to the Russian ambassador.

Through Mala's introduction Milescu met the Jesuit Ferdinand Verbiest. The two shared a knowledge of Latin, and from their first meeting Verbiest became one of the chief go-betweens and interpreters in the Manchu court's dealings with the Russian embassy. Time and again he demonstrated his willingness to aid the ambassador. Once, for instance, while Milescu was dictating the contents of the tsar's letter to Verbiest in Latin, a young man unexpectedly entered the room. Verbiest, looking at his own paper and pretending to read the Latin back to the ambassador, told him that the young man was a favorite of the emperor who had been sent to find out whether Verbiest really could converse with

Milescu in a common tongue. Verbiest had to dissemble so that the emperor's favorite would not know he was recognized.[70]

As Verbiest was chiefly concerned to open a route for Jesuit travel between Rome and Peking through Moscow, he told the ambassador that "for Christianity's sake" he was glad to serve the tsar as best he might. Milescu derived many of his opinions about the Manchus from Verbiest. The Jesuit complained of the "contemptuous treatment" meted out to foreigners by the Manchus, and he told the Russian ambassador that the Manchus "pretend that all other nations on the globe see with only one eye, they alone with two eyes." He also made Milescu promise before a holy ikon to tell no one of their conversations "nor write it down until you leave China," since as foreigners the Jesuits had already suffered many hardships "for Christ's sake" and continued under suspicion. Nevertheless, using his privileged position at court and in the Manchu bureaucracy, Verbiest on many occasions was able to convey information to Milescu concerning the court's deliberations and plans.[71]

If Milescu is to be believed, the Jesuits were motivated in part by loyalty to the Ming dynasty, whom they had served and which had been overthrown by the Manchus in 1644. As early as June 19, 1675, the Russian ambassador had been visited in Tobolsk by three Jesuit fathers—Grimaldi, Buglio, and de Magalhaens. They told the ambassador that the Manchus were "the lowest and most insignificant, the off-scourings, as it were, of other nations," who had overthrown the Ming only through treachery.[72] The fathers also offered an explanation for Manchu hostility to the embassy. Because of deteriorating conditions under the Manchus, the Chinese in the south had in 1674 started a revolt, led by Wu San-kuei and known as the Rebellion of the Three Feudatories. The Manchus feared that they would be driven from Peking and that the Mongols would also revolt. Their attitude toward the embassy was therefore ambivalent. On the one hand, if the Chinese in the south heard that an embassy from so powerful a monarch as the tsar had come offering Peking friendship, they might hesitate to strike in fear of Russian support for the Ch'ing. On the other hand, the embassy, together with events in the Amur Valley, proved that Russia's frontiers had advanced to the very borders of their own empire; any confrontation with such a powerful neighbor at that moment of weakness seemed dangerous and frightening. The latter position was the stronger in court circles.

Verbiest's single most important service to Milescu was his revelation of the Ch'ing dynasty's general strategic plans in the Amur region for the next decade. Whether the information Verbiest gave the ambassador was the result of extraordinarily clever prognostication on his part, or whether he actually had access to Ch'ing military plans and discussions, is not clear. It is clear, however, that in 1676 Milescu reported in his stateyny spisok with remarkable accuracy the course of events in the Amur for the next decade, citing Verbiest as his source of information. The Jesuit visited Milescu on August 9, not long before the embassy's dismissal from the capital.[73] The visit itself was not extraordinary: Milescu had asked the Jesuit for a Chinese grammar, which Verbiest offered to write and send to the tsar in Moscow, together with a map he had made of China. It was on this occasion that Verbiest, placing the ambassador under an oath of secrecy, divulged the dynasty's strategic military and political plans for the Amur region. According to Milescu, the transaction was to remain secret even from Verbiest's fellow Jesuits, because of Verbiest's fear of the consequences should it become known.

Although the Manchus had formerly believed that the Russians in the Amur Valley were outcasts with no support from Moscow, Verbiest informed Milescu, they now realized that Albazin and Nerchinsk were officially sponsored settlements. They also understood that the forts' main purpose was the collection of yasak from the natives, which made them a more formidable challenge to the dynasty than had previously been thought. Furthermore, the Manchus had reconnoitered the area and learned that the Albazin and Nerchinsk garrisons were weak and Moscow far away.

The Manchus planned to use the issue of Gantimur to determine Russian intentions, Verbiest continued. If at the emperor's demand the tsar returned Gantimur, "who is the chieftain of all those people," the rest of the local tribes would follow him back to China or scatter, so that it would no longer be worth the tsar's while to maintain settlements along the river. Verbiest thought that the Manchus would await one more reply on the Gantimur issue, provided there were no further Cossack raids. If, however, the tsar refused to return Gantimur, he should immediately send large numbers of troops to defend the settlements, since the Manchus then intended to go to war and capture Albazin and Nerchinsk. For that purpose they were planning a build-up of their military forces in the region. Milescu concluded his report of the conversations with Verbiest by remarking, "they, the Jesuits, were glad to serve the Tsar as they serve God, for they love not the Manchus, as they did the Chinese."[74]

The Embassy's Dismissal: The Twelve Articles

The departure of the Russian embassy from Peking was as stormy as its sojourn. The storm raged around the manner in which the court had replied to certain articles submitted by Milescu for the emperor's consideration. The ambassador's diplomatic tasks, to which the procedural and commercial problems were originally only ancillary, were embodied in the fourteen-point instructions given him before his departure from Moscow. On June 8, three days after he had presented his credentials and the tsar's letter, the ambassador abstracted his instructions in Latin in a document that Verbiest translated into Manchu. The document, which was presented to the emperor through Mala on June 16, consisted of the following twelve points.[75]

(1) The Ch'ing court should provide translations for the four letters Milescu had brought back from Moscow.

(2) One language should be agreed upon for future communications between the two empires.

(3) Both sides should write the names and titles of their respective sovereigns, according to models to be agreed upon.

(4) The emperor should send an ambassador back to Moscow in Milescu's suite.

(5) Merchants should be permitted to travel between the two empires freely.

(6) Russian prisoners in China, if any, should be set free.

(7) Forty thousand puds of silver should be sent to Moscow annually in exchange for whatever Russian goods the Manchu court wished to import.

(8) Precious stones should also be sent in exchange for goods.

(9) Chinese artisans capable of building stone bridges should be loaned to the tsar.

(10) The Russians should be permitted to purchase whatever Chinese goods they wished with the Russian goods brought to Peking; trade should take place on the open market; and customs duties should be levied (the levying of customs would, it was hoped, prevent the court from demanding special exactions or price differentials).

(11) The court should designate the most convenient route for the embassy's return to Moscow, preferably by sea and river.

(12) These articles should be accepted by the emperor in love and friendship, "for it is our desire that Their Majesties the Tsar and the Khan should dwell in love and friendship."

Less time was spent in negotiations on the twelve articles, with the exception of the tenth one, than on the more immediate procedural and commercial issues. While it is true that Mala continually avoided answering Milescu's requests for negotiations on the articles, it is also apparent that the ambassador did not pursue these issues as single-mindedly as he did the others. It is possible that the strength expended on matters of ceremony, the heat, and the prolonged confinement left him little energy, and that his experiences on the Nun-chiang and during his first days in Peking had sapped his will to insist and resist. It must also be recognized that the procedural issues involved ceremonials in which Milescu himself had to participate; they thus concerned his self-esteem more than did the political problems mentioned in his instructions.

The twelve articles were presented to the emperor as a memorial on June 26 by the emperor's own brother, Fu-ch'uan. On the same day the throne ordered that the matter be discussed by "appropriate officials" and a new memorial presented with suggestions for a reply. A month later, on July 28, the emperor received a memorial containing suggestions for Ch'ing policy, which two days later he submitted to the Grand Secretariat (Nei-ko) for discussion. The Grand Secretariat memorialized the emperor in turn on August 6 with its own policy recommendations.[76] On August 9 the emperor approved the recommendations in both documents, which outlined an answer for each point raised by Milescu.

The basic assumption underlying the recommendations made in the memorials of July 28 and August 6 was that Russia was a tributary state. At this moment Russia's tributary status was quite evidently more than a literary conceit to the Ch'ing ministers. In addition to agreeing to provide a translation of the disputed letter of 1670 and to send Latin translations with all future communications to Moscow, the ministers' policy recommendations all dealt with Russia's position and behavior within the context of the tribute system. For instance, they did not reject out of hand the tsar's proposal that Peking send an ambassador to Moscow with Milescu; instead, the matter was deferred until such time as the tsar "without interruption will present tribute annually." In such a case the dispatch of a mission to a tributary power, perhaps to invest its ruler with his seals of office, would be quite proper. The ministers were prepared to permit the embassy to sell the goods brought from Russia, but it rejected the proposal that duties be collected, since precedent was lacking. Tribute missions could customarily sell goods, but since such a sale was a tributary, not a commercial, act, duties could not be collected. Finally, the ministers refused to designate a route between Peking and Moscow, "because we do not know which roads to them are near and which are far." If the tsar wished to send tribute, however, he could memorialize to that effect and the emperor would issue a edict forbidding the molestation of Russian travelers.

Commercial relations were considered strictly upon the assum tion of Russia's tributary status. Milescu's suggestion that Chi annually export to Russia forty-thousand puds of silver as well precious stones was rejected out of hand. The memorialists thou it improper for a tribute-bearing ambassador to suggest what desired in return; besides China needed nothing from abroad. was it permissible for a tribute state to send gifts in return rewards granted upon the presentation of tribute, far less to gest the figure at which commerce should be conducted. In since trade was a usual part of the tribute process, there w need to discuss any special trading arrangements.

Again emphasizing the importance of the Gantimur affair, the ministers recommended that the request for bridge builders be deferred until a solution to the fugitive problem had been found.[77] If, however, the tsar "returns our refugees and every year without interruption sends an envoy and asks about the health of the emperor and presents tribute," he might submit memorials asking for special favors, which would be well received. Both memorials concluded with the suggestion that the decisions be carefully explained to the Russian ambassador, through whom an answer should be sent to the tsar incorporating the emperor's decisions.

Although the court had formulated its policy as early as August 9, when the emperor had sanctioned his ministers' recommendations, the Manchus were dilatory in communicating their conclusions to Milescu. On August 9, for instance, he sent an interpreter to the Board of Rites to request negotiations on his original memorial. He repeated his request on August 23, 25, and 26. As early as August 12 Mala had promised that a reply would soon be forthcoming, but as late as August 28 he could not say whether the reply would be in writing and when it would be handed to the ambassador.[78] Actually, Manchu policy on sending written communications to the tsar or providing Milescu with a written reply to the twelve articles had been determined as early as July 1, when a memorial to the throne suggested that because the ambassador "did not learn the ceremonials well, it is not proper to give him n imperial patent."[79]

On August 29 Milescu was finally summoned to the gates of the lace where, two months before, he had presented his credentials d the tsar's letter. The events of the day constituted a recapitula- n of the problems the embassy had faced ever since arriving in Manchu Empire. They resulted in a series of incidents which, se modern parlance, amounted to a break in relations between ing and Moscow. The Russian ambassador was summoned to , but not receive, a decree answering his twelve articles.[80] arrangement, he was told, was a great honor, since decrees butary states were usually issued at the Board of Rites, and s instructed to fall on his knees to hear it. Inquiring whether cree was an answer to the tsar's letter and the twleve articles, merely informed that everything was covered in it. In the absence of specific information as to the content of the Manchu declaration, he refused to kneel. At this crucial moment the tensions and divisions that had evidently been growing within the embassy itself since the conversations on the Nun-chiang, especially as a result of the restricted living conditions in Peking, came to the surface: "At that moment," Milescu later reported to the tsar, "the Moscow courtiers and the boyar-sons, and the cossacks, began calling on him [Milescu] to kneel and do their [the Manchus'] bidding. So the Ambassador placed his cushion before him and knelt."

Some time between August 9, when the emperor had approved the decision on Milescu's twelve articles, and August 29, when Milescu was called to hear the imperial decree, the court had decided to reverse its original intentions and refused to provide specific answers to the questions in Milescu's memorial. This decision may have resulted from the inconclusive discussions of the refugee problem. At any rate, on August 29 Milescu, standing in front of the palace gate, was informed by a grand secretary that the emperor would not write an answer to the tsar for two reasons. First, Milescu had been "disobedient"—in refusing, for instance, to receive the emperor's gifts on his knees "as do the envoys of other neighboring monarchs; nor indeed does anyone dare to impugn that custom." Second, the only real purpose in writing would be to obtain the surrender of Gantimur, but since that subject had already been raised on numerous occasions, and the tsar had not returned the Tungus chieftain, it was useless to write again. Nor was it possible to entertain any other questions until the matter had been settled. In fact, the grand secretary laid down three conditions for the resumption of relations between Moscow and Peking: Gantimur must be surrendered and brought to Peking by a Russian ambassador; the ambassador must be "a most reasonable man, who will do all we command him, in accordance with our customs, and oppose us in nothing"; and peace must be maintained along the Sino-Russian frontier.

This declaration, which included no reference to the twelve articles, was tantamount to an ultimatum with no time limit. Milescu, who was already in possession of Verbiest's information about Ch'ing strategy, recognized the total failure of his mission and sought immediately to defend his own actions. He entered into a polemic with the grand secretary on the spot, in front of the assembled Manchu officials and the embassy. He insisted that his refusal to accept the emperor's gifts on his knees was not an insult to the emperor but only an attempt to preserve the tsar's honor. Despite numerous arguments, the Manchu refused to give way, and members of the Russian embassy itself began to insist that Milescu seek a compromise. The grand secretary rejected a new proposal that the emperor write once more to the tsar about Gantimur on the grounds that Milescu, who had already proven his insincerity, would need a Latin translation, which could not be controlled by the Manchus and would open the way for Milescu to tamper with the emperor's titles. By now the heat of debate had evidently confused the translator, so that Milescu requested Verbiest's aid, which was given with the permission of the grand secretary. Milescu, however, still mistook the court's failure to understand his actions for displeasure and pure anger. The grand secretary's remarks, he wrote later, were "against the universal right; for nowhere is it permitted to cry out on and abuse ambassadors and envoys for upholding firmly their masters' honor."

The confrontation at the palace gate took a new and dramatic turn when, in response to repeated entreaties by Milescu for a written document, one of the court officials appealed over the ambassador's head to the embassy itself. Milescu's description of the moment betrays his own inner turmoil: the official was "calling out and asking the Moscow courtiers and boyar sons and cossacks: 'If the Great Khan writes a letter to His Majesty the Tsar, will you receive it with such honor as we demand?' And all cried out—'We will!' Now [the official] repeated that question more than once: asking them, indeed, again and again; and they gave always the same answer." This maneuver effectively destroyed the ambassador's authority with his already mutinous staff. Trying to reestablish himself, Milescu immediately turned to his embassy, which was located behind him, and declared, "if there is one dishonouring word written in the letter to the Tsar I will never accept it—it is I who have to make answer in Moscow, not you." He had lost, however, and he records that his staff informed him, "If you Sir, will not take the letter, we will—whatever its contents."[81] With no recourse, Milescu had to accept the court's decision. As he was about to leave the gate, Verbiest recommended that he make one more request for a consideration of the affair, though the Jesuit refused to intervene himself. He feared he had already been denounced for "betraying to the ambassador all their Manchu affairs."

The next day Milescu attempted to justify himself before the embassy by showing his staff the tsar's instructions, taking pains to emphasize the paragraphs dealing with the preservation of the tsar's honor. His remarks about this occasion clearly reveal the egoism that constantly interfered with his diplomatic tasks: "He showed all this to the courtiers and boyar sons and cossacks to prove that he, the Ambassador, had not demanded from the Chinese a [Latin] version of the letter arbitrarily, but by order of the tsar; so that, in the future, they should cease their opposition and not again behave as they did the day before, shouting and jabbering before the Chinese in the city, crying out that they were ready to accept anything! not, in short, to put him, the Ambassador, to shame, and worse, His Majesty the Tsar!"[82]

That same day, August 30, Mala, Verbiest, and the grand secretary who was president of the Li-fan yuan went to the embassy courtyard to make a statement to the ambassador in front of his staff.[83] The seriousness of the visit was demonstrated both by their refusal to begin until one absentee had been located and by the complicated translation procedures they had arranged: Verbiest translated the Manchu statements into Latin, which Milescu turned into Russian for another interpreter to translate once again into Mongol, which was finally translated back into Manchu for confirmation by the assembled officials. Mala informed the ambassador that the previous day's proceedings had been reported in full to the emperor's ministers, though not to the emperor himself. They had decided to make a final declaration of "our ancient custom, established for centuries in this our country." Milescu was asked to "examine and ponder" Mala's statement, to determine if he could after all accept a letter from the emperor in the Chinese fashion.

Mala's statement was a lucid description of tribute practices.

First, "every ambassador who comes to us here in China must frame his speech as if he came 'up' from a humble and inferior place to an exalted one, or throne." Second, the court officials reporting the arrival of an ambassador to the emperor state that the ambassador has come "from a lower place to Your most exalted Throne, to strike his forehead on the ground," that is, to perform the Kowtow ceremony. Third, all gifts are called tribute in official documents. Fourth, the emperor's gifts to other rulers are not called gifts, but are clearly called gratuities in return for tribute or service. These conditions must be accepted by all ambassadors and other envoys "without reserve." Mala concluded with a statement of the rationale for the tribute system which, as recorded by Milescu, was remarkable for its precision: "Nor do you, Sir Ambassador, marvel that our custom is such, but go and tell your master —for just as there is one God in Heaven, so this one God of ours on earth stands in the world's center, with all other kings and kingdoms around him. That has always been our glory and will be forever."

In a much calmer spirit than on the previous day Milescu replied that "it is a marvelous thing" that gifts sent out of love and friendship were called tribute, even though "all the world knows" that the tsar takes tribute but does not pay it. This remark brought an unusually honest admission from Mala, the closest he could come to an explanation of the reality, as against the theory, of the tribute system: "We are well aware that your master is no subject of the Great Khan's; but time out of mind, our custom has been to speak and to write in that fashion—and that applies to all countries of the world, nor can it be changed."[84] Milescu requested twenty-four hours to consider Mala's statement—not really, he explained to the tsar, to give the matter serious thought but rather to see what would develop.

For the last time Verbiest intervened to warn Milescu of Manchu intentions. Afraid to visit the embassy personally, he sent a letter by a servant later that day, in which he informed Milescu that Mala had lied in stating that the proceedings on August 29 had not been reported to the emperor. The grand secretaries, he claimed, had sat with the emperor all night, and the commission had been sent the next day unwillingly. The council decided that if Milescu accepted the emperor's letter in conformity with Mala's statements, the embassy would remain in Peking one more week to allow for the composition of the document. If Milescu refused, he would have to leave the capital immediately. The Jesuit concluded, "Their motive being mainly that the Chinese should see that, though at war with them [the Manchus], they [the Manchus] are not in awe of even so great a monarch as the tsar; nor willing to change their ancient customs [for him]."[85]

Mala and Verbiest returned to the embassy on August 31, without the president of the Li-fan yuan, to hear Milescu's decision that he could under no circumstances agree to accept Chinese customary behavior. Later that day Verbiest elaborated on the reasons behind the Manchu position. The emperor, he told Milescu, was by nature "greedy of honor and renown." He had studied many years and "learnt the wisdom of the Chinese," recognizing full well that the Chinese prized nothing so much as learning in their rulers. This learning, by implication, had taught the emperor the importance of customary Chinese procedures. Milescu asked Verbiest if the Manchus were not afraid of the tsar and the Russian approach to their frontiers. "Of a certainty they are," the Jesuit replied, "but Moscow is far off," and consequently it would be difficult for Russian armies to defend the frontier. The Jesuit also felt that the Manchus demanded Gantimur's surrender precisely because they knew that Moscow would refuse. "They will then have a good pretext for hostilities," he warned the ambassador; they could then move to destroy Albazin and Nerchinsk.[86]

Early on the morning of September 1, Verbiest informed Milescu by letter that the emperor's advisors had sat through the night and decided to dismiss the Russians from Peking that very day. An hour later Milescu, hoping to forestall any precipitate action, invited Mala to the embassy's quarters, whereupon he was informed that since the negotiations had reached a final impasse, the Russian embassy was dismissed immediately. Milescu was denied an additional twenty-four hours for preparation.

The embassy's return journey was uneventful. Shortly before recrossing the frontier, Mala, who had accompanied Milescu to the Nun-chiang, proposed an exchange of prisoners and refugees and warned that peace must be maintained along the Amur. The Cossacks at Albazin would also have to return the sables they had collected in tribute from the local tribes subject to Peking. It is evident, however, that Milescu did not really understand the true state of affairs along the Sino-Russian frontier, for in his stateyny spisok he advised, "All those natives who dwell between Nerchinsk and the Naun [Nun-chiang, well inside Manchuria] can be made subject to His Majesty the Tsar if he choose only to build a fort on the Argun, or on the Kailer; for they pay tribute to no one."[87] Verbiest's warnings had evidently fallen on deaf ears.

Chapter IV **War Along the Amur**

The development of an aggressive, positive Manchu policy toward the Russians had to await the stabilization of the Ch'ing dynasty's power inside China. With relative ease and speed the Manchus had entered China in 1644, but at least a generation passed before they succeeded in extending their control throughout the former Ming domains and beyond. The new dynasty's most formidable opposition came from Wu San-kuei and Cheng Ch'eng-kung.[1] Wu, who had collaborated with the aliens in their initial southern thrust and war of conquest, revolted against the Manchus in December 1673 and was not suppressed until 1681. Cheng, the famous Koxinga of Western literature, was a Ming general who had remained loyal to the last Chinese dynasty's lost cause. Defeated on the mainland of China, he withdrew to Taiwan, where he died in 1662, but Ming loyalists held out on the island until Manchu occupation in 1683.

The financial and personnel drain on Manchu resources during the struggle for total control of China was sufficient to prevent the Ch'ing court from developing its northern defenses and opening an anti-Russian front in the Amur Valley. Peking's annual expenditure for the support of Wu San-kuei's forces before his rebellion reached tremendous proportions. Without his Chinese troops, however, the Manchu conquest of China would have been all the more difficult, if not impossible. The struggle with Wu and Cheng not only entailed an increased outlay of limited revenues but placed a great strain on Manchu military personnel, who had to occupy as well as conquer the vastness of China. In the struggle against Wu,

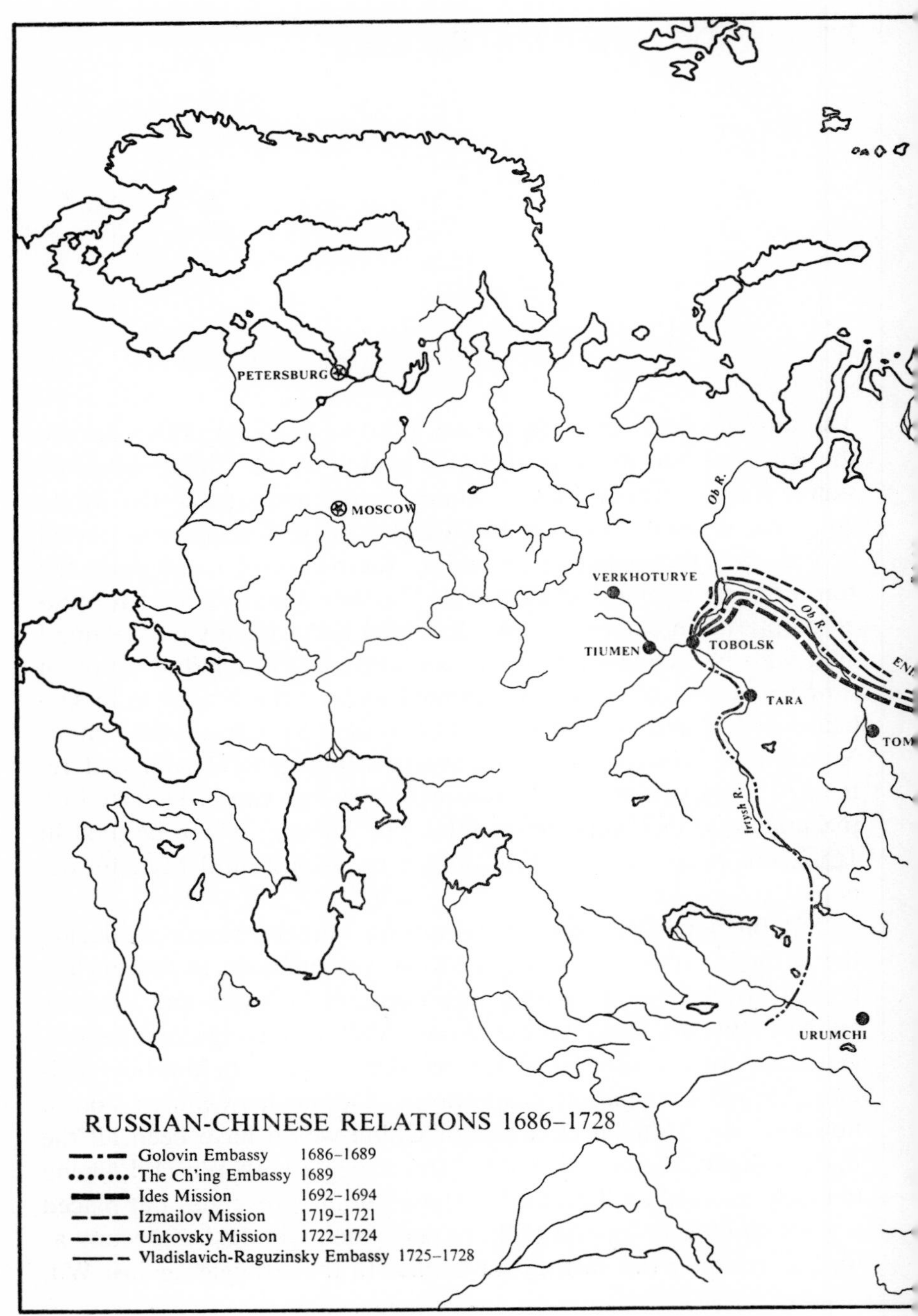

PETERSBURG
MOSCOW
VERKHOTURYE
TIUMEN
TOBOLSK
TARA
Ob R.
Irtysh R.
URUMCHI
RUSSIAN-CHINESE RELATIONS 1686–1728
Golovin Embassy 1686–1689
The Ch'ing Embassy 1689
Ides Mission 1692–1694
Izmailov Mission 1719–1721
Unkovsky Mission 1722–1724
Vladislavich-Raguzinsky Embassy 1725–1728

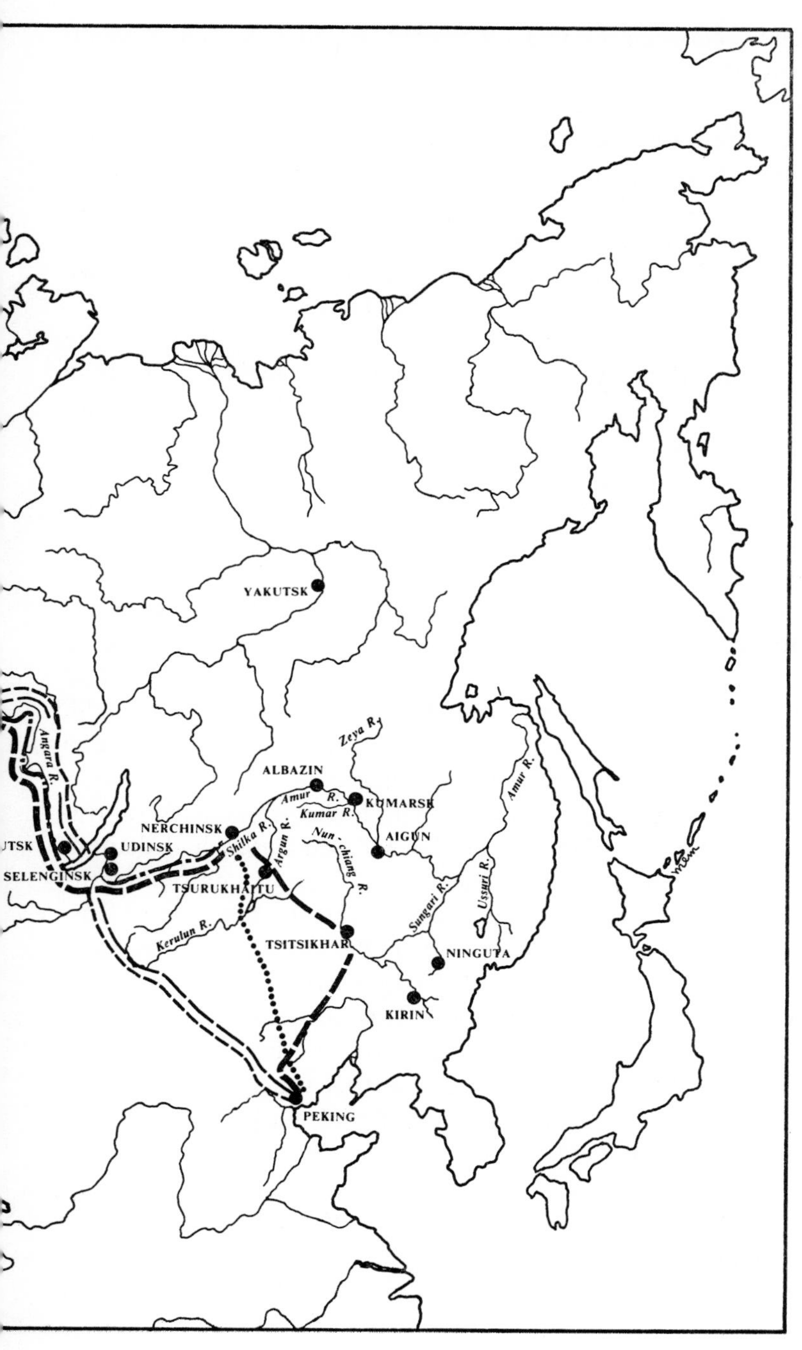

YAKUTSK
Zeya R.
Angara R.
ALBAZIN
Amur R.
KUMARSK
Kumar R.
NERCHINSK
Shilka R.
Argun R.
Nun-chiang R.
AIGUN
Amur R.
UTSK
UDINSK
SELENGINSK
TSURUKHAITU
Sungari R.
Ussuri R.
Kerulun R.
TSITSIKHAR
NINGUTA
KIRIN
PEKING

for instance, between 71 and 89 percent of all potential Manchu military manpower was engaged in battle at one time or another, and between 54 and 92 percent participated in the campaigns against Cheng.[2] Imprecise though these figures may be, they indicate the overwhelming commitment of Manchu personnel to the struggle for social stability and dynastic security inside China proper. This commitment deterred the diversion of even minimal financial and military resources for the building of an effective offensive force on the Amur until the 1680's.

The Manchus then faced two problems to the north. First, the security of the dynasty's territorial base in Manchuria must be maintained, as was impressed upon them by their difficulties with the Chinese rebels. They therefore prevented Chinese colonization of Manchuria until the end of the nineteenth century and made efforts to secure their homeland from Russian incursions. Second, as the new occupants of the dragon throne, the Manchus needed a free hand in Central Asia, particularly in Mongolia and Sinkiang, because Central Asian nomad invasions and raids were a constant threat to any dynastic power in China. As the Russians in southern Siberia maintained close contact with the Mongols and were in a position to intervene in Central Asian affairs at will, Peking needed Russia's neutrality in Central Asian politics and recognition of her own primary role in the region.

Moscow could not be dealt with within the framework of traditional East Asian diplomacy, as the Milescu fiasco had demonstrated. That embassy showed the infeasibility of combining the question of trade, which Moscow wanted, with the question of Russian withdrawal from the Amur, which Peking wanted. As early as the 1670's the Manchus indicated that they were prepared to exchange commercial privileges for Russian evacuation of the Cossack settlements along the northern frontier, but since Moscow could not control the Amur Cossacks at that time, it had to insist on treating the problems of trade and frontier separately.

A decade later the Manchus, now comparatively free from danger inside China, took measures to establish a position of strength in the north from which they could force the Russians into negotiations on Peking's terms. By military action they sought to remove the Russian threat from the dynasty's back door and, at the same time, to bring the Russians to the conference table, where trade could be exchanged for decolonization. The Ch'ing would trade commercial privileges for Russia's juridical, as well as actual, withdrawal from the Amur. Furthermore, the establishment of regular commerce would inhibit Russian interference in Central Asia, where the Manchus faced a growing threat from the Jungars.

K'ang-hsi, subtle and puissant, recognized that a position of strength along the Amur could be achieved by a demonstrable force held in reserve. East Asia's sinocentric tribute system was itself based on the "barbarians'" apprehension of China's potential, as opposed to her actual, strength. The emperor thus pursued a dual approach to Russia: while preparing a military campaign, he tried to enter into diplomatic negotiations by sending letters to Albazin, Nerchinsk, and Moscow. His military and diplomatic style were conservative and controlled. K'ang-hsi did not seek to conquer the Russians; he only sought to demonstrate to them the existence of that position of strength from which he could reach a negotiated settlement.

Military Preparations and Planning

The vulnerability of the indigenous population to Russian pressures, the creation of a military base, the development of supply resources, and the mobilization of manpower were basic problems the Manchus had to solve if they were to build a military machine capable of both offensive and defensive action in the area of contact with the Russians. Although a concerted attack on these problems was not made until the return of the emperor from an imperial progress through Manchuria to Wu-la (Kirin) and Ninguta in 1682 and the defeat of Wu San-kuei and Cheng Ch'eng-kung, certain measures taken in the 1670's provided a basis for further constructive efforts.[3] Limited in nature but permanent in character, these measures enabled the Manchus to conduct a holding operation in the north while they attended to the more immediate problems presented by the rebellions in the south. With a minimal expenditure and relying heavily on the local population for manpower and matériel, the Ch'ing court protected its suzerain position among the tribes living along the Amur in the area of most intensive and dangerous contact with the Russians.

In order to minimize contact between the Russians and the indigenes, the Manchus sometime before 1676 ordered the removal of the Soluns and the Dahurs from the Amur to interior settlements, mostly along the Nun-chiang. This move typified the strategy of a land-based empire; it resembled the removal of coastal populations along China's Pacific coast during the Manchu campaigns against Cheng Ch'eng-kung. On the one hand, it protected the local populace from Russian attack and plunder at a moment when the Manchus could not themselves provide significant protection. On the other hand, it reduced the opportunity for the tribes to cross over to Russian-held territory and transfer their allegiance and tribute payments to Moscow. The Manchus could maintain better communications with, and closer control over, the Nun-chiang than they could the Amur.[4]

In order to make their presence felt in the Amur region, the Manchus had first to establish an urban center to serve as the focal point for local power and a base for military preparations and operations. Although Ninguta, to the south, was a convenient staging ground, it was too distant from the area of contact. In the spring of 1675, therefore, the city of Wu-la was established as headquarters for the Ninguta *chiang-chün* or general, bringing the military command close to the scene of action. The chiang-chün commanded over two-thousand men, and several thousand families of exiles were settled at the new center to provide logistic support. After 1676 a 200-man naval force was employed at Wu-la in the construction of river boats and the training of sailors. Construction of such an urban center partially met the Manchu manpower shortage in the area, eliminating the population vacuum that had invited Russian intrusion.

The Ch'ing approached the problem of mobilizing available manpower in two ways. First, they organized the indigenous population into banners, or divisions of their army, called "New Manchus" (Hsin Man-chou). This policy may have originated as early as the attack on Kumarsk in 1654-1655, when Gantimur himself served with the Manchu forces. In 1671 Bahai, the field commander in

Manchuria, included in the Manchu table of military organization these native tribes, who were organized into some forty companies commanded by their own officers. In 1675 half of the 2,000-man force based at Ninguta was composed of New Manchus. Second, manpower mobilization was placed on a continuing and permanent basis through a form of conscription. Every young man was required to appear at three-year intervals before the Ninguta chiang-chün. If he was five ch'ih tall, he was immediately qualified to enter military service. Boatmen, assistant boatmen, and local militiamen were drawn from the remaining adult males under sixty years of age. In this fashion the Manchus maintained a regular military force of certain size without moving troops into the Amur Valley from regions further than Ninguta.[5]

The court initiated a program in 1668 to ensure the steady provision of supplies to its new military force. Thirty-two official farm villages (*kuan-chuang*) were established, each village composed of units of ten men and their families; one man served as headman and the others were soldiers. They gathered fuel and coal, cultivated the land, and stored supplies. Each person in the villages had an annual production quota of ten shih of grain, 300 chin of limestone, and 100 bunches of reeds.[6]

Yet these measures were insufficient to support the level of military action that the Manchus might eventually be forced to take against the Russians, and the emperor during his progress through Manchuria from March 24 to June 9, 1682, clearly recognized the need for concerted planning to expand and develop his northern military base.[7] Consequently, in September 1682 he sent down an edict ordering the two vice-lieutenant generals, Langtan and Duke Pengcun, to conduct a reconnaissance expedition into Russian-held areas.[8] In the edict, as well as in private conversations with Langtan, K'ang-hsi carefully reviewed the "Russian problem" and outlined future Ch'ing policy. The Russians, he felt, were "savage, greedy, stubborn, and ignorant,"[9] but they remained at Albazin, cultivated the land, fished, hunted, and continued to raid tributary tribes subject to Peking because past Manchu policies had been shortsighted and ill-conceived. Shortages of provisions had resulted in Manchu withdrawal before victory. "If we don't defeat them by force," the emperor concluded, "they will not fear [us] and will spread their influence."[10]

The reconnaissance mission, which entered the Amur Valley in the guise of a deer-hunting expedition, was supported by one hundred Khorchin and eighty Ninguta soldiers.[11] Pengcun and Langtan were instructed to study communications, roads, and distances, to make observations of Albazin, to consider the problem of quartering troops, and to travel along the water-routes between the Amur and the Ussuri. From the Ussuri they were to find the most direct routes to Ninguta, along which they should send a body of imperial guards (*shih-wei*) under a colonel (*ts'an-ling*). Sometime during the first part of January the expedition returned to the capital and, in a memorial that became the basis for further military planning, submitted their findings and recommendations. A force of three-thousand soldiers armed with twenty cannon would be sufficient, they thought, to overcome Albazin, which was defended by a wooden wall. However, land travel in northern Manchuria was very difficult. The "narrow and inconvenient" roads were icy in the winter and too muddy in the summer to allow passage of large numbers of men and supplies. Consequently, they recommended the use of water-routes, even though currents made such a trip between Ninguta and the Amur three months longer than by land. They proposed the construction of fifty small boats, forty large ships, and twenty-six other craft for river transport.

Ch'ing military planning now entered a new phase—a comprehensive analysis of the logistic and strategic problems presented by the confrontation with the Russians in the Amur Valley. In order to provide both a fighting force and the permanent population in frontier settlements that would deter future Russian incursions, men and matériel had to be mobilized and moved along improved transportation routes into well-constructed bases. K'ang-hsi and his advisers developed Ch'ing strength in northern Manchuria through four distinct but closely related programs: development of communications facilities, development of supply resources, mobilization of manpower, and development of anti-Russian tactics in the area of contact. Each program was articulated empirically, step by step; details were adjusted at any given moment to fit new circumstances or information. Strategically, the court established the dynasty's presence along the Amur; military tactics had to be based on the structure of that presence.

The reconnaissance mission's memorial occasioned an imperial edict, dated January 24, 1683, which set the style for the entire preparatory process. Close planning and careful use of available resources would result in great economies: warships, for instance, should also transport men and matériel; soldiers should construct ships and bases as well as cultivate land for food supplies. Of all the men sent into the area, only five hundred went for purely military purposes. Having accepted Langtan's and Pengcun's evaluation of the Amur situation, the emperor outlined the steps to be taken immediately.[12] Insisting that any solution to the Russian problem required a careful and cautious policy, he ordered the postponement of all plans for attacking Russian positions. "The use of force is, after all, not a good thing," he remarked. In order to minimize expenses in the face of the serious drain on treasury resources occasioned by the disorders in the south, K'ang-hsi ordered 1,500 soldiers, instead of the 3,000 recommended by the report of the reconnaissance mission, to go to Wu-la from Ninguta to construct warships. These men were to be armed with cannon and hunting guns. He ordered the construction of wooden towns at Aigun and Kumarsk as bases for future military operations. The ten Khorchin Mongol banners were to supply provisions and men to cultivate land near Wu-la. Until the first crop was harvested, the military colony at Hsi-po-wu-la was to supply food out of its 12,000-tan rice reserve. The emperor claimed that in this way "there will be no more shortages." Turning to transportation, K'ang-hsi ordered the construction of a post station between Aigun and the Solun villages five days distant. The Soluns were to supply the Wu-la soldiers with sheep and oxen through the station. Bahai and Sabsu, another officer, took personal charge of these operations.[13]

K'ang-hsi's decision to halve the number of troops sent from Ninguta to Wu-la was more than a simple economy measure. It was an illustration of the close attention K'ang-hsi paid to detail right up to the outbreak of Manchu-Russian hostilities in 1685. At the same time, it was indicative of a problem that was to grow in importance during the period preparatory to war: the open disagreement of the emperor's field officers and advisers with him on general as well as specific policies and measures. As a vital and vigorous ruler, K'ang-hsi was intimately concerned with administrative problems and examined minute details with great care. He personally sent orders to northern Manchuria concerning such matters as the size of boats to be built for transportation, the construction of granaries, and the size of a post station staff.[14] But since the emperor at Peking was far distant from the scene of operations, he suffered from a paucity of intelligence information. Consequently, he often issued orders that were unsuited to the situation as it was actually developing. At the same time, his field commanders, Sabsu in particular, often appeared from the Peking vantage point to be overly timid. At times disagreements arose over considerations of economy. On April 22, 1683, for instance, the emperor received a memorial recommending that officers and men leaving Wu-la for the Amur receive a month's travel rations. He replied that only a half-month's rations should be issued to each man. In May 1684, as Aigun was building its supply potential but before a permanent agricultural economy had been developed along the Amur, Sabsu memorialized that a year's travel rations should be issued to officers and men in order to ease supply problems along the front. The Board of Revenue (Hu-pu) in Peking suggested that only half that amount be issued, and the emperor agreed, remarking almost ironically that "officers and soldiers work very hard."[15]

The most serious disputes concerned tactical and developmental problems. K'ang-hsi's original plan for the erection of two wooden cities as permanent bases on the Amur at Aigun and Kumarsk met with opposition from Bahai, who memorialized that both locations were too distant from Albazin to be effective. He pointed out that Manchu forces would be divided and vulnerable, unable to aid each other in case of a surprise Russian attack. Inasmuch as Nerchinsk and other cities lay behind Albazin, if the Russians used those cities as sources of men and supplies, the Manchus would find it difficult to win total victory. Bahai therefore recommended an immediate attack before the Russians could bring up supplies. He proposed to lead a military detachment right up to Albazin to threaten and frighten the defenders into surrender. Alternatively, he suggested that a small detachment of regular troops could accompany a Russian fugitive named I-fan (Ivan) back to Albazin, reconnoiter, and make recommendations for further action.[16]

K'ang-hsi rejected Bahai's recommendation for an immediate attack on the grounds that unfamiliarity with the terrain made such a move impossible. Instead, he ordered a thorough study of the problem and the submission of a new plan. At the same time he augmented the Amur forces by sending fifty men from each banner stationed in Peking, together with military personnel from the metropolitan garrisons who had been degraded or punished for various offenses. If conditions and the state of buildup did not permit an attack in the winter of 1683-1684, he concluded, the Amur armies should return to Aigun, Wu-la, and Ninguta to await further instructions. The emperor apparently did not wish to make any military moves before all nonmilitary solutions had been exhausted or before preparations were at a sufficient stage to ensure military success. He also rejected Bahai's second proposal, even though it had the support of the council of princes in the capital, because he felt that Bahai's strategic thinking was "too loose." In the first place, he said, the Wu-la and Ninguta soldiers had no battlefield experience and lacked fighting discipline. Second, Bahai and Sabsu were not on good terms, so that any successful campaign or action would require that the two men and their forces be kept apart.[17] He ordered Bahai to remain at Wu-la, while Sabsu led detachments of regular troops to the Amur and became, in fact, the field commander in that region.

Certain elements in Peking exacerbated the dispute between the emperor and the commanders in the field. Langtan more than once pursued an independent line in the capital, where he and Duke Pengcun had direct access to the council of princes advising the emperor. On one occasion, for instance, Langtan opposed Bahai's recommendations that local tributary tribes be called on to supply the army with horses. Instead, he recommended that the Palace Stud (*Shang-ssu yuan*), or stable, supply two thousand strong horses, since the local Manchurian tribes had insufficient resources to satisfy the army's needs.[18] On another occasion the council recommended, and the emperor agreed, that Ch'ing forces be concentrated at E-su-li, a point between Aigun and Kumarsk, rather than at a place closer to Albazin, as Sabsu had recommended. Langtan believed that a wooden city could be constructed at E-su-li and manned by forces sent directly from the capital. He apparently sought to increase the court's participation in, and control of, the Amur operations; he also sought to exclude Bahai and Sabsu from participation, for he suggested that the former stay at Wu-la "under all circumstances," while the latter be sent to the Solun villages to collect horses. On receiving these new orders, Sabsu memorialized in opposition to Langtan's suggestions. Because the problems of transporting cannon and rations through the snow made a winter attack on Albazin impossible, he requested a modification of his instructions to permit him to remain at the proposed E-su-li base through the winter, attacking Albazin in May 1684. The council of princes and other court ministers approved his proposal, since the emperor himself had once entertained the thought that a winter attack might prove impossible. By appealing to this point, Sabsu was able to avoid the horse-collecting expedition among the Solun tribes.[19]

Whereas K'ang-hsi considered that Bahai's strategic thinking was "too loose" and bellicose, he thought that Sabsu was altogether too timid, unimaginative, and scheming. A principal source of disagreement was the emperor's plan to establish the E-su-li base as a symbol of Ch'ing presence along the Amur. The emperor originally instructed that five to six hundred soldiers from Wu-la and Ninguta, with four to five hundred men from the Dahur tribes, be sent to E-su-li in the autumn with their families. Grain would be brought in from outside to feed the base until fields could be sown and harvested. Langtan was sent north to consult with Sabsu about these problems, and Sabsu suggested that since snow usually began to fall at E-su-li in early September, the base's condition would be extremely precarious at the outset. He recommended, instead, that settlers come "in the spring before the autumn sets in." At first only five-hundred Dahurs should be sent, and after sowing had begun, their families could follow. To minimize the pressure on the colony's resources, three-thousand Ninguta and Wu-la soldiers should be divided into three groups, visiting E-su-li in rotation. Langtan presented Sabsu's recommendations to the council of princes, who approved, but the emperor would not, claiming that neither Langtan nor Sabsu understood the difficulties involved in such long-range planning. He now abandoned the E-su-li plan and suggested Aigun as a permanent base, where warships, cannon, and other weapons could be constructed and stockpiled. An advance base of scouts was to be established at Kumarsk to supply Aigun with intelligence. Aigun and Wu-la would be connected by a more efficient communications system, and the Amur city would become the major supply depot and military base in the north. The emperor believed that his new plan had several advantages. If the Russians attacked down-river, the boats stationed at Aigun could defeat them. Since the land around the city was broad and flat, it could be easily cultivated. "If we carry out these plans one by one," he concluded, "then the Russians would necessarily be at their wits' end and give themselves up."[20]

E-erh-sa, a secretary (*lang-chung*) of the Li-fan yuan, took the emperor's new plan to Sabsu, who, though he concurred, gently suggested that moving troops into the area, building cities, and cultivating land all at the same time "would be beyond our reach." He requested five-hundred soldiers from Wu-la and Ninguta to help in the construction of Aigun, but the emperor refused on the grounds that he had other plans for those men. Instead, he offered to send aid from the Mukden garrison. K'ang-hsi evidently felt that Sabsu's requests, first for three-thousand Wu-la and Ninguta soldiers and later for five-hundred soldiers from the same sources for construction work at Aigun, were attempts to gain control over Bahai's troops under the guise of fulfilling the emperor's own orders.[21]

On at least two occasions the emperor concluded that Sabsu's timidity and insubordination were sabotaging the buildup. As preparations proceeded, it became possible to take action closer to Albazin itself, and on August 1, 1684, Sabsu received orders to capture the Russian harvest in the vicinity of the settlement. The orders were based on a careful reconnaissance which led to the conclusion that Russian supplies were hardly sufficient to support the population; the loss of one year's harvest would therefore be a severe blow.[22] K'ang-hsi ordered an attack by water so that the boats carrying soldiers to Albazin could bring the harvest back, thereby increasing Manchu supplies as well. Sabsu, however, opposed the orders with cogent arguments. A large allotment of supplies had arrived at Aigun on July 14, but time was needed to distribute them among the soldiers and to prepare winter clothing. Russian prisoners claimed that the crops at Albazin had ripened early and the harvest had already begun. The rainy season was about to begin, which would cause the rivers to swell and make the land routes impassable. The journey from Aigun to the Russian fields was long: the men and horses would be too tired to carry out the maneuver with the necessary speed. Construction work at Aigun was incomplete, and "when we get back, it will be cold weather and very hard to do any building." Nevertheless, K'ang-hsi rejected Sabsu's objections, rebuked him sharply for failing to carry out orders, and demanded new reasons for his unwillingness to take advantage of this opportunity. Although Sabsu replied in a tone of self-accusation, the council of princes advised the emperor to delay punishment until after the campaign.[23]

Sabsu's demurral and the time required for communication between Peking and the Amur had ruined the opportunity of 1684. The emperor now had to face the fact that a full year would be lost in bringing his anti-Russian campaign to a successful conclusion if he did not modify his plans. If he cautiously ordered the destruction of Russian crops for 1685 and awaited results, he might not be able to launch a frontal attack on Albazin until 1686. Consequently, shifting emphasis, he ordered Sabsu to carry out imperial orders and sent two officials, the lieutenant-general (*tu-t'ung*) Wasan and the board president (*shih-lang*) Kuo-p'i, to Aigun to discuss with Sabsu the actual capture of Albazin. "If they refuse to surrender," he informed Sabsu, "we will start to attack their city. If we cannot take the city, we will follow the former edict to destroy their harvests and then return [to our base]."[24]

Once K'ang-hsi had decided to force the Russian issue by commanding Sabsu to attack Albazin directly, he issued orders looking to the period after the campaign. The emperor knew from the first that a military victory over the Russians would not be the final solution to his "Russian problem" but merely a means to an end. Consequently, he warned that if after victory, "we do not plan very carefully and [mistakenly] withdraw our army . . . the Russians will become even more violent." Therefore, he ordered the permanent occupation of Albazin in the event that the Ch'ing forces overcame its defenses. A fresh detachment of five-hundred soldiers was to be sent to the vicinity of the Russian settlement "to guard the city as well as to cultivate the land." Crops were to be sown in the vicinity of Albazin before the beginning of the attack and harvested after, which would assure the occupation forces a supply of food.[25] Even at this late moment, however, K'ang-hsi felt that Sabsu was sabotaging the war effort, because on or about March 1, 1685, he sent down an edict accusing Sabsu and others of gross misconduct. The Board of Revenue had memorialized that reports from Aigun indicated all the plow oxen were dead and most agricultural instruments in bad repair. This situation endangered both the support of troops in the field and the plans for the occupation of Albazin. The emperor concluded from these developments that "Sabsu and others willfully destroyed the cultivating implements and killed the plow oxen. His purpose is to delay action by all means, so that he may be expected to withdraw from the Amur . . . How could he shrink from his responsibilities and leave the task to his superior [the emperor]?"[26] Although the emperor declared that Sabsu deserved severe punishment, he deferred action until after the campaign, scheduled to begin in less than a month. Mala was dispatched to purchase new oxen, and Sabsu was instructed to see that sufficient agricultural implements were available when and where needed.

Despite disagreements between the emperor and his field officers, the establishment of a Ch'ing presence on the banks of the Amur through a military buildup in northern Manchuria proceeded with remarkable efficiency as a result of careful planning. Communications and transportation facilities were expanded for two purposes: to speed and ease the flow of food and supplies into the buildup area, and to permit the faster exchange of edicts and memorials between Peking and the Amur. The Manchus used the riverine system in a fashion resembling Russia's use of rivers and portages in its eastward expansion. The transportation network serviced military units along the Amur with supplies for future as well as for current use. By accumulating surplus grain in the front area to meet unexpected contingencies, the Ch'ing military could plan more elastically. Various methods were used to obtain sufficient quantities of grain: purchase, tribute, and military-agricultural colonies. Mala, for instance, led a purchasing mission into Manchuria to buy oxen, sheep, and grain. In order to expedite matters, the emperor ordered the Board of Revenue to provide Mala with 4,000 liang of silver to be used in place of tea and cloth for purchases. He also ordered Mala "to go quickly" but not to extort undue profits from the people, so as not to alienate any segment of the population in affected areas.[27]

Another source of supplies was the diversion of tribute from Peking to northern Manchuria. On March 2, 1685, the emperor ordered the tribute of the ten Khorchin Mongol tribes, which consisted of oxen, sheep, and grain, sent that year to Aigun instead of to Peking. In order to control the transaction, K'ang-hsi demanded a memorial detailing the conditions and amounts involved. At the same time, since the goods sent to Aigun were registered as Khorchin tribute, the customary gifts were sent by the emperor to the tributary tribes. The Li-fan yuan, as the agency in charge of relations with Central Asian tributaries, directed the operation.[28] In addition to purchase and tribute, soldiers along the frontier were ordered to till the ground for crops; supplies were drawn especially from the military-agricultural colonies established in central Manchuria.[29]

The emperor recognized that the successful creation of a Ch'ing "presence" on the Amur, based on a reservoir of manpower and supplies, had political as well as military significance. Hoping to avoid open military hostilities, he sought to use the buildup itself to persuade the Russians to withdraw. As early as April 30, 1683, almost as soon as the military concentration at Aigun had begun, K'ang-hsi ordered a detachment of soldiers sent from Wu-chu-mu-ch'ing into the Russian-occupied region, ostensibly to hunt deer near Albazin, but actually to generate suspicion among the Russians. A-mu-hu-lang, the president of the Li-fan yuan, was sent among the Soluns to announce the approach of the deer hunters and, not too secretly, to begin the preparation of military supplies. The emperor hoped that the Russians, realizing the superiority of the Manchu forces, would withdraw rather than face them.[30] The ruse failed, and Peking proceeded to use other tactics. Reconnaissance missions gathered information and prisoners for interrogation. These captured Russians were usually returned to Albazin with tales of Manchu leniency and mercy.[31]

At the beginning of 1685, as plans for the opening of hostilities were reaching full maturity, K'ang-hsi still hoped to use his military might to achieve a political solution without recourse to actual war. "The use of force," he told his council of princes, "is not a good thing. We use it only under compulsion." One last effort should be made to reach a settlement with the local Russian officials. He ordered an edict be sent to Albazin stating, "This time we send strong forces to obstruct and fight against you. With such forces, it is not difficult to destroy you." However, since the emperor could not bear "to extinguish and wipe out [the Russians] at once," he instructed them to return to Yakutsk, which would become the Sino-Russian frontier. "You can hunt sables and collect taxes there, but you may not come into our land to make trouble." He concluded with proposals for an exchange of prisoners and the establishment of frontier trade, promising, "if you still persist and refuse to obey this order, our great forces must break into Albazin city."[32] In an accompanying edict to his generals in the field, the emperor stated that if the Russians accepted these proposals, the Amur army would be stationed permanently at Aigun and advance detachments would occupy Albazin. If they refused, the army was ordered to "make advances or halt advances as the situation dictates." The emperor clearly explained the rationale for the use of diplomatic methods to solve the Amur crisis: *"If we do not instruct them,* even though we take Albazin city, when we advance they withdraw. But when we withdraw, they will advance again. Therefore, there would be no end to the use of force and the frontier people would not be peaceful."[33] The refusal of the Russians to bow to this decree made war inevitable.

The Russians on the Eve of War

Manchu military preparations did not go unnoticed by the Russians. At Albazin, Nerchinsk, and Moscow efforts were made to shore up Russia's Amur defenses. These efforts were doomed to failure because of the great distances separating the Russian home base in Europe from the Far East and the sparseness of Russian settlement in Siberia.

The Russians were aware of Manchu intentions at least as early as March 1681, when Fedor Voyeykov, voevoda of Nerchinsk, wrote the Siberian Department in Moscow that Albazin had been visited by a Manchu official from the Nun-chiang, accompanied by large military units. Although they demanded that the Albazinians join them in an open field for "conversations," the Russians, fearing for their lives, sent out only a five-man delegation. The Manchus demanded to know why a Russian fort had been built on the Zeya River, at a location used as a portage by Manchu officials when collecting tribute from subject tribes.[34] Because of this confrontation, Voyeykov decided to send a detachment of Cossacks to the Nun-chiang in June 1681 to explain to the Ch'ing officials that the Zeya fort had been built "for the planting of grain" because "along the Zeya live many Russian yasak natives of various tribes," who paid their tribute at the fort. During the conversations, which took place in special tents arranged in open fields, Yuri Laba, the leader of the Russians, informed the Manchus that the Zeya fort "was constructed by the order of the great tsar for eternity." Prior to the Russians' arrival in that region, he claimed, the land had been "nothing"; now it belonged to the tsar. Consequently, the Albazinians would not interfere with Manchu officials wishing to cross the river at that point, but neither would they destroy their own ostrog.

The Manchus kept the Russian delegation at the Nun-chiang for over seven weeks, while a report was sent to Peking and instructions were awaited. Occasional meetings were held, and at one moment four hundred Manchu soldiers were ranged alongside the conference tent, evidently as a form of intimidation. In August an official arrived from the capital with an imperial edict that constituted an ultimatum for Russian withdrawal from the Zeya. The Cossacks returned to Nerchinsk with their report at the beginning of October 1681. These events marked the beginning of Russian efforts to create some kind of defense in the Amur Valley.

In October Voyeykov called a meeting of all the Nerchinsk Cossacks at the town hall. After telling them the history of the construction of Albazin and reporting on the Nun-chiang conversations, he asked the Cossacks to decide among themselves whether or not to abandon the Zeya and to give him their written, signed answers. Voyeykov had specific instructions not to "cause arguments with China about anything," but faced with the Manchu challenge, he had to take action, for which he needed the support of the Cossacks in case of future difficulties with Moscow. He failed to gain their support, however. The inhabitants of Nerchinsk refused to accept any responsibility in the situation, on the grounds that the Zeya ostrog had been built by Albazinians, not by them, and presented the voevoda with a declaration refusing to reply to his petition.[35]

To complicate matters further, Mangutei and a Manchu force of some one-thousand men approached Albazin in the summer of 1681, ostensibly searching for fugitives but actually carrying out a reconnaissance mission, which led the Albazinians to believe that they, not just the Zeya ostrog, were now to be the object of a military attack. Voyeykov wrote another letter to the Siberian Department, pointing out that at Nerchinsk, Argunsk, and the Russian ostrogs in Dahuria there were only 202 men; guns and powder were scarce. "We cannot send anything or anyone to Albazin; and from the Bogdoy [Manchu] forces the Nerchinsk and Albazin ostrogs will not be defended by anyone, and even in the Nerchinsk ostrog they live in great fear." He incidentally complained that the Albazinians were not in the habit of obeying him.

In 1682 the Russian position grew worse. The beginning of the construction of the Manchu base at Aigun prevented the Cossacks from sailing down the Amur in search of food and tribute. The Manchus also made a minor attack on a detachment of Albazinian Cossacks, captured some prisoners, and destroyed a series of small Russian ostrogs along the Burya, Khamunua, Zeya, and Selima rivers.

The government in Moscow, recognizing that the Manchu military buildup in the area and the attacks on outlying Russian posts constituted a threat to Albazin, the key to all Dahuria, began to take action. In 1682 Ivan Astafievich Vlasov, the experienced voevoda of Irkutsk, was sent to Nerchinsk to replace the indecisive Voyeykov. Vlasov was given the right of direct communications with Moscow without having to rout his message through Eniseisk, as had previously been the custom. Vlasov and Prince K. O. Scherbatsky, the Eniseisk voevoda, were ordered "to defend with military forces all the Dahur and Baikal ostrogs." Moscow was trying to provide her Far Eastern outposts with capable leadership.

Moscow also moved during 1682 to strengthen the administrative apparatus in Dahuria and to increase the population as a defensive measure. The Amur territories were taken away from the Nerchinsk uezd and reconstituted as a special Albazin voevodstvo —perhaps as a result of Voyeykov's complaint that the Albazinians did not obey him. Aleksey Tolbuzin, the son of a Nerchinsk voevoda, was appointed the new Albazin voevoda. Shortly after his arrival he reported to Moscow that there were only 350 serving- and producing-men in Albazin and 97 peasants in surrounding villages, giving a total of 447 men. Miltary supplies were modest in the extreme: sixteen puds of powder and ten puds of lead. He estimated the Manchu force in the area at 15,000.[36]

The tsar moved quickly to increase the population even more and in a special gramota, dated April 20, 1683, ordered that 1,000 Cossacks be selected immediately in Tobolsk, Eniseisk, and the other Siberian cities and sent to Dahuria. They were to receive the tsar's wages of five rubles per person, and each Dahur regiment was to receive 5,000 rubles from the treasury for expenses and 50 harquebuses. Eniseisk would provide the newly selected Cossacks with grain.

Poor planning and bad organization, in addition to difficulties of time and place, inhibited Moscow's efforts to create a viable Amur defense. A group of six hundred serving-people from Tobolsk who had been dispatched to Dahuria mutinied en route, robbed the voevoda and other officials accompanying them, and threatened to throw them into a river. The mutineers revolted because they had been provided with poor arms and provisions. Even though these were replaced and the march continued, the group failed to arrive at Albazin before the beginning of the Ch'ing siege. The additional 400 men required by the tsar's order for 1,000 were not mobilized by the Siberian voevodas because of a "scarcity of population." During 1683, for instance, the Einseisk voevoda wrote Moscow that he had only 233 serving-people, 5 cannon, 144 harquebuses, 48 puds of lead, 30 puds of powder, and little more. Therefore, he felt that not only was he unable to help Albazin, but, should the Mongols or other nomads attack Eniseisk, he would be unable to defend it.[37]

Moscow's apparent determination to defend the Amur against Manchu attack could not overcome the multitude of problems involved in building a military machine in the face of the scarcity of able-bodied men in Siberia and the impossibly long command and logistic lines.[38] The apparent lack of interest shown by other Siberian voevodas in the Amur crisis made any success even more improbable. By the time of the Ch'ing attack on Albazin in 1685, neither population nor military supplies had increased sufficiently to allow for more than a brave but vain Russian resistance.

Albazin: 1685

After the completion of last-minute preparations Ch'ing forces attacked Albazin in the early summer of 1685. The emperor had appointed Duke Pengcun commander in chief in place of Sabsu because of the latter's failure to destroy the Albazin harvest in 1684.[39] Langtan was chief of staff, and Bandarša and T'ung-pao were staff members.[40] On the eve of the attack, K'ang-hsi outlined the strategy he intended his field commanders to follow. Because of Sabsu's failure to provide sufficient plow oxen and agricultural impliments for raising crops in the Albazin area, the Ch'ing could not occupy the entire region. Consequently, the emperor wanted the city wall destroyed and the land devastated so that crops could not be grown there again. If Pengcun could not seize Albazin by the end of the sixth month, he was to return and wait for another opportunity the following year.[41] K'ang-hsi's final instructions to Pengcun, dispatched to the front with his favorite guard-officer, Kuan-pao, demonstrated his faith in victory and his determination to win, if possible, through a show of strength rather than the shedding of blood: "War is a terrible thing, and fighting is a dangerous enterprise. Our ancestors did it only when they were compelled to do so. We rule the empire by the principle of benevolence and never by bloodthirstiness. You must instruct the officers and soldiers never to violate this edict. Because our army is excellent and our equipment strong, in the long run the Russians cannot resist us, and they must offer up our territories and return our cities. Then do not kill one single man, but let them return to their own native land. In this way, we shall demonstrate to them our sublime idea of treating foreigners kindly."[42]

The Manchu forces advanced on Albazin by river and by land. Solun scouts guided the land forces deep into the forested mountains. The Manchus had hoped to take Albazin by surprise, but unfortunately the Soluns "were not quite cognizant of the directions of the road. They only knew the general direction." When they encountered some Russian residences in an isolated region, therefore, the Manchus surrounded them, captured the inhabitants, and asked the way to Albazin. One Russian escaped and fled to the settlement to raise the alarm. Worried lest the Albazinians now have time to prepare their defenses, Pengcun decided to attack without waiting for the arrival of the naval forces.[43]

On June 23, 1685, Pengcun led three-thousand soldiers in an attack on Albazin.[44] First he read to the Russian defenders the emperor's edict demanding their surrender. Tolbuzin reportedly answered in an offensive manner, and the Manchus began preparations for the assault itself. On the morning of June 25 more than forty-five Russians tried to enter Albazin by boat to join the defenders. They were attacked and, when they refused to surrender, more than thirty were killed, while fifteen women and children were captured. That evening the Manchus prepared to build a wall to the south of the settlement as a safe place from which to shoot their arrows and make sorties into the Russian defenses. Cannon were placed to the north of the city, and troops armed with cannon prepared attacks on both the right and left flanks, while naval forces were to attack by water. An indecisive battle began on the morning of June 26 and raged well into the evening. The Manchus thereupon piled dry wood at the base of the settlement's wooden wall on three sides, while their navy held the fourth, facing the river. When the Manchus began to light the tinder, cutting the Albazinians off on all four sides, Tolbuzin sued for surrender.

During the surrender negotiations at least six hundred and probably almost all of the Russians requested permission to return to Nerchinsk. They were permitted to take their belongings with them and, as one report put it, "Tolbuzin and his people bowed low when the imperial favor was communicated to them." A Manchu detachment accompanied the Russians as far as the Argun River, where about forty-five men decided to surrender to the Manchus with their families rather than return to Russian territory. "Moved by our great generosity," it was reported, "they wished to become the subjects of our magnanimous emperor." Albazin and the other Russian settlements in the area were destroyed, and the harvest collected. Some of the "pacified" Russians were sent to Mukden, but others went to Peking, where they became that city's famous "Albazinians."[45]

K'ang-hsi received the news of the victory on July 5, 1685, during an imperial progress in Manchuria. A-erh-ni, the new president of the Li-fan yuan, presented the victory memorial to the emperor, and K'ang-hsi's exultant reply indicated that he had no misgivings about his last-minute decision not to occupy Albazin permanently. He took the occasion to assert that it was he himself who had made the major decisions leading to victory, often over the objections of his advisers and lieutenants in the field—an obvious reference to Sabsu.[46] In a series of ceremonial dialogues with his ministers as part of the court's victory celebrations, K'ang-hsi drew attention to the fact that careful planning in state affairs and the imperial virtue of magnanimity were the basis for the victory over the Russians and the successes of his reign.[47]

Clemency continued to be applied to Russian prisoners in the months following the attack, as a basic element in K'ang-hsi's Russian policy. Before the attack on Albazin one I-fan (Ivan—not to be confused with the I-fan who deserted to the Manchus earlier) had been sent with three companions to persuade Li-k'e-ting-ko, a chieftain of the E-lo-ch'un tribe, to desert to the Russian side. I-fan was captured and sent to the capital, where K'ang-hsi ordered his and his comrades' execution. The execution was not carried out, however, and on August 20, 1685, the emperor extended his clemency policy to the four hapless prisoners by abrogating their death sentences and sending them home with a final communication to the Russian authorities, which requested the return of a certain fugitive and demanded that the Russians never again invade

China's frontiers. At the same time in a gesture toward his own vassal tribes the emperor decreed that Li-k'e-ting-ko and others be rewarded for their steadfast loyalty to the Manchu throne.[48]

Peking took steps between August and October 1685 to transform the Manchu position in the north into a permanent "presence" without committing the government to a perpetual military confrontation with the Russians in the area around Albazin or somewhere between Albazin and Nerchinsk. The continuous occupation of distant Albazin would have required larger expenditures than K'ang-hsi was willing to tolerate. He ordered the improvement of post and transport stations between Wu-la and Aigun and the establishment of a military colony at Mo-le-ken in the region of the Nun-chiang.[49] His failure to perceive the critical geographical and psychological importance of Albazin to the Russians in eastern Siberia, however, was a failure of judgment that would lead him, within the year, into another military campaign in the north. In this regard the stabilizing measures taken after the conclusion of the conflict of 1685 stood the Manchus in good stead as part of a new military buildup.

Albazin: 1686

There is an historical irony in the phoenix-like rise of Albazin from the ashes of defeat and destruction, for while K'ang-hsi was striving to force his lieutenants at the front to carry out his bold policies, the tsar's officials were disobeying Moscow's stated policy of withdrawal from the Amur. The government at Moscow, prompted by the receipt of three letters from the Far East, decided in the second half of 1685 to abandon its Amur lands in the face of superior Manchu power. The first letter was Vlasov's report of the fall of Albazin. In reply, he was instructed to extend his jurisdiction to include the Albazinians and all state property in their possession, and to send Tolbuzin to Eniseisk.[50] The other two documents were Latin versions of letters written to the tsar in K'ang-hsi's name. Both letters were dated May 6, 1685, and requested the evacuation of Albazin, but since they were not delivered to Moscow until November 15 by two Russian Cossacks who had earlier fallen into Manchu hands, their mission had been overtaken by events. Nevertheless, the confluence of the news of Albazin's fall and the letters from Peking holding out hope of reconciliation caused Moscow to lose no time. By November 26 it was decided to send an embassy to Peking; the very next day two messengers, Venyukov and Favorov, were ordered to proceed to Peking to make official announcement of the embassy. They left Moscow on December 21, 1685, and arrived at Peking only on October 31, 1686.[51] Meanwhile, the second phase of the struggle for Albazin in this pre-telegraphic age had begun.

On July 10, 1685, shortly after their arrival at Nerchinsk, the Albazinian refugees petitioned the voevoda, Vlasov, for permission to return to Albazin to harvest the crops they had sown in the spring and to reestablish the settlement. Vlasov, "in order not to lose the state lands in Dahuria," sent a scouting expedition downriver. The scouts reported that the crops at Albazin were intact and that nowhere had they encountered any Manchu troops. In spite of his orders from Peking, Sabsu had not destroyed the crops, and in Siberia's food-scarce economy Vlasov could ill afford to miss this opportunity to gather in the harvest. The voevoda permitted 669 men to return to Albazin, under Tolbuzin's leadership, arming them with five cannon, powder, lead, and other supplies, and assigning eight newly-conscripted soldiers to accompany them.[52]

Vlasov's instructions to the Albazinians indicated that he was also interested in permanently reestablishing the Albazin outpost and even in expanding Russian activities in the Amur region. He told them, through Tolbuzin, that after harvesting the grain they should proceed down the left bank of the Amur in search of a better location than Albazin for the construction of a new ostrog, which was to be located near both forest and water. In that way there would be sufficient building material close at hand, and in time of siege water could be drawn from wells inside the settlement. The new ostrog was to be built with all necessary protective walls, since the old Albazin had fallen because it was badly protected and located in a place difficult to defend. In actuality Vlasov's instructions were only partially fulfilled. Tolbuzin and his Albazinians arrived at their former home on August 27 and proceeded to harvest the grain, but because of the lateness of the season Tolbuzin decided to rebuild the old settlement rather than find a new location. An earthen city wall over three meters high and eight meters wide was built; there was no time to make it higher since the ground had already frozen.

With Albazin reestablished, Vlasov pursued a policy of extending Russian influence and control to its pre-1685 limits. He instructed Tolbuzin to bring former yasak-paying tribes back under Moscow's power and to put more land under cultivation than was the case before the fall of the settlement. Vlasov's essentially irredentist policy led directly to renewed clashes with the Manchus. On March 7, 1686, Tolbuzin sent a force of three hundred men down the Amur to the Khumar River to find indigenes and collect yasak. The expedition returned to Albazin on March 20, bringing a "Chinese named Godoveika" and reporting that they had camped on the Khumar from March 12 to March 17, at which time a Manchu force found them and gave battle. The Russians victoriously pursued the fleeing Manchus for a distance of thirty versts and in the final hours of the day attacked and killed thirty of the enemy. The Albazinians lost seven dead and thirty-one wounded.[53] Godoveika was sent on to Nerchinsk, where he was closely questioned by Vlasov himself. Russian interrogation methods were harshly thorough. After giving Vlasov testimony, Godoveika was requestioned under torture, and Vlasov reported that since his testimony under torture was the same as before, he must be telling the truth.

According to Godoveika, a Manchu unit had been sent from the Nun-chiang to Albazin to capture some prisoners for questioning. A captured Russian peasant reported that Albazin had been rebuilt and was protected by earthern walls and 1500 military personnel, with more reinforcements expected from Nerchinsk. In order to verify this information, a unit of 40 men was sent to observe secretly the reconstruction of the Russian settlement. It was they who had found the Russian Cossacks encamped on the Khumar River. Godoveika also told Vlasov that Aigun was on the right bank of the Amur but that no Manchu authority existed on the left bank. He claimed that there were 2000 soldiers, 500 peasants, and 30 cannon in Aigun, together with women and children. An attack on Albazin was planned before the harvest could be brought in so that the Russians would be unable to winter there.[54] Vlasov learned that 3000 soldiers had been sent from China to the banks of the Nun-chiang to await the attack against the rebuilt settlement. It is therefore quite clear that by the end of April both Vlasov and Tolbuzin were aware of Manchu preparations for a second round of hostilities.

Manchu authorities probably learned of the Russian return to Albazin about one month after the fact, but Sabsu, having disobeyed his instructions to destroy the harvest, dared not report the news directly to the throne. He therefore memorialized that one of his lieutenants was reconnoitering in the direction of Albazin when he met a local native, who told him that the Russians had returned. Having covered himself in this fashion, he suggested that in the spring, when the ice melted, he would suppress the Albazinians again.[55]

Incredulous that the Russians would return and unaware that Sabsu had disobeyed instructions, K'ang-hsi refused to accept hearsay information as a basis for beginning military operations. Consequently, Man-p'i, a Secretary (*lang-chung*) of the Li-fan yuan, was dispatched to join Sabsu in an investigation of the situation. Upon receipt of Man-p'i's report, which was remarkably accurate, the emperor decided to initiate military action immediately. On March 3, 1686, he issued orders for the dispatch of troops, powder, and cannon balls to the front. Camels would transport the necessary supplies "when the grass becomes green." Four days later Sabsu was instructed to begin the construction of ships and to bring Wu-la and Ninguta units to Aigun. Soldiers from Mukden were to join in the attack, which Sabsu was to lead at the head of two thousand men, supported by four hundred special Fukienese soldiers. On April 28 K'ang-hsi sent Bandarša, Mala, and Langtan to the front. They were chosen because they had participated in the campaign the previous year and were familiar with the topography of Albazin. On the eve of his departure Langtan was instructed personally by K'ang-hsi to try to persuade the Russians to surrender peacefully; failing this, he was to threaten the Russians with death. He was further instructed that after the capture of Albazin the Manchu forces were to march on Nerchinsk to put a final end to the source of the difficulties on the Amur. The army would then winter at Albazin, maintaining the settlement's fortifications and using the crops sown by the Russians.[56]

The Manchu troops arrived at Aigun on June 23, and on July 4 a council of war was held at Mo-le-ken, where it was decided to approach Albazin by both land and water. The Manchu forces reached Albazin on July 18 and immediately demanded its surrender. The Russians replied with a cannonade and a sortie outside the defense walls, but the Manchus drove them back and seized an island in the river opposite the settlement. Having gained a fortifiable position on Albazin's river front, the Manchus deployed their forces on all sides of the city to complete its investment.[57] Guns were trained on every side and fired constantly into the city. Tolbuzin wrote Vlasov complaining that personnel, weapons, and ammunition were all in short supply, but before the receipt of this letter, the voevoda had already written Tolbuzin on July 15 with orders to defend his position, having received word from Moscow about the approach of an embassy. On July 26 Vlasov was able to report, on the basis of information brought him by a Cossack who had managed to leave Albazin after the beginning of the siege, that the settlement contained 826 armed men, 8 brass cannon, 4 cannon of another type, 112 puds 36.5 funts of powder, 60 puds 6.5 funts of lead, 140 hand grenades, and other minor supplies.[58]

The Manchus besieged the Russian settlement through the summer and autumn. Some time before October 3 Vlasov sent a seventy-man unit to reconnoiter in the vicinity of Albazin and make contact with the defenders, but they found the town completely invested and subjected to constant bombardment. In a nearby forest they met ten Russians who had been on guard duty outside the city when the siege began and were unable to return. They were the remnant of a group of thirty, the rest of whom had been captured or killed by the Manchus. They claimed that at times the smoke from the bombardment was so thick that the settlement was completely obscured. Tolbuzin was killed before November 21 and replaced by Baiton, his lieutenant. There was enough food to last through Easter, but water was growing scarce and the defenders were living in mud huts, which were less vulnerable to cannon attack than were wooden ones. Several sorties attempted to break the Manchu encirclement from inside, but all failed. The Manchu forces maintained a tight siege and gave no quarter.[59]

As the early northern winter drew near, K'ang-hsi gave orders to prepare for the continuation of the siege through the winter. At the same time, in a decree to the council of princes dated September 14 he openly expressed incredulity at the turn of events in the Amur, sought explanations, and proposed a diplomatic *démarche* by correspondence with Russia. For want of a better explanation, the emperor tried to understand the new developments in the light of theories of Russian behavior that had been discarded after the Milescu embassy: Russia did not receive his letters because it was so far away; the Albazinians were outlaws and thus not under Russian control. Although he contradictorily proposed to send the tsar a letter through the Dutch requesting Russian withdrawal from both Albazin and Nerchinsk, it is doubtful that the letter was sent. A month and a half later Venyukov and Farovov arrived in Peking to announce the appointment of a new ambassador to discuss frontier problems. They also delivered a letter to K'ang-hsi from the tsar requesting clarification of the Amur situation and expressing hope for future peace with Peking. K'ang-hsi, true to his desire to limit the scope of military action whenever possible, acted with great speed in issuing a decree on November 3, 1686, ordering the lifting of the siege of Albazin; at the same time he notified the tsar, through Favorov and Venyukov, of his action.[60]

The courier carrying the emperor's orders arrived at Albazin in December, just as Langtan was preparing a major assault against the settlement. The officer withdrew his troops and took up positions from which he could observe the Russians' activities. Obeying the emperor's instructions, he also quartered some of his troops along the river where they could command the approach to Albazin should Nerchinsk try to reinforce it. When the siege was finally relaxed, less than sixty-six men remained alive inside Albazin.[61]

In the ensuing months a strictly limited and minimal intercourse developed between the Russians and their Manchu captors. On December 25, Baiton sent one of his men to request provisions, which Langtan sent to the settlement with I-fan, a Russian in Manchu service. I-fan reported that Baiton was dangerously ill and that only a few more than twenty men remained inside, ill and undernourished.[62] Sickness raged within the settlement and spread to the Manchu soldiers. On February 20, 1689, K'ang-hsi informed Sabsu that he had heard that many Manchu soldiers fell ill after the raising of the siege: "these soldiers are all the best Manchu soldiers; I have pity for them." The emperor sent two doctors, supplied with medicines, to look after the Manchus. As a demonstration of his magnanimity, he ordered the doctors to attend any Russians who were ill as well.[63]

K'ang-hsi was particularly anxious that the impending negotiations with the Russians begin under the most favorable circumstances. Therefore, he ordered the Khalkha Tushetu-khan, whose domains lay closest to the Siberian frontier with Mongolia, to report the approach of the Russian ambassador. When the Tushetu-khan informed Peking, somewhat prematurely, that the envoy was nearing China's frontiers, the emperor on August 19, 1687, ordered Sabsu to lead the army back to Aigun and Mo-le-ken "before the weather becomes cold, in order to repair the weapons and utensils as well as to give the horses some rest in the cold winter."[64] Still distrustful of the Russians, however, and mindful of past experience, the emperor ordered the stationing of advance guards in strategic positions near Albazin. The Russian survivors of the siege were notified that the Manchu troops were evacuating the area because of the arrival of the tsar's envoy to discuss peace. In this way K'ang-hsi hoped to avoid a third Albazin crisis. Vlasov learned of the Manchu departure in October 1687, and the new ambassador received a letter from Peking in January 1688 confirming the news.[65] The military phase of the Amur confrontation between Russia and the Manchu Empire was now ended. It remained to seek a final solution at the peace table.

Chapter V The Treaty of Nerchinsk: An End and a Beginning

The Treaty of Nerchinsk, negotiated and concluded in August and September 1689, divided the two earliest periods in the history of Sino-Russian relations. In the first period the Russians and Manchus had met and jockeyed for power in the Amur River Valley; K'ang-hsi's demonstration of Ch'ing strength in the region of confrontation brought the Russians to the conference table, ending the struggle for almost 165 years. Accommodation rather than conflict characterized the second period, which began with the treaty and lasted down to the middle of the nineteenth century. The creation and successful development of institutions for conducting relations between Peking and St. Petersburg through the avoidance rather than the resolution of conflicting interests and ideologies enabled the two empires, one East Asian and the other European, to coexist along extended geographical and social frontiers despite the absence of a significant body of shared political and cultural assumptions.

The negotiations at Nerchinsk were a recapitulation and summation of the process leading to the conference.[1] The growth of Jungar power in Mongolia that had impelled the Manchus to seek Russian neutrality in Inner Asia impinged directly and immediately on both delegations to the meetings. The problems that had plagued Manchu-Russian contact from the outset dominated the negotiations: delineation of the frontier, the return of fugitives, the conduct of trade, and creation of institutions for the development of future intercourse. Stablity in Sino-Russian relations could be achieved only by solving these problems. In the end the treaty was phrased in strictly equal terms, representing conscious compromises by both sides.

The most obvious cause of Manchu-Russian friction was the lack of a clearly defined frontier in the Amur region. Both Russians and Manchus were vague about the area's geography. The Russians claimed the Amur by right of colonization, a principle generally accepted in the West; the Manchus claimed it by virtue of their suzerainty over certain native tribes, a principle valid in the East Asian international system. These rival claims were complicated by Russian assumption of suzerainty over tribes already vassal to Peking. Since fur had economic value in both Moscow and Peking, the demarcation of the frontier in even so sparsely settled a region as eastern Siberia concerned both capitals. Fugitives exchanging one sovereign for another changed the direction of their tribute payments and became not only an economic but a political problem as well, since effective tribute collections were the only measure of suzerainty. The establishment of political stability along the Amur demanded internationally recognized principles for controlling the movements of the indigenous population. The Manchus had less access to sources of fur than had the Russians and were, therefore, the more keen to find a solution to the problem.

Stability in Manchu-Russian relations depended upon the creation of effective institutions for the conduct of further intercourse, based on the vital interests of each power. Russia wanted trading privileges in China. Whereas the Ch'ing dynasty was prepared to grant Russia sufficient trading rights to take the persistent edge off Russian commercial hunger, it demanded in return Russian neutrality in Central Asia. Both Moscow and Peking gave their respective plenipotentiaries instructions dealing with all these topics.

The Russian Delegation and Its Instructions

The Russian delegation to the conference with the Manchus was composed of men obviously assembled more for their abilities than their nobilities. Prince V. V. Golitsyn, one of Russia's leading diplomats, personally undertook to select the embassy. As ambassador he selected Fedor Alekseevich Golovin, who at the time of his appointment in 1686 was only thirty-five years old.[1] Fedor Alekseevich was the son of the boyarin A. P. Golovin, a close collaborator of the tsars Alexis Mikhailovich and Fedor Alekseevich, as well as a strong supporter of Peter I. Father and son once served simultaneously as voevodas at Astrakhan, and Golovin senior was named voevoda at Tobolsk in December 1685.[2] They cooperated in the early stages of the embassy's preparation, since Tobolsk was the base for equipping the mission and the jumping-off point for its eastward journey.

I. A. Vlasov, voevoda of Nerchinsk, was appointed second envoy. Since Moscow's knowledge of the distant Amur was hazy and faulty, Golovin would have to rely heavily on Vlasov for first-hand information and experience. But according to K'ang-hsi's Jesuit translators, the Nerchinsk voevoda provided a discordant note. He had strong personal opinions about the Amur problem, which did not always accord with Moscow's policies. Semen Kornitsky, a high-ranking secretary (*diak*), was appointed third envoy, and Andrei Belobotsky, a Pole educated in Latin at the University of Cracow, was named the embassy's Latin translator. The suite also included several young courtiers, secretaries, and clerks. The embassy's military component was not inconsiderable: Golovin left Moscow accompanied by 506 soldiers, and in Siberia he obtained the services of some 1400 Cossacks, which together with the meager Russian forces available along the Amur put some 2500 to 3000 men at his disposal during the actual negotiations.[3]

Golovin left the capital with his embassy on January 26, 1686. Passing through Udinsk, where he heard about the lifting of the Manchu seige of Albazin, he arrived at Selenginsk on October 25, 1687, where he hoped to hold the conference. Accordingly, on November 19 he dispatched a messenger, Stepan Korovin, to inform the Manchu frontier authorities of his arrival and to request the emperor to dispatch his own delegates. Although willing to allow K'ang-hsi to name the place for the conference, Golovin stipulated that the delegations should approach each other "in an equal number of envoys and serving-people." After some misadventures, Korovin reached Peking and returned only in June

1688, to report that K'ang-hsi had agreed to hold the conference at Selenginsk and would immediately send an embassy of five officials close to his person, accompanied by 500 men.[4] In the event, an outbreak of hostilities in Mongolia prevented this embassy from reaching its destination.

Between the time of his appointment in 1686 and the opening of the Manchu-Russian conference at Nerchinsk in August 1689, Golovin received three sets of instructions. The first, issued before his departure from Moscow and dealing with the problems of the frontier, fugitives, diplomacy, and trade, was a monument to Moscow's lack of information concerning the Amur situation and the Far East.[5] The ambassador was given maximal and minimal positions regarding the delimitation of the frontier. He was to begin by demanding that the Amur be made the border between the two empires. Yet if necessary, he was permitted to accept Albazin as the frontier, with the settlement remaining in Russian hands and the Russians retaining trading privileges throughout the Northern Manchurian river system. Since this position was based on Russian claims to historical control of the tributary natives along the Amur River, Golovin was to ask for reparations for losses inflicted on Russian settlements by Ch'ing attacks, though he could relinquish this demand as a sign of Moscow's friendship for Peking. Moscow was prepared to return fugitives demanded by the Manchus, with the exception of Gantimur and his descendants, who were now Christians. Peking was to agree, by treaty, to pay all diplomatic honors to Russian embassies and messengers, to provide them with provisions and transport, and to refrain from placing on them any constraints. The tsar and emperor would address each other by the titles prescribed by custom, with one exception: the emperor would not call himself "Lord of All the World," nor would he use expressions indicating his own superiority and the inferiority of the recipients of his letters. Peking was to agree to send "Chinese" envoys to Moscow, not messengers from states tributary to China. These envoys were to bring goods and gifts consisting of valuable stones, as well as "pure and good silver" in amounts ranging from 1000 to 3000 puds for exchange on the open market or, preferably, sale to the state treasury.

New instructions were issued to the ambassador on July 17, 1687, probably as a result of reports by the messengers Venyukov and Favorov, who had by then returned from Peking. The new document dealt almost exclusively with the problems of frontier delimitation. To make its demands more attractive to Peking, Moscow was now prepared to agree that each side should punish with the death penalty transgressions arising from the settlement of disputes. The tsar was also willing to agree to neutralization of the Albazin area: neither side would build settlements in the region or station military or civilizan groups there, and all walls and buildings still standing would be torn down. Should the Manchus reject the proposal, Golovin was instructed to suggest the postponement of negotiations, with the subjects of each side enjoying the right of free trade in the Albazin area during the interim. These new instructions had but one aim: the delay of a final decision on the Amur. What Golovin's first instructions proposed to accomplish by treaty, the second would accomplish by an agreement to delay negotiations: Russia would gain time to build up her forces in East Asia so that a final solution could be sought later on more favorable terms.[6]

Moscow modified its stand even further in a third set of instructions issued to Golovin on October 29, 1688. Now more concerned with Golovin's approach to the negotiations than with policies to be pursued, Moscow instructed its envoy to make immediate contact with the Manchus, probably in the neighborhood of Albazin; under no conditions was he to enter China itself. Moscow apparently hoped in this way to maintain the strictest equality and avoid any appearance of submission to China. If the Manchus refused to accept any of Moscow's proposals, the ambassador was to announce Russia's unilateral delimitation of the frontier along the Amur and Moscow's willingness to fight and maintain it. If the Manchus refused to meet with Golovin at all, he was to send a declaration of Russian policy to the nearest Ch'ing officials and dispatch Ivan Loginov, who had brought Moscow's third set of instructions to the ambassador, to Peking with full powers to conclude a treaty: Golovin was to give Loginov three treaties to offer the Manchus. On the assumption that the failure of the first Ch'ing embassy to arrive at the frontier signified K'ang-hsi's reluctance to enter into direct negotiations, Loginov went to Peking and, arriving May 13, learned almost immediately that a new embassy was about to start north.[7]

The Mongols: A Third Force in East Asia

The nomadic Mongol tribes of Inner Asia, together with a few Mongol settlements around lamaseries, were a third force in the development of seventeenth- and eighteenth-century Sino-Russian relations. During the interim between the first Ch'ing embassy's failure to reach the frontier and the dispatch of the second, they posed severe problems for the Russian embassy. At times, in fact, they appeared to hold the balance of power between the two empires.[8] Russian-Mongol relations strikingly paralleled Russian-Manchu relations, both in the Russian challenge to the Mongols, the latter's response and the forms of contact. Although in Moscow's efforts to reach Peking, she required the acquiescence of the Mongol khans, who controlled the most important routes of access to North China, tensions developed along the Siberian-Mongolian frontier as a result of Russian colonization in southern Siberia.

The construction of Russian ostrogs, particularly in the Selenginsk region, directly challenged the authority of the Mongol khans by offering to their subject tribes alternative sources of local power and objects of allegiance. The khans could not remain unconcerned about the growth of Russian population and authority in the Selenga Valley, where a large number of the members of Buryat, Tabungut, and Evenki tribes began paying yasak to the newcomers.[9] The Mongol khans responded to the challenge with both diplomatic and military activities. As early as 1672 the Tushetu-khan sent an embassy to Moscow to complain about the construction of the Selenginsk ostrog and to request its removal elsewhere. In 1675 the Tushetu-khan sent another embassy to Moscow to complain about Cossack attacks on his vassals for the collection of yasak and to request negotiations at Nerchinsk. The embassy was well received by the Russians since good relations with the Mongols were necessary to safeguard the Russian position in Selenginsk and to assure a safe route to China, but no solutions were found to the problems raised.[10]

In the late 1670's and through the 1680's Mongol opposition to Russian incursions moved more and more onto the military plane without a cessation of diplomacy. Embassies were continually exchanged with protestations of friendship, while Cossacks raided Mongols and Mongols counterattacked against Russian settlements. Since the Tushetu-khan and other Mongol princes were themselves Manchu tributaries, this worsening of Russian-Mongol relations was a direct function of developments in the Far East. In 1684, for instance, when an envoy from the Tushetu-khan went to Russia to complain about Cossack depredations and to demand the return of Buryats who had fled into Russian suzerainty, he emphasized his khan's close relationship with K'ang-hsi, who at that very time was encouraging the Tushetu-khan to take a strong position toward the Russians in view of the development of Ch'ing power along the Amur.[11]

Golovin had been instructed to seek the cooperation of the Mongol khans as supporters and mediators in his negotiations with the Manchus, for which purpose he carried gramotas written by the tsar to the Tushetu-khan and the Undurgegen, the Khutukhtu, or chief lama and incarnate Buddha of Urga.[12] In the spring of 1687 the ambassador was met at Rybny by Venyukov and Farovov, who were en route to Moscow from Peking; they had passed through Mongolia, where they had an audience with a leading Mongol feudal lord, the Ochiroi-sain-khan, who insisted repeatedly that the Russians return his vassals who had fled into Siberia. The two messengers informed Golovin that K'ang-hsi had sent several messages to the Tushetu-khan and others proposing their participation in the Manchu-Russian conflict. Golovin feared that the Mongols would agree because of their grievances against the Russians, but he received no support when he asked Moscow to return the Buryats to the Tushetu-khan's control.[13]

Golovin's main concern was the clarification of Mongol policy in the Manchu-Russian conflict and the establishment of peaceful relations with the nomad princes as a means of using or neutralizing them in the struggle. His task was complicated by the common interests of the Mongols and the Manchus. Consequently, he decided not to transmit the tsar's gramotas to the Tushetu-khan, because the documents contained suggestions that the Mongols ally themselves with the Russians against the Manchus; the Tushetu-khan would certainly have informed Peking of this sign of Russian hostility, which would have increased Golovin's difficulties in the impending negotiations. His efforts to make contact with the Mongol authorities were complicated by their technique of combining diplomacy with raiding. In the autumn of 1687, for instance, a Mongol embassy visited Golovin at Udinsk.[14] After agreeing to maintain contact with the Russians, the Mongols on the night of their departure stole a hundred horses and fifty head of cattle from the Russian embassy's stockade. Raids continued despite Russian complaints, even while the Russians were waiting at Selenginsk for the arrival of the first Manchu delegation. Golovin could not take forceful action in his own defense, however, lest he endanger the peace negotiations with the Manchus.

Russian-Mongol tensions reached a crisis during the visit of Golovin's special envoy, Ivan Kachanov, to the Undurgegen at Urga, for at the same time K'ang-hsi sent a special mission to the Undurgegen's court, after which the Mongols laid siege to Selenginsk. The siege, which prevented Golovin's departure, began on January 25, 1688, and lasted until March 25, when the ambassador received reinforcements.[15] During the siege Russians were prevented from leaving the ostrog altogether; their provisions diminished, their animals weakened. If the Mongols did not actively participate in the siege of Albazin, their action at Selenginsk aided K'ang-hsi by putting Golovin's embassy under considerable pressure and endangering its physical condition. Immediately after the siege had been lifted, Golovin left for Udinsk, where he spent the summer fortifying that ostrog against a possible future attack.

At prescisely this moment Mongolia's internal political situation underwent a radical change: control of the country passed from the pro-Manchu Khalkha princes, including the Tushetu-khan, to the anti-Manchu leader of the Ölöt tribe, Galdan. Galdan was khan of the Jungars, a tribe of Ölöts in western Mongolia whose military power had been created by Galdan's father, Khotokhotsin. Galdan became a threat to the Manchus when his power spread to the Moslem communities of Sinkiang, but K'ang-hsi was unable to organize the feuding Khalkha Mongol princes into an anti-Jungar alliance. By killing Galdan's brother, the Tushetu-khan provoked Galdan into a frontal attack. After a series of furious battles the Jungars completely routed the Khalkha forces under Tushetu-khan, who sought refuge in Inner Mongolia, while tens of thousands of Khalkhas fled south to Manchu protection. It was this conflict that prevented the first embassy sent by K'ang-hsi from reaching Selenginsk. Notified of this on August 1, 1688, Golovin proceeded to Nerchinsk, where from October 1688 to May 1689 he received many Khalkha refugees from the Jungars into Russian citizenship.[16]

The situation in Mongolia was extremely precarious by the autumn of 1689 when the Nerchinsk conference opened. Galdan, now master of the larger part of Outer Mongolia, prepared for war against the Manchus, who were giving refuge to his enemies. In an exchange of letters with Peking, Galdan demanded the surrender of the Tushetu-khan and the Undurgegen.[17] This developing Ölöt-Manchu conflict was a traditional barbarian threat to China along her northwestern frontier; it also gave the Russians an opportunity to acquire an ally against the Manchus. K'ang-hsi, at first anxious to use the Khalkhas against the Russians, could no longer tolerate the rise of Galdan as a possible threat on his frontier. Consequently, he decided to conclude a quick peace with Moscow in order to release his energies and resources for the struggle with Galdan's strong and militantly united people. The unexpected and rapid shift in the Inner Asian balance of power had thus forced K'ang-hsi to pursue a policy of neutralizing Russia in the Far East in order to avoid a Russo-Jungar alliance against the Manchus. That his fears were well founded was demonstrated in July 1689, when on the eve of the Sino-Russian peace conference Galdan sent an envoy to Irkutsk to contact the Russians; he continued his efforts to form an alliance with Moscow for many months.[18]

The Manchu Delegation and Its Instructions

Korovin's earlier arrival in Peking with the announcement that Golovin awaited the Manchu embassy at Selenginsk had prompted

K'ang-hsi to name his representatives and formulate his own policies for the negotiations. The importance that he attached to the conference was demonstrated by his appointment to the embassy of men from circles closest to his own person. The two chief delegates were imperial relatives. Songgotu was a chamberlain of the Imperial Bodyguard who had served in many bureaucratic positions, including grand secretary, but most important, he was the uncle of the empress and the great-uncle of the heir-apparent. He had a reputation for being haughty and lacking self-control. After the conclusion of the Treaty of Nerchinsk, Songgotu took part in the campaigns against Galdan; he died in 1703. The other chief delegate, T'ung Kuo-kang, was an uncle of the emperor on his mother's side. In 1690, after the conclusion of the treaty, T'ung Kuo-kang served as commander of the artillery corps in the anti-Galdan campaign and was killed at the battle of Ulan-butung.[19]

The three other Manchu delegates selected were also persons of importance. One was A-erh-ni, the president of the Li-fan yuan.[20] Maci, the governor of Shansi, was another delegate. Although he participated in the first abortive attempt to reach Selenginsk, he remained behind during the second successful embassy as a result of his promotion in 1688 to president of the Censorate. In 1690 Maci was made a member of the Council of Princes and High Officials, becoming later that year the acting president and then president of the Board of War. He was closely connected with the preparations for war against Galdan. The last member of the delegation was Mala, now a captain-general, who had dealt with Milescu as a junior vice-president of the Board of Rites and was one of the court's leading "barbarian experts," specializing, along with A-erh-ni, in Russian affairs. The carefully selected delegation thus included two members of the imperial family, two specialists on "barbarian affairs," and a leading member of the regular, heavily Chinese bureaucracy. Yet all were Manchus, and Maci, who was then senior vice-president of the Censorate, memorialized the emperor suggesting that it would be advisable to name some Chinese (Han) to the staff as well. The emperor ordered the Chinese officials to select several delegates, but those chosen declined to serve because of age or illness. The emperor angrily discharged them and appointed two officials of his own choice: Ch'en Shih-an, junior metropolitan censor of the Board of War, and Chang P'eng-ko, director of the Police Office. Chang was appointed governor of Chekiang in 1689 and did not join the second embassy. The Jesuits Gerbillon and Pereyra, who were French and Portuguese respectively, were appointed the embassy's Latin interpreters with the rank of colonel (*ts'an-ling*). The embassy was supported by eight hundred troops under the command of several officers, including Langtan and Bandarša. Wen Ta, a vice-president of the Li-fan yuan, was ordered to precede the expedition as it traveled through the nomadic areas, and A-erh-ni was sent ahead to Urga to meet the Living Buddha and explain the embassy's purpose so as to avoid disturbing the sensitive Khalkhas.[21]

The emperor issued instructions to the embassy before its departure from Peking on May 30, 1688.[22] The document provided the embassy with a precise statement of the court's demands and of the reasons behind them. Nerchinsk, it maintained, was the original camping-ground of the Mao-ming-an tribe, a Manchu tributary. Albazin was the home of Pei-le-erh, a Dahur chieftain and another tributary to the Ch'ing. Consequently, those areas were neither Russian nor uninhabited; they rightly belonged to the Manchus. The Amur River was even more important, however, than the immediate disposition of Nerchinsk and Albazin. It was the key to the entire river system in northern Manchuria. Moreover, tribes tributary to Peking inhabited its banks. "If we do not take [these places] completely, [our] frontier people will never have peace." As the upper and lower reaches of the Amur and all its tributaries were considered Manchu territory, "we cannot abandon them to Russia." The instructions concluded that the court was prepared to negotiate the demarcation of the frontier, allow trade, and return fugitives claimed by the Russians only on condition that Moscow return Gantimur and other unspecified fugitives claimed by Peking.

Manchu policy as outlined in these instructions was realistically maximalist, based on certain clearly implicit assumptions. First, the Amur and its tributaries were of strategic importance to the Manchus because they constituted one great river system providing access directly into the heart of Manchuria to the south and the Pacific to the east.[23] Second, the balance of power in the Amur rested on the allegiance of the native population, as implied by the statement that the territory was inhabited by tribes vassal to the Manchus. This claim was, on the one hand, an effort to establish legitimacy for Manchu claims along the river while, on the other hand, it indicated a realization that the Manchu position there inevitably rested on the support of the local tribes. The need for such support stimulated the court's concern to establish peace for the frontier people. Any feudal social relationship—and certainly the tribute system can be interpreted as such—had to be two-way. The responsibility of the suzerain toward the vassal had to be as clear, if not as explicit, as the responsiblity of the vassal toward the suzerain if the relationship was to be sufficiently meaningful to survive. Unless Peking could fulfill its obligations as a suzerain power along the river by providing peace for the local tribes, they could be expected to turn toward the Russians. K'ang-hsi's instructions to his delegates were formulated with this possibility in mind.

It was the outbreak of the Ölöt-Khalkha war that prevented the embassy from reaching Selenginsk. The emperor himself ordered the envoys' return to Peking out of consideration for the physical safety of so many of his relatives and close advisors. Not only was the embassy in danger of capture by Galdan, but the Jungars had so ravaged the countryside that travel was much more difficult than usual. The Ch'ing envoys sent a letter to Golovin at Selenginsk detailing Manchu complaints against the Russians and explaining their inability to continue the journey.[24]

Loginov's arrival at Peking prepared the way for K'ang-hsi's appointment of the second embassy, sent to Nerchinsk. The number of delegates was changed, and the supporting staff greatly increased. Songgotu and T'ung Kuo-kang remained as chief delegates, along with Mala. Sabsu was ordered to take 1,500 soldiers to Nerchinsk to provide a symbol of Ch'ing power. The war in Mongolia directly influenced Ch'ing policy toward the negotiations. On or about June 13, 1689, Songgotu memorialized the emperor suggesting that his original instructions be kept in force.[25] But K'ang-hsi, well aware of the significance of the struggle taking place on his northwestern frontier, was prepared to modify his stand of the previous year in order to reach faster and greater accommodation with the Russians. The very short edict that was his reply to Songgotu contained two important points of departure from the previous year's instructions. First, the emperor now gave the delegation legitimate authorization to conduct negotiations with the Russians. The original instructions had envisaged a comparatively simple situation in which the Ch'ing representatives would make a statement to the Russians; if the latter rejected the statement, the Manchus would withdraw from the negotiations and return to Peking. The new modification specifically stipulated that negotiations were to take place and that the Manchu representatives should hold an alternative policy in readiness. The second departure, the admission that Nerchinsk might remain in Russian hands, involved the conscious recognition that trade would develop. Whereas a year before trade had been made conditional upon Russian surrender of Nerchinsk to the Manchus, Nerchinsk was now recognized as something more than a simple lever in the negotiations. This was the significance of the court's rationalization of its possible acquiescence to Russian control of Nerchinsk: Nerchinsk in Russian hands would facilitate trading operations.

The embassy left Peking on June 13 and arrived at Nerchinsk toward the end of July 1689. Golovin was delayed until August 1—perhaps for diplomatic reasons—and negotiations did not begin until August 22, when the Russian and Manchu envoys met for the first time.

The Procedures of Diplomacy

The Russians demanded meticulous observation of the principle of equality between the two parties at the Nerchinsk peace conference. As early as August 2 a young Russian representative visited the Manchu camp to insist that during the meetings each side be represented by the same number of officials and each party be accompanied by no more than five hundred soldiers. Although the Manchus objected to certain Russian demands, the first meeting of delegates on August 22 was conducted with scrupulous attention to equality. Each delegation was accompanied by an equal number of men, stationed an equal distance from the place of meeting. The soldiers carried only swords, and each side searched the other for hidden weapons. The tents of the two parties were placed side by side and open to each other so that each delegation could sit in its own tent.[26] This arrangement obviated the question of who was to visit whom first. These detailed arrangements for the preservation of equality represented a significant departure from the difficulties of precedence attendant upon Milescu's meeting with Mala on the Nun-chiang thirteen years before. Two reasons may be advanced for this Manchu willingness to compromise on ceremony. First, the confidence inspired by a successful military campaign and the demonstration of Manchu superiority on the Amur allowed the Ch'ing court to abandon its ceremonial pretence to superiority without injury to its position vis-à-vis the Russians. Second, the conclusion of peace had become an issue of sufficient urgency that the Manchu envoys could not allow ceremonial difficulties to interfere with their diplomatic tasks.

The first meeting of the diplomats was resplendent in its simplicity, but it began badly.[27] The Manchus crossed the river to the meeting place with more soldiers than the five hundred agreed upon and stationed them too close to the tents. The Russians complained. The Jesuits Gerbillon and Pereyra went over to the Russian side to explain that the Manchus were inexperienced in the ways of diplomacy: either the Russians would have to make concessions to Manchu inexperience, or the negotiations would be broken off before they had even begun. The Russians agreed, provided the Manchus brought no more men up, and the Jesuits returned to the Manchu camp, where they had some difficulty persuading Peking's envoys to relent. "After all," Gerbillon wrote in his diary, "we had some difficulty to prevail on our Ambassadors to cross the River, on account of the Jealousies raised in them, particularly by the General of the Emperor's Troops in Eastern Tartary [Sabsu], who had often been deceived by the Russians when he had any affair to transact with them."

With this initial contretemps overcome, the envoys met in their first session. The Russians approached the meeting tents with great pomp and circumstance. They paraded their soldiers with drums, fifes, and bagpipes, and the ambassador and his staff rode up on horseback dressed in their finery, with much cloth of gold and black sable fur in evidence. The Russian tent was floored with Turkish carpets, and a silk-and-gold Persian carpet covered the ambassador's table, upon which stood his papers, an inkstand, and a clock. The Manchus had approached the tents with equal pomp, "in all their Robes of State, which were Vests of Gold and Silk Brocade, embroider'd with Dragons of the Empire," but upon hearing of the Russians' regalia, the Manchus decided to use understatement to symbolize their magnificence. They removed all marks of dignity except one great silk umbrella carried before each official. Their tent contained a plain bench covered with a cushion of simple cloth, whereas the Russians sat in "Chairs of State" or stood in array behind the ambassadors. In order to carry equality to its logical extreme, the envoys of each side dismounted, entered their tents, sat down, and called out their first greetings simultaneously. Belobotsky, the Russians' Latin translator, opened the proceedings with a formal statement of greeting to the Manchus. He called on them to reply with their own statement, but Songgotu, obviously trying to use the occasion to squeeze out any possible Russian recognition of Manchu superiority, declined to speak before the Russians had presented their proposals. An argument ensued, each side trying to persuade the other to accept the "honor" of speaking first, until the Russians offered to show the Manchus their accreditation documents and asked to see the Manchus'. The latter declined to look at the Russian papers or to show their own (they probably had none), in order to preserve the image of equality.

The conference met in plenum session only three times during the negotiations. After the first ceremonial meeting of August 22, when basic propositions were exchanged, a meeting the next day failed to produce results. This second session was taken up entirely with proposals and counterproposals concerning frontier demarcation. The third and last plenum was held on September 7 for the purpose of signing the treaty itself. The real work of the negotiations was conducted through messengers of secondary rank who went from one camp to the other to mediate the differences between the two sides. Orthodox Russian suspicion of Roman Catholic Jesuits forced Golovin at one point to seek to communicate with the Manchus directly through the Mongolian language, but the Mongolian translators on each side were so poor that the negotiations reverted to Latin almost immediately. Thus, the task of actually negotiating the Treaty of Nerchinsk fell chiefly on the shoulders of the Pole Belobotsky, the Frenchman Gerbillon, and the Portuguese Pereyra. Each side used coercion to hurry the negotiations forward. At various moments one or the other would threaten to withdraw entirely from the conference, and between August 24 and September 6 the Manchus virtually besieged the Russian camp at Nerchinsk, while other Manchu troops threatened the beleaguered Russians at Albazin.[28]

The Treaty as Compromise

The final treaty represented a distinct compromise between the extreme positions assumed by both Moscow and Peking in the years before 1689 and in the first sets of instructions issued to their respective embassies. The successive modifications of each side's instructions over a period of time provided the basis for compromise, which was extended by a further agreement at the very first plenum session to "let bygones be bygones" and to attend to matters at hand. The Jesuit Pereyra claimed responsibility for this first compromise, which the treaty itself both explicitly and implicitly took as its point of departure.[29] The body of the treaty dealt in great detail with the delineation of the frontier and then with the declaration of regulations and institutions that would promote continual and peaceful contact between the two empires.

The final delineation of the frontier was a compromise more favorable to the Manchus than to the Russians. As K'ang-hsi authorized in his second set of instructions to Songgotu, the Russians kept Nerchinsk, and the frontier was drawn between it and Albazin. Albazin was explicity to be demolished and the survivors of the siege removed to Russian territory, along with their property and military equipment. The treaty did not prevent the Manchus from garrisoning the area and explictly forbade hunters from crossing the frontier, which eliminated all possibility of keeping open the question of ultimate sovereignty over Albazin. Similar compromises were reached on most other frontier areas, though in some cases geographical knowledge or instructions were too meager to allow of a decision.[30]

The agreement to ignore the past in negotiating the future was particularly important to reaching a compromise on the question of fugitives. Although the instructions guiding both delegations took diametrically opposed positions on the return of Gantimur and his relatives, that question played only a minor role in the negotiations. This was partly due to the agreement about the past, but even more was it the result of the protracted difficulties encountered in dealing with the delineation of the frontier. An agreement was finally reached that all fugitives could remain where they were when the treaty was signed, and "no claims for their rendition will be made on either side."[31] While this effectively disposed of Gantimur, an agreement was made that in the future all fugitives would be returned to their original jurisdiction. When the subjects of either empire committed crimes while legitimately traveling in the other empire, they were to be returned to their own officials, who were instructed by treaty to "inflict on them the death penalty as a punishment of their crimes." Outstanding cases would be settled by diplomatic negotiations "in an amicable manner."

The inclusion of a clause dealing with the handling of fugitives and criminals in the future implied that Sino-Russian contact would increase. The treaty also made careful provision for the conduct of trade, stipulating that either empire's subjects were permitted to cross the frontier and carry on commerce provided they held proper passports. This point was a Manchu concession to the Russians. Although K'ang-hsi had foreseen the development of trade as a rationalization for allowing the Russians to remain at Nerchinsk, the Manchu negotiators were not eager to include such a stipulation in the text of the treaty itself.[32] They flatly rejected Russian proposals concerning the forms for future correspondence and the treatment of ambassadors and messengers, arguing that they had no instructions on the matter and that it was not their business to regulate the style of the emperor's correspondence. Instead, they gave the Russians verbal assurances that their ambassadors would always be received at Peking "with Distinction." The treaty was therefore more permissive than descriptive concerning the development of forms for the conduct of future relations between the two powers. It left the actual details to be worked out on a pragmatic basis. The permissive quality of the treaty resulted largely from the circumstance that while Golovin's instructions contained detailed plans for institutions for future contact, Songgotu's instructions chiefly concerned the demarcation of the frontier, mentioning trade only as a means of obtaining a peace settlement based on a negotiated frontier rather than as an objective in itself.

The Treaty as an Instrument of Diplomacy

Using a combination of "favor and over-awing," or concession backed by successful military action, the Manchus negotiated a treaty solving the problems that had originally led to their conflict with the Russians. The frontier was delimited, and the problem of fugitives was settled, and the Russians were forced to withdraw from their advance positions. Manchu control of the Albazin region meant strategically that they controlled Russian access to the Amur River system. The Manchus recognized that their occupation of Nerchinsk would have been superfluous to their immediate local objective: prevention of Russian incursions into northern Manchuria. They accepted and utilized the treaty for their own diplomatic purposes. The Russians, too, accepted it, despite initial objections by the Ambassadorial Department in Moscow.[33] Peter the Great, now on the throne, was seriously occupied with other matters.

The treaty immediately began to operate as a weapon of Ch'ing policy in Central Asia. When Galdan sent a specific proposal for a Russian-Jungar alliance to Golovin in February 1690, it was already too late to take joint military action against the Manchus. Eight or nine months earlier Golovin had himself considered trying to establish contact with Galdan, but now Peking and Moscow were bound by the treaty. K'ang-hsi learned of Galdan's efforts to conclude a treaty with the Russians and immediately ordered this information made known to Grigory Lonshakov, who was in Peking as a Russian messenger. The court ordered Lonshakov to send two men to Nerchinsk immediately with an aide-memoire concerning the new treaty, pointing out that since the Khalkhas were subjects of the Manchus, any military action against them by Galdan with Russian support would violate the treaty.[34] K'ang-hsi's invocation of the treaty in 1690 illustrates his precise political intentions in negotiating the treaty in the first place. Relations between Moscow, the Mongols, and the Jungars worsened. The Russians no longer considered it feasible to receive Mongol envoys in Moscow, since they were Manchu vassals. By 1696 K'ang-hsi had defeated the Jungars, and with Galdan's death in 1697, probably by suicide, Khalkha reverted to its Mongol overlords under Manchu suzerainty. The Mongols were no longer a third force in Inner Asia.

The treaty's provisions for the exchange of persons crossing the frontier illegally and for the conduct of trade by persons holding official passports required the development of institutions on both sides of the frontier to conduct correspondence and to control and inspect both passports and the merchants carrying them. In other words, the treaty created situations requiring working institutions, but it left to each side to establish them in accord with its own interests. These institutions, multiplying with time, provided the foundation for Sino-Russian relations between 1689 and the breakdown of the treaty system in the middle of the nineteenth century.

The Ch'ing Historical View of Nerchinsk

The few available documents concerning the Ch'ing court's reaction to the conclusion of their first treaty with a European power offer a significant, albeit microcosmic, study of the role played by Chinese court terminology in assessing the political realities of the international arena in which Peking found itself, as well as in developing an historical view of the event. If nothing else, these documents demonstrate the extreme care that must be taken in any attempt to judge the Chinese apprehension of reality through the terminology used to describe discrete events.

Songgotu reported the Nerchinsk negotiations to the emperor in a memorial that reflected, to an admittedly limited extent, the actual event: *"Nei-ta-ch'en* [Grand Secretary] Songgotu and others arrived at Ni-p'u-ch'u [Nerchinsk] and held a conference with the envoy arrived from Russia, Fei-yao-to-lo-e-li-k'e-hsieh [Fedor Alekseevich]. They [the Russians] first claimed that Ni-p'u-ch'u and Ya-k'e-sa [Albazin] were places of their expanded territory. Therefore, they insisted on this and hotly debated. Songgotu and others stated that the Argun and Nun-chiang and Ni-p'u-chu and other [places] were territories originally belonging to our Mao-ming-an tribes. Ya-k'e-sa was the place where our A-erh-pa-hsi [Albazi] and others lived of old. Later, it was grabbed [by the Russians]. We told them the whole story in detail and enlightened them and condemned their invasions. Moreover, we announced to them the imperial benevolence of preserving their men's lives. Therefore, Fei-yao-to-lo and other Russians all agreed sincerely and followed [us]. They showed us their maps and we clarified the frontier problem. Accordingly, we made a common oath to live forever in harmony."[35]

Although this memorial reflects a tendency to claim more credit for the imperial virtue than was perhaps its due, it intimates the actual equality that characterized the diplomatic process at Nerchinsk. The documents subsequent to it, however, illustrate how this memorial and the relevant situation were taken by the court bureaucracy and interpreted in such a way as to make reality consonant with accepted Ch'ing terminology and the official view of the world. The emperor ordered the court to discuss Songgotu's memorial. The council of princes and others memorialized in a form that shows how the requirements of court usage changed the very substance of the event, as originally apprehended by the officials immediately involved, and translated it into the form required for entry into the official records of the dynasty: "The Russians secretly occupied Ya-k'e-sa and other places and disturbed our frontier people for more than thirty years. The emperor, sympathizing with [the Russians'] ignorance, could not bear to launch military expeditions against them. He sent officers and men to be stationed in Hei-lung-chiang [Aigun] in the hope that [the Russians] might realize the crimes [they had] committed. Because they obstinately adhered to error, he then ordered that they [the Manchu troops] attack and take Ya-k'e-sa city. All the prisoners captured were released. Shortly, the Russians came again to Ya-k'e-sa and built up the walls. Again the emperor ordered the soldiers to besiege the city. The situation [of the Russians] was extremely dangerous. At that moment their king sent an envoy to make peace. The emperor thereupon permitted the raising of the siege. Moreover, he ordered some great officials to enlighten them with reason. The Russians began to feel grateful for all the great favor and mercy he granted them and decided to turn toward civilization. They followed the previous instructions of our ministers, pointing out the [correct] borderline. This caused several thousand *li* in the northeast not previously included in China's territory to be included on our map. This all is arrived at as a result of the careful planning of the emperor as well as the spread of the Imperial Virtue and Awe to far-away places."[36]

This memorial, which was approved by the emperor, was obviously a gross exaggeration not only of the real situation at Nerchinsk but of the intent of Songgotu's original memorial as well. Songgotu's memorial did not contain such expressions as "turning toward civilization," so typical of documents of the tribute system, nor did it emphasize the view that the Manchu envoys had dictated the conditions of peace to the Russians. The council of princes' remarkable statement that considerable territory not previously included in the Manchu Empire now came under Peking's control must also be noted: were the document in question meant for anything more than court use, such a statement would have been inadmissable, since it completely cut the ground out from under the original Ch'ing contentions regarding Russian occupation of Manchu territory. The vocabulary of the tribute system was a conceit used inside the court, often consciously and conspicuously at variance with reality, even as the Manchus themselves understood it.

The official record of the Amur conflict, the *P'ing-ting Lo-ch'a Fang-lüeh,* concludes with an extremely interesting essay explaining the Ch'ing historical assessment of the treaty and the events leading up to it. Although it is impossible to date the composition of this work, it was probably completed before 1722, the year of K'ang-hsi's death, or at the latest before the conclusion of the Russian-Manchu Treaty of Kyakhta in 1727.[37] The last pages of the record indicate the historical interpretation put upon the event by the Manchu court approximately one generation after the conclusion of the treaty itself.

Once court verbiage is cleared away, the essay is extraordinarily candid in its analysis of the bases for Manchu policy toward the Russians. The disturbances caused by the Russians among the Soluns and Dahurs were an important problem to the Manchus, and the Shun-chih emperor failed in his efforts to settle the problem. K'ang-hsi, however, clearly understood that "the places occupied by the Russians were extremely near the native place of the present dynasty," and that the Manchu had no choice but to "pacify" the Russians. Since it was preferable not to engage in a military action, K'ang-hsi, in addition to accepting Russian envoys and conferring generous gifts on them, "used trade [in order] to be on good terms" with them. This use of commerce as a diplomatic tool—a basic aspect of the entire tribute-system international order—is here stated explicitly. The attempt failed, however, and the emperor finally realized that "because their [the Russians'] nature was similar to that of animals, they could not be brought to terms unless both favor and awe were used in combination."[38] In other words, K'ang-hsi clearly understood that a military victory alone would not suffice to solve the Russian problem. It was his willingness to make necessary concessions, or "favor," that enabled the treaty to be concluded. The projection of this policy through time provided the basis for the regularization of the Sino-Russian relationship.

Chapter VI The Sino-Russian Treaty System

The Treaty of Nerchinsk was more a statement of problems to come than a solution to past problems. The treaty created a need to develop an institutional framework for the conduct of Manchu-Russian relations, particularly in the field of commerce. The treaty itself was only vague and permissive, leaving to each of the two participating governments the determination of how to relate the newly sanctioned Sino-Russian commerce to its own interests and society. In the course of time the commerce carried on by Russian caravans traveling the trade routes between Moscow, Siberia, and Peking became the most important operative element in the Sino-Russian relationship. Irregular at first, the treaty-sanctioned caravan trade developed rapidly after 1689, only to fail commercially within two decades. Nevertheless, the relationship had been established on a permanent basis, and most of the institutions of the Nerchinsk treaty system survived to become part of the revised system introduced by the Treaty of Kyakhta in 1728.

Sino-Russian Trade Before Nerchinsk

Although the Treaty of Nerchinsk regularized Sino-Russian trade by placing it on an official footing, direct or indirect commerce between Russians and Chinese had taken place at least as early as 1639, if not before. Of the three trade routes between Siberia and China the earliest went from Tobolsk to Lake Yamysh and on through Jungaria into China. The second ran from Selenginsk through Outer Mongolia to Urga and thence to Peking. The third route started at Nerchinsk and reached into Manchuria through the Amur's western tributaries. Each route flourished because of specific geographical or political features. Before Nerchinsk, the western route was the main artery for both direct and indirect Sino-Russian trade. Tobolsk had been established in 1587 at the confluence of the Tobol and Irtysh rivers, with the Irtysh providing a convenient access to China from western Siberia. The focus of commercial activity moved east to Nerchinsk after 1689, and from 1698 the state monopoly on the China trade restricted the movement of caravans along all others routes until 1727. There are early indications of a thriving trade along the central route, beginning in the region of Lake Baikal, but it did not become really important until the establishment of the Sino-Russian trading post at Kyakhta-Maimaichen after the signing of the Treaty of Kyakhta in 1727.[1] Afterward the central route eclipsed all others in importance, holding its position well into the middle of the nineteenth century.

As Russians replaced native Tartars along the western Siberian stretches of the complex system of existing trade routes, indirect commerce between Russia and China developed, with the Bukharans playing the role of middlemen.[2] Rapid Russian expansion, the difficulties involved in transportation over the long new lines of communication, and the agricultural underdevelopment of pre-Russian Siberia resulted in great logistic problems for the early Russian colonizers.[3] Conscious of its inability to guarantee supplies to Russian settlers in Siberia, Moscow encouraged them to trade with the Bukharans, who could supply basic commodities in return for Siberian furs. The Bukharans and the Nogais, a seminomadic people in southwestern Siberia, were granted special commerical privileges, such as free trade in, and passage to, cities like Tobolsk and Tyumen.[4] Although these privileges were reduced as the Russian position in western Siberia improved with the development of local agriculture,[5] the economic growth of the new settlements was not sufficient to provide for all the needs of the growing population. During Russia's "Time of Troubles," for instance, the Russo-Siberian supply lines atrophied, and in 1610-

1611 Siberia received almost nothing from Russia. Afterward Moscow again encouraged trade with Central Asia by lowering customs levies.[6]

Bukharan caravans arrived annually at Tobolsk between 1639 and 1674, while Moscow was still making tentative efforts to establish direct commercial ties with Peking. The route through Bukhara was only the earliest of a small complex of western routes along which indirect Sino-Russian trade took place. A second route from Tobolsk to China passed through Jungaria to Suchow and Peking. The journey from Tobolsk to Suchow alone took about four and a half months.[7] Between 1639 and 1695 Russian and non-Russian merchants imported cotton and silk cloth, ready-made clothes, medicinal goods, tea, and various kinds of rhubarb along this route.[8] Whereas Bukharans dominated the trade route through Bukhara, Kazan, and Tobolsk, Tartars dominated the Jungarian route, though Bukharans and even Russians sometimes traveled it. Between 1639 and 1658 almost all the goods carried directly from China to Tobolsk went by the Jungarian route.[9]

The most important direct route between Tobolsk and China went to Lake Yamysh and then over the Tarbagatai Mountain range to Urga. Baykov was the first to travel this route, on his way to Peking, and Perfilev and Ablin also took it there. By the middle of the seventeenth century it had eclipsed the routes through Bukhara and Suchow.

Two factors accounted for the rise of this route. First, the journey from the Irtysh River to Urga took only sixty days, making it much shorter than the other routes.[10] The second factor was the development of a market at Lake Yamysh in conjunction with the salt industry there.[11] As a rule, this market opened on August 15, the Day of the Assumption of Our Lady the Virgin, and continued for two or three weeks. Merchants from Tobolsk, Yaroslavl, and Veliki Ustyug, as well as Greeks and representatives of such great gosts as O. Filatev, journeyed down river with the salt expeditions, bringing a wide variety of Russian and foreign goods which they exchanged for Chinese and Central Asian products brought to the market by Kalmuk and other Central Asian merchants.[12] Caravans traveling through the Mongol and Jungarian steppes brought Chinese silks, linen, rhubarb, tea, porcelain, and even cattle to market. Trade ended by the end of August or the beginning of September (only occasionally did the market stay open later), and about the middle of October the Russian and Tartar merchants returned to Tobolsk with the salt expedition. The market on Lake Yamysh was also the point of departure for a direct trade with China carried on by Russian, Siberian, and Central Asian subjects of the tsar. Profits were such that many merchants were prepared to ignore Moscow's stringent strictures against unlicensed participation in direct trade with China. In 1668 and again in 1670 groups of Russians and non-Russian subjects of the tsar arrived at Tobolsk from China via Lake Yamysh. There were other notable instances of Russian subjects who, in an effort to avoid Moscow's proscriptions on the China trade, placed themselves physically beyond the reach of Russian law and traded directly between Yamysh and China without entering Siberia at all.[13]

The traders using the Yamysh route were geographically more diversified than those using any other route between Tobolsk and China. They included Tartars from Kazan and Tobolsk, burghers and military personnel from Tobolsk, and merchants from Bukhara and Central Asia as well as from such widely scattered Russian and Siberian cities as Vashsk, Vyatsk, Lalsk, Moscow, Solvychegodsk, Veliki Ustyug, Yarensk, Yaroslavl, Eniseisk, Irbit, and Nitsynsk. They even included some state and privately-owned serfs from Suzdal, Tarsk, and Ufimsk. Central Asian merchants dominated the Yamysh route until the end of the seventeenth century, but by 1703 Russians dominated the China trade there.[14] Russian merchants also competed with Siberians for primacy in the importation of Chinese goods. From 1668 to 1676 Siberians imported more Chinese goods into Tobolsk through Yamysh than did the Russians, who dominated the market after 1683. The route itself declined after 1689, however, and by the turn of the century it was supplying only the local needs of the Tobolsk region. The Jungarian wars having cut Tobolsk off from China proper, the great Siberian and European Russian merchants were trading through Nerchinsk.

Central Asian political conditions strongly influenced Russian imports of Chinese goods. Whereas goods originating in China never fell below 51 percent of the total value of "oriental goods" imported through Yamysh and Tobolsk, at least in years for which records are available, Chinese goods fell in absolute ruble value from a recorded high of 1,913 rubles in 1683 to a recorded low of 628 rubles in 1703.[15] The steady supply of Chinese goods at the Yamysh market depended particularly on circumstances in Jungaria. After the Manchus had begun to subjugate Galdan, Jungar merchants were unable to go to Yamysh as frequently as before, much less guarantee a steady supply of Chinese goods. Between 1688 and 1691, for instance, Russian goods brought to Yamysh for export to Central Asia and beyond simply remained unsold.[16] Although the reestablishment of peace in Jungaria was reflected in a sudden growth of trade at the beginning of the eighteenth century, by then trade with China had shifted to the east, so that Chinese goods played almost no role at all on the Yamysh market.[17]

The central trade route leading from Eniseisk, Irkutsk, and Selenginsk through the Khalkha Steppe into China was the only other important route before 1689. It may have been used as early as 1648-1649, when Chinese goods, chiefly cloth, appeared on the Eniseisk market, but the first Russian caravan did not use it until 1674 when one Porshennikov led more than forty merchants from Selenginsk to Peking, including the great gost G. Nikitin, who at the time was an agent of the Filatev family. Milescu originally intended to take this route to China, and at the time of his visit to Selenginsk the settlement had already become an established emporium in the China trade. The Bukharans also traded along this route as far as Tomsk and Krasnoyarsk. In November 1684, for instance, a Bukharan caravan arrived at Irkutsk with ninety camels; it traveled in the guise of a convoy for a Jungarian diplomatic mission and brought nankeens, tea, tobacco, and other goods for sale. In the trading season 1686-1687 so many merchants arrived at Irkutsk to trade with Bukharan caravans that warehouse space was in short supply.[18]

In eastern Siberia some local trade developed between Russian and Chinese merchants along the Amur, although there is no evidence of direct trade between eastern Siberia and Peking through Manchuria before 1689. In 1684, for instance, Prince Scherbatov, the voevoda of Nerchinsk, reported that Russian traders were exchanging Siberian furs for Chinese cloth in the Dahur lands along the Amur. This local trade in Chinese goods, which continued even during the period of Russo-Manchu armed conflict, attracted the great Russian gosts despite the fact that eastern Siberia was not a rich fur-producing region.[19] Agents of S. Luzin, O. Filatev, I. Ushakov, and G. Nikitin participated in trade at Nerchinsk and Albazin before 1689. However, the peace negotiations at Nerchinsk between the Manchu and Russian representatives, raising prospects for legal trade, were reflected in the eastern Siberian commercial scene. In 1689, on the eve of the signing of the treaty, Nerchinsk ceased exporting fur pelts to Siberia and Russia and began importing them in preparation for the approaching trade.

Direct long-distance Sino-Russian trade at Nerchinsk started with the arrival of the Manchu embassy. As early as September 1689 agents of S. Luzin and O. Filatev went to Russia with large quantities of Chinese goods, probably purchased directly from the embassy. Since 1,416 rubles were collected in customs tithe at Nerchinsk in 1689, at least 14,160 rubles' worth of goods were imported that year from China through the new frontier trading post.[20] Moscow was already issuing passports for direct trade with Peking in November 1689, but the uncertainty regarding trade conditions was reflected in the fact that some of the passports indicated routes through Albazin while others mentioned Selenginsk. The contents of the Nerchinsk treaty were not yet known in Moscow, of course, and each merchant was left the final choice of route. In December 1689 the first Russian caravan sanctioned by the treaty set out for China. Including agents of O. Filatev, S. Luzin, and G. Nikitin, it went from Nerchinsk to an ostrog on the Argun River and on to the Nun-chiang in Manchuria, following Milescu's route, which remained the most important Sino-Russian trade route up to 1727.

Petrine Commercial Policy

The reign of Peter the Great (1682-1725), during which the Sino-Russian treaty system began to assume stability and final form, was characterized by the tsar's penchant for warfare on both land and water. Klyuchevsky, the great Russian historian, computed that during the forty-three years of Peter's reign, only the last full year, 1724, was wholly free from war, and that during the preceding thirty-four years Russia had been at peace for no more than thirteen months. Peter's vast war machine required great expenditures, as he clearly recognized when he wrote to the Senate in 1711, "Collect money as possible, because money is the artery of war."[21] Throughout his reign Peter was faced with a rising tide of expenditures, requiring increased government revenues and new sources of funds. Peter's trade policies and even his desperate effort to open gold mines in Jungaria, which almost led to war with China, must be seen against the background of these financial problems.

In both internal and foreign commerce Peter sought to develop policies and institutions that would maximize government income from the collection of customs duties, the sale of monopolies, or the establishment of direct state monopolistic enterprises. In a comprehensive economic edict in 1711, for instance, he amended the Code of 1649 to permit "people of all social groups" to "engage freely in commerce," provided they paid the customary taxes.[22] He had an obviously fiscal motive: by opening commerce to all classes, a large proportion of commercial activity that had theretofore escaped taxation was brought back under the fiscal regulations of the state.

State monopolies were another important source of income for Peter. The salt monopoly was established in 1705, under which the state resold salt at an almost 100 percent profit.[23] An English monopoly on tobacco that had been established in 1698 was reclaimed by the state in 1705. Articles such as tar, chalk, fats, fish oil, potash, caviar, and bristles either continued as or became new state monopolies. Oak coffins were collected by the state from the makers and sold in the monasteries at four times their original price. Private merchants struggled against the restrictive aspects of the state monopoly system, with the result that after 1714, when they reached their peak development, a general decline of monopolies set in. The state monopoly on the China trade, however, persisted until 1728.

Peter was particularly concerned with the development of foreign trade, including trade with China, and frequently acted to increase the state's income in this sector. While in Europe on the "Great Embassy," he constantly corresponded on this subject with the authorities in St. Petersburg and with his agents in other areas. On December 31, 1697, he sent instructions concerning the conditions for trade-farming, or selling trading privileges for specified payments, to foreigners. From Amsterdam he ordered the government to bring order to the Siberian trade because violence and coercion in Siberia impeded the commercial development of that vast land. He issued a decree in December 1697 from western Europe that voevodas who hindered caravans en route to China were to be severely fined. On February 17, 1698, Peter ordered, this time from England, that merchants not be forced to journey all the way to Moscow to obtain papers for travel to Peking, lest they "lose time and suffer losses."[24]

Not only did Russia's general historical commercial traditions and Peter the Great's specific economic policies influence the growth of Russia's China trade, but so did the problems, conditions, and policies obtaining in Siberia. Siberia was, on the one hand, a source of wealth to meet the expenditures of the state. On the other, it was the royal preserve of the tsar, to be exploited by his agents. These were the purposive and operative sides of the same coin. But as Siberia's population grew toward the end of the century, the tsar found it impossible to control all necessary economic activities through his agents. A paradoxical situation developed: while the tsar jealously tried to maintain the state's monopoly on such things as fur, salt, rhubarb, and tobacco, he was increasingly obstructed by illegal competition from private merchants who were often acting as agents for his own representatives in Siberia. Three factors contributed to the tsar's inability to take decisive measures against private merchants in Siberia: it was nearly impossible to enforce royal decrees at such a great distance from the capital; the bureaucracy was often more interested in its own private ventures than in the tsar's business; and private commerce had become vital to the well-being of the Siberian population. A compromise evolved between public and private interests: private trade was allowed and at times even serviced by the state within the limitations of the royal monopolies, wherever they were enforceable; the state at the same time tried to control the specific activities of private traders. The problem was immeasurably complicated by the fact that long-distance trade between Moscow and its Siberian colony was principally conducted by the very individuals who were engaged in the state's service in Siberia.

Peter the Great's reign saw a lively development in Siberian commercial activities. The population growth was accompanied by increased commerce in salt, grains, spirits, tobacco, and Chinese goods, as well as in other items not produced by the Siberian economy itself. Although the amounts actually traded may not have been large compared to the commerce of European Russia, Siberian commerce showed diversification, expansion, and even nascent specialization. Solikamsk, for instance, specialized in salt exports, while Nerchinsk was a major entrepot for Chinese goods.[25] Internally, Siberia's commerce was extremely localized: local commodities were exchanged over limited territorial expanses, and imported commodities were distributed to the local population through the larger settlements. In the first quarter of the eighteenth century Tomsk was probably the most important commercial center of Siberia because of its location on the main overland routes from western Siberia to the east and north. Tobolsk was next, having become the center of a lively local trade in Chinese goods. Irkutsk, the third one, developed its importance in Siberia's external trade as a transit point for the China trade.

Siberia's external trade, together with the Sino-Russian transit trade through Siberia, was more important than the internal trade of the country in terms of the variety of commodities, the total value of the trade, and the number of persons occupied full-time with it. However, since it was a major source of customs revenues for the state, it probably contributed little to the Siberian bureaucracy itself. Chinese goods were to be found, however, on the market at local fairs. At Irbit, for instance, tea (green, black, and brick), various kinds of cloth (nankeens, foulards, damask, brocade, silk, and cotton), tobacco pipes, pictures, china, enamel and porcelain ware, were already available at the end of the seventeenth or beginning of the eighteenth centuries.[26]

The state attempted to maintain its primacy in the Siberian market by involving the merchant in a web of services and obligations that tended severely to restrict his freedom of commercial action. For instance, it provided postal service between Tobolsk, Yakutsk, Nerchinsk, and Moscow three times a year. It erected and supervised warehouses, merchant halls, and market places, and organized annual fairs at designated places. These facilities offered opportunities at low cost for storage, display, and the sale of goods, with a certain degree of protection, while the state protected its own interests by preventing trade in contraband or monopolized goods. The state was also able at the fairs to collect more taxes at a higher rate than would otherwise have been possible. In return for these facilities, which private merchants would have been unable to provide for themselves, the state imposed restrictions and obligations. Passports and customs houses were utilized to control merchant movement. Individuals engaged in the service of the state were forbidden to bring into or out of Siberia articles that might be traded with the Siberian population or shipped to China. Corruption and circumvention, however, were more the rule than the exception in the observance of state regulations. In the long run, the state never effectively controlled its own officials' commercial activities.[27]

Establishment of a State Monopoly in the China Trade

With the signing of the Treaty of Nerchinsk, Moscow now faced the necessity of initiating the officially sanctioned trade with Peking and of maximizing the state's benefits from it. It is apparent that at the beginning Moscow had no clear idea concerning the state's role in the commerce. However, in the four decades between the Treaties of Nerchinsk and Kyakhta, three distinct tendencies emerged, each aimed at establishing a rigorous state monoploy in the China trade. These tendencies were the progressive monopolization of participation in the trade, the continuous effort to maximize the state's gold and silver income from the trade, and the creation of state monopolies in those commodities that were profitably exported to or imported from China. As the state's role in the trade increased, private merchants and public officials struggled to evade the state monopoly in order to benefit personally from trading with Peking. This conflict between state and private interests did not abate until the conclusion of the Kyakhta treaty and the complete overhauling of the Manchu-Russian commercial machinery.

Moscow first acted on the permissive clause of the Nerchinsk treaty in 1693 when it issued comprehensive new regulations for the collection of customs in Siberia.[28] In effect, these regulations governed participation in the China trade. In compliance with the treaty, the state required every merchant traveling to China to carry an official passport granting permission for the trip and listing the bearer's merchandise. At each state of the journey, passport and goods were examined, and any goods not listed were confiscated. Two-time offenders were subjected to the knout, and their relatives and households were tortured, if necessary, to uncover other attempts at fraud. In an obvious attempt to discourage corruption, government officials, voevodas, clerks, customs heads, and their near kinsmen were exempted from these regulations, and soldiers accompanying trading caravans to China or stationed at customs houses had the right to invest up to fifty rubles with the merchants. Customs duties were to be collected at Verkhoturye, the major port of entry from Russia into Siberia, and at Nerchinsk, the port of exit to China. A tithe was collected in kind on units of ten furs and pieces of stuff, but cash was collected for other items. Passports carried customs receipts to prevent the collection of duties twice from the same goods.

Three unwanted developments forced the government to issue a new set of regulations in 1698.[29] First, participation by the Russian and Siberian merchant class in the China trade was not as widespread as the government had wished, whereas non-merchants were taking part illegally in the trade to the detriment of the state's income. Second, non-Russians had entered the trade, which violated the state's mercantilist economic theories. Third, the demand for Russian products on the Peking market had declined, diminishing the profits of the individual caravans, because too many caravans had exported too many goods to China. The new regulations of 1698 stipulated that only merchants could participate in the China trade and specifically excluded all other classes, including members of the church hierarchy. Non-Russians, both Christian and Moslem, were equally interdicted. The state sought to control the value of Russian goods on the Peking market by inducing scarcity: the new regulations specifically limited trade caravans to a bi-annual schedule. Private enterprisers were free to join the caravans, but the state took over the responsibility for organizing and administering them. Chiefs and tselovalniks to conduct the caravans and manage the state's trade were chosen from among the gosts and the merchants of the gostinaya sotnya, the next lower merchant rank. Because increased private trade meant increased customs collections, the state extended special services to private merchants participating in the caravans, such as inexpensive storage facilities and postal services.

The regulations of 1698 constituted a compromise between the state and the private merchants. The state needed such merchants to provide it with commercial agents and to pay customs duties, but it also had to control the trade sufficiently to prevent private competition from injuring its own commerce at Peking. The competition increased rather than diminished, however, and in 1706 the state took rigorous action, which harshly and conclusively established its complete monopoly over the caravan trade to Peking in order to preserve and increase its profits. In a letter dated January 28, 1706, the voevoda of Eniseisk and all Siberian officials were strictly prohibited from permitting anyone to go to China for any purpose whatsoever, including commerce, unless he carried specific documents issued directly by the Siberian Department or the tsar in Moscow.[30] The Eniseisk voevoda was further instructed to inform all the officials "in the forests, and in the settlements, and in the winter quarters," that death awaited transgressors of this new regulation.

As the state tightened its control over the conduct of trade, it also gradually monopolized the commodities involved in the commerce with Peking. These fell into three categories. The first included goods of a political rather than economic significance: arms and munitions. As Central Asian politics grew more intense and dangerous, Moscow recognized, which K'ang-hsi had intended, that any interference on her part would disturb the commerce based on the Nerchinsk treaty. Arming the Jungars would endanger commercial profits and might eventually threaten Russia herself. The government, therefore, forbade the export of military supplies to the Jungars in article 15 of the 1693 trade regulations and imposed severe penalties for trading in arms, lead, and powder. The customs regulations of 1698 extended the list of items forbidden for export to Central Asia to include gold, silver, powder, lead, cannon, wicks, harquebuses, rifles, and any other items useful in military campaigns. Lest the arms carried for defense by the caravans journeying to Peking fall into Jungar, or Manchu, hands, strict inspections were instituted to ensure that the same arms carried out from Nerchinsk were brought back. Upon the caravan's return each soldier had to account for the arms he carried, which had been listed before his departure, or pay a remarkably stiff fine.[31]

The second category of goods monopolized by the state in the China trade consisted of gold, which within the context of the Petrine era's economic theories was the chief object of commerce, the support of the national wealth and state, and the raison d'être of the China trade. Even though the general statutes prohibiting the export of gold applied to China as to other areas, the state took special measures to encourage and even force the importation of gold from Peking. The customs regulations of 1693 stated that duties on gold should be paid in gold, although duties on other goods could be paid in kind. On December 5, 1697, Moscow took a step further by instructing the Nerchinsk customs that all duties were payable only in gold and silver, except when a merchant's goods were valued at less than one thousand rubles, in which case it was assumed that the merchant could not purchase or otherwise obtain gold for the payment of duties. Whatever gold remained after the customs were collected was registered for Moscow's immediate information. The 1698 customs regulations confirmed and extended these arrangements, fixing the prices at which the state would purchase gold from merchants. This policy, which forced merchants to obtain gold in China if they hoped to import other goods, was fairly successful. When in 1723 Moscow learned that there was more gold circulating in Siberia than it had previously realized, it proceeded to complete its monopoly of the metal. In a special decree the state declared that all gold brought from China had to be examined, weighed, and registered in the name of the owner, who thereafter was permitted to sell his gold to no one but the state treasury, under pain of death.[32]

The third category of goods under the state monopoly included three important items: rhubarb, whose root was wanted for its antiscorbutic properties, tobacco, and fur pelts. The sale of rhubarb and tobacco on the Siberian and Russian markets did not increase the country's specie reserve, but it did increase the state's income. In other words, the economic role of these two plant products differed from that of gold and silver, the objects of trade, or from that of fur, the means of carrying on the China trade. Imported Chinese tobacco and rhubarb were valued by the state only insofar as they increased the state's income from the Russian economy itself. Consequently, the state at first farmed out the monopolies on these two items to enterprising merchants in return for specific cash payments. It reclaimed the monopolies only when commerce in rhubarb and tobacco became so prosperous that the state treasury could no longer ignore them.

In 1691 I. Isaev, a merchant of the gostinaya sotnya, obtained an exclusive monopoly on the Siberian rhubarb trade for five years. He agreed to engage in no other commerce in Siberia and to import no more than fifty puds of rhubarb annually. The import was duty-free, and the death penalty was to be exacted against illegal rhubarb trade by third parties.[33] Isaev's monopoly ended on May 17, 1695, and Matvei Poppe, a Hamburg merchant, acquired it next, under the same conditions.[34] The appearance of contraband rhubarb on the market indicates that the trade in this product was quite profitable, and by September 1697 Moscow had to prohibit private traffic in rhubarb from Siberia to Russia.[35] Contraband rhubarb probably entered Siberia through the market on Lake Yamysh, where considerable trade in Chinese goods was conducted by Bukharans. The rhubarb edict of 1697 required the Siberian officials to examine, weigh, and register by name of owner and quality of product all rhubarb brought into the country outside of Poppe's monopoly. In other words, the state had begun to recognize the value of this trade, and in 1704 it acted to reestablish its own monopoly of the product. In that year an edict ordered Larion Senyavin, the son of Akimov, to go to Turfan (in modern Sinkiang) and other cities "where rhubarb may be produced" to purchase three hundred puds of the plant for the state. He was given one thousand rubles to purchase Russian leather for use in the commerce, and in Siberia he received cash and fur pelts for the same purpose. The edict declared the death penalty for anyone else found trafficking in rhubard, and Senyavin himself was given a specific salary, including two hundred pails of plain wine annually, "so that he, Larion, seeing His Great Majesty's grace towards him, will make more profit in the purchase of rhubarb as compared to former times."[36] By the time that the Kyakhta trade began to develop after 1728, the state had already established an office at that settlement as the sole point of import for rhubarb and maintained complete control over its sale and distribution.

The Siberian tobacco monopoly was a clear illustration, on the one hand, of competition between Chinese and Western products on the Siberian market and, on the other, of the conflict between official and private trade with China. By its very nature, tobacco is a product quickly and easily consumed, after which it is no longer available for inspection or the collection of customs duties. The state therefore depended for profits on a strictly regulated monopoly. It adopted the form of monopoly-farming, granting it first to Martyn Bogdanov, a member of the gostinaya sotnya, for one year beginning December 1, 1696. During this period Bogdanov was freed from customs payments but was required to build stores for the sale of tobacco and liquor, upon the public sales of which a tax would be levied. Bogdanov, in turn, had the right to grant retail privileges to other merchants, who after the expiration of the one-year monopoly could continue selling tobacco, subject to taxation. By June 1697, however, the state had to modify the monopoly grant to preserve other interests. For instance, it interdicted the sale of tobacco to natives, who bought it with fur pelts and thus hindered the collection of yasak furs for export to China. Bogdanov's original grant was extended on June 1, 1697, on condition that he pay customs and submit to the supervision of tselovalniks, which indicated the rapid growth of profits from the tobacco trade.

Five months later, on April 16, 1698, an Anglo-Russian commercial treaty signed in London gave the Marquis of Camarthen, Lord Sir Thomas Osborne, sole right for seven years to import annually ten thousand casks of "the nicotine herb" from America into Russia, in return for payments to the Russian court. The first year's sales went slowly, however, and at the end of the second year the English company refused to renew the agreement for an additional five years as allowed by the treaty.[37] The failure of the English tobacco venture in Russia is explicable in terms of the competition from imported Chinese tobacco. Camarthen's representative in Russia had requested permission for the English to import Chinese as well as American tobacco, but a Russian investigation in 1700 revealed that the use of Chinese tobacco was so widespread among the Siberian population that the state's customs duties acquired from its import would be seriously curtailed if Chinese tobacco were forbidden or granted to Camarthen's monopoly. The English request was rejected. When the state resumed the English tobacco monopoly, it also extended that monopoly to Chinese tobacco, and finally in 1706 it forbade all private trade in "the weed."[38]

The mercantilist prohibition of the export of gold and silver placed Russia's trade with China on a strictly commodity export basis. Because fur pelts were the chief export to China, and because the state sought to increase its trade profits by monopolizing goods intended for export to, as well as import from, China, the state monopoly on fur pelts developed faster and sooner than on other goods. However, as the state's participation in the caravan trade to Peking grew, requiring more pelts of higher price and better quality, it was led to monopolize not only the export of certain kinds of pelts to China but the trade of these pelts inside Siberia and Russia as well. As early as 1692, for instance, the treasury complained that it was receiving poor quality furs in payment for customs duties, and the 1693 customs regulations forbade the export to China of pelts valued at more than forty rubles per forty skins. In this fashion the treasury planned to raise the quality of pelts received from customs payments and reserve to itself the right to export the high quality pelts to Peking. This was the first step in the establishment of a state monopoly over the export of fur goods. In 1697 the crown's monopoly was completed by a series of decrees reserving all trade in certain types of fur, particularly sable pelts and black-fox skins, in order to prevent competition from cheaper-priced, poor-quality skins of the same variety, and no merchant could export fur not purchased directly from the state treasury. By 1700 these prohibitions were extended to include sales of fur pelts to anyone who might resell them to China, including Bukharans, Kalmuks, and Mongols.[39]

The court's monopoly, however, was constantly undermined by the cupidity of its Siberian officialdom. A constant stream of edicts from the tsar complained of abuses. An edict of 1697 explained that voevodas themselves engaged in the fur trade at the expense of the state, and another one in the same year complained of conspicuous official consumption of fur by local Siberian officials at the state treasury's expense.[40] In 1701 a voevoda of Nerchinsk was accused of illegally profiting from the China trade by transgressing the fur monopoly. Siberian officials had great freedom of action by virtue of their distance from Moscow, of which they took advantage.

The state monopoly of the institutions and content of the China trade was a pragmatic development rather than the result of any preconceived national plan. It was forced on the state in large measure by competition from private merchants and corruption on the part of public officials. Whatever the vagaries of Peter's immediate commercial policies, he had one basic concern: an intense need to maximize his government's revenues by whatever means. He was a creature of his times as well, so that his economic policies reflected the mercantilist theories of Europe.

Trade and Diplomacy between Treaty and Monopoly

The thirty-eight years between the Treaties of Nerchinsk and Kyakhta can be divided into three periods, based on the balance between state and private participation by Russia in the China trade. Private capital, which in fact initiated the treaty-sanctioned trade, predominated in the first period, from 1689 to 1697. Growing profits enticed the state to move in and establish a state monopoly on participation in the China trade during the second period, 1698-1705. The third period, between 1705 and the Treaty of Kyakhta, witnessed the operation of the state monopoly on a decreasingly profitable basis. Its diminishing profits were the result, on the one hand, of an oversupply of Russian goods on the Peking market and, on the other, of illegal private competition, in which Moscow's Siberian officialdom connived with private capital. Commercial and diplomatic activities coalesced during the intertreaty period, until with the establishment of the state monopoly, trade and diplomacy became complementary aspects of a single process of international communication rather than supplementary facets of closely related but distinct activities. The development of direct state participation in the China trade was a gradual process, however, and the monopoly took over existing patterns of economic relationships between Nerchinsk and Peking that had been created primarily by the investments and activities of private Russian merchants. The state substituted itself for private capital as a source of investment; it did not radically alter the form or content of the trade, nor did it influence Manchu participation in any way.

During the intertreaty period Peking remained the primary Chinese market for the sale of Russian goods, but after 1689 Nerchinsk became the chief emporium and entrepot on the Russian side, as well as eastern Siberia's most important commercial center. Nerchinsk's population consisted of two discontinuous groups united in pursuit of the profits from the China trade. The first group was the settlement's permanent population, numbering about 1,000 persons. The second group included merchants, workers, and porters who came to Nerchinsk on a seasonal basis to participate in the trade. They grew in number from 172 in the 1691-1692 trading season to 572 in 1697. Of these, perhaps only 30 to 50 were merchants each year; the rest provided the basic labor force for the conduct of trade and the staffing of the caravans.[41] The growth of Nerchinsk's ambient population is an index of the settlement's role in the trade.

The first Russian caravan left Nerchinsk for Peking at Golovin's instigation in December 1689, immediately after the conclusion of the treaty. The ambassador wanted to test the provisions of the treaty concerning commerce and the exchange of diplomatic personnel; he therefore sent with the caravan Grigory Lonshakov, a boyar son, to negotiate with the Manchus about the relocation of the Argun ostrog and the return of the yasak-paying natives who had crossed into Manchu territory from the Shilka after the conclusion of the treaty. The speed with which this private merchant caravan was organized attested to the interest that the China trade aroused among the Russian merchants.[42] Although since 1653 Manchu commercial regulations had theoretically permitted only one Russian caravan to visit Peking every three years, between 1689 and 1698 official caravans were sent to Peking annually, and it is probable that unofficial caravans also made the journey every year.

Participation in the caravan trade was a prolonged undertaking, requiring great capital, a large staff of agents and workpeople, and arduous travel. The distance from Moscow to Peking was over 5,900 miles, and the trip there and back lasted no fewer than three years. Dmitry Grigorev Grechenin, for instance, received one of the first passports issued in Moscow for the new legalized trade in November 1689. He left Nerchinsk for Peking in June 1691 and did not return to the frontier until March 1692, the journey from Nerchinsk to Peking and back taking, on an average, ten to twelve months.[43] As Nerchinsk itself was chiefly a transit point and local market, lacking resources for equipping caravans, most of the caravans were made up before their arrival at the settlement. The high cost of cattle and camels east of Baikal forced merchants to obtain beasts for transportation at the Balagansk ostrog before reaching the frontier.[44] The caravans went from Nerchinsk along the Argun River to the Nun-chiang and thence to Peking, taking some three months.[45] The most difficult leg of the journey occurred between the Argun and the Nun-chiang, a region very sparsely populated, with little local agriculture and a superabundance of brigands.[46] The Russians had to provision their own caravans as far as the settlements on the Nun-chiang, where the Manchu authorities then assumed responsibility for securing transport and provisions. In Peking the caravans were housed in the O-lo-ssu kuan (Russian Inn), where they received provisions from the government.[47] This arrangement was an early instance of the kind of institutional compromise that characterized the development of the Sino-Russian treaty system. Customarily the Ch'ing government provisioned and transported tributary delegations from the frontier to Peking, where they were housed and maintained at government expense. In this respect the Manchus were treating the Russian trade caravans as tributary missions, though the Russians were not required to perform tributary ceremonials at the capital. The Russians, in turn, were not displeased at the Manchu assumption of costs of transportation and provisions over a considerable distance and of their maintenance at the capital. Since most of the caravan workers remained at the Nun-chiang while the merchants went on to Peking, the cost to the Manchus of supporting the caravans was not excessive. In addition, a limited local trade developed along the Nun-chiang (again within the tributary tradition, which permitted frontier trade), although the area remained primarily a transit point.

The caravans assumed diplomatic functions that were directly related to their commercial tasks. They were convoyed by military personnel, whose commander usually carried instructions empowering him to negotiate for transport and provisions with Manchu officials on the Nun-chiang and to deal with other problems requiring official representation. In Peking he presented documents to the "near people" of the emperor, attesting the caravan's *bona fides* and requesting permission for free trade. The commander was usually a man of experience, who often had previous knowledge of China.

Seven caravans in all journeyed officially from Nerchinsk to Peking between 1689 and 1697 (no official caravans went in 1690 or 1694). A caravan's staff usually included representatives of the gosts or the gostinaya sotnya, minor traders, workers, and a military convoy. Most of the staff of the caravan, as well as the individual merchant participants, were hired in Moscow, where the merchants received their passports for travel to China. The staff was nevertheless fairly fluid in composition. Merchants often hired additional local workers to assist in defense, loading, packing, and other activities, and they often left some porters at Nerchinsk or on the Nun-chiang, to be picked up on the return journey. Although labor costs at Nerchinsk were quite high, anyone who succeeded in making the journey all the way to Peking undoubtedly found it profitable, because a certain amount of unregistered petty trade was permitted.[48]

The conditions of the caravan trade to Peking restricted private merchant participation. The costs of transport over long and difficult trade routes and the fact that a merchant could not expect to earn a profit on his initial investment for approximately three years eliminated nearly all but the greatest merchant houses.[49] The caravans were dominated by four great merchants or their families: O. Filatiev, S. Luzin, I. Ushakov, and G. Nikitin. These men regularly sent large quantities of goods to Peking.[50] Before the final establishment of the state monopoly on the export of fur, these four families were also the most important merchants on the private Siberian and Moscow fur markets, where they could easily obtain sufficient quantities of fur pelts for export to Peking. For the Filatiev interests, for instance, participation in the China trade was a logical extension of their general commercial activities in Russia and Siberia.[51]

Gavril Romanovich Nikitin was one of the most interesting of the four great merchants participant in the caravan trade, and not atypical. He began his career as an agent of the Moscow gost Ostafy Filatiev, for whom he traded in fur on the Sol-Vychegodsk market. As a Filatiev agent, he also obtained considerable experience in the China trade before the Treaty of Nerchinsk. In August 1674 Nikitin went from Selenginsk through the Khalkha Steppe to China on the first caravan to reach Peking through the central or Mongolian route. The caravan was received in Peking as an embassy, lodged in the ambassadorial court, given provisions, and received in an imperial audience, where it presented gifts.[52] With this experience behind him, Nikitin entered the gostinaya sotnya by February 1679 and in 1681 became a gost. His participation in the post-treaty China trade was, therefore, not only one aspect of his general commercial activities in Siberia but a logical development of his own career as an agent of the Filatiev family.

The Filatievs and Nikitin were Moscow merchants, but Ivan Ushakov and his brother Aleksey were Siberians, members of a new merchant class just emerging in the colony in the second half of the seventeenth century. Their interests were extremely widespread, and they entered the China trade through contact with F. A. Golovin, the Russian ambassador at Nerchinsk, who granted them supply contracts. Semen Luzin, about whom little is known, probably entered the China trade through his interests in the fur trade. He sold Siberian fur pelts to western European merchants at Arkhangelsk and in partnership with his brother Andrey, an appraiser of furs at the Siberian department, carried on an extensive and steady fur trade in Siberia.[53]

These petty merchants who succeeded in participating in the China trade through Nerchinsk came by and large from cities closely related through the fur trade to both Moscow and eastern Siberia: Lalsk, Yarench, Ustyug, and Sol-Vychegodsk. Often of peasant origin, they began their commercial careers as agents for the great merchants and saved small amounts of capital, which they invested in Siberia; usually they settled there. Such petty merchant families as the Oskolkovs and Savateevs participated in the China trade on a limited scale at an early date. Other European Russian merchants traded to China only episodically, and those who did had close ties either with the Siberian market or with important insitutions like the Siberian Department. Even more rarely did local settlers in Siberia participate in the trade, despite their geographical proximity to Nerchinsk. One exception was the burgher I. Shtinnikov, who supplied wine to Irkutsk on a contractual basis and rented salt-works and arable land on the Ushakov estates. He made one journey to China in 1695 to trade at Peking.[54]

The lack of cheap and organized credit in seventeenth-century Russia and Siberia was an important factor limiting petty merchant participation in the caravan trade to China. In 1699, for instance, a group of merchants at Nerchinsk petitioned the local voevoda not to delay the departure of the annual Peking caravan. They were participating in the caravan on the basis of goods and money borrowed at a high rate of interest from the great gosts, for which they had signed themselves into short-term indenture. The willingness of the great merchants to make loans to petty merchants participating in the caravans was an intelligent choice of means to control competition. The amount of Russian goods, measured by value, exported to China after the Treaty of Nerchinsk rose steadily, if erratically, from an estimated 7,563 rubles in the caravan of 1691 to a high of approximately 49,300 rubles in the summer of 1696. The value of imports from China rose from about 14,473 rubles in 1689 to a high of about 240,000 rubles in 1693. On an average, more than 50 percent of the goods, measured by value, carried into or out of China by any given caravan in the years 1691 to 1696 belonged to the four great gosts. Only in the caravans of 1696 and 1697, the last ones before the imposition of the state monopoly, did they control less than 50 percent, which is explained by the increased participation of petty merchants, often on loans from the gosts, and the ancilliary trade carried on in small amounts by members of the caravan staff.[55] After 1698 these marginal petty merchants, unable to compete with the gosts, supported the state monopoly, since by becoming the state's agents they could share in its profits. Among the names of the leaders of the state caravans to Peking from 1698 to 1719 only one, P. Khudyakov, does not appear among the petty merchants participating in the private caravan trade up to 1697.

The Sino-Russian caravan trade was based primarily on the exchange of Russian fur for Chinese cloth. Fur, the basic source of Siberian wealth, was in demand in the harsh winter climate of North China, where few fur-bearing animals lived, whereas good Chinese cloth was in great demand in Moscow's aristocratic and court circles, and the poorer quality cloth circulated widely in Siberia, which did not produce much cloth for itself. With the opening of the treaty trade, fur pelts began to flow into Nerchinsk from central and eastern Siberia, from Eniseisk and Yakutsk through Irkutsk. Irkutsk developed into an important transshipment center on the trade routes that met at Nerchinsk and continued on into China. By 1695 the demand for fur in Nerchinsk rose beyond the supply available for export from Siberia to China, so that furs were diverted from the European market or even purchased in European Russia for export to China. By 1696, 73.2 percent of the fur pelts, by value, exported to China through Nerchinsk was obtained by commercial agents in European Russia.[56]

Small amounts—three to four thousand rubles annually—of Russian and western European manufactures also appeared on the Nerchinsk market, and whatever was not consumed locally was exported to China. Although these manufactures constituted a very minor item in Russian exports to Peking, they facilitated the participation of petty merchants in the caravan trade. By selling such manufactures along the Russo-Siberian trade routes, petty merchants often defrayed their expenses and even purchased small quantities of fur for export. The small amounts of manufactured goods actually exported to China supplied only limited demands on the Peking market or were consumed by the caravans themselves. Stockings, shoes, dyes, flax cloth, hatchets, knives, writing paper, and musket powder were all needed on the way to Peking. Western European, Russian, and even Persian handicrafts and manufactures were used as gifts to Manchu administrative personnel; these items included the better quality broadcloths, clocks, mirrors, telescopes, gold lace, and silver dishes.[57]

The caravans brought back from Peking a wide variety of Chinese goods, particularly luxury items for consumption by the higher social classes in Siberia and Moscow. Between 1689 and 1698 Russian merchants explored both the Chinese and the Russian-Siberian markets to determine what Chinese goods could be imported profitably through Nerchinsk, and as time passed, a larger variety of Chinese items appeared in Russia. Precious stones, pearls, articles of gold and silver, and tea in small amounts were brought back from Peking or obtained on the local market at Nerchinsk and along the Amur, but the commodity in most overwhelming demand was cloth of various types, colors, sizes, and qualities. Damasks, silks, and cottons (the nankeens of the Canton trade) were imported in such quantities that the prices they commanded in Russia fell by more than 50 percent by 1697.[58]

Chinese manufactures played a minor, though not unimportant, role in Russian imports from Peking: knives in casings, fans, silver saltcellars and pitchers, wooden vessels lacquered or painted, jasper, porcelain, and similar items were in high demand among Moscow's court circles. Chinese household articles even came into common use among the Siberian merchant and aristocratic classes by the middle of the eighteenth century. Teas and spices such as cardamom and saffron, which came into China from India, also found their way into the Russian market, where the demand was small and the price high.[59]

The caravan trade with China attracted private merchants by holding out hopes of high profits. In 1697 the value of Russian exports to China exceeded 240,000 rubles at Moscow prices, which was greater than Russia's trade with all of Central Asia. The volume of goods traded grew to such an extent that by the end of the seventeenth century, the Nerchinsk *gostiny dvor* or permanent marketplace could no longer store all the goods brought from China. Inns, huts, and private warehouses were pressed into service, and in 1699 Moscow ordered the construction of a stone gostiny dvor large enough to handle all the trade's needs. Significant profits could be made even on a small volume of trade because of the considerable price differential between Nerchinsk and other places in Siberia and Russia. Russian handicraft products were priced 25 to 30 percent higher in Nerchinsk than in Eniseisk and 150 percent higher than in European Russia or Tobolsk. Hops rose two and a half times in price when brought from Tomsk and Eniseisk to Nerchinsk, and cattle driven to Nerchinsk from Balagansk increased four times in value. Fur pelts from Yakutsk, Ilimsk, Ust-Kirensk, Krasnoyarsk, Irkutsk, Eniseisk, and Mangzeya rose from one and a half to four times their value in their place of origin. Annual profits in the internal Siberian fur trade alone averaged 22 to 25 percent. Profits were larger when furs were exported through Nerchinsk to Peking. In 1698, for instance, despite unfavorable market conditions, a thousand squirrel skins costing 15 rubles in Nerchinsk purchased enough nankeens in Peking to bring 72 rubles at Nerchinsk or enough satin to bring 40 rubles. Lynx fur was four times more valuable in Peking than at Nerchinsk, fox fur three times, polar fox two to two and a half times, and ermine twice as valuable.[60]

Prices on imported Chinese cloth rose in ratio to the distance from Nerchinsk, which was the reason merchants preferred to transport their goods away from the frontier before offering them for sale. In 1694-1695, for instance, an end of satin of the widest width brought 7 rubles in Nerchinsk and 8.5 rubles in Moscow, while satin of medium width was priced at 3.5 rubles and 6.5 rubles respectively. An end of nankeen that brought 75 kopeks at Nerchinsk brought 1.2 rubles on the Moscow market.[61]

Profit expectations were sufficiently higher in the China trade than in the internal Siberian market or the commerce between Siberia and Russia to attract well-established merchant capital to Nerchinsk and Peking, despite the risks involved and the length of time required to realize a profit on an initial investment. Profits before the payment of customs duties could be expected to reach as high as 48 percent in the caravan trade to Peking.[62] This expectation of high profits, which had prompted the state to establish a monopoly over the China trade, was substantiated by its initial experiment in direct trade with Peking, the Ides mission.

The Ides Mission

The state's interest in direct participation in the caravan trade to Peking was manifested as early as 1692, when Moscow sent an exploratory mission to China to investigate the possibilities of developing state trade for the treasury's profit. The Ides embassy, which left Moscow in March 1692, reflected the amorphous state of Russian society in general at the time, lacking clear distinctions between private and public commerce or between foreign diplomacy and foreign trade. The mission was institutionally and temporally transitional. Institutionally it bridged the gap between state diplomacy and private trade, on the one hand, and state diplomacy and state trade, on the other. Temporally, it was the last of the series of missions, of which the Milescu embassy was the archetype, to combine diplomacy and commerce, and it was the first to achieve the second goal. The Ides embassy was also the first state caravan to Peking, though the tentativeness of the state's interest was indicated by its limited investment in the venture.[63]

Eleazar Isbrant Ides was a merchant, born in Denmark, who in 1676 and 1677 prospered in the sea trade at Arkhangelsk, and by 1688 had a large house in Moscow and estates in the suburbs. After 1689, however, he began to suffer severe commercial losses, and he petitioned the court for permission to trade to China with state subsidies in the hope of resuscitating his fortunes. His petition to the throne provided the state with an opportunity to investigate, against the background of Peter's general monopolistic commercial policies, the value of the China trade for the state's treasury. The court went beyond Ides' original request and appointed him envoy to China, "for the affairs of Their Majesties," in order to send a gramota or letter to the emperor. To facilitate his commercial activities, he also received an advance of three thousand rubles in silver and three thousand rubles in sable pelts and other furs from the Siberian Department. The official nature of this diplomatic-commercial venture was re-emphasized by the direct participation of the state in the caravan's organization. In the first days of March 1692 a secretary of the Ambassadorial Department, two sublieutenants, and a medical officer were added to the caravan's staff. On March 7 the court ordered the Tobolsk voevoda to assign a Mongolian interpreter, a secretary, and forty or fifty soldiers to the caravan; it was also freed from the usual payment of customs duties, which was itself a recognition of the official nature of the undertaking. Ides was given the full complement of official documents: a passport, dated March 8, a letter of recommendation to the Urga Khutukhtu and the Mongol Prince Ochiroi-sain-khan, as well as the tsar's gramota, dated March 19, 1692.[64]

What began, therefore, as a fairly routine request for permission to trade to China and for an official passport, as required by the treaty, turned into an official embassy to explore the role the state might assume in the lucrative China trade. Ides' instructions, which primarily concerned commerce and only secondarily diplomacy, were a mixture of the traditional instructions issued previously to Milescu and Golovin and of new ones highlighting the state's interest in the recently established commerce.[65] For instance, Ides was to make the usual request that Chinese merchants be allowed to go to Moscow with a thousand or more puds of silver, as well as precious stones, embroidered materials, spices, and other valuable Chinese goods. Beyond this, however, he was instructed to survey carefully and secretly the China market, informing himself "exactly and sufficiently" concerning such matters as China's products in general, the location of and routes to mines for precious stones, her other trading partners, and Chinese products that might advantageously be imported into Russia. Most important, he was to estimate current and future profit expectation in the China trade. In order to gather this information, which he was to record meticulously in his official journal, Ides was ordered to request the freedom of Peking, particularly of its mercantile sections. He was to inspect closely the commercial streets of Peking, to determine the exact and true prices of each type of merchandise offered for sale in the city's marketplaces, and to study the goods consumed by the Chinese themselves.

Ides' diplomatic instructions concerned, first, problems the solutions to which were clearly defined in the Nerchinsk treaty and which required only a demand for action and, second, the gathering of information about the operations of the treaty and the future intentions of the Ch'ing government. In the first category, after Ides had assured the emperor that Moscow meant to keep the treaty and ascertained whether the Manchus were obeying it, he was to deal with a series of questions arising from the treaty provision on fugitives. The second category concerned a subject that the Nerchinsk treaty had specifically avoided: delineation of the frontier along the Ud River. While making it quite clear that he himself was not empowered to conclude agreements concerning the frontier, Ides was to determine Manchu intentions in that region, for which he was given two hundred rubles' worth of sable pelts to use as bribes, if necessary. The only issue on which Ides was to undertake anything approaching direct diplomatic activity was to request a site for the construction at the tsar's expense of a Russian church in Peking. Finally, the envoy was specially instructed to fulfill all the requirements of Chinese etiquette, an injunction derived from previous lessons.

Traveling by way of Nerchinsk and Manchuria, the embassy arrived at Peking on November 3, 1693, where it was well received and encountered none of the difficulties that had attended Milescu's sojourn there.[66] After depositing his credentials with the emperor's ministers, presumably at the Li-fan yuan,[67] Ides was first received in an imperial audience on November 14, 1693. Although the tsar's letter was returned as a result of his name having been placed before the emperor's,[68] Ides and members of his embassy were received by the emperor on at least four additional occasions, and they were often entertained with food from the emperor's table.[69] Conversations took place between Ides and the Manchus, and the envoy was permitted to circulate in the city and collect the commercial information that was his mission's chief objective. He left Peking on February 19, 1694, having been received in a farewell audience by the emperor on February 16 and been given an answer to his instructions on the day of his departure. He arrived at Moscow a year later, on February 1, 1695, almost three years after he had set out.

The Ides mission afforded the Ch'ing court an opportunity to take stock of its relations with Russia after four years of operation of the Treaty of Nerchinsk. The definite, though minor, diplomatic implications of the mission awakened Peking to the fact that the treaty was permissive, not explicit. Like the Russians, therefore, the Manchus had to consider the exact nature of the relationship and establish regulations for the conduct of intercourse, particularly on the commercial level.[70] The Ch'ing response to the Ides mission illustrated the delicate balance Peking tried to create in its relations with Moscow. Whereas the problem of correct ceremonial raised by errors in the form of the tsar's gramota to the emperor would previously have given rise to serious altercations, now, anxious to maintain the Nerchinsk peace, Peking moderated its approach and followed a middle path between acceptance and rejection. The Li-fan yuan returned the envoy's credentials and refused the tsar's gifts, but K'ang-hsi granted Ides audiences. Although he refused to write a letter to the tsar, the emperor sent him gifts and complied with his request that Ides be given the freedom of the city.[71] There is little doubt that Ides encouraged this accommodation by performing the kowtow at the audiences he had with the emperor.[72] The two most important results of the Ides mission were that the Peking government undertook to codify the regulations governing all aspects of its relationship with Russia and that Moscow received a great deal of valuable information about China and its commerce, on the basis of which it decided to enter the trade and establish a monopoly over it.

At exactly what moment in the thirty-second year of his reign K'ang-hsi promulgated the regulations governing the Russian trade is not clear, but it was probably during Ides' sojourn in Peking. In traditional fashion the regulations moved from specific issues to generalities. In other words, faced with particular problems, the Manchus customarily established precise regulations to deal with them as precedents for future action. The regulations fell into three distinct but related categories.[73] The first two dealt with general specifications for the caravan trade and the reception of Russian envoys and documents at Peking. Whether the regulations placing limitations on the caravan trade were meant to cover diplomatic missions as well is not clear, but since trade and diplomacy were almost inseparable, the issue quite possibly never arose. Caravans were to include no more than two hundred men, nor were they to come to the capital more than once every three years (although this regulation never became operative). En route the Russians should provide their own horses and camels and cover their own traveling expenses. They were forbidden to trade in contraband articles and were not granted living allowances in Peking. Furthermore, they were to begin their return journey within eighty days of their arrival at the capital. Although these regulations were restrictive, they were ameliorated somewhat by provisions that no customs duties could be collected on their imports or exports and that, while at Peking, they would be housed at the O-lo-ssu kuan. In consonance with the times, these regulations were a mixture of commercial and diplomatic practices, for while the caravans were to be treated as purely commercial undertakings, they were to be housed in quarters traditionally reserved for visiting tributary delegations. Nevertheless, the regulations made it clear that the caravans were not considered tribute missions, since diplomatic envoys were subjected to special regulations.

The specific diplomatic regulations promulgated by the Ch'ing court came in response to Ides' unacceptable memorial. Although it was decided to reject the document and gifts, which were styled as tribute in deference to tradition, certain allowances were made, rationalized on the basis of Russia's great distance and of its ignorance of the Chinese customs-system. The errors of form in the gramota were explained to Ides, but the peaceful conduct of Sino-Russian relations required the avoidance of similar situations in the future. Consequently, the Tartar general of the Amur was empowered to open all Russian communications and to return them if they contained errors of form—a task usually reserved for officials of the Li-fan yuan at Peking. This extension of accepted practice was intended to avoid conflicts arising through direct communications between tsar and emperor by empowering secondary officials to play the key role. The dangers of conflict were further diminished by physically removing the task of opening memorials and issuing denials from Peking to the frontier. Once a Russian envoy had passed the frontier and traveled to Peking, other regulations were needed to govern his immediate confrontation with the Manchu court. The form outlined was strictly in accord with tributary practice, but because of the general post-Nerchinsk reluctance to send diplomatic envoys of high rank from either side to the other, the necessity of testing these regulations in practice was avoided. Indeed, between the treaties of Nerchinsk and Kyakhta only one envoy in addition to Ides went to Peking from Moscow, and after Kyakhta the Manchu embassies to Russia clearly demonstrated that the Manchus were not adverse to reciprocating their ceremonial demands where necessary by acceding to Russian court ceremonials.[74]

The third category of regulations promulgated at this time dealt with the extradition of fugitives, the major diplomatic issue that Ides had raised with Peking. The Manchus themselves were not without complaint, and the court issued specific orders concerning the apprehension of Russians committing crimes inside Manchu territory, which were basically a restatement of the principles enunciated by the Nerchinsk treaty.[75]

Ides' embassy was a political failure in that he obtained no agreements concerning the fugitive problem other than these new regulations. As Songgotu pointed out to him, it would be impossible to determine who was a fugitive until the entire frontier was defined. The court also refused Moscow's request for land on which to build a Russian church, and it maintained that all Russians in China who wanted to return home had already done so. Ides was assured by a French Jesuit, however, that K'ang-hsi intended to keep the provisions of the Treaty of Nerchinsk, and he learned further from the Jesuits that the emperor had ordered the construction of strong fortifications on the Amur, below Albazin near the mouth of the Zeya.[76] The embassy must at the same time be judged a commercial success. Although the Manchus still refused to permit Chinese merchants to travel to Moscow, Ides gathered valuable commercial information, on the basis of which he made detailed recommendations concerning goods suitable for export to China.[77] Ides himself was convinced that great profits could be gained from the China trade,[78] and the 48.1 percent profit he made on the state's investment in his caravan supported that conclusion. As a result, after Ides' return to Moscow in 1695 the state decided to enter the trade on a permanent basis.

The State Monopoly in the China Trade: 1696-1719

Between 1696, when the state organized its first real caravan to Peking, and 1719, when the Manchus once again turned their attention to adjusting their relations with Russia in the light of Peter the Great's renewed interest in Central Asia, nine state caravans made the long journey to China.[79] The first one, organized as a consequence of Ides' commercial success, established the pattern followed by later caravans with only minor deviations. The state itself appointed the head of the caravan and his assistants, ordered the Siberian authorities to provide the caravan with fur pelts for the Peking market, dictated the route it was to travel, and disposed of the caravan's goods upon its return.

As early as June 14, 1696, the tsar ordered the chief of the Ambassadorial Department to send Spiridon Yakovlev Lyangusov to China with sables and other furs belonging to the state treasury.[80] For some reason, however, the organizational procedures were not completed until the first months of 1697.[81] In February 1697 orders were sent to the voevoda of Irkutsk to supply Lyangusov with fur pelts from the yasak tribute and the tithe tax. An aide-memoire sent to the Nerchinsk customs chief in the same month added that Lyangusov was to take sables and black fox pelts to Peking to exchange for gold, silver, damask, and nankeens, on all of which he was to pay the usual customs duties upon his return to Siberia. A further aide-memoire to Nerchinsk in June 1697 described the procedures to be followed when the caravan returned from Peking. An exact report of the gold ingots brought back from China was to be made and a copy sent to Moscow. Rigorous punishment awaited any attempts to prevent the entire shipment from reaching Moscow. Gold owned privately by any participants in the caravan was to be purchased by the customs or confiscated if anyone refused to sell. These regulations emphasized the mercantilist nature of the entire operation.[82]

The caravan itself consisted of 289 "travelers," secretaries, domestic servants, and other employees, in addition to 189 merchants and "workmen," or about 478 persons in all. On April 8, 1698, Lyangusov delivered his credentials and orders to the voevoda at Irkutsk, and he was in Nerchinsk by July 15, 1698. He probably arrived at Peking in about October or November of that year, and returned to Nerchinsk in July 1699. I. Savateev, one of Lyangusov's assistants, upon his return made a detailed report to the voevoda of the caravan's experience in Peking. He gave details concerning the current Peking prices for furs such as squirrel, ermine, fox, and lynx, and for Russian hides, as well as the purchase prices for the two principle imports from China, silk (damask) and cotton (nankeens). He claimed that in Peking silver was mixed with copper and did not have "hall-marks," while gold was rare and expensive. Regular Russian commodities were already superabundant on the Peking market as a result of too frequent Russian caravans. No duties had been collected by the Chinese on transactions, and despite an evident slackness in business, the Russians had encountered no major obstacles to the completion of their mission.[83]

The Lyangusov caravan did not escape as easily in Russia as in China. In the years after its return there were repeated complaints of fraud, deceit, and robbery at the government's expense. An edict of January 22, 1699, ordered the Nerchinsk voevoda to apply the customs tariff of 1698 to all merchants, including those in the state caravans. This general order was specifically applied to Lyangusov's caravan in a gramota to the Nerchinsk voevoda, dated April 30, 1699, which stated that the government regretfully ordered all the caravan's Chinese merchandise deposited in a wooden warehouse immediately upon its return from Peking. Even this instruction was not strictly obeyed, and a new set of instructions sent to the Nerchinsk voevoda in 1701 enumerated the malversations and transgressions of the voevoda's assistants and subordinates. Among them was a complaint that Lyangusov's caravan had imported tobacco and various other "native commodities" from China, which Petr Khudyakov, the Nerchinsk customs chief, had passed without levying the required duties.[84] From the very first, Moscow encountered corruption and even competition from its own caravan officials.

A rather desultory and fugitive air also characterized the caravan trade from its beginning. The "caravan system" existed only by virtue of the fact that all caravans followed a basic pattern of organization and procedure. Each caravan was directed by a "caravan head," who was assisted by at least three other persons: an aide or "companion," and two tselovalniks. The state treasury carried all the caravan's expenses and supplied the furs for trade in Peking. Despite a general uniformity in basic operations, each caravan was a discrete unit, organized as a specific enterprise, drawing on the personnel and experience of previous caravans but having no institutional or organic connection with them. Although two organs of the central state, the Ambassadorial Department and the Siberian Department, were interested in the caravan trade, there was no institution such as a "caravan office." The patterns of behavior that characterized successive caravans were more the result of accumulated responses to similar problems than of any over-all organizational scheme.

The state utilized important merchants, drawn from all over Russia, as its agents in the caravan system. The caravan head was, as a rule, selected from the ranks of the gosts or the gostinaya sotnya, and he carried the title *kupchina* (merchant) until 1710, when the position was renamed *komissar* (commissar) in view of certain new functions accruing to the office. Usually a caravan head had served an apprenticeship in some post related to the China trade and was therefore a member of a small but growing group of Russian experts on China. More often than not he first served as an aide or tselovalnik under an older caravan head and, once appointed, usually led two caravans to Peking under his own authority. I. Savateev, for instance, served in Lyangusov's caravan of 1697-1699, then as director in 1704 and 1709. Oskolkov was Bokov's aide in 1700-1701 and caravan head in 1703 and 1714. Khudyakov had served as customs chief at Nerchinsk before he was appointed caravan head in 1705 and again in 1709, and Gusyatnikov served as one of Bokov's tselovalniks in 1700-1701, assistant to Oskolkov in 1703, and finally director in 1714-1719.[85]

The caravan heads handled minor diplomatic business for Moscow, such as negotiations concerning the size of the caravans and the routes to be followed between Siberia and Peking; they also carried diplomatic correspondence between Moscow and Peking. Ivan Savateev carried three letters from the Li-fan yuan to Andre Vinius, director of the Ambassadorial Department in Moscow.[86] The first concerned fugitives, and the second, replying to a letter from Vinius to Songgotu requesting passage for Savateev's caravan, discussed the regulation of official correspondence. In effect, it restated provisions contained in the Manchu regulations of 1693 governing correspondence and insisted that Russian official letters not be addressed to Songgotu. The third letter concerned the opening of new caravan routes between Siberia and Peking. The Nerchinsk-Manchuria-Peking route had been officially recognized at a time when political conditions made a Central Asian route impossible. By the time of Savateev's first caravan, however, a Central Asian modus vivendi had developed because of K'anghsi's victories over the Jungars, and it became possible to consider opening an alternative and shorter route to Peking from Selenginsk through Mongolia. The Li-fan yuan's letter explained that it had permitted Savateev to return to Siberia through Kalgan, the Orkhon River, and Selenginsk, at his own request.

Peking's willingness to consider opening new trade routes was conditioned by two circumstances: the problem of controlling the size of the caravan and the court's desire to remove the center of "barbarian control" from Peking. The caravans were generally sizable undertakings. Savateev's caravan, for instance, included no fewer than 400 people by the time it arrived at the Nun-chiang. It was so large that its departure from Nerchinsk took place in several stages between June 28 and July 11, 1703.[87] Thereafter, the Li-fan yuan informed Vinius, all caravans taking the Mongolian route were to be stopped by the Tushetu-khan, who would inform Peking of the number of men in the caravan before it was allowed to proceed.[88] Peking eventually raised to 220 the statutory number of Russians permitted to join the caravans inside China. This use of the Tushetu-khan also transferred the responsibility for "barbarian control" to one of Peking's Mongol vassals. Inasmuch as the new route required only seventy travel days from the Siberian frontier to Peking, it was much preferable to the Nerchinsk route and eventually became the sole authorized route between Siberia and the Chinese capital.[89]

Each caravan was affected by the problem of competition, which also adversely influenced the Peking market. Competition developed from the contradiction inherent in the state monopoly of the China trade, namely, that the state had to employ members of the private merchant community as its monopoly caravan agents. Competition with the state was compounded of four elements: the method of payment of the caravan officials, illegal participation of private merchants in the state caravans, corruption of Siberian customs officials, and other caravans.

In lieu of salary, the various caravan officials, including the kupchina, were allowed to carry certain amounts of fur for sale on the Peking market. Theoretically they were not allowed to sell their furs until the completion of the state's business, but it is apparent that these privately owned furs were a factor of great importance on a market already beginning to be surfeited with Russian goods. Savateev's first caravan, for instance, carried 15,500 rubles' worth of such private goods. It was a small sum compared with the total value of the caravan's cargo (223,319 rubles), but the sale of privately owned goods at the beginning of the commercial process took the edge off demand and depressed prices, to the disadvantage of the state's trade. In 1706 the state moved against competition from private merchants not in its employ by decreeing the death penalty for transgressions of the monopoly,[90] but since the caravans were individual government units under the kupchina's authority, he could, and often did, permit the introduction of private merchants and private capital into his enterprise.

Competition from the caravan agents themselves continued to be a problem even after the state tried to eliminate private capital. Oskolov, leading his second caravan to China in 1714, received sables in payment of his salary, which placed him in a position to compete with the very state goods he was to trade on the Peking market.[91] Gusyatnikov, who led the caravan of 1716-1717, was allowed to take into China "for his food" duty-free goods in the amount of 3,500 rubles. His tselovalniks were permitted to bring 2,000 rubles' worth of goods into Siberia from Russia, but they could take only 1,000 rubles' worth through Selenginsk to Peking, which represented an attempt to force at least the tselovalniks to make their private profits in Siberia rather than at Peking. A similar system was employed in the collection of duties on Chinese goods personally imported by the staff of a returning caravan. Gusyatnikov could import, duty-free, 3,500 rubles' worth of goods, with a 10 percent duty collected on anything beyond that amount. Tselovalniks were allowed 1,000 rubles' worth under the same conditions.[92] However, the agents of private merchants obtained positions as tselovalniks, soldiers, and workers with the caravans, and profits were sufficient to allow payment of duties without harm to private commerce. In 1717, for instance, Prince Gagarin, the governor general of Siberia, ordered the Irkutsk customs head to collect duties on all private merchandise in Gusyatnikov's caravan, above the amount that he and his tselovalniks were legally allowed to import and export duty-free.[93] Gusyatnikov himself paid duties on 20,000 rubles' worth of goods, and other members of his staff exported to China about 23,630 rubles' worth of goods above their legal limit. The entire caravan exported approximately 65,000 rubles' worth of goods in addition to its duty-free privileges, constituting about 40 percent of the caravan's total value. The state had lost its battle to control competition.

Adverse market conditions developed in Peking itself as a direct consequence of both the state's inability to enforce its monopoly inside Siberia and the flow of goods into Peking from non-Russian sources. Third parties like the Bukharans were free to trade with Peking, and Russian goods could reach the capital through the comparatively unrestricted market at Urga, where Russian and Chinese merchants met in fairly free circumstances. As Russian goods glutted the Peking market, the price level declined. The situation reached a crisis in the Gusyatnikov caravan of 1717, which was in Peking from November 11, 1716, to August 26, 1717. This unusually long period was occasioned by the declining market and severe competition. En route to Peking, Gusyatnikov had encountered a caravan led by one Nadein, who was either a Bukharan or an agent of a Siberian merchant, or both. Their meeting took place inside the Manchu frontiers, so that Gusyatnikov lacked authority to prevent Nadein's journey to Peking. As a consequence, the caravans engaged in a price war at the Manchu capital.[94]

The decline of the Peking market was described in a series of summaries of market conditions drawn up by Ides in 1695, Savateev in 1699, and others, including Gusyatnikov.[95] In the twenty years between 1698 and 1717 the selling price for Russian merchandise on the Peking market fell from 5 to 60 percent, depending on the commodity, while Chinese goods remained at approximately the same price level. Furthermore, the Chinese demand for specific Russian products, such as squirrels, ermines, and various kinds of fox, sable, and lynx, remained fairly constant during the two decades. This factor, combined with limitations imposed by nature, prevented the Russian merchants from diversifying their exports and led to oversupply. The critical market conditions resulting from Gusyatnikov's caravan were further exacerbated by the arrival at the frontier of a small private caravan, evidently under Prince Gagarin's personal protection but without Moscow's permission, led by Vasily Ifin, who carried a letter from Gagarin to the Li-fan yuan. Ifin's arrival at the frontier so shortly after Gusyatnikov forced the Li-fan yuan to take action to clarify market conditions. It wrote the governor general of Siberia that because of the glut of Russian furs in Peking, Chinese merchants had gone into debt to the Russians, and arguments had ensued. It also informed Gusyatnikov that if he could find no cash purchasers for his goods, he would have to take them back to Siberia.[96]

The Li-fan yuan also made specific proposals to the governor general to alleviate the situation. Official caravans should be spaced at greater intervals than in the past to allow time for the absorption of goods already available on the market. The Manchu authorities would henceforth receive only the regular state caravans along the new route, at Kalgan and at Peking as before. Any other caravans or individuals "who come with letters or for the conduct of minor commerce" would have to go to Nerchinsk and take the Manchurian route through the town of Tsitsikhar. The new regulations would have the effect of lightening the burden of the frontier inhabitants responsible for supplying forage and horses for the Russians on their way to Peking. The letter containing these proposals was sent to the Tushetu-khan, who was to find Ifin on the frontier, where he was trading, and ask him to transmit it to Governor General Gagarin.[97] Without waiting for a Russian reply, the Manchus immediately proceeded to put the new regulations into effect, and when Prince Cherkasky, who replaced Gagarin as governor general of Siberia, requested permission for the admission of a new caravan under the direction of Fedor Istopnikov in 1719, he was refused.

The Moscow market also reflected the declining profitability of the caravan trade. There was a steady and marked rise in trade profits up through Khudyakov's first caravan in 1708. Savateev's profits in 1710, however, were considerably below Khudyakov's. Just as a glut of Russian goods developed on the Peking market, so too by the time of Khudyakov's second caravan in 1709 the Russian treasury began having difficulties disposing of the Chinese goods brought back from Peking. As early as May 1709 certain goods such as tobacco were removed from the list of reserved retail commodities, and by 1710 special measures were required to dispose of other Chinese products. Unable to sell them in Moscow, even on a free and open market, because of the small Russian demand for the expensive luxury goods in which the caravans specialized, the state took drastic measures, permitting their re-export to the Baltic provinces and other areas.[98]

Within twenty years of the establishment of the state monopoly on the China trade, therefore, the caravan system had spent itself and ceased to return a profit. The Manchus also began to find the caravan trade something of a burden. Yet the problem of developing a viable system of intercourse based on commerce, which would not generate its own destruction, remained a vital issue for both empires. The Istopnikov caravan provided the context within which the reorganization of the Sino-Russian treaty system could begin.

The Institutions of the Treaty System

The decay of the commercial aspects of the Sino-Russian relationship dealt a severe blow to the Nerchinsk treaty system but did not destroy it completely. The five institutions that made up the treaty system after 1689, none of which were mentioned in the treaty itself, survived the Russo-Manchu commercial and political crises of the second and third decades of the eighteenth century to provide continuity and become an integral part of the new arrangements that emerged from the Kyakhta conference in 1727. They can be divided into two groups, according to their function within the institutional complex. The first group included the caravan trade and the O-lo-ssu nan kuan or Russian South Hostel (the inn in Peking where Russians lodged). These were institutions of contact: they were vehicles for commercial and political confrontation. The second group consisted of the Russian and Chinese experts, the O-lo-ssu pei kuan or Russian North Hostel (the Russian church in Peking), and the O-lo-ssu wen kuan or Russian language school.[99] These were catalytic institutions: they facilitated contact and were the institutional reaction of each side to its own requirements. As the Russians needed an unofficial corps of China experts to treat with Peking, so the Manchus needed specialists in Russian affairs. Men like Songgotu and Mala were considered "barbarian experts." But the growth of contact required even greater specialization, so that the Ch'ing court established the O-lo-ssu wen kuan to train Peking's first "Kremlinologists." Finally, the presence during a religious age of Russian *émigrés* in Peking required a religious institution where they could worship, and the caravan staffs worshipped there too.

The lack of any cohesive organizational structure under one directorate for all the Russian caravans to Peking—even their accounting was done individually—was counterbalanced to some extent by the development of the group of men who through participation in the caravan trade became Russia's earliest "old China hands" or amateur China specialists. Savateev, Oskolkov, and Khudyakov, each of whom averaged three trips to Peking, acquired experience and knowledge not dissimilar to that of the English and American "old China hands" in the nineteenth century. The most outstanding member of this group was Lorents Lange, a Swedish engineer in the service of the Russian government, who eventually became the first Russian consul in Peking. Although it is not clear how he came to Russia and entered the tsar's service (he may have been a prisoner captured in the Swedish wars), his career in China is well documented.

Lange was a literate man with a fine eye for description and detail; he recorded what he saw in diaries, most of which were published in the course of the eighteenth century.[100]

Lange made his first trip to Peking in the company of Thomas Carwin, an English physician at the Russian court.[101] About the end of August 1713 Tulishen, who was the Manchu envoy to Ayuki, the Torgut khan on the Volga, transmitted to Gagarin, the governor general of Siberia, a request from K'ang-hsi for the visit of a physician. In August 1715 the court at St. Petersburg responded by sending Carwin to Peking. One can only surmise why Lange was appointed to accompany him. If Carwin was to go to Peking in the company of Gusyatnikov's caravan, which had already left for China, he would have had to catch up with it before it crossed the frontier, and Lange may have gone along as an aide. Or, since Lange was an engineer and Peter the Great was anxious to obtain a stove made of Chinese porcelain, he may have taken advantage of Carwin's journey to send Lange to Peking to purchase one. At any rate, upon his return Lange impressed Peter to such an extent that he was appointed the tsar's commercial agent inside China.

Lange and Carwin left St. Petersburg on August 18, 1715, and toward the end of the following year arrived at Peking, where they had more than one audience with the emperor. During the first audience Carwin administered to the emperor's needs by taking his pulse and declaring him to be in perfect health. The problem of the stove was a bit more difficult, but eventually, through the intercession of a French priest, K'ang-hsi promised to have one made according to Peter's specifications and sent on to Petersburg. Lange was particularly impressed by K'ang-hsi who, he said, had "great Strength, of Body as well as Mind. He abstained from Wine, Women and Sloth, and though according to the national Custom he took many Wives, yet he was hardly ever observed to go among them in the Day time."[102] Lange and the other China experts provided some sense of continuity, because outgoing caravans often met returning caravans somewhere en route in Siberia, and these men could exchange the latest information and gossip from Moscow and Peking.

At Peking Sino-Russian contact took place in an atmosphere of greater institutional continuity than in Moscow or St. Petersburg because of the existence of the O-lo-ssu nan kuan, the O-lo-ssu pei kuan, and the O-lo-ssu wen kuan. The O-lo-ssu nan kuan or Russian South Hostel was located on the Tung chiao-min hsiang in the southeastern section of Peking's Tartar city.[103] The building in which it was located was originally called the Hui-t'ung kuan and belonged to the Board of Rites, which used it to lodge tribute bearers. The Hui-t'ung kuan, built in 1441 during the Ming dynasty, was composed of two parts: the Nan Hui-t'ang, located in Tung Chiang-mi hsiang, and the Pei Hui-t'ung kuan, located on Ch'eng-ch'ing-fang-ta-chieh. Both served the same tributary purpose. After the Manchu conquest, however, the Pei Hui-t'ung kuan became the hostel for visiting Mongol and Manchu dignitaries, whereas the Nan hui-t'ung kuan was used for other tributary envoys.[104] These envoys generally brought merchandise for trading on the Peking market, and after the completion of official ceremonies they were allowed to conduct commerce on the Hui-t'ung kuan's grounds for a specified number of days.[105] The Hui-t'ung kuan became the lodging for all Russian diplomatic and commercial caravans in Peking, and since they were in the capital more often than the representatives of any other non-Asian nationality, it became known as the O-lo-ssu kuan or Russian Hostel sometime in the last years of the seventeenth century. The appellation was first officially used in 1693, at the time of Ides' mission, when K'ang-hsi promulgated the regulations governing Sino-Russian trade, according to which all Russian caravans were to be lodged there. It continued in use for other nationalities when the Russians were not in Peking until about 1727, when it was assigned to the Russians' exclusive use.[106] The O-lo-ssu kuan was a vast building, containing 387 rooms at the time it was built in the Ming dynasty.[107] According to one description, in 1720 it contained three courts and by the next year had already begun to fall into decay from great age.[108] It became, together with its compound, the site for the erection of a Russian Orthodox Church, as stipulated in the Treaty of 1727, on which construction was begun by the end of the year.[109]

With the arrival of a Russian caravan in the environs of Peking, the emperor customarily appointed a high-ranking court officer to the position of Tsung-li O-lo-ssu shih-wu or Superintendent of Russian Affairs, who was charged with the caravan's affairs for the duration of its sojourn at the capital. However, his general responsibilities were never specifically defined, and the O-lo-ssu kuan was actually directed by a *chien-tu* or superintendent, appointed by the Li-fan yuan to supervise its affairs and, therefore, the affairs of the Russian residents. The chien-tu became the most important intermediary between the Russian caravans and Manchu officialdom, and all communications between the two passed through his office. He did not live in the hostel but visited it frequently. The Li-fan yuan also appointed two porters to guard the hostel's entrance and keep out undesirable visitors. The court itself appointed a *yü-shih* or censor to live inside the hostel to guard against espionage by the Russians and, perhaps, to spy on the other Manchu officials working there. The caravan was protected by 260 officers and soldiers stationed inside its walls, who accompanied the Russians when they went abroad.[110]

The O-lo-ssu pei kuan or Russian North Hostel was the first Russian Orthodox church in Peking and was located in the northeastern extremity of the Tartar city. It was built to serve the Albazinians who had emigrated to Peking after the first siege of the Amur settlement. These Albazinians were organized into a Russian company under the Manchu Bordered Yellow Banner, a division of the Manchu forces, and allotted residences in the northeastern corner of Peking where the Bordered Yellow Bannermen lived. K'ang-hsi treated the Russian bannermen generously and granted them, in addition to government housing, annual pensions and permission to follow their own religion.[111] Because the Treaty of Nerchinsk stipulated that fugitives should remain where they were when the treaty was signed, the Albazinians remained in Peking.

Maksim Leontev, the priest who founded the church, was himself an Albazinian, captured by the Manchus in 1685. Although it is impossible to determine when the church was constructed, it was consecrated in 1690 or 1692 and named after St. Nikolay or the Trinity. Sometime in the eighteenth century it was renamed the Church of the Assumption. In its own neighborhood in Peking, however, it was called the Lo-ch'a miao or Russian Temple. The priest was under the jurisdiction of the metropolitan of Tobolsk, who sent new priests to Peking as needed. For instance, a deacon, Lavrenty Ivanov, was sent from Tobolsk to Peking in 1696, and in 1712 Khudyakov requested permission from Peking to bring some priests to assist the lone and aging Mi-ti-li (Dmitry?), a curator who had served the church from at least 1696. K'ang-hsi agreed, and Tulishen, returning to Peking from the Volga in 1715, brought in his train a staff consisting of the archimandrite, a monk, a deacon, and seven other priests. Hilarion Lezhaysky, the archimandrite, died in 1719, and the Russian government appointed Inokenty Kulchitsky to replace him; but when the Istopnikov caravan, in whose train Kulchitsky was to travel to Peking, was refused entry into the Manchu Empire in 1722, Kulchitsky, too, was unable to proceed.[112]

The exact date of the establishment of the O-lo-ssu wen kuan or Russian Language School is unknown, but indirect evidence suggests that it was sometime in K'ang-hsi's reign. In 1670, when Milovanov visited Peking, no one at court read Russian, but in 1693 the Nei-ko or Grand Secretariat had Ides' letters translated from the Russian for the emperor. Furthermore, Ides brought back to Russia in 1695 a long folio of Chinese paper sealed in an envelope with the imperial vermilion seal and containing a very poor Russian translation of another letter he carried, written in Latin. By 1694, therefore, the Manchu court either provided its own translators or used Russian residents in Peking for that purpose. The Russian traveler Timkowsky, who visited Peking in 1820, believed that the school had been established immediately after 1689.[113]

The school was located on the west side of Pei-ch'ih chieh, just outside the Tung-hua-men, the eastern gate to the Forbidden City, and was administered jointly by the Nei-ko and the Li-fan yuan. It represented both bodies' interests: the Nei-ko was charged with the translation of official documents from foreign countries, and the Li-fan yuan was responsible for Russian affairs. Each organization appointed one *t'i-t'iao,* or proctor, from its own staff. The Nei-ko t'i-t'iao had charge of academic studies, while the Li-fan yuan t'i-t'iao administered the school. Two *chu-chiao,* or professors, and two *fu-chiao-hsi,* or assistant professors, made up the instructing staff. In the school's early days the instructors were chosen from among the Russians in the Manchu banner forces, but as the Albazinians became more assimilated, Russian priests and even Manchu students were appointed. The Russians received considerable financial remuneration.[114]

Students for the school were chosen exclusively from among the eight Manchu banners, and there were only twenty-four in all classes at any given time.[115] The students took monthly, quarterly, and annual examinations, but the quintennial examination was by far the most important. The students were given official ranks according to their examination results, and these ranks led to positions in the bureaucracy, either at the Li-fan yuan or on the frontier, where a knowledge of Russian was needed.[116] The students in the school received stipends of three taels a month, but those who succeeded to official ranks through their examinations received fixed salaries of between thirty-two and forty taels a year.[117] Although the school never produced fine scholars and the level of language instruction fell sharply and decisively to incompetence by the beginning of the nineteenth century, it did for a while provide trained officials to serve Peking's relations with Russia.

Chapter VII **Trade and Diplomacy: The Balance Upset**

The decline of the caravan trade weakened the web of economic ties in which the Manchus had sought to involve Russia and upset the balance between economic and political interests by which K'ang-hsi had hoped to neutralize Russia in Central Asian politics. Peter the Great's revived interest in Central Asian affairs toward the end of his reign grew out of this decline of Sino-Russian commerce and constituted a direct attack on the viability of the Nerchinsk treaty system. Consequently, between 1718 and 1728 the Ch'ing court again sought the element of stability in its relations with Russia that had eluded it after Nerchinsk. A renewed Jungar threat and the possibility of a Russian-Central Asian *rapprochement* and anti-Manchu alliance formed the background to this decade of negotiations, ending in the complete reform of the treaty system, the opening of a vastly increased market for Russian goods inside the Ch'ing empire, and the stabilization of Sino-Russian interests and institutions. The revised treaty system endured, virtually unchanged, for more than 130 years.

Russia, the Manchus, and the Jungars

Galdan's failure to make contact with Golovin in February 1690 deprived him of an important ally and prevented the expansion of his offensive potential. It did not, however, hamper his activities.

Early in 1690 Galdan invaded Outer Mongolia (Khalkha) and, meeting no resistance, spent the summer on the lower Kerulun River. Marching toward Peking at the end of the summer, he was defeated by a Ch'ing army at the battle of Ulan-butung, but he gained time by initiating negotiations and then fled northward unpursued. Although his defeat at Ulan-butun was indecisive, it was sufficient to make the Khalkha Mongols acknowledge Manchu suzerainty. K'ang-hsi received the homage of all the important Khalkha leaders at Dolonor in 1691; thereafter they remained loyal to the Ch'ing throne.[1]

Upon his return to his headquarters at Khobdo, Galdan found a new power rising in Jungaria, his nephew Tsewang Araptan (1643-1727).[2] However, he invaded the Khalkha lands again in 1694, probably as a result of severe famines in his own territories. K'ang-hsi now decided to eliminate Galdan altogether as a threat to Manchu security. While Sabsu's forces guarded Mongolia's eastern frontiers, the emperor personally led eighty thousand men in three armies to the north. Galdan tried vainly to avoid battle, but his forces were crushed at Jao Modo on June 12, 1696. Some of the Jungar survivors joined Tsewang Araptan, but Galdan, with about one thousand men and three thousand women and children, wandered aimlessly in the Altai Mountains. K'ang-hsi led a second expedition against him in the spring of 1697. Unable to escape, Galdan fell ill on May 3, 1697, and died the same day.

Galdan's disappearance did not solve the Manchus' Jungar problem. Tsewang Araptan, who inherited both his uncle's title, Kontaisha, and his power, soon extended Jungar hegemony over parts of Siberia, western Mongolia, and the whole of eastern Turkestan, with the exception of Hami. His conquests in Tibet brought him into direct conflict with the Manchus, who could not allow the seat of Lamaism to fall into hostile hands. Although Peking had recovered most of Tibet by 1720, it was unable to overcome completely Tsewang Araptan's flourishing power. Brought into conflict with the Russians through his expansion to the west and north, Tsewang Araptan's forces repulsed Russian attempts to penetrate Jungaria in 1715, and by 1720 the Jungars and Russians had arrived at a modus vivendi.

After Tsewang Araptan's death in 1727, his successor, Galdan

Tseren, successfully campaigned against the Manchus, completely routing a Manchu army under Furdan in 1731.[3] But unable to bring his anti-Manchu wars to a decisive and favorable conclusion, Galdan Tseren signed a treaty with the Manchu Ch'ien-lung emperor designating the Altai Mountains as the boundary between Jungaria and the Ch'ing empire. Civil war among his successors at last allowed the Manchus under Ch'ien-lung to settle their Jungarian problem, and by 1757 Peking had firmly established its dominion over all Jungaria. The final Manchu victory in eastern Turkestan was greatly facilitated by the Kyakhta treaty, which ended Russia's dalliance with the Jungars.

Commerce was the most important element in the development of Russo-Jungar relations. The Bukharans, who ranged far and wide along the caravan routes and were Inner Asia's chief merchants and the major suppliers of Chinese goods to western Siberia before 1689, were supporting Galdan economically and politically by 1679. Consequently, although the Russians after Nerchinsk were not about to enter into an alliance with Galdan, neither were they prepared to turn their backs on the Bukharans' Jungar patrons. In the next decade Moscow continued to grant important commercial privileges to the Bukharans in Siberia, which indicated an attitude of passive benevolence toward the Jungars.[4] Galdan's death did not change Russian policy in Central Asia, and Bukharans resident in Siberia as farmers or as merchants at Tobolsk received the same treatment as Russians of a similar social status.[5] By the end of 1698, however, Russia had extended privileges to the Bukharans above and beyond those accorded Russian merchants, apparently in an effort to curry favor with Tsewang Araptan. For instance, Bukharans paid only a 1/20 duty on the value of their business transactions, whereas Russian merchants continued to pay 1/10. Furthermore, merchants going to Siberia specifically in the kontaisha's name were freed from all customs payments.[6] In June 1699 a "gentleman of some standing" went to Lake Yamysh to negotiate with the Jungars for laborers and animals to transport salt to Tobolsk; he was also instructed to construct forts for the protection and regulation of the official slave traffic.[7]

Over the next fifteen years the Russo-Jungar commercial modus vivendi was endangered by Tsewang Araptan's expansion to the north and west. On June 20, 1713, the governor general of Siberia ordered Ivan Dmitriev Cheredov, a cossack from Tara, to deliver a letter to Tsewang Araptan's headquarters enumerating Russian grievances and complaints: the Jungars had pillaged the populations of several Russian settlements, destroyed other settlements, and plundered and assassinated the agent of an important merchant.[8] Tsewang Araptan finally received Cheredov in audience twice and presented the emissary with his own bill of complaints against the Russians: they had invaded and settled Jungarian territory and plundered his subjects. He would return the plundered merchandise but was inclined to levy a 10 percent duty on it. Having achieved little, Cheredov returned to Siberia in October 1714 accompanied by a Bukharan caravan and two Jungar envoys carrying a letter to Moscow. In accordance with the spirit of the Nerchinsk agreements, however, the Jungar envoys were not admitted into European Russia.

Peter's decision to undertake a military expedition in territory claimed by the Jungars and to open a mining enterprise there further complicated the Central Asian picture. From 1712 on Gagarin had heard reports of gold in Turkestan, and he claimed to have seen gold powder circulating among the Tobolsk Bukharans, who said that it came from the region of "Erket." Since this name was unknown to the Russians, they required further information. In 1713 Gagarin dispatched Grigory Truchnikov, a Tobolsk boyar, to the villages "Selim and Daba," situated to the southeast and reported to be gold-mining centers. On May 22, 1714, Peter, anxious to investigate further, ordered a Lieutenant Colonel Bukhholts to take fifteen hundred men from Tobolsk, as well as engineers and mining experts from among Swedish prisoners of war in Siberia, and go directly to Lake Yamysh to construct a military outpost. Bukhholts wintered on Lake Yamysh and in the spring of 1715 reached "Irket" or "Erket", looking for the fabled gold-bearing sands.[9]

Peter now considered a radical shift in Russian policy toward the Manchus and the Jungars in favor of the latter. In 1715 he ordered Gagarin to search for mines at Lake Zaisan on the upper Irtysh and to construct settlements in that region. If Tsewang Araptan would not oppose this undertaking, Peter was prepared to conclude an offensive alliance with the Jungars; it was obvious that the Manchus were the only possible object of such an alliance. At first the tsar considered supporting his proposal with a threat to conclude an anti-Jungar alliance with Ayuki, the Torgut khan on the Volga, and other nomadic leaders if Tsewang Araptan refused, but this threat was suppressed in the final draft sent to the kontaisha.[10] Events quickly outstripped the time needed for communications, however, when the Jungars destroyed their opportunity for a Russian alliance by going over to the offensive.

Bukhholts returned to Tobolsk in November 1714 and in July 1715 took 3000 men as well as 1500 soldiers back to the Irtysh. As soon as he arrived at Lake Yamysh on October 1, he began the construction of a military fort there, but the work was not finished until the end of April 1716. Fearing the growth of Russian strength in the area, Cheren Donduk, one of Tsewang Araptan's generals, wrote a threatening letter to Bukhholts in February 1716, following it with an attack in which the Russians, outnumbered, were routed and finally compelled to retreat down the Irtysh after destroying the Yamysh fort. Bukhholts constructed a new base, the present city of Omsk, below the first fort and left it in the command of a subordinate on December 22, 1716. He himself returned to Tobolsk on December 31, and by September 2 of the next year he had reached St. Petersburg to explain his expedition's disastrous conclusion. Gagarin sent the tsar's proposal for an alliance to the kontaisha in March 1717, after the destruction of the expedition it was meant to support. A further collision of interests was averted by a Manchu attack on Hami, which turned Tsewang Araptan's attention from the Yamysh. Gagarin, hoping to regain Russia's position there, was preparing a second expedition when the tsar, irritated by the turn of events, relieved him of his duties and recalled him to St. Petersburg. There, together with Bukhholts, he was interrogated on January 22 and again on February 8, 1719.[11]

Gagarin and Bukhholts gave information at St. Petersburg that only intensified the mystery surrounding the origin of the gold they had seen at Tobolsk and underscored the lack of precise knowledge of the area in question. Peter decided to make a more intensive examination of the situation and in January 1719 appointed Ivan Mikhailovich Likharev, a major of the guard, to make an on-the-spot investigation. Likharev left Tobolsk on May 8, 1720, with two doctors, two students of geography from the Academy of Sciences, and enough silver and tobacco to pay the mission's expenses.[12] He returned there in the middle of October, after engaging the Jungars and establishing the settlement of Ust-Kamenogorsk, although he did not succeed in crossing Lake Yamysh.

By September 1720 Tsewang Araptan's position was precarious: he had been defeated in Tibet and a Manchu embassy demanded his acknowledgement of Ch'ing suzerainty. Although he had thwarted the Russian attempt to advance into his territory, he feared an alliance of his enemies, and thus he initiated a move to try to set them against each other. On June 28, 1719, after his appointment but before his departure from Tobolsk, Likharev had dispatched a messenger to Tsewang Araptan with a bill of complaints and a suggestion that the kontaisha submit to Russian suzerainty—evidently a revival in modified form of Peter's proposal for an offensive alliance. The messenger was arrested and detained for a full year, but when the Jungar position worsened, the kontaisha released him and received him in audience in November 1720.[13] Tsewang Araptan explained to the messenger that he feared a Sino-Torgut anti-Jungar alliance, and he reproached the Russians for allowing K'ang-hsi's envoy, Tulishen, to pass through Russia on his way to meet the Torgut khan, Ayuki, on the Volga. He also protested Russian forced baptism of the Lamaist Torguts. From this position of righteous indignation he refused to accede to Russia's demand for submission, but neither did he close the door on the possibility. Instead, he conditioned his submission in such impossible terms that, while there was little danger of meeting them, there was still a real possibility of arranging an alliance: "As his Majesty the Tsar has conferred the Mungats on the Khan Ayuki, let him confer on me the Mongols who have risen against me, and then we will tell where the gold is to be found." In short, he made an outrageous demand for control of large parts of Siberia's population, but at the same time he reminded Peter that Jungaria might be rich in gold, which could be had for a price.

The kontaisha then sent an ambassador to Russia to defend Jungar interests and prevent Russia from entering an alliance against him. Arriving at St. Petersburg on September 6, 1721, the ambassador was immediately received by the tsar, and the next day at the College of Foreign Affairs he offered the Russians free passage for prospectors in exchange for a defensive alliance against the Manchus. Peter evidently accepted this proposal, because two months later the ambassador left St. Petersburg accompanied by a special messenger, Captain of Artillery Ivan Unkovsky, who was charged to receive Tsewang Araptan's formal act of submission.[14] Peter was apparently prepared to pursue a course of action leading to a Jungar alliance at the expense of the declining Peking trade. The Unkovsky mission represented the high point in Russo-Jungar relations and posed a great danger to the Manchus.

There is a remarkable contemporaneity in Unkovsky's instructions, dated December 31, 1721, in that they envisaged a Russo-Jungar mutual assistance and economic aid treaty. This policy represented the most extreme position taken by Russia toward the Manchu Empire since the military conflict along the Amur. Moreover, it was the result of conscious decisions in St. Petersburg, whereas the Amur conflict and its results had derived from historical chance. Unkovsky was to promise the kontaisha a Russian *démarche* against Peking in return for his submission and the right to exploit Jungaria's gold resources. St. Petersburg was prepared, if necessary, to make a military demonstration against the Manchus if Tsewang Araptan would sign a treaty of submission. Unkovsky was to use gifts as a means of creating an amenable atmosphere at the court. The tsar also sent mining experts with Unkovsky, who was to tell the kontaisha that Russian exploitation of his natural resources would benefit him and his people as well as the Russians: he would receive a percentage of the enterprise's profits, while his subjects would receive employment as workers and miners. Unkovsky was also instructed to obtain the cession of some territory for the construction of a line of forts, to bring Siberia into direct communication with advance Russian outposts in Jungaria and protect the mining enterprise. The Russian envoy left Moscow on February 25, 1722, arriving at the kontaisha's encampment in November; he returned to Tobolsk over a year later, on January 23, 1724, and reached Moscow in April of that same year.[15]

Peter's policy changes came too late to achieve positive results. K'ang-hsi's death on December 20, 1722, and the accession of the new emperor, Yung-cheng, provided the Manchus with an opportunity to make a diplomatic countermove against the Russians: an embassy was dispatched to the kontaisha to offer peace in the name of the new emperor. The kontaisha no longer felt that submission to St. Petersburg was an immediate condition for his survival. His advisors were also deeply divided over the question of submission to the tsar; Unkovsky later reported to the College of Foreign Affairs at St. Petersburg that the Jungar court was racked by violent discussions of this issue. Tsewang Araptan's wife, the daughter of Ayuki, supported a pro-Russian policy, but his son and successor, Galdan Tseren, and the general who had defeated Bukhholts, Cheren Donduk, stoutly opposed a Russian connection.[16] Without the immediate necessity to make a decision, and with his own court seriously divided, Tsewang Araptan avoided a final commitment. Unkovsky returned to Russia with indecisive results: an exchange of prisoners was arranged, and vague promises of a protectorate were exchanged for even vaguer promises of future submission. The kontaisha trod a narrow path between Peking and St. Petersburg, acceding in general terms to each but conceding nothing specific to either.

Peking's well-timed peace proposals prevented for the time being the development of a Russo-Jungar alliance but did not remove the threat. The Manchus needed a more long-range accommodation with St. Petersburg to free their hands in Central Asia. The Ch'ing court therefore proceeded to exert such pressures on the Russian position in Peking that St. Petersburg itself requested new Russo-Manchu negotiations. In the meantime, however, the most important dramatis personae in the situation were disappearing from the scene: K'ang-hsi died in 1722, Ayuki in 1724, and Peter at the beginning of 1725. Tsewang Araptan died in 1727, just as the Manchus were completing the process of neutralizing Russia in Inner Asia in order to destroy the Jungars.

The Beginnings of Diplomacy

Although the Nerchinsk treaty system operated too unsatisfactorily to prevent a revival of Russian interest in Central Asian politics, the continued existence of the caravan trade, despite its declining profits, gave the Manchus considerable leverage in St. Petersburg. The Ch'ing strategy was aimed at bringing Russia to the point where she would consider negotiations essential to the continued operation of the caravan system; it consisted of decreasing commercial contact and thereby reducing the expectation of a revival of the trade and of state profits. The maneuver was effected by three letters written by the Li-fan yuan to the governor general of Siberia. The first, dated August 27, 1717, and delivered through Gusyatnikov, suggested that because the latter's caravan had traded unsuccessfully at Peking, several years should be allowed to elapse before another caravan was dispatched. Moreover, the next caravan should be sent only to the frontier regions outside the Great Wall, presumably to Urga, rather than to Peking. The arrival of Ifin's caravan at the frontier provided Peking with the opportunity to back up its expressed intentions with action, and Ifin was not permitted to enter the empire. This development was explained in a second letter to Gagarin.

The Istopnikov caravan was the occasion for the third and final letter in the series. Little is known about this caravan, but Prince Cherkasky, Gagarin's successor as governor general of Siberia, wrote Moscow in July 1718 that in compliance with the tsar's edict Fedor Stepanovich Istopnikov had been sent as commissar of a trade caravan to China, accompanied by the tselovalnik Petr Lobachkov, and "with them were sent some goods and five men, working people." Istopnikov also carried a letter of recommendation to the Manchu authorities, signed by Stepan Rakitin, voevoda of Irkutsk.[17]

The Li-fan yuan responded to Rakitin's recommendation in a letter dated June 3, 1719, and addressed to Gagarin because Peking had not yet been informed of his removal. This letter was the clearest definition of Manchu policy to date. The Li-fan yuan announced that trade with Russia was both unnecessary and unprofitable and was therefore to be prohibited. Manchu trappers in the north and European ships at Canton adequately supplied Peking's needs for fur pelts and foreign goods. Russian prices were too high, and Russian merchants sold inferior pelts to the imperial court, involved Chinese merchants in debt, and misbehaved at the capital. The Li-fan yuan also gently reminded Siberia and St. Petersburg of the Central Asian problem: "Now in our state it is a time of war, so is it worthwhile for us for your Russians who come here for the purpose of trade always to tie up state funds in this fashion?" However, the door was not completely closed, for the Li-fan yuan issued a clarion call for negotiations by demanding that the Russians consult the tsar to determine "what belongs to great commerce . . . and when about that you will receive an answer, at that time we shall see what should be done."[18] Thus, although Istopnikov's caravan was not permitted to enter the Manchu Empire, Peking made it clear that its primary interest was not in the cessation of trade but in halting Russian activities in Central Asia. The letter was forwarded to St. Petersburg from Tobolsk on December 20, 1719.

Izmaylov's Embassy

Peter decided to enter into a new round of negotiations with Peking in the first part of 1719, at least two months before the Li-fan yuan wrote its third letter. He was deeply involved in the long struggles with Sweden that characterized his reign, and he had just become fully aware of the setback his Jungar policy had suffered in 1716. These two factors ruled out any immediate possibility of engaging in a Far Eastern military conflict, even assuming his government could solve the logistic problems that had made Albazin's defeat inevitable almost thirty-five years earlier. For both economic and political reasons Peter needed a modus vivendi with Peking.

Fearing total exclusion from the China market, Peter decided to lay a careful groundwork for the successful conclusion to the negotiations. Consequently, the tsar's gramota to K'ang-hsi, accrediting Lev Vasilevich Izmaylov as his personal envoy and dated March 20, 1719,[19] was written with a view to ensuring its reception in Peking. Aware from past experience of Manchu sensitivity about the use of titles in direct communications to the emperor, the gramota opened without the usual recitation of the tsar's titles or, indeed, any mention of the tsar at all. It was addressed simply: "To the Emperor of the Great Asiatic Nations, the most Absolute Monarch, the very Bogdy and Chinese Khan, Our friend, fond congratulations."[20] In the body of the gramota K'ang-hsi was most often referred to as "Your Khan's Majesty"; it concluded, "Your Majesty's good friend," and was signed by Peter's own hand, with the state seal affixed. The use of such a self-denying formula indicated the importance Peter attached to Izmaylov's mission.

Lev Vasilevich Izmaylov was born in 1686. On Peter's orders and as part of the tsar's program to Europeanize the Russian army, he had served in the Danish army, rising to the rank of captain by 1707. Upon his return to Russia he was named captain in the Preobrazhensky Guard regiment. In April 1710 he again went to Denmark, this time on a diplomatic mission. Although Izmaylov had no direct knowledge of China, his personal background included both the military and the diplomatic training important in carrying out missions to Peking.

The appointment of Lorents Lange as his first secretary compensated for Izmaylov's lack of experience in the Far East. Other members of his suite included a second secretary, a subofficer of the Guard Corps who was presumably in charge of the embassy's security, a Scottish doctor who styled himself John Bell of Antermony, two surveyors from the Academy of Sciences, a private secretary, an interpreter, and two gentlemen who were senior attendants, almost colleagues, of the envoy himself, as well as soldiers and domestic servants. Antony Platkovsky, a cleric assigned to the Orthodox Church in Peking, joined the embassy at Irkutsk, and Izmaylov hired three interpreters of Mongolian at Selenginsk. Nikolay Khristizy, a representative of the College of Commerce, was commerical counselor.[21]

The instructions issued to Izmaylov by the College of Foreign Affairs on June 4, 1719, put commerce in first place among those subjects recommended to the embassy's attention.[22] They envisaged a vast reform of the existing Sino-Russian commercial system along lines that were strikingly advanced for the age. Consisting of thirteen articles, Izmaylov's instructions dealt with three distinct topics: first, the journey to Peking and the intelligence information to be gathered en route and in the city itself; second, the posture to be adopted by the ambassador toward the Peking court, ensuring the creation of a cordial atmosphere for negotiations; third, the proposals to be put forth during the negotiations. Whereas peaceful negotiations were the embassy's prime objective, Peter also sought information that might be useful should the negotiations fail and the necessity for military action arise.

Three out of the thirteen articles of the instructions dealt with ceremonial procedures. They constituted an effort to avoid as many of the problems of the past as possible. Upon his arrival at Peking, Izmaylov was to note the location of the emperor's residence—evidently to forestall his being received elsewhere—and to demand an immediate audience, attended by every honor due the tsar's representative, but all the while stressing the tsar's desire to strengthen the formerly friendly relations and continue advantageous exchanges. Izmaylov was given great leeway in ceremonial affairs. He could present his credentials before the audience, stressing the use of "Majesty" in reference to the emperor rather than "Highness"; he was not required to deliver the tsar's letters into the emperor's own hands; and he was allowed to make a grandiloquent speech at the imperial audience, stressing Russia's friendship for Peking and requesting the appointment of councilors to meet with the embassy for negotiations. If ceremonial difficulties arose, he might cite Persian examples—since Persia, being Asian, was somehow thought to be relevant—but he was also permitted to request Jesuit intercession at court, in return for which he could promise free passage through Russia for Jesuit correspondence between Rome and Peking—a goal the Jesuits had long sought.

The instructions contained specific proposals for the reconstruction of the entire commercial system. St. Petersburg sought the total abolition of all restraints on commerce and the negotiation of a free trade agreement, including permission for Russian merchants to travel freely throughout China and to trade without hindrance at free market prices. The Russians were prepared to pay all their expenses in the Manchu Empire, requesting only that the emperor grant them complete freedom to purchase horses, camels, provisions, and forage at market prices. According to accepted diplomatic usage, envoys would continue to receive transport, forage, and maintenance. No time limits were to be placed on the length of a merchant's sojourns in China. Such a free trade system, Izmaylov was to emphasize, would profit the subjects and treasuries of both empires. He was empowered to sign a treaty to this effect, should the Manchus agree.

One of the most important paragraphs in the instructions proposed the establishment of a permanent Russian consulate or commercial agency at Peking to represent Russian interests and handle arguments and disagreements between the subjects of the two empires. The consul would have command over all Russian subjects in China, though the exact degree of his control was not specified in this particular set of instructions.

The last paragraph represented an attempt to meet unforeseen contingencies, particularly Manchu indictments of Russian policies in Central Asia. Izmaylov was instructed not only to refuse to discuss any subject not specifically mentioned in his instructions (he could agree to report such subjects to the tsar), but also to reject any Manchu complaints concerning the construction of Russian forts at Lake Yamysh and Lake Zaisan, on the grounds that those forts lay well within Russian territory, were necessary for the defense of Russian subjects from predatory attacks by Central Asian nomads, and were too distant from Peking to constitute a danger to the Manchus.

The College of Commerce issued special instructions to Izmaylov clarifying the commercial provisions contained in the College of Foreign Affairs instructions. In a decree dated May 8, 1719, Lorents Lange was designated first Russian consul in Peking if the Manchus acceded to Russian wishes. The College of Commerce gave Lange a special set of instructions outlining his duties and responsibilities in nineteen articles. He would appoint vice-consuls, open consulates with coats of arms above the doors, convene and chair a council of leading Russians in Peking, and handle commercial affairs. He was given full judicial authority, short of inflicting the death penalty, and could expel Russians from the Manchu Empire.[23]

Taken together, these three sets of instructions constituted St. Petersburg's proposals for the creation of a free trade zone, to include the total areas of the Russian and Manchu empires. At the same time that restrictions existed in Russia's bilateral trade arrangements with her western European partners, St. Petersburg proposed what amounted to the abolition of any commercial system whatsoever between Russia and China. The instructions also contained a proposal for the establishment of an adumbrated form of extraterritoriality, which in its classic sense would not come into existence until the Opium War 120 years later. These proposals assumed the institutional equality of the two empires and total reciprocity.

Armed with his instructions as well as with merchandise for trade and gifts for the Ch'ing court, Izmaylov and his embassy left St. Petersburg on July 16, 1719.[24] He arrived at Irkutsk on March 30, 1720, where he received a fourth set of instructions, dealing with the Istopnikov caravan. He was informed of the Li-fan yuan's third communication and told to press the matter of the caravan in Peking. He entered the capital on November 18, 1720, conducted thither from the frontier by Tulishen, the Ch'ing ambassador to the Torguts on the Volga, who had recently returned from Russia and was acting as a Russian expert for the Manchu court. His presence was a mark of honor and a sign of the Manchu intention to enter into serious negotiations with the tsar's representatives. The embassy remained in Peking for more than three months, from November 18, 1720, to March 2, 1721, during which time the emperor received Izmaylov a dozen times.[25] In the first audience K'ang-hsi personally received the tsar's letters and Izmaylov's credentials, and the Russian embassy performed the kowtow. "Great pains were taken to avoid this piece of homage, but without success," Bell reported. "The master of ceremonies stood by, and delivered his orders in the Tartar language, by pronouncing the words *morgu* and *boss*; the first meaning to bow, and the other to stand; two words which I cannot soon forget."[26]

Lavish entertainments, both private and state, audiences with the emperor, considerable freedom of the city and mingling with the local population—all characterized the embassy's sojourn in Peking. At every turn Manchu authorities tried to impress the embassy with the strength of their military and political institutions and the splendor of their adopted culture. K'ang-hsi also tried to impress Izmaylov with his peaceful intentions. At the envoy's second audience with the emperor on December 2, 1720, K'ang-hsi expressed his "concern" that Peter exposed himself too frequently to the dangers of ocean voyages—not a surprising remark to come from the monarch of a continentally oriented empire. He also spoke of maintaining peace between the two empires. Russia, after all, was a cold and distant land, he said, and if the Manchus tried to conquer it, their armies would freeze. China, however, was hot, and the emperor pointedly remarked that if the tsar tried to conquer it, his armies would die of heat prostration.[27]

Negotiations began in a spirit of cooperation and accommodation on December 18, 1720, and continued until the following March 2, the day on which Izmaylov left Peking.[28] On the first day of the conversations the Russian envoy submitted for Manchu consideration a draft commercial treaty, which was identical with his instructions. The Ch'ing court rejected the treaty but was prepared to discuss separately one of its articles, the establishment of a Russian consulate in the capital. Although Izmaylov promised that Lange would conform to Chinese custom and dress, he urged that the Russian state pay the consul's expenses and that Lange be permitted to retain his own religion. After prolonged discussions the court agreed by February 5 that Lange could remain in Peking, but at the emperor's not the tsar's expense, which from the Manchu point of view placed him within the context of the tribute system. Istopnikov's caravan would also be allowed to trade at Peking, provided it conformed to the regulations of 1693. Lange would probably have to return with the Istopnikov caravan, but thereafter caravans could continue to trade at Peking under the 1693 regulations. No commercial treaty could be concluded, however, until the settlement of certain frontier and fugitive problems.

The Li-fan yuan informed Izmaylov on January 2, 1721, that more than seven hundred Mongols, subject to Peking, had committed crimes and fled into Russian territory. The Manchus demanded that he depute a personal representative to accompany their own messenger to the governor general of Siberia to demand the return of the Mongols under the provisions of the Treaty of Nerchinsk. Izmaylov acquiesced on February 4, and the next day he reached an understanding with the court on the consulate question, permitting Lorents Lange to remain in Peking. The court also evinced concern over the increase in Russian settlements along their own frontier. They mentioned Selenginsk, Udinsk, Nerchinsk, one hundred Russian settlers in the Manchu-controlled Urianghai (Tannu-tuva) lands, and settlements along the Irtysh. Now that the Jungar wars were drawing to a close, the Li-fan yuan suggested that the Manchus build a fortress of their own on the Irtysh, staffed by the military, as a center and source of protection for commerce and a station for envoys and caravans traveling to or from Peking along the Altai route. The problem of correspondence between emperor and tsar was raised, but no new solution to the problem of the use of titles was forthcoming. In the end Izmaylov had to reject a direct answer from the emperor to the tsar's letters when the Li-fan yuan informed him that it must be couched in traditional suzerain-vassal terminology.[29]

Izmaylov returned to Moscow on January 2, 1722, having failed to achieve the embassy's goals set out in his various instructions. His concrete achievements were also limited: Istopnikov's caravan was permitted to trade at Peking, and Lange remained there as Russian commercial agent. The embassy's actual importance lay in the role it played throughout the following decade of negotiations, when the two empires were seeking a degree of institutional stability in their diplomatic and commercial relations: it was a summation of the past and an intimation of the future. The Li-fan yuan made it patently clear that peace could be purchased only by the solution of outstanding frontier problems, which the Treaty of Nerchinsk was incompetent to solve. A clearly delineated frontier between Siberia and Mongolia would presumably prevent Russian penetration of Jungar lands and the formation of an anti-Manchu Russo-Jungar alliance. If Russia were prepared to pay the price of noninterference in Central Asia for commerce with Peking, Peking was prepared to pay the price of commerce for Russian noninterference in Central Asia.

The embassy also demonstrated that Russia's free trade and extraterritorial proposals were unrealistic in terms of Sino-Manchu economic and social thought. The Ch'ing court rejected them at the beginning of the eighteenth century when offered by Russia, just as it would reject similar proposals a hundred years later when presented by England. Great Britain's maritime technology and Indian base, however, permitted her to go to war to support her proposals, whereas Russia in the 1720's was too weak in Siberia and too involved with Sweden for Peter seriously to contemplate military action against Peking. The Manchus understood this situation: K'ang-hsi had hinted to Izmaylov of his awareness of Russia's military involvements by expressing concern for the tsar's health and "fear" that the tsar was exposing himself to unnecessary physical dangers. Peking countered St. Petersburg's proposals with her own, aimed at the close control of Sino-Russian commerce. Although the Ch'ing court was prepared to continue the caravan trade under the strict observance of the 1693 regulations, it was their proposal for a fortress on the Irtysh as a Sino-Russian commercial emporium that became the basis for finally achieving Sino-Russian institutional stability.

Lange's Consulship

Lorents Lange was the first commercial agent from either Russia or the West to reside officially at Peking, where he remained until the middle of July 1722. St. Petersburg considered the permanent residence of a commercial agent at the Ch'ing capital an integral part of her proposed free trade system. The consul would represent Russian interests, supply vital political and commercial intelligence, and provide a degree of Russian institutional continuity on the Chinese end of the long caravan route. Although the Ch'ing court did not agree entirely to the consular system St. Petersburg sought to establish in the Manchu Empire, Lange attempted to carry out these duties during the seventeen months he spent at Peking. The arrival of the Istopnikov caravan divided his stay into two periods. From March to the end of September or the beginning of October 1721, Lange was concerned primarily with establishing his consulate on a regular footing and fulfilling his consular duties, including preparations for the caravan's arrival. From the beginning of October 1721 to the next July, he was occupied mainly with the caravan's affairs. His sojourn ended with a series of discussions with Manchu officials, clarifying the outstanding issues between Peking and St. Petersburg but culminating in his expulsion from the Ch'ing empire.[30]

Lange confronted four basic problems in the creation of a consulate. He had to establish his own legal position, find physical quarters for the consulate, assure himself and his staff a supply of provisions, and maintain communications with the nearest Russian government officials at Selenginsk. Recognizing the uniqueness and novelty of his position, Lange believed that the only way to confirm his "public character" was to present his credentials to the emperor himself, so as early as March 22, 1721, he raised this question with the Li-fan yuan. Despite his claim that the credentials took the form of letters from the tsar to the emperor, the Li-fan yuan refused to cooperate. On more than one occasion Lange found himself in the emperor's entourage, and they even exchanged pleasantries, but the consul never succeeded in actually presenting his documents to K'ang-hsi.[31] The importance Lange personally attached to this matter derived from his own image of a consul in the European tradition, but his account makes it patently clear that in the eyes of the Manchu officials his credentials meant nothing. His official position rested solely on their willingness to treat with him and not on his accreditation.

The consulate's physical establishment was an even more pressing matter, in view of the imminent arrival of Istopnikov's caravan. Lange was lodged at the O-lo-ssu kuan, which was in such great disrepair that it could not satisfy the needs of the caravan. Lange told the Li-fan yuan that he wished to hire separate quarters for himself so that the O-lo-ssu kuan, "which from age, were gone to ruin and might be entirely beat down by the approaching rainy season," might be repaired. The Li-fan yuan responded immediately and precisely: no one would dare suggest to the emperor that the quarters allotted for Lange's residence were unsatisfactory, which would imply that "the Bogdoi-Chan had not an inhabitable house for a foreigner." This issue confronted Lange with the same problem that had confronted other Russian representatives in Peking before him: intersocietal communications. He maintained that "it was acting contrary to the common right, allowed by the world," to restrain a public official from hiring lodgings at his own expense without prior application to the emperor. The Li-fan yuan replied, according to Lange, that each country had its own customs and that they would not alter theirs "on any consideration whatever." Meanwhile, the condition of the O-lo-ssu kuan had deteriorated still further, until about midnight on April 30 a windstorm blew down one wall of the consul's bedchamber, which, he remarked, "made me very apprehensive for what remained." The Li-fan yuan also refused to permit Lange to repair the building at his own expense, so that when Istopnikov arrived, the caravan had to leave its cargo in the middle of an unprotected courtyard until, in the first half of October, the Li-fan yuan began repairs.[32]

The problem of supplies and provisions was even more complicated, because it infringed upon the pecuniary prerogatives of the Li-fan yuan. Despite his own instructions and inclinations, Lange had to acquiesce to customary behavior. To all intents and purposes he was a guest of the Manchus and was treated as a tributary envoy, even though in fact he was not considered one.[33] His position was equivocal at best. On March 7, 1721, for instance, he observed a man dressed as a beggar enter the O-lo-ssu kuan, carrying some starved fowls, salted cabbage, and rice wine, which he deposited in the courtyard. He informed the consul that he had contracted with the Li-fan yuan to supply Lange with a certain amount of foodstuffs every nine days. Lange, in dismay at the condition of the chickens but not yet having succeeded in establishing his "public character," decided to use this issue to initiate formal relations with the Li-fan yuan. He demanded negotiations on the supply question, insisting that the emperor himself should specify what provisions the consul would receive, and that he would prefer to receive their value in cash. Lange suspected that the officials of the Li-fan yuan planned to eat a part of his provisions. Eventually the court sent down the desired specifications, and Lange was given silver for the value of the fish, fowls, sheep, and milk included in the provisions, because otherwise the Li-fan yuan itself would have had to purchase them for ready cash.[34] Lange reckoned to receive in provisions and cash the equivalent of 48 liang of silver monthly, which was insufficient for all his needs. Forage, for instance, was dear in Peking. Moreover, when Lange tried to purchase it anyway on the open market for the caravan's animals, the Li-fan yuan instructed the guards at the O-lo-ssu kuan's gate to drive away the peasants delivering the hay.[35] It evidently felt that Lange, with semi-official status as a state guest, should not be permitted to establish economic ties with the population outside those channels the Li-fan yuan itself could control.

Lange's most difficult organizational problem was establishing communications between his consulate and Selenginsk, the nearest Russian settlement. Couriers traveling in either direction had to traverse Manchu-administered territories and therefore needed official passports. This problem was never resolved, partly because of Manchu suspicion of Russian motives in sending messages back and forth, and partly because of political and bureaucratic inefficiency.[36] The issue played a significant role in Lange's final conversations at court before his departure.

The consul's activities fell into three general categories: he represented Russian commercial interests in general and the St. Petersburg court in particular; he dealt with the exchange of personnel, including the issuance of passports; and he gathered information. His principal commercial duties involved the collection of debts owed by Chinese merchants to the Russians and the provision of funds for the approaching Istopnikov caravan. Claiming that he needed funds to make purchases for the tsar, Lange repeatedly raised the debt issue with the Li-fan yuan and solicited its aid. At first the Li-fan yuan put him off, claiming that the debtors had retired to the countryside, but when the consul's interpreter met one of the debtors on the street, Lange raised the issue again. Two debtors finally appeared before him on March 26, 1722. They informed him that a third, who owed Gusyatnikov 1,400 liang of silver, had died the previous year. Lange insisted on the principle of collective responsibility, and long arguments ensued. He collected almost no debts and came to the conclusion that the merchants, who were already "very poor and indigent," bribed the Li-fan yuan's officials from time to time not to press the matter.[37]

The approach of the Istopnikov caravan involved Lange, unawares, in the court intrigue surrounding the imminent succession to the aged K'ang-hsi. On August 14, 1721, Lange received a letter from Istopnikov announcing the arrival of the caravan and begging the consul to secure a loan of 2,000 liang for him from the Li-fan yuan, payable at the Kalgan customs house. The caravan had been detained so long at the frontier that Istopnikov had run out of cash for operating expenses; he promised to repay the loan as soon as trade began at Peking. The Li-fan yuan refused the request, but the next day the emperor invited Lange to join him and his retinue at Jehol, where they were vacationing. Lange arrived on August 21, and four days later Joao Mourao, a Portuguese Jesuit, informed him that a "person of quality" wished to offer the Russians 10,000 liang of silver as an advance on the caravan's arrival. Lange was free to use the funds as he saw fit. Mourao would not at first tell Lange the identity of the "person of quality," but after much questioning he admitted that it was K'ang-hsi's ninth son. Lange refused the offer but eventually accepted 1,000 liang as a token of good faith, and on September 7 he dispatched his interpreter to Kalgan with 1,500 liang in silver for Istopnikov's needs. Yin-t'ang, the emperor's ninth son, was a contender for the throne, but more important, he became a supporter of K'ang-hsi's fourteenth son, Yin-t'i, whom the emperor had placed in charge of the campaign against the Jungars. K'ang-hsi favored Yin-t'i and wished to give him this opportunity to distinguish himself. Yin-t'ang contributed heavily to Yin-t'i's purse and had a large stake in his future. His offer to Lange may well have been an effort to establish the basis for future influence with the Russians, particularly in view of Yin-t'i's Central Asian responsibilities.[38]

Lange had other duties as well. On occasion he acted as the Peking representative for Russian merchants, making purchases for them at the capital, and he was the tsar's personal commercial agent. For instance, he purchased a tapestry, japanned ware, and other items desired by Peter.[39] On at least one occasion he was asked to provide passports for Ch'ing officials planning to visit Siberia. The Li-fan yuan told the consul that on the "Occa," an affluent of the Angara, there had been found an ancient Buddhist statue, held in high esteem by Tamerlane and praised to the emperor by the Urga Khutukhtu. K'ang-hsi wanted to send four officials to procure the statue or at least make an accurate description of it. Lange at first refused to grant the passports because, as he remarked in his journal, "I could well penetrate the grounds of their errand." Upon his return from Jehol the consul had visited an aged Jesuit who had been appointed to accompany the mission to the "Occa" but had declined because of his great age and the strains of such a long and arduous journey. The Jesuit informed Lange that the mission's real object was to plant border-markers along the frontier against the day when negotiations for the delineation of the border would take place. The Manchus would then support their claims on the basis of ancient landmarks and border stones. Lange finally relented, however, when vague threats were made against him at court. In return, he exacted a promise of unlimited trade for Istopnikov's caravan—a promise rarely kept.[40]

In addition to his administrative duties, the consul gathered extensive commercial and political information of a general nature for the use of St. Petersburg's policy-makers. In his journal he described in detail the commodities of the Sino-Korean trade and the nature of the Ch'ing-Korean tributary relationship, as well as the Chinese trade with Southeast Asia, Bukhara, and Sinkiang.[41] He also sent St. Petersburg pertinent political and military information. On December 21, 1721, for instance, he wrote the tsar that the war with the Jungars was going badly for Peking. Contagion was spreading through the ranks of the Manchus' 200,000-man army; provisions were in such short supply that the army was eating its diseased camels, horses, and cattle; and the Mongols were alarmed over the course of events.[42]

Lange carried out his duties in the face of numerous obstacles placed in his path. The Li-fan yuan tried to restrict his movements by denying him the official horses used by the Izmaylov embassy, so that the consul had to purchase and maintain his own at great expense. He consistently had difficulties obtaining interviews with Li-fan yuan officials, and even the Jesuits feared to be seen too often in his company. The soldiers stationed at the gate of the O-lo-ssu kuan complicated matters. For instance, both before and after Istopnikov's arrival they forced all merchants arriving to trade with the Russians to pay an "exit fee" even before they had entered the compound. Although entry itself was free, no regulations governed exit from the O-lo-ssu kuan, so the soldiers could make exactions as they wished.[43]

Bureaucratic cupidity created new problems when Istopnikov arrived at the capital on September 29, 1721. Some court officials had tried to delay the caravan at Kalgan until the court could return from its Jehol vacation, since in its absence Peking's merchants would have first choice of the caravan's better goods. Lange prevented this, but court officials then succeeded in delaying the opening of trade in Peking itself in an effort to obtain gifts and special prices on the caravan's goods for the court. The Li-fan yuan supported their demands. On December 2, for instance, the trade was declared open, but at the same time the soldiers at the gate were ordered to search any merchants leaving the premises and to confiscate goods the court might desire. The trade was thus stopped before it had even begun. Lange still refused to give in to the court's demands, and on December 15 the Li-fan yuan placed two hundred thousand sable pelts from the emperor's own stores on public sale at prices far below the caravan's. As the caravan could not afford to compete, the public demand was satisfied by the emperor's sables. The next day the Li-fan yuan began levying entrance, as well as exit, fees at the O-lo-ssu kuan. These conditions continued during the caravan's entire Peking sojourn.[44]

With the passage of time the Ch'ing court, aware of Russia's interest in Central Asian affairs, grew increasingly suspicious of Lange's activities at the capital. On April 16, 1722, Lange learned that "some weeks ago" the court had ordered the Tushetu-khan to expel both Russian and Chinese merchants from Urga; he was to make it appear that he himself had issued the order rather than Peking. The trading season at Urga had been the busiest and most profitable on record, and the expulsion was more symptomatic of Manchu distrust of Russian intentions than a direct attack on Russian interests. Lange was not overly displeased at this particular move because he recognized that the private market at Urga menaced the state's interests at Peking.[45]

As information concerning Peter's approaches to Tsewang Araptan reached Peking, the Manchus came to believe Lange was acting on behalf of a developing Russo-Jungar alliance. As early as April 1721 the court warned the consul not to send so many messengers out of Peking, and a year later it acted to cut his communications with Siberia. This was the issue over which the final crisis of Lange's consulship developed. On April 6, 1722, he requested the Li-fan yuan to detail some soldiers to escort a consular messenger to Kalgan. Lange planned to send money to that city to purchase forage for the caravan's animals, which had been left there according to custom. The next day the Li-fan yuan rejected his request, warning that it suspected him of ulterior motives prejudicial to the dynasty's interests. Lange threatened to send his messenger without official permission. On the night of May 4 two officials directed the guards to pull Lange from bed and take him to an interview with the president of the Li-fan yuan. The interview turned into a midnight interrogation, in which the president demanded a record of all Lange's past correspondence with Selenginsk and copies of all his private correspondence in future. Finally he showed the consul "a small letter," which turned out to have been written in Russian by an interpreter at Selenginsk and sent to Urga for forwarding to Lange at Peking. The president demanded that Lange open it in his presence, and he summoned two translators to read it with the consul and make copies. Lange refused, returned the letter unopened, warned the president that his actions might result in serious consequences, and stalked out of the Li-fan yuan. During the next two days various officials visited the O-lo-ssu kuan, but Lange would not modify his stand. On May 7 he was given the letter, unopened, with the explanation that the president had only taken "the liberty of having a little pleasantry with me; not altogether without flattering himself, that I might not be averse to comply with his desires."[46] Lange thereupon opened the letter and, voluntarily and without duress, verbally communicated its contents to the Li-fan yuan's messengers. He may have thought that this gesture would end the matter.

Just how serious the incident was in the eyes of the Ch'ing government became apparent the next day when Peking virtually broke off relations with St. Petersburg, to use modern parlance. A representative of the Li-fan yuan visited Lange at the O-lo-ssu kuan and informed him that the emperor had terminated all commerce with Russia until the settlement of all frontier problems. Furthermore, because the emperor felt it would be a long time before another Russian caravan visited Peking, Lange was to be expelled from the empire and to return to Russia with Istopnikov. If Sino-Russian commerce was reopened, Lange would be permitted to return.[47]

Lange fully understood the importance of Peking's new move. Between May 8 and his final audience with the emperor at Jehol on July 17, 1722, he tried to explore the immediate reasons for Peking's abrupt action and to clarify the outstanding difficulties between the two empires. He began by officially protesting the Li-fan yuan's announcement and requesting an interview with the president of that body. The president refused to receive him but agreed to accept any messages the consul cared to send. Lange sought clarification of five points. The first three dealt with his own difficulties at Peking: he asked the emperor to receive his credentials and to write a letter to the tsar before the consul left China; he requested a satisfactory explanation for the expulsion of the Russian merchants from Urga; and he sought an explanation for the government's interference with his correspondence with Siberia. Fourth, he asked, "What should I say to the Czar, my master, regarding the perpetual peace between the two empires?" And last, Lange inquired whether he would have to provide his own transportation to the frontier. On May 10 he was informed that the decision to break relations was irrevocable.[48]

On May 15 Lange, having received no answers to his five queries, decided to seek an interview with the emperor's "first minister." When the interview was refused, he virtually forced his way into the minister's home: with Lange standing in the middle of his courtyard, the minister could hardly refuse to receive him. The consul explained that since the situation concerned the problem "of peace and war between the two nations," he felt it only proper to give the Ch'ing government a full exposition of Russia's policies.[49] He then repeated his earlier complaints. The minister, in turn, referred again to frontier problems, by which he meant Jungaria, and concluded that the emperor "was tired of receiving the law, in his own country, from foreigners, of whom his subjects reaped no profit." If Russia delayed in changing its attitude, the emperor "should be obliged to do it himself by such ways as he should find most convenient." Lange replied to this veiled threat of war with one of his own: since the tsar was about to conclude his Swedish wars honorably, if he had not done so already, nothing prevented him "from turning his arms to this side, in case they [the Manchus] exercised his patience too much." Once the tsar decided to make war on Peking, all difficulties would vanish, because he "did not suffer himself to be hindered by difficulties." The Manchus "might then have sufficient cause to repent their having despised the friendship of a monarch who was not accustomed to receive offenses with impunity." Lange, however, realized that "this discourse was not at all to the [president's] taste" and, protesting his good intentions, insisted that he was not threatening the Manchus but only explaining reality to them. He concluded by saying that further attempts at mutual understanding were in vain: "therefore, the game must go on, seeing the dice was thrown already."

Lange spent the month of June preparing for his departure. Tulishen was appointed to conduct him to the frontier and to furnish him with all necessary provisions. On July 9 Lange had a final stormy interview with the president of the Li-fan yuan. The president explained that the court had nothing against him personally and was, in fact, much satisfied with the consul's deportment. The two men parted with wishes that they might meet again soon. On July 12 Lange left Peking for Jehol, where on July 17 he took leave of the emperor in a formal audience. He arrived at Selenginsk on August 26, 1722, "after having resided near seventeen months at the court of China."[50]

Lange's sojourn at Peking as official Russian representative had been a unique concession to St. Petersburg. Even Korea, which most approximated a classic tributary power, was not permitted to keep permanent representatives at the Ch'ing capital. The concession was a symbol of Manchu willingness to enter into negotiations with Russia. At the same time, Lange's expulsion was instrumental in bringing about those negotiations. St. Petersburg was expected to be loath to lose the unique concession of consular representation at Peking once it had been granted; in fact, K'ang-hsi believed the tsar would go to great lengths to retain it. Furthermore, the emperor was in receipt of news concerning Peter's embassy to the Jungars, and Lange's expulsion was meant to shock St. Petersburg into a recognition of what Peking assumed were its true interests in Asia. Lange was, in short, a tool held in reserve by the Manchus, which they decided to use in the middle of 1722.

Lange reported his expulsion to the tsar in a letter from Selenginsk dated September 3, 1722, which was received by Peter on February 2, 1723.[51] He explained his expulsion in terms of the Jungar situation: a Ch'ing official waiting at Selenginsk for a reply from St. Petersburg concerning some fugitives had learned of Peter's embassy to the Jungars and reported it to the Li-fan yuan.[52] Inasmuch as St. Petersburg had already received considerable information about relations with Peking from Prince Cherkasky, the governor general of Siberia, it was well aware by the middle of 1722 that some action was needed to protect its interests on the Manchu frontier. As early as April 12, 1722, Peter had visited the Senate and, reviewing the pertinent documents, decided that Russia would conform to the Nerchinsk treaty's provisions concerning fugitives; an edict to that effect was issued on July 4. At the same time, however, St. Petersburg issued two edicts with a strongly anti-Manchu tone. Cherkasky was instructed not to tolerate the presence of Ch'ing officials in Siberia if they caused any inconvenience, and K'ang-hsi's officials sent to search for the Buddhist statue on the "Occa" were refused entry to Siberia. Cherkasky received these edicts at Tobolsk on September 4 and October 22, 1722, and immediately sent Stepan Fefilov of Tobolsk to make investigations at Selenginsk.[53]

By the time Fefilov arrived at Selenginsk on April 1 or 2, 1723, a decided change appeared imminent in Peking's policy. Tulishen had forwarded a letter to Prince Cherkasky from the Li-fan yuan, dated July 22, 1722, repeating the complaints made to Lange at Peking earlier in the year. In the meantime, a merchant from Urga had brought to Lange, who was still at Selenginsk, news of K'ang-hsi's death on December 20, 1722, and although Lange was not sure of his informant's reliability, he communicated the news to St. Petersburg on March 8, 1723. On receipt of the notification on November 26, 1723, St. Petersburg decided almost immediately that the death of the old emperor and the accession of a new one provided an opening for the resumption of negotiations. An edict of January 29, 1724, appointed Lange head of a commission to regulate frontier and fugitive problems with Peking and placed Lieutenant Colonel Bukhholts, with one thousand cavalry and another thousand infantry, under his command. The edict gave Lange specific instructions on how to open the negotiations. Most important, he and Bukhholts were empowered to speak in the name of the College of Foreign Affairs and to report to Cherkasky, rather than St. Petersburg in order to speed up the political process.[54]

Russia's *démarche* was matched by a distinct modification in the tone of Manchu communications to Cherkasky. A letter from the Li-fan yuan dated June 13, 1723, six months after K'ang-hsi's death and the accession of Yung-cheng, which claimed forty Jungar fugitives had fled to Siberia, was extremely polite and moderate in tone. Lange himself noticed the change and reported to the tsar that two Manchu officials had arrived at Selenginsk on November 1 to be apprised of the results of Fefilov's investigations. Lange requested proper credentials, and the two officials immediately left, promising politely to return with the documents as soon as possible. On February 22, 1724, the Li-fan yuan asked Lange to inform the Tushetu-khan of the results of the inquiry, after which a Manchu commission would be sent to Selenginsk. Lange complied with Peking's request, and in mid-July two negotiators arrived from Peking with full powers to discuss all outstanding questions. In the meantime, Lange had received Fefilov's report, as a result of which he extradited eighty-four fugitives to China. He also informed the members of the Manchu commission that he had full authority to negotiate with them but that a special ambassador would soon be sent from St. Petersburg to conduct negotiations at a higher level.[55]

Chapter VIII Sava Vladislavich and the Search for Stability

Almost simultaneous succession crises in the Ch'ing and Romanov dynasties increased the need for stability along the Sino-Russian frontier in the third decade of the eighteenth century. The new Ch'ing emperor, Yung-cheng, and the new tsarina, Catherine I, were both deeply involved in retaining their thrones and in achieving success on the international stage in those areas of primary importance to each: Yung-cheng in Central Asia and Catherine in Europe.

Yung-cheng was K'ang-hsi's fourth son. When late in 1722 the emperor took ill and kept to his bed at his country villa, he designated Yung-cheng as his representative at the Winter Solstice Sacrifices, because his favorite, Yin-t'i, was in the northwest guarding the frontiers against the Jungars. Although these festivities usually ended December 22, Yung-cheng was at his father's side when the emperor died on December 20, and according to official accounts K'ang-hsi named him his successor just before he expired. During the first years of his reign Yung-cheng consolidated his power by appointing his own supporters to key posts and by watching, imprisoning, or executing his brothers.[1] Internationally, Yung-cheng sought to pacify the frontier regions, which were traditionally the most important problem in continental China's foreign policy. Like his father before him, the new emperor understood that the Jungars were the chief threat to the Manchu position in China and that the key to Ch'ing domination of Central Asia was peace with Russia.

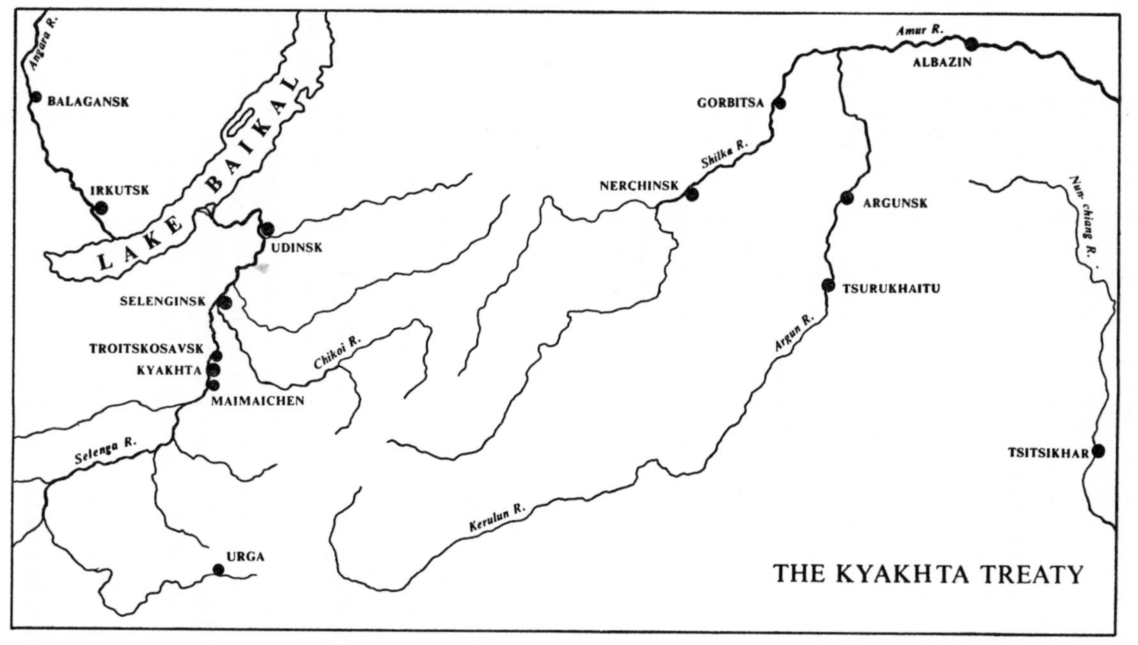
Angara R.
BALAGANSK
IRKUTSK
LAKE BAIKAL
UDINSK
SELENGINSK
TROITSKOSAVSK
KYAKHTA
MAIMAICHEN
Chikoi R.
Selenga R.
URGA
Amur R.
ALBAZIN
GORBITSA
Shilka R.
NERCHINSK
ARGUNSK
TSURUKHAITU
Argun R.
Nun-chiang R.
TSITSIKHAR
Kerulun R.
THE KYAKHTA TREATY

On January 28, 1725—two years, one month, and eight days after K'ang-hsi's death—Peter the Great died from stone and strangury. He was survived by a congeries of relatives with claims to the throne, since the traditional order of succession, which pointed to his nine-year-old grandson Peter (the son of Tsarevich Alexis, whom Peter the Great had assassinated), had been replaced by decree on February 5, 1722, which permitted the sovereign to name his successor. When it became clear that the tsar was about to die without naming a successor, government dignitaries assembled at the palace on the night of January 27 and, under the influence of the Guards, with whom she was popular, named Peter's wife Catherine empress of Russia. During the next thirty-seven years the Russian crown changed hands several times. Andrei Ostermann, whom Catherine I appointed vice-chancellor after her accession, guided Russia's foreign policy until 1740, basing it on a close alliance with Austria and hostility toward France, which opposed Russian interests in Sweden, Poland, and Turkey. Europe was divided into two hostile camps, each anxious to win Russian support. On August 6, 1726, Osterman concluded a military alliance with Austria, by which Russia became a member the Austro-Spanish league.

While Yung-cheng needed peace with Russia to dominate Central Asia, Catherine and Ostermann needed peace with the Manchu Empire to free Russia's hand in European politics. Consequently, Russia's new government was prepared to proceed with Peter's plan for an embassy to China. Lange was sent a decree, dated March 3, 1725, stating that the special ambassador's first diplomatic task would be to extend felicitations to the new Manchu emperor and to announce Catherine I's accession to the Russian throne.[2] Peter had begun the preparation of the embassy, and his death provided the most propitious moment for it to begin its work.

The Formation of the Russian Embassy

Although the decision to send a full-scale embassy to China had probably been made a year before Peter's death, not until October did the College of Foreign Affairs express the opinion that the time seemed right for its dispatch. The appointment of the embassy's staff had taken place in the middle of 1725, and Sava Vladislavich was named ambassador on June 18, 1725.[3]

Sava Lukich Vladislavich followed directly in the tradition of merchant-diplomats like Ides and Lange. He was born into a princely family in Bosnia in January 1668. His father fled the Turks, first to Venice and then to Ragusa, where he took the surname Raguzinsky, meaning "of Ragusa." Sava Vladislavich became a merchant in Constantinople, where he also served as a secret agent for Russian interests. He went to Russia at the end of the seventeenth or beginning of the eighteenth century and on January 1, 1703, requested permission to open a commercial house in Azov, trade freely in Russia for ten years, pay only the regular duties collected from Muscovite merchants, and sell fox skins. These privileges were granted in July 1703 and were extended two years later to include free passage for his goods into Little Russia and the Ukraine. By 1708 Vladislavich had apparently come to the tsar's attention, because Peter gave him a house in Moscow that year and in 1710 appointed him an aulic councilor of Russia, count of Ragusa, and awarded him estates in Little Russia. In 1711 he accompanied Peter in the campaign of the Pruth, and in 1712 he traded at Arkhangelsk and financially aided the construction of ships at St. Petersburg. Between 1716 and 1722 Sava Vladislavich visited Ragusa, Venice, and Rome on Peter's behalf, purchasing, among other things, statues for the Summer Garden at St. Petersburg and the tsar's palace at Peterhof.[4] In other words he was just the type of European-oriented merchant that Peter valued in the service of his Europeanization program. Consequently, upon his return to Russia Vladislavich was appointed a titular councilor of state and, soon after, "Envoy Extraordinary and Minister Plenipotentiary to China." By that time he was about sixty years of age and personally acquainted with the procedures of commercial negotiations and diplomacy.

The rest of the embassy was made up largely of specialists appointed in August and September 1725. Lorents Lange was given new credentials and appointed Vladislavich's China expert, and Ivan Bukhholts commanded the embassy's military contingent.

The ambassador's two chief assistants, therefore, had considerable experience in the embassy's two areas of chief concern: China and Jungaria. Stepan Kolychov, named frontier commissioner, was a master of requisitions for the Senate who had just taken part in the demarcation of Russia's frontiers with Poland and Turkey and was thus acquainted with the problems of geographical surveying. Wherever possible, specialists or men with experience in China were apppointed secretaries, topographers, priests, or to other posts. Izmaylov's secretary, Glazunov, was appointed secretary to the new embassy.[5] The Academy of Sciences provided topographers and geodesists, but Vladislavich disapproved of them and hired new ones in Siberia. The bishop of Pereyaslavl, Inokenty Kulchitsky, who had been appointed to Peking as early as 1721, was named head of the religious mission that the court hoped to establish in Peking. He was accompanied by several priests and two students of Moscow's ecclesiastical academy, who were to study Chinese at the Ch'ing capital. Vladislavich was dissatisfied with these too, however, because they were too old; one he used as his Latin translator, and the other he replaced with a younger man. All told, the embassy included 120 staff members and 1,500 military personnel.[6]

The total cost of the embassy came to about 100,000 rubles. In addition to his own salary of 6,000 rubles per annum for two years, the ambassador was given 10,000 rubles for presents to the emperor and 3,000 rubles for gifts to the emperor's ministers and others who might prove of aid to the embassy. Most of this amount was received in the form of goods, including clocks, pendulums, telescopes, mirrors, and fur pelts. In the tradition of Russian embassies to China, the ambassador and his suite were permitted to export private merchandise for sale in Peking at a value of no more than 20,000 rubles.[7]

Vladislavich prepared carefully for his tasks. The list of documents given him for study occupied ten pages of his official journal. He read the official journals written by Golovin, Ides, and Izmaylov, as well as the documents and communications of the years 1722-1724, just prior to his own embassy. He was furnished with abstracts on religious affairs and Russian commerce in Mongolia, a cypher code, an official gramota to the emperor, credentials investing him with full powers, and a passport.[8] The precise concern for organization and detail that characterized the entire embassy was especially evident in the instructions he received before his departure for Peking.

Vladislavich's instructions from the College of Foreign Affairs, dated September 14, 1725, and written in forty-five paragraphs, were a complete description of what the government considered an optimal settlement with Peking and of the embassy's behavior ancillary to the negotiations.[9] In the month after receiving them, the ambassador studied each paragraph closely and continually sought clarification of vague points and modification of unrealistic ones. The theme of accommodation ran throughout. Whenever the formulators of the instructions thought Manchu opposition probable, they recommended compromise and even surrender of earlier positions. For instance, Vladislavich was to ask permission for a commercial caravan to accompany him into China, but if the Manchus refused, he should enter China without it.[10] If Peking refused permission for the embassy itself to enter, Vladislavich was to remain on the frontier and write St. Petersburg for new instructions. If he succeeded in entering China, he was to leave the frontier commissioners behind, so that they might survey the border while the embassy proceeded to wherever the emperor was. He was to compromise on ceremonial questions, never refusing to take part in required rites, including the kowtow, but keeping detailed notes on everything. His primary concern, however, was the preservation of the tsarina's honor, and of his own as her envoy. He was also allowed to give copies of all his documents to the emperor's ministers before the first imperial audience, making it clear to them that in the tsarina's letter the emperor's title alone had been used, whereas the tsarina simply signed her name at the end.[11]

The instructions' commercial articles duplicated Izmaylov's. The ambassador was empowered to sign a commercial treaty creating a Sino-Russian free trade zone, and Lange was again appointed consul in Peking. The College of Foreign Affairs recognized, however, that commercial agreements with Peking required prior resolution of the frontier and fugitive problems. The Nerchinsk treaty was to be used as the basis for negotiations on the issue of the return of fugitives, although the ambassador was explicitly told not to break off negotiations should Manchu demands in this regard prove beyond the competence of his instructions: deferred decisions were preferable to no agreements at all. His instructions concerning the frontier were extremely detailed, aimed at providing answers for any contingency. En route to the frontier Vladislavich was to collect whatever information he needed about the frontier and to have maps made of all places in undemarcated territory that were considered necessary to Russian security. He was also to invite the creation of joint Manchu-Russian commissions to survey the borderlands, since St. Petersburg assumed that the Manchus lacked the detailed information available to Vladislavich. If worse came to worst and Peking refused all recommendations, the ambassador could rely on his own judgment and promise to represent Manchu interests in St. Petersburg if satisfactory agreements were concluded on other subjects. However, he was to reject out of hand Peking's assertions to Izmaylov that Selenginsk, Udinsk, and Nerchinsk were located on Manchu territory and that a Manchu fort should be constructed on the Irtysh. Finally, Vladislavich was to request a grant of land for the construction of an Orthodox church in Peking and the admission of a bishop with all the privileges granted the Jesuits; all Russian activities would be paid for by St. Petersburg.[12]

The College of Foreign Affairs also gave Vladislavich two secret instructions.[13] The first enjoined him and his suite to collect vital military intelligence between the frontier and Peking: location and size of cities, distribution of military forces, the size and armaments of those forces, details of fortifications, important geographical data. The second secret instruction concerned Peking itself, where, in addition to gathering intelligence data, Vladislavich was to make a careful study of Ch'ing relations with neighboring countries.

Two weeks after receiving the public and secret instructions, Vladislavich submitted a list of fifteen questions involving matters that he felt needed immediate clarification, since later he would be too far away in Peking to seek clarification.[14] His questions and the college's replies emphasized still further the need for accommodation with the Ch'ing court. The important point, the college maintained, was to reestablish commercial relations, and it implied its readiness to go to great lengths to achieve this goal. Vladislavich wanted more detailed instructions in case the Ch'ing court, refusing to receive him as it had Izmaylov, required ceremonies beyond the kowtow. "Strive as much as possible," the college told him, "but be satisfied that you have received that which is possible."

Among Vladislavich's questions on frontier problems, one in particular demonstrated the logical quality of his mind. The question concerned the proposed Manchu fortress on the Irtysh. If the entire river was located in Russian territory, he argued, the Manchu proposals were of course inadmissible. However, if the sources of the river lay in Mongol or Jungar territory, and if the local rulers permitted the Manchus to build such a fortress, or if they themselves had accepted Manchu suzerainty and the fortress was built by right of rule, how could Russia forbid its construction? He noted that in Europe there were numerous rivers, like the Danube, that flowed through the territories of more than one state, implying that each had the right to fortify its section of the river. The college, ignorant of the peace just concluded between the Manchus and the Jungars, replied reasonably that the Manchu-Jungar wars made it highly unlikely that the Jungars would permit Peking to construct a fortress in their territory.

The same orderliness and lucidity of thought characterized Vladislavich's comments on the instructions he received from the College of Commerce.[15] Whereas the instructions stated Russia's maximum desires concerning the organization of the China trade, Vladislavich sought and obtained, point by point, a description of Russia's minimum requirements, which left sufficient room for negotiation and interpretation of his instructions. He also asked for a closer definition of his personal responsibilities. The instructions, for instance, called for Lange to build a house in Peking that would serve as the consulate, a warehouse, and his private residence. Vladislavich, conforming to his own need for precision, asked for size and cost specifications. The College of Commerce agreed that if Lange were not granted European consular privileges, he should live according to local customs and regulations.

The College of Commerce's instructions also detailed the Russian proposal for a Sino-Russian free-trade zone in which the subjects of both empires would be permitted free, unlimited trade and residence in each other's country, although Russians in China would be under the control of their own consul, with extraterritorial privileges, and would be provided with military convoys when traveling into or out of the country. Vladislavich's critique of the Russian scheme displayed his concern for justice and realism. He worried that excessive Russian demands might make the Manchus so suspicious that they would refuse to trade at all. The Nerchinsk treaty only mentioned free trade, he pointed out; it did not give Russians permission to travel all over the Manchu Empire. Even in Europe many of the Russian desiderata would have been considered unjust. It was not customary, for instance, to give military convoys to merchants. Moreover, the demand for trade free of all duties and taxes was unreasonable, because the collection of duties was legitimate in Europe and even in Russia. The college replied with a statement of its minimal demands: resumption of trade on the basis of the caravan system. The college was even prepared to accept the levying of duties, if they were not heavy, and to concede all its maximum demands, relying on the principle that what was not possible was not possible. Vladislavich could only try to maximize Russia's advantage; he could not be held responsible for the outcome of the negotiations.[16]

Armed with these detailed instructions, the embassy left St. Petersburg on October 12, 1725, and arrived at Peking one year later, on October 21, 1726.[17] Vladislavich's chief concern during the journey was the gathering of information about the frontier regions. Siberia itself deeply impressed him,[18] but the collection of geographical data was no easy task. Prince Dolgorukov, the governor general of Siberia, had ordered the preparation of maps of the frontier areas that were to be delineated in the coming negotiations, but Vladislavich found the maps so inadequate that he sent the team of surveyors back to perfect their knowledge and draw new ones.[19] Lange joined the embassy at Irkutsk in April 1726, and Vladislavich recognized in him a capable and valuable addition to his staff.[20] Lange had sent his secretary to Peking in February 1726 to announce the approach of Vladislavich's embassy, and when the secretary returned to Selenginsk in May, he informed Lange that the Li-fan yuan was sending two officials to meet the embassy at the frontier.[21] In the meantime, Vladislavich also communicated directly with Peking, requesting permission to enter China. He even tried to contact the Jesuit Parrenin at Peking, writing him a secret Italian letter requesting his services for intelligence purposes. As he crossed the frontier, the Russian ambassador sent a lengthy report to the College of Foreign Affairs. He would continue to insist on the entry of the commercial caravan, he wrote, which was a more important issue than the establishment of a religious mission at the Manchu capital. He felt that conditions were favorable for a successful conclusion to the negotiations: one of the two officials sent to meet him was Lungkodo, the emperor's uncle, who would remain at the frontier while Vladislavich journied on to Peking. He then took the opportunity to make his first policy recommendation concerning Sino-Russian commerce: in the interests of developing Russian trade on the Peking market, he advised the complete interdiction of Russian commerce in Mongolia.[22]

The Embassy in China

Vladislavich and his embassy entered the Ch'ing capital ceremoniously and remained six months, until April 25, 1727, longer than any other Russian embassy except Lange's consular sojourn. Yung-cheng received the ambassador in audience on November 4, 1726, at which the Russian presented his credentials in tribute fashion, kowtowing and holding his documents above his head on a small tray covered with yellow cloth. The emperor, in a speech addressed to the president of the Li-fan yuan and translated by one of the Jesuits, reaffirmed Ch'ing interest in peace and friendship with Russia and expressed his hope that the forthcoming negotiations would lead to such an end. He appointed three representatives, whose high position at court affirmed the importance his government attached to the conference with Vladislavich: T'e-ku-t'e, the Manchu president of the Li-fan yuan; Tulishen, vice-president of the Board of War; and Chabina, minister of the imperial household.[23]

The first session of the Sino-Russian conference lasted the

entire time the embassy was in Peking. Twenty different drafts of the proposed treaty were presented, discussed, and rejected. Each side presented a bill of complaints, which the other rejected. Relations between the negotiators became so strained at times that the Russian embassy was denied food and for more than a month was given only brackish water, which caused over half the staff to fall ill. When Vladislavich himself finally sickened, the emperor sent three of his own physicians to attend him. Nevertheless, by March 21, 1727, both sides had agreed on general principles for a final settlement. At the same time Yung-cheng recognized that the major issue, the demarcation of the frontier, could not be resolved in Peking, where there was little available data concerning the topography of the areas in dispute; he recommended that the negotiations be adjourned to the frontier itself.[24]

The general conditions agreed upon at the Peking sessions approximated the minimal desiderata listed in Vladislavich's instructions, with the exception of frontier demarcation, which was to be decided by a joint commission. Fugitives would be extradited on the basis of the principles of the Treaty of Nerchinsk. Russian caravans would be admitted to China once every three years, at their own expense. Two new trading centers were to be established directly on the frontier in place of the markets at Urga and Tsitsihar on the Nun-chiang, which had been unofficial markets outside the caravan system; in this way, it was hoped, trade could take place without the difficulties resulting from the presence of Russians in places of Chinese or Mongol settlement. No Russian agent would be allowed permanent residence in Peking itself, but one could come and go with the caravans, which was merely a continuation of the commissar system. In order to avoid disputes over forms of address in correspondence, letters would be exchanged only between the Peking Li-fan yuan and the St. Petersburg Senate—this, too, was a continuation of established practice. Passports bearing official seals would continue to be required, and ambassadors, diplomatic agents, and couriers would be received as before, without hindrance. Vladislavich went to take leave of the emperor on April 19, 1727, accompanied by Lange and his secretary, Glazunov. Yung-cheng reiterated his desire for peace and promised the resumption of trade once the frontier issue had been settled. On April 23 the embassy left for the frontier.[25]

The Embassy at the Frontier

Vladislavich arrived at the Bura River near Selenginsk on June 14, 1727, but it took him another three months to conclude a frontier agreement. Although geographical data were scarce, the Russians had been preparing maps based on the personal observations of the embassy's geodesists, and Kolychov, the frontier commissioner who had been waiting at Selenginsk since January 8, 1727, had collated all other information available.

The Manchu delegation to the frontier sessions of the Sino-Russian conference consisted of Tulishen, Tsereng, and Lungkodo.[26] Tulishen provided continuity with the Peking sessions and a certain amount of expertise on Russia. Tsereng was an expert on Jungaria, the background to the negotiations. A Mongol, he was a member of the Borjigit clan and a twenty-first-generation descendant of Genghis Khan. His Khalkha family surrendered to K'ang-hsi for protection when Galdan invaded Mongolia in the 1680's. As a Mongol prince enjoying the Manchus' confidence, he was brought to Peking in 1692 to study in the palace, and in 1706 he was married to K'ang-hsi's tenth daughter; it was the sort of royal marriage often used to preserve the loyalty of the frontier peoples to the imperial center. Between 1715 and 1725 Tsereng participated in the struggle with the Jungars, serving with such distinction that in 1725 he was ordered to organize his relatives into a new khanate, known as Sain Noin. This made him independent of the Tushetu-khan. Tsereng's participation in the commission, however, was only partly due to his intimate knowledge of the Jungar problem. As a Mongol loyal to the Ch'ing imperial house by marriage, he could bring the Mongols into the Sino-Russian picture, making them a party to the negotiations and hence to the settlement. Since the settlement was in reality a vehicle for the eventual defeat of the Jungars, Peking must have considered Mongol participation essential.

Lungkodo was a Manchu, the third son of T'ung Kuo-wei, whose elder brother, T'ung Kuo-kang, had participated in the

Nerchinsk negotiations. Lungkodo was K'ang-hsi's cousin and an uncle of Yung-cheng on his mother's side. T'ung Kuo-wei's family had supported Yin-ssu as K'ang-hsi's successor, but Lungkodo had at the last minute joined Yung-cheng's faction. He was one of the attendants at K'ang-hsi's deathbed who claimed that K'ang-hsi had named Yung-cheng his sucessor. Lungkodo was responsible for order in Peking when Yung-cheng returned to the capital with his father's body, and his military power aided the new emperor in successfully opposing his brothers. He was rewarded on Yung-cheng's enthronement day with appointment as one of the four officials to supervise all state affairs, including K'ang-hsi's funeral. By 1725 he had fallen from favor, however, and was sent to Alashan in Ninghsia to direct the construction of forts and cultivation of land in preparation for the anti-Jungar campaigns. He suffered further disgrace in 1726, ostensibly for corruption but actually for refusing to testify against certain opponents of the emperor. To afford him an opportunity to redeem himself, he was appointed to the boundary commission, where his overzealousness led to difficulties, although as the emperor's blood relative he was meant to lend weight to the proceedings.

The Russian and Manchu commissions met for the first time on June 23, 1727. Lungkodo, perhaps out of ignorance of the real situation and in an effort to impress the emperor, made extreme territorial demands, insisting that Russia leave the Amur completely, cede Nerchinsk to Peking, and draw the frontier between the Bura and Selenginsk. On June 19 Vladislavich ordered Bukhholts to send out military reinforcements. When Lungkodo persisted in refusing to modify his position, Tulishen, realizing that a dangerous impasse had been reached, promised Lange on July 11 to inform Peking of Lungkodo's obstinacy; two days later he accepted a letter from Vladislavich to the emperor on the same subject. This brought quick results. Lungkodo was recalled on August 8, Tulishen was made chairman of the Manchu commission, and within two weeks, on August 20, a Sino-Russian frontier agreement, the Treaty of the Bura, was signed.[27]

On the day that he signed the frontier agreement, Vladislavich sent a report to the Senate and the College of Foreign Affairs giving his explanation of the agreement's speedy conclusion. The recall of Lungkodo was quite important, but no less so were the services of Father Parrenin and Maci, to whom he had sent presents, and the help of one Galdan, who gave him secret information for payment. The presence of Bukhholts' troops had contributed to the settlement, as had the repair of Siberian fortifications authorized by St. Petersburg. He had held forty-eight conferences with the Manchu commissioners, in which he had often referred to the fact that Russia, being at peace in Europe, could turn her attention to Asia. When the trade caravan that had been waiting on the frontier since 1722 left for Peking in 1727 with three students, who were going to study Chinese, Manchu, and Mongolian at the capital, Vladislavich sent with them gifts of 1,000 rubles to Maci and 100 rubles to Parrenin.[28]

The Treaty of the Bura was a detailed description of the frontier agreed upon by the frontier commissions, but the line itself had to be drawn and marked with frontier stones to a greater degree of exactitude than was possible on paper, given the knowledge available to the negotiators. Joint Sino-Russian frontier survey commissions were therefore formed to define the frontier's precise location at all important points. The first commission completed its work on October 12, 1727, when it exchanged documents describing in detail the frontier between the Kyakhta and Shabindobagom rivers.[29] The second commission exchanged protocols defining the frontier between the Kyakhta and Argun rivers on October 27.[30] Appended to each protocol was a register of the precise definitions of the boundary, area by area,[31] and sixty-three "beacons" were set up as border stones at vital points, with a description of the border inscribed on each in Russian and Chinese.[32] A neutral strip of land, "according to the comfort of local conditions, from five to thirty *sagenes* in width," extended on either side of each marker.[33] The way was now open for concluding the definitive Sino-Russian treaty itself, covering political and economic as well as frontier affairs.

The Treaty of Kyakhta

The Treaty of the Bura, the instrument that Peking required before it would sign any other agreements with Russia, was itself incorporated into the Treaty of Kyakhta,[34] a Latin draft of which reached the frontier from Peking on November 13. Although it was supposed to have been based on the political and commercial principles agreed upon at the Peking sessions, much to Vladislavich's surprise the draft treaty varied from the original Peking understanding as well as the Bura treaty and its protocols in two important ways. First, the draft treaty made no mention of the caravan trade to Peking. Second, the entire Ud River region, which was to have remained undemarcated, owing to an insufficiency of geographical data, was assigned to China, and all Russian habitations in the region were to be destroyed.[35] The Manchu commissioners insisted that this version must be approved and signed, since the emperor himself had already sanctioned it, but Vladislavich refused. Appealing over the commissioners' heads, he wrote directly to Lange, who was in Peking with the trade caravan, instructing him to intercede at court. At the end of the year, when Vladislavich learned that Catherine I had died on May 6, he informed the Manchu delegation that Russia's rulers were changing, but not her policies. Finally, on June 14, 1728, a new draft of the treaty arrived from Peking: it conformed completely to the original understandings and the frontier protocols. The commissions exchanged copies of the treaty that same day. Vladislavich and Glazunov signed for Russia; Chabina, T'e-ku-t'e, and Nayentai (specifically representing the Li-fan yuan) signed on behalf of Tulishen.[36] Ratifications were exchanged near the Kyakhta River, hence the treaty's name.

The Treaty of Kyakhta consisted of eleven articles, ranging over all aspects of the Sino-Russian relationship.[37] Articles I and XI declared eternal peace and friendship between the two empires and discussed the language and ratification of the instrument. The other nine articles, constituting the Sino-Russian settlement itself, dealt with six specific problems: demarcation of the frontier (III, VII), exchange of fugitives (II), commercial relations (IV), a Russian religious establishment in Peking (V), forms of diplomatic intercouse (VI, IX), and settlement of future disputes (VIII, X). Article II delineated the entire frontier on the basis of the Treaty of the Bura, with the exception of the territory along the Ud River, east of the Gorbitsa, which according to agreement would be demarcated in the future "by ambassadors or by correspondence." The provisions concerning fugitives were identical with those in the Treaty of Nerchinsk.

The heart of the settlement was the commercial system, which according to the preamble to Article IV was specifically established in return for the frontier and fugitive settlements, that is, for Russian neutrality in Central Asia.[38] It consisted of two distinct elements: trade by caravan and frontier trade. The caravan trade was to be resumed under the Manchu regulations of 1693. No more than two hundred merchants could go to Peking once every three years in a single caravan, which would pay all its own expenses and receive no subsidies from the Ch'ing government, though no duties or imposts would be collected by the government from sellers or buyers. Each caravan was required to notify the Manchu frontier authorities in writing of its arrival, whereupon officers would be designated to guide the caravan to Peking and supervise its affairs. Russian merchants were free to buy or hire camels, horses, and provisions between the frontier and the capital. The Russians would appoint a caravan chief, responsible for all its affairs, who would settle arguments among the Russian merchants themselves. If he was of high rank, he would be accorded due honors. The only goods restricted in trade were those defined as contraband by the laws of the two empires. When the caravan returned to Russia, no one would be allowed to remain behind without specific agreement between the caravan chief and the Manchu officials charged with Sino-Russian relations. The property of any Russian merchant dying in China was to be turned over to the caravan chief. The treaty thus incorporated the basic elements of the Nerchinsk commercial agreement, the Ch'ing regulations of 1693, and specific aspects of Vladislavich's instructions about matters that would normally have been the concern of a consular agent.

The Kyakhta treaty established a new form of legitimate commerce in addition to the caravan trade, as opposed to the extralegal Urga market. Two regular Sino-Russian frontier commercial emporia were to be created, one at Kyakhta on the Selenga River, the other at a spot near Nerchinsk. They would be surrounded by fences and palisades for protection. In order to restrict the frontier trade to those two places, the treaty stipulated that all merchants going there for trade had to follow "direct routes," and that merchants trading elsewhere would suffer confiscation of their goods. An equal number of officials under chiefs of equal rank were to be charged by each side with the responsibility for the defense and commerce of these two emporia, and disputes between them would be decided in the fashion described in the treaty. While this was a distinctly new departure in Manchu-Russian relations, it brought the commercial system into harmony with more traditional tribute practices: trade often took place at the frontier while a tribute mission visited Peking, and frontier markets were structurally, though not ideologically, autonomous. The frontier trade regularized by the treaty was an addition to the caravan system, not a substitute for it, and was in large part a political institution designed to increase Russian desire for stable relations with Peking by enlarging the market accessible to Russian commercial penetration. It also would keep Russians from penetrating physically into Mongolia or Sinkiang. A location for the second emporium had already been chosen by the time the treaty was ratified: an exchange of letters, dated May 17, 1728, designated Tsurukhaitu, on the right bank of the Argun River near Nerchinsk.[39]

St. Petersburg also obtained certain religious concessions in exchange for the frontier settlement. The O-lo-ssu kuan was specifically assigned as the Russian hostel in Peking, and a church was to be built on the premises, with the assistance of a court official appointed to oversee relations with Russia. One priest, called a "lama" in the treaty, who was already in Peking with the caravan, would be assisted by three others, to whom the treaty granted permission to reside at the Ch'ing capital; they would all receive subsidies from the Manchu government in the form of provisions, and they had freedom of religion "according to their own laws." In addition, four young students who could speak and read both Russian and Latin were permitted to reside at the O-lo-ssu kuan for the purpose of language study, but unlike the members of the religious establishment, they were to be maintained by the Russian government. Upon completion of their studies, they would be replaced by new students. This was the beginning of the famous Russian Ecclesiastical Mission in Peking.[40]

The Treaty of Kyakhta projected the entire treaty system into the future as a permanent feature of Sino-Russian relations by creating the necessary machinery for the settlement of such disputes as might arise between the two empires and by describing in detail the forms for further diplomatic intercourse. The treaty charged each empire's frontier commanders or chief officials with the settlement of all disputes "according to the laws of justice," and delays caused by the officials' self-interest would be punished "according to their own laws." The creation of judicial machinery in the form of joint responsibility by both empires' frontier officials required, however, a common definition of "justice" in a situation where no common concept of "law" existed and where accepted punishments for specific crimes differed according to each society's legal assumptions. Consequently, Article X of the treaty defined specific crimes and legislated mandatory punishments in terms of the norms of each social system. Criminals escaping across the frontier, or others who crossed with arms and committed brigandage or murder, were to be executed wherever they were found. Those who crossed with arms but did not commit any crimes were punished "as they should be," that is, according to the customs of their own empire if they did not carry valid passports. Soldiers who deserted and robbed their sovereign were to be hanged if they were Russian, strangled if they were Chinese, and the stolen property would be returned to their respective governments. Men crossing the frontier to steal cattle or other animals were to be turned over to their own frontier authorities for punishment by fines on a prescribed sliding scale: ten times the value stolen for the first offense, twenty times for the second offense, and death for the third offense. Those who crossed the frontier without passports for legitimate activities, such as hunting and fishing, would have their earnings confiscated for the benefit of their sovereign. Common people who crossed the frontier were also to be punished, though no penalties were specified; presumably this referred to people straying across the border by accident. This article, perhaps the most interesting in the entire treaty, was a conscious effort to bridge the cultural barrier between Chinese and Russian society.[41]

The treaty tried further to resolve cultural differences by stipulating the manner in which Sino-Russian correspondence was to be conducted and diplomatic personnel received. The negotiators apparently realized that the achievement of stability in their relationship depended in part on the avoidance of those specific problems of form that had bedeviled Moscow's and later St. Petersburg's relations with Peking from the beginning. Article X, therefore, stipulated that the Li-fan yuan in Peking and the Senate in St. Petersburg were corresponding bodies for the central authorities, and that all documents had to carry official seals to be recognized: Russian correspondence to China had to bear the seal of the Russian empire or of the governor at Tobolsk, who as senior official in Siberia could also, according to the treaty, receive letters from the Li-fan yuan and correspond with it. All letters concerning frontier problems, the commercial entrepots, deserters, robberies, and the like had to be personally signed and sealed by the Tushetu-khan and the Wang Danjin-dorji, both Khalkha Mongol princes, if they originated with the Manchus, and by the frontier commander if they came from Russia. Couriers were permitted to travel only along the Kyakhta road, unless an emergency required a more direct route. Arriving at the frontier, the couriers would present their documents, properly sealed, to the frontier officials, at which time they would be provided with transport, provisions, and guides. The frontier authorities would inform each other of transgressions of these regulations, confer together, and punish the culpable parties.

If the necessity arose to dispatch envoys, they too would have to conform to treaty regulations. Upon arriving at the frontier, an envoy, regardless of rank, would inform the authorities on the other side of his rank and the purpose of his mission; officials would then be sent to receive him and conduct him to his destination. As soon as envoys had crossed the frontier, they were to receive transportation, provisions, and protection; at the capital they would be lodged at their host's expense. However, if the mission occurred in a year when no regular commercial caravan was scheduled, it could not import merchandise for commercial purposes. The treaty also created sanctions to encourage the quick dispatch of mutual business, allowing each side to invoke force against the other to ensure that its obligations were met: if correspondence was delayed at forwarding points, or if answers did not arrive within a reasonable period of time, either side could refuse entry to ambassadors and merchants from the other, and normal relations would be resumed only upon settlement of the outstanding difficulties. This provision was invoked three times between 1728 and 1860.

The contrast between the Nerchinsk and Kyakhta treaties is striking. The former was no more than an enabling act—a description of a situation and a statement of intention. Kyakhta, however, was an extraordinarily specific diplomatic instrument. The negotiators tried to foresee all possibilities and to create institutions, or at least regulations, to cover any eventuality. Their success and foresight is reflected in the fact that, with only minor modifications, the Treaty of Kyakhta remained the essential basis for Sino-Russian relations down to 1860, when it was superseded by the radically different Treaty of Peking.

Vladislavich, Dolgorukov, and Lange: The Future of Sino-Russian Relations

With the conclusion of the Treaty of Kyakhta, St. Petersburg had to consider giving content to the new commercial and political system. As early as September 28, 1727, Vladislavich pointed out in a report to the College of Foreign Affairs that the pre-Kyakhta *ad hoc* arrangement permitting local Siberian officials great latitude in the conduct of relations with Peking had led to disaster, and before his departure from the frontier he undertook to reorganize frontier administration.[42] He placed Colonel Bukhholts, who had long experience on the frontier, in charge of general frontier affairs and security, under the authority of the voevoda of Irkutsk and the governor general of Siberia. Bukhholts was also charged with completion of the construction work on the two new trade emporia in Kyakhta and Tsurukhaitu. Troops were permanently stationed at strategic points along the frontier. Bukhholts was instructed to forbid and prevent the export to Mongolia of cattle, which might be used to provision the Manchu armies fighting the Jungars and hence be construed by the Jungars as interference and cause for attack. He was to keep in touch with Lange on all diplomatic affairs, corresponding in code, to represent Russia in correspondence with the Tushetu-khan on current business, and to maintain the relationship with Galdan, the spy who had aided Vladislavich at the negotiations, by paying him an annual honorarium.

Vladislavich also appointed commissioners for Kyakhta and Tsurukhaitu, who were under Bukhholts' orders and were responsible for police and judicial affairs as well as for the commercial supervision of their respective emporia. Each was assigned a specific section of the frontier, along which he must travel on annual summer tours of inspection, examining the frontier stones and searching for fugitives and contraband. They received further instructions concerning the preservation of Russian interests among the indigenous population. Lamas, for instance, were forbidden to immigrate to Russian territories, and marriages between Russian and Manchu subjects were interdicted. If necessary, the commissioners were allowed to send Russian Buddhist subjects among the Mongols to take ecclesiastical orders, so as to protect Russian interests and provide necessary intelligence.

The ambassador clearly understood that the success of his arrangements required the loyalty of local military forces and sufficient funds to meet the needs of the frontier administration. Consequently, he instructed the voevoda of Irkutsk to pay the troops regularly, as a form of control. False declarations or prevarications about customs collections, misuse of funds for construction at Kyakhta and Tsurukhaitu, or any other misdemeanor concerning border controls were to be punished severely. Because the Buryats, who still formed the most substantial element in east-central Siberia's frontier population, depended on trade in horses and cattle for income, and because the new frontier regime would inflict hardships on them by limiting their territory for transmigration, the ambassador ordered that they be permitted to come and trade at will in Kyakhta. But he placed high export duties on horses and cattle, making it difficult, though not impossible, for the Manchu armies to use the Buryats as a source of supply.[43]

Vladislavich left Selenginsk on July 3, 1728, and on December 18 arrived in Moscow, where four days later, Peter II received him in audience. By March 8 of the following year he had completed the process of turning over to the authorities the emperor's gifts to the tsar, the instruments of the treaty, maps, and other state documents, and sometime in 1729 he submitted a report of his embassy's achievements, paralleling point by point the paragraphs of his original instructions.[44] This accomplishment did not end his interest and participation in Manchu-Russian relations, however. Until his death in St. Petersburg on June 17, 1738, he continued to submit to the government his ideas concerning Russia's Far Eastern policies.

In 1731 Vladislavich submitted a two-part memorial considering the problem of war and peace with China.[45] While counseling prudence and mature reflection, he discussed the merits and demerits of a limited war to obtain control of the Amur. It would be a glorious and valuable campaign, he claimed, but not an easy one. The logistic effort required would be great, the results negligible. Russia, he concluded, should "maintain everything according to the provisions of the treaty" and not enter into great arguments for small results. In the second part of the memorial, however, the former ambassador discussed the possibility of waging total war against China. If by God's grace Russia had a long period of peace in Europe and accumulated "several millions of money above expenditures in the treasury," St. Petersburg could seriously consider the military conquest of China, which was the richest and most abundantly provided state in the Asian or European world. First, although the Chinese were industrious, numerous, and prepared for war, they were not a warlike people. Second, the Manchus then ruling China numbered no more than four million (an exaggeration on his part), whereas the Han Chinese suffering under the harsh Manchu regime numbered about two hundred million. A Russian invasion from the north would encourage them to rise against the Ch'ing dynasty, engulfing many provinces in an internal war. The Manchus would then have to divide their forces into three parts: to maintain garrisons, to fight the invading Russians, and to suppress the Chinese rebels. With the vast majority of the Chinese population on Russia's side, she would defeat and conquer China easily.

Despite Vladislavich's sanguine view of the possibility of conquering the Manchu Empire, the Russian government remained interested in peace because of the commerce that it encouraged. The government's need of a deliberate policy to maximize profits from that commerce by means of the rational organization of the China trade was debated by Sava Vladislavich, Prince Dolgorukov, the governor general of Siberia, and Lorents Lange. As early as September 1727 the ambassador had raised the entire question of organization and administration of Sino-Russian commerce in a report to the College of Foreign Affairs.[46] More than one-third of the total value of goods exported in the state's Peking caravans was privately owned, he declared, because the state permitted the caravan staffs to export goods in lieu of salaries. Moreoever, the private merchandise was usually first-rate goods, while the state's goods were inferior. The state was paying for the transportation of the private goods, however, and they were usually traded first on the Peking market, because of the cupidity of the caravan staffs. He proposed several measures to remedy this situation and increase the caravans' profits. No one except the state should export fur pelts to Peking, and the caravan staff should be given fixed salaries and forbidden to conduct any kind of trade inside the Manchu Empire. The caravans should be convoyed by regular military units of fifty to one hundred men, who would also form the caravan's labor force. Any private merchandise discovered in the caravan when it returned from Peking should be confiscated "without pity." He also recommended that greater continuity be established between caravans and that each caravan chief communicate Peking's market conditions to the next caravan's director, which would permit a more judicious Russian purchasing policy.

Vladislavich also considered the problem of the private Siberian trade with China and pointed out that certain noncommercial considerations must be taken into account. The inhabitants of the frontier zone depended on commerce for their livelihood, and the soldiers, who arrived unprovided with basic necessities, needed to trade, although some years previously they had been forbidden to engage in commerce.[47] Merchants, who contributed nothing to frontier defense, were enriched "in the twinkling of an eye," whereas the soldiers were reduced to such ruin that they could not afford to maintain their horses or arms in a usable condition. The chief recipients of the benefits of private commerce were the great European Russian merchants, who successfully avoided the payment of customs duties. Vladislavich made several proposals to remedy this situation. Free trade should be established at the two frontier commercial centers created by the Kyakhta treaty, and the inhabitants of the frontier zone should be permitted to trade in all commodities except fur pelts and cattle. However, European Russian merchants should not be permitted to trade at the frontier, which would be reserved for the Siberians "who do not know other trade routes and have no other trade." Finally, Colonel Bukhholts and the military should exercise control over the collection of customs in order to ensure that no evasions were permitted by the customs officials. He concluded, "This disposition [of affairs] cannot be contrary to anyone except the local commissioners, who prevaricate fraudulently."

Vladislavich was concerned primarily with maximizing state income from the China trade, but Prince Dolgorukov, as the tsar's chief official in Siberia, was more interested in the problem of financing the state's activities in Siberia and in customs collections. When asked for his comments on the ambassador's proposals, he criticized them from this viewpoint.[48] In contrast to Vladislavich, the governor general felt that the interdiction of all but state commerce in furs would result in a severe deficit in the levy of customs duties. He proposed, instead, that the Senate in St. Petersburg nominate two commissars to govern the caravan trade. The first would travel to Peking with a caravan while the second was preparing the next caravan in Siberia. They would be able to watch and control each other's activities. He agreed that the caravans should not be permitted to trade privately in Peking but did not agree with Vladislavich's proposed salary solution which, he maintained, would require an outlay of 13,200 rubles for each caravan in addition to expenses for workers. It would represent a considerable dispensation of unearned funds. Besides, Russian silver rubles had less value in Peking than in Russia. Dolgorukov, who had a more positive view of human nature than Vladislavich, proposed a different solution: the Irkutsk voevoda should give the caravan staff fixed salaries in fur pelts and goods of his choosing, which could be exported to Peking under written guarantees that they would be sold on the market only after the caravan had completed the state's business. The caravan tselovalniks would be charged with the purchase of these export fur pelts so that they could not complain of being given pelts of poor quality to sell at Peking.

As a bureaucrat and administrator, Dolgorukov believed that state control and supervision were necessary to enlarge profits from the China trade, most particularly from the sale of Chinese goods inside Russia. The problem as he saw it was to determine a just price at which to sell the Chinese commodities. Since the caravan staff was composed of experts acquainted with the value of Chinese goods, it should be responsible for pricing and selling the goods that its caravan imported. Dolgorukov also severely criticized Vladislavich's proposal to restrict frontier trade to the Siberians. Because they lacked the means to import large quantities of Chinese merchandise, they would be unable to distribute goods widely. Unless European Russian merchants, with their command of capital resources and trade routes, were permitted to trade on the frontier, commerce and customs collections would decline sharply.

Vladislavich's recommendations, together with Dolgorukov's criticisms and suggestions, were submitted to Lange in 1730 when he returned from Peking with the first post-Kyakhta caravan. In reply, Lange wrote a long critique of Russia's China trade policy, which showed in every line a basic concern with the entire commercial process and an understanding of the need for planning in terms of the market itself, rather than simply in terms of an organizational solution to the problem of increasing profits. If at the present time, he wrote, conditions on the Peking market were as good as they had been in earlier years, trade would be profitable. However, the caravan of 1728, which had been under his direction, had proven an almost total failure. Dividing the history of the caravan trade into "earlier" and "later" periods, he illustrated the market's decline through figures that showed a rise in the purchase price of fur pelts in Siberia between the two periods, but a decline in the selling price at Peking.[49] This imbalance, he continued, resulted from an oversupply of fur pelts on the Peking market, which in turn came about because of too many caravans supplying that market and because of the very successful competition by the Urga market with Peking. If proper remedial measures were taken immediately, Lange counseled, the market might recover in a decade or so. The objective of any policy must be to change the balance of supply and demand in Peking now to maximize profits later. Supply had to be cut off at the source, so that the Chinese received no fur at all for the time being. State caravans might continue to travel to the Ch'ing capital once every three years for the next decade, but their purpose should be political, not commercial: to keep open the trade routes and prevent the Manchus from suspecting that commercial relations had been suspended. These small "political" caravans could trade without profit, though hopefully without loss too, until prices on Russian goods at Peking rose to a satisfactory level. Then, predicted Lange, Sino-Russian trade would be important and lucrative for the state, "as it should be."

Lange proposed three immediate steps to encourage a rise in prices in Peking. First, a considerable portion of the fur supply should be kept in storage in Siberia, without profit, for a number of years. Second, all customs collections on the frontier should be canceled immediately, to encourage trade in other commodities. Third, trade with Mongolia should be controlled, but not forbidden, in order to weaken the Urga market without permitting the development of contraband commerce. These proposals were audaciously different from the suggestions of Vladislavich and Dolgorukov, but Lange supported them with long and closely reasoned arguments. He alone of the three participants in the debate was aware of the distinction between immediate, short-range policy and long-range policy planning. He urged the state to make a continuing study of the Peking market to determine what profits could be expected and whether customs duties collected from private trade could possibly become a more important source of state income than the state's actual participation in the commerce. On the strength of such a study, Lange thought, it might not prove unreasonable for the state to withdraw from commerce in favor of creating a special commercial company, probably on the model of the various East India companies in western Europe. Lange was a "practicing economist," who sought explanations for specific phenomena in historical and market analysis.

All three men believed the caravan system would prove to be the primary instrument of Sino-Russian commerce, and all three were wrong. Both Vladislavich and Lange failed to perceive the real economic and political significance of the institutional innovations in the treaty that they themselves had negotiated with the Manchus. In the event, Kyakhta, not the caravan trade, provided the key to stability and commercial growth.

The Transition to Stability

The Treaty of Kyakhta envisaged Sino-Russian commerce proceeding on two courses: triennial caravans and frontier markets. It was a mixed system, combining the elements of three different traditions of experience. The Russian trade caravans resembled tribute missions but were not, and in their case the Manchus made a clear distinction between trade and tribute. Both Russia and the Ch'ing dynasty had extensive experience with both. The establishment of commercial emporia on the frontier was the outgrowth of a third tradition: the use of frontier markets to control the barbarians. Nor was Russia a stranger to frontier emporia. Astrakhan, for instance, located where the Volga flows into the Caspian, was a venerable commercial city where Russians, Caucasians, and Persians traded together.

Despite the fact that the treaty described a dual commercial system, the caravan trade did not long survive establishment of the Kyakhta frontier trading-post.[50] The triennial caravans were unable to compete with Kyakhta commercially, and the entire caravan trade died a natural death. That this would happen became evident when the very first caravan reached Peking after the conclusion of the new treaty. Organized while Lyangusov's caravan of 1719 was still at Peking, it was refused permission to cross the frontier when it reached Selenginsk in June 1724, and suffered tremendous losses before it finally left for the Ch'ing capital in September 1727.[51] Despite its losses, it was the largest caravan to date, with an investment of approximately 334,210 rubles. Its goods were carried to Peking on 637 wagons, accompanied by 1,650 horses, 565 cattle, and 205 men.[52] The caravan traded badly in Peking, where it remained under Lange's direction for six-and-a-half months. Lange sold less than a quarter of the one million squirrel skins the caravan had imported, and those at little profit. The market simply could not absorb additional Russian goods. When Lange arrived at Kyakhta on September 30, 1728, he turned over the caravan's unsold stores to the local frontier commissioner for sale at the new frontier trading-post.[53] Neither did the caravan succeed in disposing of its Chinese goods until 1735, by which time it had realized only 244,000 rubles, considerably less than the initial investment. The next caravan made a profit of only 15,000 rubles, and the third did little better.[54] By 1755, when the last Russian caravan wended its way to Peking, the caravan trade had ceased to be of commercial interest to the Russian treasury.

The Manchu government had recognized much earlier the failure of this portion of the Kyakhta settlement. In the second year of Ch'ien-lung's reign (1737-1738), the superintendent of the O-lo-ssu kuan, the censor Ho-ch'ing, memorialized the throne to the effect that trade with Russia should be limited to the frontier, and that Russians residing at Peking should be excluded from commercial activities.[55] Kyakhta had begun to prove its commercial value.

Sava Vladislavich himself founded "The Sandy Venice," as Kyakhta was sometimes called in literature. For the construction of the new trading post he chose a spot directly on the frontier, 5.43 miles from the Troitskaya fortress (the future Troitsko-savsk), which was itself being constructed as part of the frontier defense system. By the time the first stone had been laid at Kyakhta, the nearby fortress already contained several houses, a customs shed, barns, a prison, and a small wooden church. At first Kyakhta was simply an outpost of the Troitskaya fortress.

The ambassador charged a Captain Knyaginkin with the construction of Kyakhta and left him 350 soldiers of the Yakutsk regiment and thirty Cossacks to carry on the work, which was completed in the winter of 1728-1729. The small settlement at first consisted of thirty-two huts for the residence of merchants who were expected to gather for trade. In the middle of the huts was a marketplace, which included twenty-four shops, above which were storerooms.[56] Both Kyakhta and Troitskaya were inconveniently situated on a sandy steppe where there was an insufficient supply of water. The short, shallow Kyakhta River usually dried up in the summer, when the settlement's residents had to rely on drinking water drawn from deep wells. The traveler Gmelin, who visited Kyakhta in 1735, felt that Vladislavich would have been wiser to construct the trading post on the Bura River, and Pallas, who visisted it in 1742, was equally critical.[57] A significant factor in the choice of the Kyakhta may have been that it is the only river in the area that flows from north to south, all others flowing in the opposite direction: by locating the settlement on a river that flowed from Russian into Chinese territory, Vladislavich may have been trying to avoid presenting the Manchus with the temptation to pressure Kyakhta by cutting off the river's flow.[58]

Commercial activity at Kyakhta had begun by the second half of 1728. In April, even before the exchange of treaties, the Russian frontier administration received a letter from a group of Chinese merchants who had arrived at Urga in expectation of the opening of frontier trade. They proposed going to the Kyakhta River, and the Russian authorities agreed, then issued a decree informing all Russian merchants in the Transbaikal region that they could proceed to Kyakhta "to trade freely in any goods they wished, except provisions and furs, with the payment of the usual customs duties."[59] They were to go first to Selenginsk, where their goods would be inspected by the customs authorities, before proceeding to Kyakhta. However, several months of indecisiveness followed. Between August 1 and September 2, only ten Russian merchants passed through the Selenginsk customs on their way to Kyakhta. Nor did the Chinese rush to the frontier, despite their letter. By August 25 only four Chinese yurts were to be seen in the neighborhood, but at the end of September Lange delivered his unsold furs to the settlement and the Kyakhta trade began.[60] On the Russian side it was controlled by a small staff of officials. A superintendent collected duties, assisted by a cofferer and several serving-people. Russians residing at Kyakhta were charged thirty kopeks per person per trading season for the use of the state-constructed and owned buildings, and Knyaginkin kept a special register of all the funds he collected.[61] Colonel Bukhholts reported in 1729 that trade at Kyakhta was well begun, but Tsurukhaitu was being abandoned as unsuitable. Chinese merchants from Urga began to construct a trading post directly across the river from the Russian settlement. This merchant community, known as Mai-mai-ch'eng or Trade Town, was sufficiently well established by 1735 for Gmelin to describe the interiors of the Chinese living quarters with great detail and accuracy.[62]

Sino-Russian trade through the Kyakhta-Mai-mai-ch'eng complex developed rapidly. While the caravan trade declined, the export of fur to China through Kyakhta on a strictly barter basis increased from 423,035 rubles in 1735 to 1,175,364 rubles in 1759, only four years after the last Russian caravan had traded at Peking.[63] Between the opening of trade at the end of 1728 and the devising of a greatly expanded treaty settlement in the middle of the nineteenth century under the influence of the Opium Wars, only three major and five minor interruptions in commercial relations took place, lasting altogether fifteen years and seven months. These interruptions, all of which took place before the end of the eighteenth century, were caused by various problems, including the return of fugitives from justice, the levying of customs duties, and personal conflicts between merchants in Kyakhta and Mai-mai-ch'eng. Commerce was never interrupted for strictly economic reasons, such as a sharp decline in supply or demand. In order to resolve the difficulties that gave rise to the interruptions, two more agreements were signed, in 1768 and 1792, without the use of force by either side. The agreement of 1768 dealt chiefly with frontier problems, and that of 1792 involved a minor adjustment of the trade regime. In 1851 the Treaty of Kuldja extended the Kyakhta system to Sinkiang, at Kuldja and Chuguchak, but in no way modified the regime obtaining at Kyakhta.[64] It was an extension of the trade system to a new area, which had grown in importance as Russian interest in Central Asia developed after the first quarter of the nineteenth century. The extension was a testimony to the essential stability of the relationship negotiated by Vladislavich and institutionalized by the Treaty of Kyakhta in 1727.

An Hypothesis as Epilogue

This book began with a description of the traditional East Asian world order, and for two reasons it must end with some remarks about the West. First, the East Asian world order was eventually defined as "traditional" by the West not because of changes that took place in East Asia but because of changes occurring in Europe long after the period of this study. Therein lies one of the chief significances of early Sino-Russian relations. The *dramatis personae*—Baykov, Milescu, Golovin, Lange, and Sava Vladislavich—did not consider China either "traditional," underdeveloped, quaint, picturesque, or "native." Although China and East Asia differed from Europe, the difference was thought to be cultural and customary, not developmental. During the age of these men, whose diplomatic acitivites in the Far East encompassed less than a century, China came to be considered more civilized and advanced than Europe. Chinese arts were in the late seventeenth and eighteenth centuries translated into a European aesthetic chinoiserie affecting Peter the Great and Catherine the Great much as it did the monarchs and aristocracy of western Europe. Chinese law and custom, particularly the remarkable Confucian examination system, were held up as models of an advanced society, which Europe had yet to become. But within a century and a half of concluding the Treaty of Nerchinsk, the West had begun to knock at China's doors, demanding that she change her ancient ways and "modernize" the conduct of her international relations. To "modernize" meant to Europeanize. This remarkable shift in attitudes resulted in part from changes in Europe's assumptions concerning the world order.

The second and perhaps more important reason for concluding with some brief remarks about the West concerns the current problem of Western intercourse with the "non-West." Because we live in an age when the West—particularly the North Atlantic community but increasingly the Communist West, too—is entering upon a major struggle with China, research on East Asia will be less than fully valuable if it does no more than add to the "fund of knowledge." Such knowledge can only be the prelude to the understanding that must be acquired, and acquired quickly, if we are to live peaceably with China. Equally necessary is the heightened perception of ourselves that comes from a study of those who are radically different. The Western student of China is thus in a superb position to look inward on himself, outward on his society, and backward on his past, so as to judge the development of contemporary Western behavior patterns. The student of Sino-Western intercourse also faces the difficult task of evaluating not only the course of China's relations with the West but the sources of policy on each side as well. In such an effort the student's own intellectual position must be removed in sympathy from both China and the West as far as possible. No study of Sino-Western contact through history can concentrate only on the changes that have taken place in China, ignoring changes that have taken place in the West, and still hope to convey the significance of its story.

The Western assault on the East Asian world order that began in the nineteenth century, and has yet to be concluded, took many guises, but it concentrated on the problem that has been egocentrically and erroneously termed "China's entry into the family of nations." The conflict stemmed from far more than the new European and American developments in military and transportation technology or their rapidly expanding commercial interests. Equally important was the growth at the end of the eighteenth and beginning of the nineteenth centuries of new Western concepts of the intellectual order. The intellectual revolution that accompanied technological change transformed the European view of the international system, emphasizing elements that had not been important when the Russians and Dutch, for instance, approached China in the seventeenth century. From a European point of view, the Sino-Russian Nerchinsk and Kyakhta treaty system rested primarily on two pillars. The first was the prevalent Western concept of international law; the second was the viability and flexibility of the treaty system's institutions. The system broke down in the middle of the nineteenth century when the West's assumptions changed and the institutions of the Kyakhta treaty could no longer accommodate the new technology by which the West was subjecting East Asia to its new concept of world order.

In the latter part of the eighteenth century European jurists and legal historians began to systematize and summarize the basic theories of the law of nations that had dominated Western thinking since the seventeenth century, when Hugo Grotius initiated the codification of international law as the Law of Nations under the Latin expression *jus gentium. Jus gentium* had its primary theoretical basis in natural law, which was "both creative and organizing." It posited a moral system to guide relations between states and provided for the systematic application of law to all states.[1] The *jus gentium naturale,* or basic natural law of nations, applied to all nations, whether or not they were "civilized," that is, to European and extra-European alike. The law stressed the equality and independence of all nations. In the practice of interstate relations, however, this universal natural law was expanded or contracted. A modified natural law of nations developed, called by Christian Wolff the *jus gentium voluntarium,* or volitional law of nations, which was based on the nations' *consensus presumptus,* the presumed or pre-existent agreement on particular matters of all nations, that is, of all rulers of men. The *consensus presumptus* was "revealed irrespective of agreement or express submission to legal rules." The natural law of nations was further modified by the customary laws founded on tacit consent, or by specific treaties, which constituted the *jus gentium pactitium,* or law of nations as revealed in their treaties with one another. It was within the context of *jus gentium voluntarium,* which included, for instance, "the prohibition of use of poisoned weapons or the systematic application of privileges and immunities to diplomatic envoys,"[2] that Milescu appealed to Mala in his debates over proper audience ritual. These prohibitions or regulations, based as they were on a supposedly universal concept of natural law, were assumed to appear in many parts of the world under various guises that would obtain in relations between individual states. This explained Milescu's insistence that all sovereigns permitted foreign envoys to follow their own customary procedures in greeting the sovereign to whom they were accredited.

The natural law of nations provided the context within which Russia, as a European and Christian nation, tried to enter into relations with China. That law was the intellectual precondition for the growth of relations between states whose customary norms of behavior differed as radically as did the Russian and the Dutch, or the Russian and the Manchu-Chinese, but whose technology did not permit the imposition of one side's assumptions on the other. All sovereigns were equal by virtue of natural law. Consequently, when Johann Christian Lünig published at Leipzig in 1719 his two-volume study and compilation of ritual, the *Theatrum ceremoniale historico-politicum,* he included a section on Chinese, Japanese, and Siamese ritual without suggesting that the practices of those nations did not in any way conform to accepted international behavior.[3] Unusual they may have been, but under the natural law of nations the European did not recognize any inequality between sovereigns because of unorthodox practices or institutional differences.

The natural law of nations had practical application to the immediate development of Europe's relations with Asia and China before the end of the eighteenth century. Because all sovereigns were equal, for instance, the subjects of one could accept positions under another and serve loyally as long as the particular interests of the two did not clash. Englishmen served Indian rulers, and the East India Company ruled portions of the Indian subcontinent as the vassal of Indian potentates. In China, the Dutch and eventually the Russians could begin to accept Chinese ceremonial, such as the kowtow, as a custom that did not imply, within the European context, anything more than recognition under natural law of the emperor's dignity in his own land. The natural law of nations was, in short, the ideational basis for the compromise inherent in the Nerchinsk-Kyakhta treaty system.

The changes that began to take place in European thinking concerning the law of nations at the end of the eighteenth and beginning of the nineteenth centuries had far-reaching consequences for the West's relations with China that persist down to the present day. "The eighteenth century," wrote the legal historian C. H. Alexandrowicz, "was at the same time one of expanding world commercial relations and one of contracting international legal conceptions."[4] Many legal writers began to assume the legal existence of a European community of nations (*Rechtsgemeinschaft*). According to them, the European community was based on a common tradition and a geographical continuity of interstate relations, which justified "the conception of a positive European law of nations based on treaties and [European] custom." The legal positivists, who represented one part of a larger intellectual movement in Europe, placed the law of nature and its concomitant natural law of nations in a subordinate position, or even outside the law entirely. They were more juridical and more concerned with concrete situations as the basis for developing the family of nations than were the naturalists. The compilations of treaties published with increasing frequency toward the end of the eighteenth century were themselves legal texts illustrative of the positivist trend in international jurisprudence, which previously had been subordinate to natural law.

This change in the character of European international law was by no means abstract. The Congress of Vienna, the concept of the Concert of Europe, and the growth within the European community of the codification of specific practice as "international law" reflected in practice the new theoretical developments. In Europe's relations with the Far East the new positivist concept of the "family of nations" materially changed the situation. Whereas under natural law the "family of nations" was presumed to be a universal continuum, under the developing positive law it was redefined as those states that adhered to accepted international legal practice as proclaimed by the European states acting in concert. Entry into the family of nations was formalized and symbolized by "recognition," a concept that is purely European and positivist, meaning essentially that the member nations accepted a new member by virtue of its adherence to their regulations and institutions. The first extra-European states to be admitted, on the occasion of their independence, were the United States of America,

Haiti, and Liberia. Their geographical location outside Europe ensured the universalization of European regional practice. That they were new states did not alter the principle, but their intellectually European origins strengthened it. This Europeanization must be kept in mind when analyzing the "modernization" of international systems.

The tribute system was no less modern and no more traditional from the eighteenth-century European point of view than from the Asian. "Modernization," in the sense of Europeanization, was not then required for participation in the international community, because Europe was not, and did not consider itself, the standard or norm for international behavior. Since all sovereigns were loyally equal, the diplomatic process entailed the development of institutional compromises on immediate issues that did not impinge on the practices of the participants, except insofar as specific compromises were required for the resolution of discrete issues. Only in the nineteenth century did the diplomatic process between Europe and extra-European nations involve a necessary "modernization" of the non-European international system.

As the concept of the "family of nations" was shared by both the naturalist and the positivist views of international law, China's "entrance into the family of nations," which was the primary problem of her external relations in the nineteenth century, did not signify admission *sensu stricto,* because she had never actually been excluded.[5] Rather, it was an adjustment in Chinese institutions and concepts made necessary by the changes in international juridical doctrine that had occurred in Europe in the course of the late eighteenth and nineteenth centuries. The growth of positivist legal doctrine was eventually accompanied by a growth in Europe's technological ability to insist on, and even force, China's adherence to Europe's legal innovations.

The change in legal theory in the West is an important factor in explaining British behavior in China in the nineteenth century in contrast to Russian behavior in the seventeenth and eighteenth. Originally, acts of recognition were not required for the development of full relations on an *ad hoc* basis. For example, the Russians sought Lange's residence at Peking as consul not for the purpose of legalizing the Sino-Russian relationship but simply for the sake of commercial convenience. Lange sought recognition of his consular status by the emperor not so that he could act as consul but so that he could obtain the emperor's permission to remain permanently at Peking; he could, in fact, act as consul without any question of the "legality" of his activities occurring to either the Russians or the Manchus, because he was *ipso facto* a consul, the law of nations requiring no specific act of recognition of his legal personality. In the nineteenth century, however, recognition became a specific substantive act required by international law as the first step in establishing full interstate relations. Because European practice by then specified that recognition take the form of the permanent exchange of residential ministers, non-European states entering the family of nations had to accept ministers at their capitals.

This new concept of recognition was the reason for the representation controversy between the European powers and China in the nineteenth century and explains why the Europeans insisted that China accept resident ministers at Peking. Entry into the family of nations, or adjustment of non-European institutions to European innovations, was not necessarily voluntary on the part of the non-European power. From England's viewpoint, for instance, the development of commerce between England and China required adherence to international law, since the orderly growth of trade could take place only within the context of the sanctions and guarantees provided by law. China's initial refusal to recognize the importance of accepting European practices was a logical inconsistency that could not be tolerated by Europe, for it denied and negated the most fundamental assumptions of the entire Europe-centered positivist approach to the law of nations. Consequently, China's adherence to the law of nations, even if forced by English guns, was viewed as a progressive and civilizing step in both London and Manchester.

It is interesting in this respect that the Macartney embassy to China in 1793 to seek expansion of English trade came at a moment when naturalist and positivist thinking coexisted on the European legal stage. This coexistence may account to some extent for the apparent indecision on Macartney's part concerning the proper form of behavior to be assumed by him at Peking and the peculiar interpretations placed on his behavior back in Europe. The issue of whether or not he had kowtowed to the Ch'ing emperor was important precisely because, while kowtowing was acceptable under natural law, it was not acceptable according to the emerging positivist approach. The influence of the positivist approach can be seen in England's insistence that she had a right to a permanent ambassador at Peking because the Russian ecclesiastical mission, which had been established by the Kyakhta treaty, was really an embassy. What the British did not understand at the beginning of the nineteenth century, because they were reading present assumptions into the past, and what the Manchus did understand within the context of their own view of the world order, was that the religious mission was not a permanent embassy, whatever may have been its diplomatic functions. The British, by demanding permanent ministerial representation at Peking, implied historically that the Kyakhta system could not survive the loss of the body of assumptions that had structured the world under natural law.

Seen from another, more functional point of view, the specific institutions created at Kyakhta were viable, flexible, and thus responsive to changing commercial demands as long as they intentionally eschewed those areas of ideological, cultural, and customary conflict that had previously bedeviled Sino-Russian relations. The Kyakhta treaty system allowed for the development and modification of commercial institutions. As conceived by the negotiators, Sino-Russian commerce was to have taken place through two distinct channels: the triennial caravan to Peking and the permanent market on the frontier at Kyakhta. The caravan trade died a natural economic death for reasons that can only be suggested here. The system allowed to both the Russians and the Chinese the opportunities appropriate to traders carrying merchandise over a distance, as opposed to the opportunities permitted to purely sedentary wholesale or retail merchants. The Russians, however, were unable to take advantage of this opportunity within the caravan system. The profits did not live up to Russian expectations because of the restrictions placed on the caravan trade by the treaty's stipulations, such as limitations on frequency, size, and the duration of the trading period. Extralegal restrictions prevailed as well, such as the Manchu-controlled access to the market while the caravans were in Peking. Had an accounting procedure existed for the Sino-Russian trade as a whole, however, or at least for a series of caravans over a period of years, the caravans might have appeared more profitable to Moscow.

In the final anlysis, the permanent market at Kyakhta proved more attractive to both state and private Russian commercial entrepreneurs than the caravan trade. The Kyakhta market allowed the Russians the opportunity to boost their profits as producers without taking the risks of long-distance trade. Furthermore, the shift of the center of gravity to Kyakhta and away from the caravans had the advantage of displacing the high cost of transportation between the frontier and the Chinese markets onto the shoulders of the Chinese merchants. The Chinese were apparently satisfied with this arrangement, probably owing to their lower transportation costs.

The freedom of economic forces to shift the center of trading activity from an apparently uneconomic to a more profitable commercial institution was only one factor making for the commercial viability of the Kyakhta settlement. The second factor was implicit in the Kyakhta market itself. Although the intensity of commercial activities varied with the season, the market operated the year round. There were no regulations on either side concerning the number of merchants allowed access or the amount of goods that could be traded. Moreover, Kyakhta's comparative proximity to the Russian sources of fur, and to Urga on the Chinese side, permitted merchants of both nations to abstain from the market until they felt conditions were suitable—an ability the Russians lacked at Peking. Freed from the extremely intense but short-lived moments of confrontation that characterized Sino-Russian contact at Peking, the two empires could now settle down to a more natural level of intercourse, rising or falling as conditions demanded. Contact became a permanent feature of the Sino-Russian relationship, whereas previously it had been only spasmodic.

Probably the most important element in the development of Sino-Russian stability was the "cultural neutrality" of the institutions of the Kyakhta treaty system. For purposes of continuing contact with China, all participants in the East Asian world order accepted some ritual recognition of Peking's universal paramountcy, either cosmological or political. Although the Russians rejected the Confucian dicta, reality required that Peking in its own interest continue and even develop its relations with Moscow: not only were the Russians pressing at the back door of the Ch'ing dynasty's Manchurian homeland, but the possibility of a Russo-Jungar anti-Ch'ing alliance in Central Asia was a clear and present danger to the dynasty's position inside China. This situation was exacerbated by the ideological conflict implicit in the encounter of the European and East Asian international systems in the form of Sino-Russian contact. The Treaty of Kyakhta, however, obviated the inevitability of conflict by creating institutions that in and of themselves lacked cultural implications and avoided precisely those forms of contact in which intellectual or institutional conflict had already taken place. Questions of titles and form were avoided by instituting correspondence between officials other than the tsar and the emperor. Russian caravans in Peking were not required to perform tribute ceremonials. The treaty itself provided specific punishments for certain crimes.

The institutions of the Kyakhta treaty system were "neutral" by virtue of the fact that they could be incorporated into each society's structure of assumptions without infringing upon the prerogatives or sensibilities of the other. For instance, Russian commercial caravans to Peking could be entered in the official dynastic records as tribute missions if the court wished, but the court did not treat the caravans as tribute missions. This inconsistency allowed for foreign intrusion into Chinese society without upsetting its internal intellectual balance. At the same time, the Kyakhta treaty institutions permitted the level of Sino-Russian contact to fluctuate at will, because the institutions themselves imposed no levels. Not only could trade increase or decrease as needed, but frontier officials could correspond with each other freely about problems of mutual concern. Indeed, they were required to do so. Neither party to the arrangement felt that it had to step outside the treaty system to adjust its relations with the other —that is, the treaty system was self-adjusting, and war was avoided. The settlement even included specific sanctions to be employed by either side against the other if necessary, such as the unilateral suspension of trade when correspondence remained unanswered.

Politically, the treaty system rested on the equation of dissimilar elements on the international scene. Peking granted the Russians commercial concessions in exchange for Russia's political neutrality in the Manchu-Jungar struggle in Central Asia. Finally, the Kyakhta treaty system established very narrow paths of access from each society into the other and permitted each to control those paths on its own side. The negotiators recognized that open societies constituted a threat to international stability, since free access might upset either side's internal socio-cultural equilibrium. At the same time, access was sufficient so that neither party felt the need to go to war to obtain greater access to the other empire. The same principle functioned before the nineteenth century at Canton or at Deshima in Japan.

The Sino-Russian and Sino-Western commercial system broke down in the middle of the nineteenth century under the onslaught of western European and American settlements with Peking in the wake of the Opium Wars. The system did not disintegrate because of China's growing weakness. China had been weak before the Opium Wars, but the tribute system protected the Ch'ing dynasty behind a façade of moral and cultural superiority reinforced by Europe's concept of the natural law of nations. Nor did it disintegrate because the Canton system could no longer sustain the current volume of Sino-Western trade, although lack of capital and Chinese merchants' debts to Westerners hampered commercial development. More important contributing factors were the introduction of opium into the Canton trade and Peking's inability to prevent its importation owing to the superiority of Western arms. And in the final analysis, these were different aspects of the basic cause of the tribute system's demise: the refusal of Europe and America to acquiesce in it. Instead, with their new concepts of world order, they demanded open societies, free trade, and license to spread their new and aggressive ideas in China at will. Their legal positivism and economic liberalism brooked no compromise with the Confucian tribute system, which crumbled before them, exposing now "traditional" China to the corrosive ideology of the West.

Appendix   Notes   Bibliography   Glossary   Index

Appendix: The Sino-Russian Treaties, 1689–1728

There were five basic diplomatic instruments of Sino-Russian relations during the period 1689-1728. Because the original manuscripts are not available for study, my translations are based on a comparative analysis of the various Russian texts published in the following works: *Treaties, Conventions, etc., Between China and Foreign States* (2 vols.; Shanghai, 1917), I, 3-60; Godfrey E. P. Hertslet, *Treaties &c. Between Great Britain and China; and Between China and Foreign Powers; and Orders in Council, Rules, Regulations, Acts of Parliament, Decrees, &c., Affecting British Interests in China* (2 vols.; London, 1908); N. Bantysh-Kamensky, *Diplomaticheskoye sobranie del mezhdu rossiyskim i kitayskim gosudarstvami s 1619 po 1792 god: sostavlennoye po dokumentam, khranyaschimsya v Moskovskom Arkhive Gosudarstvennoy Kollegy Innostrannykh del, v 1792-1803 godu,* ed. V. M. Florinsky (Kazan, 1882), pp. 335-373; *Russko-Kitayskie otnosheniya, 1689-1916: ofitsialnye dokumenty,* ed. L. I. Duman (Moscow, 1958), pp. 9-22. I checked my translations against the English language versions contained in the papers of Robert J. Kerner, which are available at the Bancroft Library, University of California, Berkeley; the Kerner Collection is not yet catalogued. For various Chinese and Latin texts of these treaties, see *Treaties, Conventions, etc., Between China and Foreign States,* which served as the point of departure for comparing the published versions of the treaties. The magistral article by Walter Fuchs, "Der Russisch-Chinesische Vertrag von Nertschinsk von Jahre 1689," *Monumenta Serica,* 4.2:546-591 (1939–1940), discusses the textual problems associated with the first Sino-Russian treaty. For English translations of Chinese documents relevant to these treaties, see *A Documentary Chronicle of Sino-Western Relations (1644-1820)*, compiled, translated, and annotated by Lo-shu Fu (2 vols.; Tucson, 1966), I, 99-103, 150-152.

In making these translations, I endeavored to represent the original texts as closely as possible. Textual modifications are based on a comparison of the published texts. Syntactical and grammatical changes have been introduced only when required for the sake of clarity and intelligibility. Neither the grammar nor the representation of non-Russian words is consistent within or between these documents. All spellings of personal names, place names, and titles have been retained as given, with all their inconsistencies and errors. The reason is simple: the Russian texts demonstrate internally the paucity of Russian geographical knowledge about the frontier areas demarcated in 1689 and 1727, as well as the meager Russian knowledge of Manchu, Chinese, and Mongolian names and titles. Any attempt to standardize them in translation would falsify the nature of these diplomatic instruments as historical documents representing the era in which they were composed. For the same reason, the documents have been translated in such a way as to preserve as completely as possible the structure and flavor of the originals, which differ markedly in style from the exact, legalistic documents that characterize international relations in the modern age.

The Treaty of Nerchinsk, August 27, 1689

The record of the treaty that was enacted by the boyar Fedor Alekseevich Golovin and the Ambassador of the Chinese Khan, Councilor Sumguta, and associates, at the conference on the frontier near Nerchinsk in 7197 [1689].

By the divine grace of the Great Sovereigns, Tsars and Great Princes, Ioann Alekseevich and Petr Alekseevich, Autocrats of all the Great and Little and White Russias and of the many states and lands, eastern, western, and northern; of their fathers and forefathers heirs, lords and freeholders; the Great and Plenipotentiary Ambassadors of Their Royal Highnesses, the Minister of the Presence and Lieutenant Governor of Briansk, Fedor Alekseevich Golovin, and the Chamberlain and Lieutenant Governor of Elatomsk, Ivan Ostafevich Vlasov, and the clerk Semon Kornitsky, who were at the ambassadorial conference near Nerchinsk,

And the Great Ambassadors of the Great Asian Countries, of the Autocratic Monarch who of all the Bogdoi lords is the Most Wise Administrator of the Law and Guardian and Glory of the affairs of the society of the Chinese people, of the Actual Bogdoi and Chinese Bugdykhan Highness: Samguta, Commander of the Imperial Bodyguard and Voevoda of the Interior Chamber and Councilor of the Kingdom, and Tumke-Kam, Voevoda of the Interior Chamber, Prince of the First Rank and Lord of the Khan's Banner, and Ilamt, the Khan's uncle and Lord of One Banner, etc.,

Enacted and confirmed these articles of the treaty:

I

The river called Gorbitsa which going down falls into the Shilka river from the left side near the Chernaya river is decreed the boundary between both states.

Likewise, from the upper reaches of that river the power of both states is thus divided by the stone mountain chain which begins from the upper reaches of that river and extends even to the sea, along the heights of those same mountains; so that all rivers, small and great, that fall into the Amur from the southern slopes of those mountains are under the dominion of the Khin state.

Likewise, all rivers that flow from the other slopes of those mountains shall be under the power of the tsarish majesty of the Russian state. Those other rivers that lie in the middle between the river Ud under the dominion of the Russian state and the delimited mountains which are located near the Amur of the domain of the Khin state, and which fall into the sea, and every land within that area between the above-mentioned river Ud and the mountains which lie up to the frontier remain undemarcated for now, since for the demarcation of those lands, the great and plenipotentiary ambassadors, not having a decree of the tsarish majesty, will leave them undemarcated until that propitious time when, upon the return of the embassies of both sides, the tsarish majesty is pleased, and the Bugdykhan Highness agrees, to send ambassadors or envoys with amicable correspondence, and then through either embassy or letters those named undemarcated lands calmly and properly can be set to rest and demarcated.

II

Likewise, the river called Argun which falls into the river Amur is thus decreed the frontier, so that all lands that make up the left side, going along that river to its very sources, are under the dominion of the Khin khan; likewise, all lands contained on the right side are in the domain of the tsarish majesty of the Russian state, and all buildings on the southern bank of that river Argun shall be moved to the other side of that same river.

III

The town of Albazin which was built by the tsarish majesty will be destroyed to its foundations and those people living there with all military and other supplies shall be returned to the side of the tsarish majesty, and none of their losses [i.e., effects], however small the things, shall be left there.

IV

Fugitives, whether they were, up to this peace decree, from either the side of the tsarish majesty or from the side of the Bugdykhan highness, are [permitted] to be on either side without being exchanged, but those who after this decreed peace shall pass over, such fugitives shall be expelled without delay from either side and [turned over] immediately to the frontier voevodas.

V

Whatever people with [i.e., who possess] documents of passage from either side, for the [sake of the] presently inaugurated friendship, may freely come and go to both states for their affairs on either side and may buy and sell what is necessary to them and it shall be [so] ordered.

VI

Formerly, before this decreed peace, there were quarrels between those living on the frontier for trade between both states. [Now if] traders shall pass and thefts or murder will be committed, such people, having been caught, shall be sent back to that side whence they came, to the border towns, to the voevodas, and for them who commit such crimes the punishment shall be severe. [When] people band together and commit such crimes as the above-mentioned thievery, such willful ones, having been caught, shall be sent to the frontier voevodas, and for those who commit such crimes the punishment shall be death. And warfare and bloodshed shall not be resorted to by either side for such reasons or for the offenses of those living on the frontier. Instead, it shall be written about such disputes by the side on which the thieving occurs and reported to the sovereigns [of both powers], and disputes shall be settled by special diplomatic note.

Regarding these articles of the agreements about the frontier decreed by the ambassadors, if the Bugdykhan highness wishes on his part to place markers at the border and to record on them these articles, we shall allow it at the discretion of the Bugdykhan highness.

Given at the frontiers of the tsarish majesty, in the Daur lands, August 27, 7197 [1689].

This letter was written by the hand of Andrei Belobotsky in the Latin language.

Counter signature of the secretary Fedor Protopov on the document.

The translator, Foma Rozanov, read from the original copy.

The Bura Treaty, August 20, 1727

Of the Russian Empire Ambassador Extraordinary and Plenipotentiary Minister of State, Acting Councilor, the Illyrian Count Sava Vladislavich,

And of the Middle Empire Councilor and General, State Administrator and brother-in-law of the Khan, Tseren-van,

And Chief of the Chamberlains, the *Dariamba* Besyga,

And of the Military Department, the *Askhanema* Tuleshin,

Have agreed on the division of land of both empires and have fixed the frontier.

From the north side of the Kyakhta river [where stands] the guardhouse of the Russian Empire, [and] from the south side where the guardhouse sign of the Middle Empire [stands] on Orogoitu hill,

Between that guardhouse and [that] beacon [i.e., sign], the land must be divided equally. The first demarcation mark will be placed in the middle. And there the frontier merchantry['s activities] of both countries will take place.

From there commissars will be sent in both directions for the determination of the boundary.

Beginning on the left side of the extreme summit of the Burgutei hill furthest to the south, [the frontier shall run] along the mountain chain to the Keransky guardhouse.

And the frontier shall be a small part of the Chikoi river from the Keransky guardhouse [to] Chikta, [and] Arakhudar, up to Ara Khadain-Usu directly along those four guardhouses and beacons.

From Ara Khadain-Usu to Ubur Khadain-Usu to the guardhouse and the beacon.

From Ubur Khadain-Usu to the Mongolian guardhouses and beacons of Tsagan Ola is the possession of the subject peoples of the Russian Empire. The Mongolian guardhouses and beacons belong to the Middle Empire, [and] all empty land will be equally divided between them as it has been done here on the Kyakhta.

If in the vicinity of the territories of the subject peoples of the Russians there are such hills, mountain chains and rivers, those hills, mountain chains and rivers will be considered as the frontier.

If near the Mongolian guardhouses and signs there are such hills, mountain chains and rivers, they also will be considered as the frontier.

And where there are no hills, mountain chains or rivers, but there is contiguous steppe, it will be divided equally in the middle, and markers will be established, and it will be considered as the frontier.

From Tsagan Ola, from the guardhouse beacon, to the Argun river, to the bank, there are Mongol guardhouses and beacons, [and] along the guardhouses and beacons, in the vicinity, several people will go, agreeing to set up signs, and it will be considered as the frontier.

To the right side, starting from the first marker which is between the Kyakhta and Orogoitu, the border will be across Orogoit Ola,

Tymen Kudzuin, Bichiktu Khoshegu, Bulesotu Olo, Kuku Chelotuin, Khongor Obo, Yankhor Ola, Bogosun Ama, Gundzan Ola, Khuturaitu Ola, Kukun Narugu, Bugutu Dabaga, Udyn Dzoin Norugu, Doshitu Dabaga, Kysynktu Dabaga, Gurbi Dabaga, Nukutu Dabaga, Ergik Targak Taiga, Toros Dabaga, Kynze Mede, Khonin Dabaga, Kem Kemchik Bom, [and] Shabina Dabaga.

They will adhere to the tops of those mountain chains, which will be divided in the middle and will be considered as the frontier. If any mountain chains cross between them and rivers adjoin, the mountain chains and rivers will be cut in two and divided equally.

In accord with all the above-described division, from Shabina Dabaga to the Argun, the north side will belong to the Russian Empire, and the south side will belong to the Middle Empire.

Lands, rivers and markers will be written down [and] entered by name on a map, and the emissaries of both Empires will exchange letters [with this information] among themselves and will take them to their superiors.

During the establishment of the frontier of both empires, if some people ignorant of recent [developments] surreptitiously migrate and erect their yurts inside [the other country's territory], whoever they may be, they shall be earnestly sought out [and] each [country] will bring [them] back to its side.

People of either Empire who err by their migrations, whoever they may be, shall be justly and earnestly sought for, and each side shall to itself take its own and settle them inside [its territory], so that the border may be equally clear.

The Uriankhy [people], to whichever side they pay five sables of yasak, on that side they shall remain and continue to pay [the yasak].

Those Uriankhy [people], however, who paid one sable to each side, from the day the frontier is established, will never again be required [to pay it]. Thus it was established by agreement.

The last project [was] presented by the Russian Ambassador in Peking on March 21, and in the second month of this year according to the moon [i.e., lunar calendar], [the treaty] consisting of ten articles and an eleventh article about the frontier. Everything that was written in the ten articles was agreed to in Peking, and to these ten points the frontier treaty will be added, and it will have to be sealed and affirmed in Peking by chop and brought hither for exchange. And then the entire treaty consisting of eleven articles shall be in force.

This treaty has been signed by the hands [of the representatives] of both countries, and they exchanged [it] at the river Bura in the year of Our Lord 1727, the month of August, the 20th day.

The original at the exchange was signed thusly:

Seal. Count Sava Vladislavich

Secretary of the Embassy Ivan Glazunov

Translator: Foma Rozanov, who read a copy.

Letter Concerning the Demarcation of the Frontier Between Russia and China, Exchanged at Abagaitu Hill, October 12, 1727

Of the Russian Empire Border Commissar and Secretary of the Embassy, Ivan Glazunov, and High Chamberlain of the Middle Empire, Khubitu, and *iz Kherakhavan* [Askani amban?] Nayantai of the Ambassadorial Mongolian Department [Li-fan yuan?], by strength of the established peace treaty concluded through Ministers Plenipotentiary of both Empires on the Bura river on August 20, 1727, accordingly established and confirmed the frontier between both Empires. Lands and rivers they divided to the end of the frontier, and boundary beacons were erected. Beginning from the southernmost Burgutei hill, from the summit, to the Diretu territory, four beacons [were established] opposite the four guard posts of the Middle Empire, [at] Keransk, Chiktai, Ara Kudiura, [and] up to Ara Khadain-Usu. Part of the Chikoi river was considered as the frontier, and on the south bank of the Chikoi river were erected six beacons, and the border commissar of the Russian Empire, following the peace treaty, destroyed two Russian winter camps, so that the border might be clear: one which stood on the south side of the Chikoi river, on the upper end of Shabaga meadow, beneath the newly erected boundary beacon, the other at the mouth of the Ara Kudiury, on the south bank of the Chikoi river. Likewise, some Russian subjects, the Bratsky, migrated up along the Kudiury [and] beyond the guard posts of the Middle Empire, and he brought them with their encampments back to the north bank of the Chikoi.

Concerning the six beacons that were established along the bank of the Chikoi river for the prevention of quarrels, the border commissars agreed that Russian subjects are not to cross to the south bank of the Chikoi river opposite these six observation towers; and an order was given to the guard officers of the Middle Empire about inspection and maintenance.

From the boundary beacon of Ara Khadain-Usu to Ubur Khadain-Usu and to Tsagan Ola, by virtue of the peace treaty, where there was empty land between the furthest possessions of the subjects of the Russian Empire and the guard posts and beacons of the Middle Empire, it was divided equally and 48 boundary beacons were erected on suitable hills, ridges, and other landmarks which were in the vicinity of the furthest possessions of the subjects of the Russian Empire. Boundary markers were uniformly erected where suitable hills and ridges and other notable landmarks occurred. Along the northern side, in the vicinity of the guard posts and beacons of the Middle Empire, subjects of the Middle Empire, the Tungus, migrated in the Chindagan area in the upper regions of the Keru river. And the commissars of the Middle Empire, following the treaty, brought them with their encampments back to their own side. From the guard beacon of Tsagan Ola to the upper reaches of the Argun river five boundary beacons were erected in the vicinity of the guardhouses of the Middle State, and they were considered as the border, and so that no one crossed the border strict orders were given to the guards of both Empires. And thus they confirmed [the position] along the entire border, and for the prevention of border quarrels in the future, [and] in order that people should not thievishly move the boundary beacons from one place to another, placards were written in Russian and in Mongolian on paper, were secured to wood and were secretly buried in the ground between the boundary beacons, and on those placards were named the ridges, mountains and rivers from the summit of the Burgutei hill to the upper reaches of the Argun river, where boundary beacons were erected and their number, as follows below:

The first boundary beacon was erected on the summit of the southernmost of the Burgutei hills. The second boundary beacon was erected on top of a hill, to the north opposite Lake Tsaidam, directly to the east opposite the Burgutei hill. The third boundary beacon was erected on the summit at the end of the Khurlik chain, to the south opposite a salt lake. The fourth boundary beacon was erected on the summit of a hill, on the right side, opposite the Diretu lands [and] opposite the Chikoi. The fifth boundary beacon was erected on the upper end of the Sherbaga meadow on the bank of the Chikoi river. The sixth boundary beacon was erected on the summit of a hill at the mouth of the Chiktai on the bank of the Chikoi river. The seventh boundary beacon was erected at the mouth of the Khazai river on the bank of the Chikoi river. The eighth boundary beacon was erected at the mouth of the Ara Kudiura on the bank of the Chikoi river. The ninth boundary beacon was erected at the mouth of the Uilga river, where the Ilimovoi meadow is, on the bank of the Chikoi. The tenth boundary beacon was erected at the mouth of the Ara Khadain-Usu on the bank of the Chikoi river.

An old beacon stands on a spit of the Ara Khadain-Usu at the Lyleya river; the eleventh boundary beacon was erected on the north side of that river, on the bank of the river. The twelfth boundary beacon was erected on the summit of a hill opposite an old beacon on the north side of Ubur Khadain-Usu. The thirteenth boundary beacon was erected on a summit of the northern slope of the Kumuryun chain, at an old beacon. The fourteenth boundary beacon was erected on the spot of an old beacon, over against the Kumuryun at the end of the chain opposite the Kue river. The fifteenth boundary beacon was erected to the north of an old beacon opposite the Gungurtei river at the end of the Kumuryun chain. The sixteenth boundary beacon was erected on a summit to the north of a guard beacon in the vicinity of the upper reaches of the Ashangaya river, on the north side of the Onon river. The seventeenth boundary beacon was erected near the summit of a hill to the north of the abandoned Kharyaguta beacon. The eighteenth boundary beacon was erected on the summit of a hill on the north side of the Khasulak river, to the north of the Khasulak guard beacon. The nineteenth boundary beacon was erected on the summit of Monko hill, on the right side [and] to the north of the abandoned beacon of Baldzhi-Batukhad. The twentieth boundary beacon was erected by the Kumulei guard beacon on the northern sand bank, on a hillock, on the southern side of the Baldzhi-khan river, to the west.

The twenty-first boundary beacon was erected on the summit of a hill by the abandoned Galdatai beacon of one of the Galdatai mountains, called Belchir. The twenty-second boundary beacon was erected on the summit of a hill on the left side of the Kirkhun river, to the north of the Kirkhun guard beacon. The twenty-third boundary beacon was erected on top of the high Khalyu range, on the left side of the abandoned beacon to the north of the Bukukun river. The twenty-fourth boundary beacon was erected on the summit of Bain Zyurik Hill, to the north of the Gilbiri guard beacon of the Gilbiri river. The twenty-fifth boundary beacon was erected on the Buyuktu range on the north side of the abandoned Altagan beacon. The twenty-sixth boundary beacon was erected on the summit of the very last mound of a sand bar on the northern side of the Khormoch river, by the guard beacon of the Agatsui river. The twenty-seventh boundary beacon was erected by the abandoned Nirkyuru beacon, on the north side of the Gozolotoi river, on the southern side of a crest. The 28th boundary beacon was erected on the summit of Adarga hill, on the northern shore of the Keryu river, to the left of the northern Tabun Tologoi guard beacon. The 29th boundary beacon was erected on the summit of a hill north of the abandoned Khongaru beacon. The 30th boundary beacon was erected north of the Ulkhuts guard beacon, by the side of a natural stone on the end of a knoll on the summit.

The 31st boundary beacon was erected on the summit of Ara Bain Zyurik hill, on the left (i.e., eastern) side of the Onon river, opposite the northern end of the Ulkhuts boundary beacon. The 32nd boundary beacon was erected on the summit of a black hill to the north of the abandoned beacon of Ubur Bain Zyurik Bituken. The 33rd boundary beacon was erected on the summit of the Byrkin range north of the Byrkin guard beacon. The 34th boundary beacon was erected on the range along the north side of the abandoned Khursi beacon. The 35th boundary beacon was erected on a summit at the end of the range to the north of the Mangutnuk guard beacon. The 36th boundary beacon was erected on the summit of a hill on a sand bar of the big Turgin river, north of the abandoned Kul beacon. The 37th boundary beacon was erected on the summit of Tosok hill north of the abandoned Tosok guard beacon. The 38th boundary beacon was erected on the crest of

Kho hill, north of the abandoned Dzuchin beacon. The 39th boundary beacon was erected on a hill on the Khorin Narasun sand bar north of the Khorin Narasun guard beacon. The 40th boundary beacon was erected on Shara hill, to the north of the abandoned Sendurtu beacon.

The 41st boundary beacon was erected on top of the range at Toktor hill, on the left side of the Toktor river, north of the guard beacon of Ubur Toktor. The 42nd boundary beacon was erected on the summit of a black hill, north and to the right of the abandoned Kuku Ishig beacon. The 43rd boundary beacon was erected on the summit of a hill of the Turken range, along the north side of the Uburbyrka river, north of the Turken guard beacon. The 44th boundary beacon was erected on top, on a high place, on a crest, north of the empty left (i.e., east) Turkenek beacon. The 45th boundary beacon was erected on the right (western) side of Tsagan Nor on the top of a hill of the crest, north of the Dorolgo guard beacon. The 46th boundary beacon was erected on top of Kuku Tologoi hill, north of the abandoned Imalkhu beacon. The 47th boundary beacon was erected on the summit of Khara Tologoi hill, on the north bank of the Imalgu river, on the left (eastern) side to the north of the Ulintu guard beacon. The 48th boundary beacon was erected on top of a hill of the crest on the left (eastern) side north of the Imalkhu river, north of the abandoned Iryn beacon. The 49th boundary beacon was erected on two mounds in the steppe, on the left (eastern) side north of the Obotu guard beacon. The 50th boundary beacon was erected on the summit of a hill in the steppe north of the abandoned Nipse beacon.

The 51st boundary beacon was erected on a summit at the end of the range, north of the Mogydzyg guard beacon. The 52nd boundary beacon was erected on a high place in the steppe, along the north side of the abandoned Tsiptu beacon. The 53rd boundary beacon was erected on a summit at the end of the range north of the Dzerentu guard beacon. The 54th boundary beacon was erected on the summit of a hill in the steppe north of the abandoned Inke Tologoi beacon. The 55th boundary beacon was erected in the steppe along the northern side of the Munku Tologoi guard beacon. The 56th boundary beacon was erected in the steppe north of the abandoned Angarkhai beacon. The 57th boundary beacon was erected in the steppe north of the Kubeldzhiku guard beacon. The 58th boundary beacon was erected in the steppe north of the empty Tarbaga Dakhu beacon. The 59th boundary beacon was erected on the summit of Shara Ola, to the north near the Tsagan Ola guard beacon. The 60th boundary beacon was erected on the summit of Boro Tologoi hill north near the abandoned Tabun Tologoi beacon.

The 61st boundary beacon was erected on the summit of a hill, to the north near the Soktu guard beacon. The 62nd boundary beacon was erected on top of a mound to the north near the abandoned Irdyni Tologoi beacon. The 63rd boundary beacon was erected on the summit of Abagaitu hill, situated on a sandbar on the right (i.e., west) bank of the Argun river, opposite the middle estuary of the Khailar.

Here the new frontier is joined with the old former frontier, which was confirmed at Nerchinsk. In accord with the entire boundary agreement and the erection of boundary beacons, beginning from Burgutei hill to the upper reaches of the Argun river, the entire north side is of the Russian Empire and the south in like manner is of the Middle Empire, as is explained in the peace treaty. And by virtue of it, the hills, rivers, lands and waters were divided between both empires, and beacons were erected on the frontier. Whatever people erred by their migrations, each was brought back to his own side. The manifest love of both Empires was affirmed. Regular supervision of the border was effected in order that there [may] be no quarrels for evermore. Two concording letters which were written and affirmed by hand and by seal were exchanged on the upper reaches of the Argun river on Abagaitu hill in the year of Our Lord 1727, 12 October.

The original was signed thusly: Ivan Glazunov, Secretary Semen Kireev.

[Addendum:] Registry of boundary beacons, newly erected between the Russian and Chinese Empires by border commissars named by both Empires, beginning from the first beacon, near the Bura river, between Kyakhta and Orogoitu, to the east up to the upper reaches of the Argun river; with an indication of those boundary beacons where guard posts were newly established along the frontier on the Russian side.

Boundary beacons:

1. On the summit of the southernmost of the Burgutei hills.
2. Directly east of the Burgutei hill, north of Lake Tsaidam, on a summit.
3. On a summit at the end of the Khurlik chain, south of a salt lake.
4. On the summit of a hill, on the right side, opposite the Chikoi and opposite the Diretu lands.
5. On the bank of the Chikoi river on the upper end of Sherbaga meadow.
6. On the summit of a hill on the bank of the Chikoi river at the mouth of the Chiktai.
7. On the bank of the Chikoi river at the mouth of the Khazai river.
8. On the bank of the Chikoi river at the mouth of the Arakud-yury.
9. On the bank of the Chikoi, on Ilimovoi meadow, at the mouth of the Uilga river.
10. On the bank of the Chikoi river, at the mouth of Arakhadain-Usu.
11. On the north side of the river, on the bank, where an old beacon stands on a sand bar of the Arakhadain-Usu at the Lyleya river.
12. On the summit of a hill to the north opposite the old beacon of Ubur Khadain-Usu.
13. On a summit of the northern slope of the Kumuryun chain, at an old beacon.
14. North of an old beacon of the Kue river at the end of the Kumuryun chain.
15. At the end of the Kumuryun chain, north of the old beacon of the Gungurtei river.
16. On the summit north of the guard beacon on the upper reaches of the Ashanagai river, near the north side of the Onon river.
17. On the summit of a hill north of the abandoned Kharyaguta beacon.
18. On the summit of a hill on the north side of the Khasulak river, north of the Khasulak guard beacon.
19. On the summit of Monko hill, to the north on the right side of the abandoned beacon of Baldzhi Batukhad.

20. On the south side of Baldzhi Khan river, to the west, on a hillock on a sand bar, north of the Kumulei guard beacon.

21. On the summit of a hill of the Galdatai mountains, called Belzir, north of the empty Galdatai beacon.

22. On the summit of a hill on the left side of the Kirkhun river, north of the Kirkhun guard beacon.

23. On top of the high Khalyu range, on the left side to the north of the abandoned beacon of the Bukukun river.

24. On the summit of Bain Zyurik hill, north of the Gilbiri guard beacon of the Gilbiri river.

25. On the Buyuktu range north of the abandoned Altagan beacon.

26. On the summit of the very last mound of a sand bar of the Khormoch river, north of the guard beacon of the Agatsui river.

27. On the south side of a crest of the Gozolotoi river, north of the abandoned Nirkyuru beacon.

28. On the summit of Adarga hill, on the north shore of the Keryu river, to the left of the northern Tabun Tologoi guard beacon.

29. On the summit of a hill north of the abandoned Khongaru beacon.

30. By the side of a natural stone on the end of a knoll on the summit north of the Ulkhuts guard beacon.

31. On the summit of Arabain Zyurik hill, on the left (i.e., eastern) side of the Onon river, opposite the northern end of the Ulkhuts boundary beacon.

32. On the summit of a black hill to the north of the abandoned beacon of Ubur Bain Zyurik Bituken.

33. On the summit of the Byrkin range north of the Byrkin guard beacon.

34. On a crest in the range along the north side of the abandoned Kurtsy beacon.

35. On a summit at the end of the range to the north of the Mangut Nuk guard beacon.

36. On the summit of a hill on a sand bar of the big Turgin river, north of the empty Kul beacon.

37. On the summit of Tosok hill north of the Tosok guard beacon.

38. On the crest of Kho hill, north of the abandoned Dzhuchin beacon.

39. On a hill on the Khorin Narasun sand bar north of the Khorin Narasun guard beacon.

40. On Shara hill north of the abandoned Sendurtu beacon.

41. On top of the range at Toktor hill, on the left side of Toktor river, north of the Ubur Toktor guard beacon.

42. On the summit of a black hill, north and to the right of the abandoned Kuku Ishig beacon.

43. On the summit of a hill of the Turken range, on the north side of the Ubur Byrki river, north of the Turken guard beacon.

44. On top of a high place, on a crest, north of the left (i.e., eastern), abandoned Turkeneku beacon.

45. On the right (western) side of Tsagan Nor, on top of a hill of the crest, north of the Dorolgo guard beacon.

46. On top of Kuku Tologoi hill, north of the abandoned Imalkhu beacon.

47. On the summit of Khara Tologoi hill, on the north bank of the Imalgu river, on the eastern side to the north of the Ulintu boundary beacon.

48. On top of a hill of the crest on the left (eastern) side north of the Imalkhu river, north of the abandoned Iryn beacon.

49. On two mounds in the steppe, on the left (eastern) side north of the Obotu guard beacon.

50. On the summit of a hill in the steppe north of the abandoned Nipse beacon.

51. On a summit at the end of the range, north of the Mogadzyk guard beacon.

52. On a high place in the steppe, along the north side of the abandoned Tsiptu beacon.

53. On a summit at the end of the range north of the Dzerentu guard beacon.

54. On the summit of a hill in the steppe north of the abandoned Inke Tologoi beacon.

55. In the steppe north of the Munku Tologoi guard beacon.

56. In the steppe north of the abandoned Angarkhai beacon.

57. In the steppe north of the Kubeldzhiku guard beacon.

58. In the steppe north of the abandoned Tarbag Dakhu beacon.

59. On the summit of Shara Ola, to the north near the Tsagan Ola boundary beacon.

60. On the summit of Borotologoi hill, north near the abandoned Tabun Tologoi beacon.

61. On the summit of a hill, to the north near the Soktu guard beacon.

62. On top of a mound to the north near the abandoned Irdyni Tologoi beacon.

63. On the summit of Abakhaitu hill, opposite the middle estuary of the Khailar, on the right (i.e., western) bank of the Argun river.

Guard posts:

1. From the three tribes of Tsongolov, Ashekhabatsy, and Tabunutsy, on the Keran in five yurts with a chief. But opposite the fifth beacon on the north bank of the Chikoi river there is a village where blacksmiths live, and here there are three Russian [military] serving people for guarding. Supervision of the frontier was thus assigned to them by decree.

2. From the same three tribes in five yurts with a chief, and they were ordered to stand opposite the Kudyura [river's] mouth on the north bank of the Chikoi river.

3. From the eleven Khorin tribes in ten yurts with two elders. They are to nomadize on the Menza river until they come to the meadowlands opposite the Kumuren [river's] mouth.

4. From the Saradul tribe of [T]Unguzy in five yurts with an elder under the supervision of *Zaisan* Gurdbei of that tribe; they are ordered to stand on the Baldzhikhan river.

5. From the same Saradul tribe in five yurts with an elder under the supervision of the same *Zaisan* Gurdzei; they are ordered to stand opposite the Gilbiri beacon on the Altan river.

6. From the Sartil tribe of Tungus in five tents with an elder, under the supervision of *Shulenga* Intuna of that tribe; they are ordered to stand on the Keryu river near the boundary marker of Tobun Tologo.

7. From the Tsamtsagin tribe of Tungus in five yurts with an elder, under the supervision of *Shulenga* Khonton of the same tribe; they are ordered to stand on the Tyrna river near the Ulkhuts marker.

8. From the Pochegat tribe of Tungus with an elder, Kobu, under his supervision in five yurts; they are ordered to stand near the Mangut marker.

9. From the Ulzut tribe of Tungus in five yurts with an elder under the supervision of *Zaisan* Dugar of that tribe; they are ordered to stand on the Uchirkhubli river at the boundary marker of Khorin Narasun.

10. From the Ogunov tribe in five yurts with an elder under the supervision of *Zaisan* Sonom of that tribe; they are ordered to stand on the upper reaches of the Dorolgo river and Tsagan Nor, near the Dorolgo boundary marker.

11. From the Balikagir tribe of Tungus in five yurts with an elder under the supervision of *Zaisan* Birchi of that tribe; they are ordered to stand on Imalgu river near the Obontu boundary marker.

12. From the Ulyats tribe of Tungus in five yurts with an elder under the supervision of *Zaisan* Shid of that tribe; they are ordered to stand at Lake Tari near the Mogyd Zyg boundary marker.

13. From the Nomyat tribe of Tungus in five yurts with an elder under the supervision of *Shileng* Ildunu of that tribe; they are ordered to stand at Lake Tarbag Dagu near the boundary marker.

14. From the Chelpgir tribe of Tungus in five yurts with an elder under the supervision of *Shuleng* Umuchan of that tribe; they are ordered to stand at Lake Khalsutai near the Tsagan Ola boundary marker.

15. From the Dolots, Naimats and Konur tribes of Tungus under the supervision of *Shulengs* Buguluk, Derzh, and Abid of these tribes; they are ordered to stand at the Argun river, near the boundary marker, opposite the middle estuary of the Khalar, on the sandbar hill of Abagatu. They are also to observe down the Argun along the left side to the ford, which is opposite Khaulastu hill. There, at that place indicated as the place for border trade, the guard is assigned from the Nerchinsk [military] serving people and their chief-of-fifty, Dmitry Mylnikov, and his comrades.

Letter Concerning the Further Demarcation of the Frontier Between Russia and China, Exchanged October 27, 1727

Chamberlain of the Russian Empire and Commissar of Frontier Affairs, Stepan Andreevich Kolychov, and Chief Chamberlain of the Middle Empire, the *Dariamba* Besyga, and the *Tusulakchi Tushemel*

Pufu, and the *Det Zergen Taizhi* Arapatan, agreed on the Bura river in accordance with the treaty of August 20, 1727, concluded by the Ambassador Extraordinary, Actual State Councilor, the Illyrian Count Sava Vladislavich and by Tsyrenvan of the Middle Empire and by other dignitaries, who [all] concurred, negotiated as follows:

The frontier was started between the Kyakhta and Orogoitu, and a marker was erected there; from the new marker [continuing] to the right, they erected two markers on Orogoitu hill. And from that Tymen Kudzuin Khoshegu [place] [the frontier] continues and crosses the Selenga river and two markers were erected on the left end of the top of Bulesotu Ola. Two markers were erected on a hill at the rear end of Kukuchelotuin and on the south side of Yankhor Ola, where they meet. Two markers were erected on Khongor Obo. Bogosun Ama was crossed, and two markers were erected on Gundzan-Ola on a spit between the southern slope of Zormlik hill and the northern slope of Mertsel hill. The Ziltura river was crossed between Khutugatu and Gundzan, and two markers were erected on the left end of Khutugatu Ola. Two markers were erected above the Burkhold river, at a high point on the range between the right end of Khutugatu Ola and the left end of Kukun Narugu. Two markers were erected at a high point on the road by the left end of Udyn Dzoin above the Kutsuratai river. Two markers were erected on the road, on a high point on the road, above the Tsezha river. Two markers were erected on the road on a high point above the Modunkuli river. Two markers were erected on the road on top of Bogutu Dabaga above the Burula river. Two markers were erected on a high point on the road at Doshitu Dabaga by the left source of the Keketa river. Two markers were erected on a high point on the road at Kysyniktu Dabaga, by the right end of Udynzon on the left end of Gurbi on the right source of the Myunkyu Keketa river. Two markers were erected on the top of Gurbi Dabaga above the Ura river. Two markers were erected on a high point on the road on a peak on the right end of Gurbi above the Khankhi river. Two markers were erected on a high point on the road at the top of Nukutu Dabaga above the Narinkhoro river. Two markers were erected on a high point on the road at the left end of the top of Ergik Targak Taiga above the Tengis river. Two markers were erected at a high point on the road on the top of Toros Dabaga, above the Bedikema river. Two markers were erected on a crest at Kynzemeda, at the right end of Ergik Targak Taiga above the Us river. The Us river was crossed, and two markers were erected [there]. Two markers were erected at a high point on the road on top of Khonin Dabaga. Two markers were erected at Kem Kemchik Bom. Two markers were erected at a high point on top of Shabina Dabaga. With the marker erected on the Kyakhta a total of 24 markers were erected, which is recorded in the treaty. Each country erected one marker apiece as a landmark on top of these crests, and they divided the territory in the middle. Those ranges and rivers that run across [the frontier] were intersected by the erected markers and divided equally. From the Kyakhta to Shabina Dabaga ranges and rivers and all forests on the north side of the newly erected markers will belong to the Russian Empire. Ranges, rivers and all forests on the south side of the newly erected markers will belong to the Middle Empire. We, the dignitaries of both Empires, agreed in a friendly manner and reached terms in all truth. The exchanged letters were written by both countries[' representatives] and were signed with our own hands for the sake of correctness and were confirmed and completed.

The original letter was thus confirmed: Stepan Kolychov confirmed this letter, October 27, 1727.

[Addendum:] Registry of the boundary markers, newly erected between the Russian and Chinese Empires through establishment by the boundary commissars named by both countries, and also of those markers where new guard posts have been established on the Russian side of the frontier.

Boundary markers were erected along the newly traced frontier from the right side of the Kyakhta river to the last landmark of Shabina Dabaga:

1. Opposite the hill named Burgutui on the right side along the Kyakhta river.

2. On the very top of the crest of Obogoitu Evskim, to the left side of that crest, from the Bura river and along that crest to the Selenga river, through the territories of Vymen Kudzuin, Bichektu, and Khoshegu [sic], and across the Selenga river to Buleyutu Ola hill.

Guard posts were established opposite these markers:

I. These two markers are in the keeping of the guards appointed to *Taishi* Lupsan of the Tsyngalov tribe and his tribe.

A. An aide-memoire about the establishment of guard posts at these markers and about the maintenance of these markers was sent on September 23, 1727, from the Commissariat for the Chinese frontier settlement to the Irkutsk Government Chancery.

3. On the left end of the Bulesotu Ola region on the left side along the Selenga river.

4. On Yankhor Ola hill, there where both the rear end of Kuku Chelotoin and the south end of Yankhor Ola converge.

5. On the Khongom Obo territory, where an old Chinese marker had been erected.

II. The maintenance and keeping of the markers at these places had been previously assigned to the guard post of the Selenginsk [military] serving-people of Ivan Frolov, and a decree on this subject was issued them on September 3, 1727. The *Zaisangs* Mondai and Amur Andykhaev of the Ataganov tribe and their tribe are in charge of the same above-described three markers, and a decree on this subject was given to them on January 6, 1728.

6. In the Guidzan Ola region, across the Bogusun Ama on a spit between the south end of Zyurmlikan hill and the north end of Mertsel hill.

7. On the left end of Khutugaitu Ola on the crest.

8. Between the right end of the same Khutugaitu Ola crest and the left end of the Kukun na Rugu above the Ubur Kholod river.

III. At these three markers *Zaisan* Dulkitsa of the Sartakhov tribe and his tribe are commanded to establish guard posts. A decree on this subject was given to them on January 6, 1727.

9. On the left side of the Udyndzoin river above the Kukurata river.

10. Above the Tsezha river.

11. On Bugu Dabaga crest above the Burula river.

14. [sic]. On Udyndzon crest, on the right end of Gurbni, on the left side of the Myunke Irket river, on the right peak, on Kysynktu Dabaga.

IV. The maintenance and keeping of the guard posts at these six markers was assigned to *Shulenge* Khrudei of the Turaev tribe, *Shulenge* Nagarai of the Khorzhutsk tribe, *Shulenge* Obo of the Zeikhtaev tribe and *Shulenge* Chanka Raka of the Saetsk tribe and their tribes, [all under the jurisdiction] of the Irkutsk department. A report about the establishment of these guard posts was sent to the Irkutsk provinical chancery on September 23, 1727.

15. On Gurbi Dabaga crest above the Ura river.

16. On the right end of Gurbi crest above the Khankha river.

17. On Nukutu Dabaga crest above the Ryakh Ro river.

18. On the left end of Ergik Targak Taiga on the crest above the Tengis river.

19. On Toros Dabaga crest above the Bedikema river.

The maintenance and keeping of the guard posts at these markers was assigned to the yasak foreigners of the Udinsk ostrog of Eniseisk province. An aide-memoire about the establishment of guard posts at these markers was sent to the Eniseisk voevoda's chancery on April 17, 1728.

20. On the right end of the crest of Ergik Targak Taiga on the Kynzymeda river above the Us river.

21. Along the right side of the Us river, where it was crossed.

22. On Khonin Dabaga crest.

23. At the mouth of Kemkemchik Bom river.

V. The maintenance and keeping of the guard posts at these markers was assigned to the yasak foreigners of Krasnoyarsk. An aide-memoire about the establishment of guard posts at these markers was sent to the Krasnoyarsk voevoda's chancery on April 19, 1728.

24. At Shabina Dabaga. This marker is ordered to be completed in accordance with decreed measurements, and the maintenance of the guard post is assigned to the yasak foreigners of the Kuznet district, to the *Yasauls* Malkish Magalokov and Aechak Azylbaev of the Biltirsk tribe and to the *Yasauls* Kashtymen Tylbichekov and Kukchelei Kushteev of the Tsagaisk tribe. A decree was given to them about the completion of this marker and about the establishment of a guard post, on November 24, 1727.

VI. The supervision of the completion of this marker was assigned to Vasily Kuznetsov, the [military] serving[-man] of Kuznetsk. A decree about this was sent to the Kuznetsk governor, Boris Seredinin, on January 6, 1728.

[Three and a half months later the members of the commission on frontier demarcation who represented the Russian side composed the following]

Deposition of those who were present at the frontier demarcation:

On February 13, 1728, at Selenginsk, in the field chancery of the embassy of the Chinese expedition, those of the Chinese Frontier Demarcation Commissariat who were attached to the Commission for this demarcation, the undersigned, along with Chamberlain and Commissar Gentleman Kolychev, [all the] undersigned bear witness that in accordance with the treaty between the Russian and Chinese Empires of last year [of] August 20, 1727, according to which a frontier was created and boundary markers were established from the southernmost Borgutei hill to the right side of Shabina Dabaga, that that border was created opposite the previous territory of the subject peoples of the Russian Empire and a great distance from the Mongolian territory and that much land was delimited which had never been before [in Russian possession], namely: from the Khan-Tengeri river a distance of approximately eight days horseback-ride in length and in width three days to the Abakana river, and these places had never been under the domination of the Russian Empire. When the Russians of the Kuznetsk department used to come to those places to trap wild animals, [and] both Russian traders as well as yasak people went to those places of Chinese possession, the Sochty [Soiots?] of Tsytsenvan killed and robbed them, because those places are most profitable for trapping wild animals. In those places they hunt sables, foxes, squirrels, gluttons, otters and beavers. Russian subjects, yasak people as well as Russian hunters, are greatly satisfied with the thus determined and extensive frontier, and are happy that with the help of God and the pleasure of Her Imperial Majesty the frontier thus was determined.

Secretary Nikifor Kondratiev.

Captain Ivan Zhizhin of Kuznetsk ordered a Selenginsk serving man, Grigory Protasov, to sign for him.

Selenginsk serving men, Grigory Shishmarev, Semen Surgutsky, Yakim Tarkov, Sergei Sanzhinov, Mikhailo Strelkov, Yakov Shipunov; by request of the above a converted yasak person of Selenginsk, Nikita Rakhmanov, has signed too.

Signature of *Shulenga* Mergen.

Signature of Chieftain Babai.

Signature of *Zaisan* Dulkitsa
Signature of Elder Petrusha
Signature of *Shulenga* Yugor

The Treaty of Kyakhta, October 21, 1727

By decree of the Empress of All the Russias, etc., etc., etc., the Illyrian Count Ambassador Sava Vladislavich, who was dispatched for the renewal and greater strengthening of the peace which was formerly concluded between both Empires at Nipkov [Nerchinsk], agreed with the appointed dignitaries of the Emperor of the Empire which is called Taidzhin, [who were] Chabina, dignitary, Royal Councilor, President of the Mandarin Tribunal and Director of the Chamber of Internal Affairs; and Tegute, dignitary, Royal Councilor, President Director of the Tribunal of External Provinces, and Lord of the Red Banner; and Tuleshin, Second President of the Military Tribunal. They agreed as follows:

I

This new treaty was especially concluded so that the peace between both Empires might be stronger and eternal. And from this day each government must rule and control its own subjects, and, greatly respecting the peace, each must strictly gather and restrain its own so that they do not provoke any harmful affair.

II

Now, consequent to the renewal of peace, it is not fitting to recall previous affairs between both Empires, nor to return those deserters who had fled before this, and they will remain as they were. But henceforth, if anyone flees and cannot be restrained in any way, he will be diligently sought out by both sides and caught and handed over to the frontier people [i.e., frontier authorities].

III

The Russian Ambassador, the Illyrian Count Sava Vladislavich agreed together with the Chinese dignitaries:

The boundaries of both Empires are an extremely important

matter, and if the locations are not inspected, they [the boundaries] will be impossible [to settle]. Therefore, the Russian Ambassador, the Illyrian Count Sava Vladislavich, went to the frontier and there agreed with Shusak-toroi kun vam khoksoi Efu Tserin, general of the Chinese State, and with Besyga, dignitary of the Royal Guard, and with Tuleshin, Second President of the Military Tribunal, and the borders and territories of both Empires were established as follows:

From the Russian guard post building which is on the river Kyakhta and the Chinese stone guard post which is on the hill Orogoitu, the land lying between those two points was divided equally in two, and a beacon was erected in the middle as a sign of border demarcation, and a place of commerce for both states was established there. From there commissars were sent in both directions for boundary demarcation.

And beginning from the aforementioned place [and going] to the east, [the boundary was drawn] along the summit of the Burgutei mountains to the Kiransky guard post, and from the Kiransky guard post along the Chiktai, Ara Khudara, and Ara Khadain Usu, [and] opposite these four guard posts a part of the river Chikoi was made into the boundary.

As was decided at the place called Kyakhta, from Ara Khadain Usu up to the Mongolian guard post beacon of Ubur Khadain Usu, and from Ubur Khadain Usu to the Mongolian guard post beacon of the place Tsagan Ola, all empty places between the lands possessed by Russian subjects and the beacons of the subject Mongols of the Chinese kingdom were divided equally in two, in such a manner that when mountains, hills and rivers occurred near places inhabited by Russian subjects, they were made into a sign of the border; conversely, when mountains, hills and rivers occurred near the Mongolian guard post beacons, they too were made into a sign of the border, and in flat places without mountains and rivers [the land was] divided equally in two, and boundary markers were erected there.

People of both states who have traveled from the guard post beacon of the place called Tsagan Ola up to the bank of the Argun river, after inspecting the lands that are located behind the Mongolian beacons, unanimously approved this boundary line. And beginning from the frontier beacon which was erected as the border between the two places Kyakhta and Orogoitu, proceeding to the west, [the boundary runs] along the mountains of Orogoitu, Tymen Koviokhu, Bichiktu Khoshegu, Bulesotu Olo, Kuku Chelotuin, Khongor obo, Butugu dabaga [i.e., pass], Ekouten shaoi moulou, Doshitu dabaga, Kysynyktu dabaga, Gurbi dabaga, Nukutu dabaga, Ergik targak, Kense mada, Khonin dabaga, Kem Kemchik bom, Shabina dabaga.

A division was effected along the summits of these mountains, in the middle, and it was considered as the frontier. Those ranges and rivers which lie across them [i.e., the summits], such ranges and rivers were cut in two and equally divided in such a manner that the north side will belong to the Russian State, and the south side to the Chinese State. And people sent from both sides clearly described and traced the division, and [they] exchanged letters and drafts among themselves and took them to their own dignitaries. During the affirmation of the frontiers of both Empires some base people deceitfully migrated, having taken possession of lands, and they erected their yurts inside [those lands]; they were sought out and brought back to their own camps. Thus the people of both states who fled thither and hither were sought out and forced to live in their own encampments. And thus the frontier area became cleared.

And those Uriankhy [people] who paid [yasak of] five sables to one side will henceforth be left as before with their leaders. But those who gave [yasak of] one sable will henceforth [and] nevermore have it taken from them, from that day when the boundary treaty was completed. And thus it was decided, about which it was confirmed by written witness and delivered to each country.

IV

Now with the establishment of the boundaries of both states, it is not necessary for either side to retain deserters. And consequent to the renewal of peace, as was decided with the Russian Ambassador, the Illyrian Count Sava Vladislavich, trade shall be free between the two Empires, and the number of merchants, as we already established before this, will not be more than two hundred men, who every three years can go to Peking once. And because they will all be merchants, therefore they will not be given provisions, as was done previously, and no duty shall be taken, neither from sellers nor from buyers. When the merchants arrive at the frontier they will write and announce their arrival. Then, upon receipt of the letters, mandarins will be sent out, who will meet and accompany them for the purposes of commerce. And if the merchants desire to buy camels, horses and provisions along the road and to hire workers for their own maintenance, then they shall buy and hire. The mandarin or leader of the merchant caravan shall rule and administer them, and if any quarrel arises, he shall settle it justly. If that chief or leader is of noble rank, he is to be received with respect. Things of all descriptions may be sold and bought, except those that are forbidden by decrees of both Empires. If someone desires to remain secretly [on the other side] without official consent, it will not be permitted him. If someone dies of illness, whatever remains of his, whatever may be his rank, it shall be given over to the people of that state, as the Russian Ambassador, the Illyrian Count Sava Vladislavich, decided.

And in addition to [this caravan] trade between both States, another convenient location shall be chosen on the frontier for lesser trade at Nipkov (Nerchinsk) and on the Yyakhta [river in the region of] Selenginsk, where houses shall be built and enclosed with a fence or with a stockade, as occasion may require. And whoever desires to go to those places for trade, he will go there only by direct route. And if anyone, straying, leaves it [the direct route], or goes to other places for trade, then his merchandise shall be confiscated for the Sovereign. From one side and from the other, an equal number of soldiers shall be stationed [there], and officers of equal rank will [be in] command over them, who will guard the place as one man and will settle disagreements, as was decided with the Russian Ambassador, the Illyrian Count Sava Vladislavich.

V

The *koen* or house that is now at the disposal of the Russians in Peking shall be for Russians arriving in the future, who will themselves live in this house. And what the Russian Ambassador, the Illyrian Count Sava Vladislavich, recommended about the construction of a church, it was done in this house with the aid of the dignitaries who have supervision over Russian affairs. One lama (priest) who is at present in Peking will live in this house, and three other lamas (priests), who will arrive, will be added, as was decided. When they arrive, provisions shall be given to them, as are given to him who arrived earlier, and they will be established at that church. The Russians will not be forbidden to pray and to honor their god according to their law. In addition, four young pupils and two of older age, who know Russian and Latin and whom the Russian Ambassador, the Illyrian Count Sava Vladislavich, desires to leave in Peking for the learning of languages, shall also live in that house, and provisions shall be given to them on the royal account. And when they have completed their studies they will be free to go back.

VI

Sealed passports are absolutely necessary for communications between both Empires. Therefore, whenever *gramoty* are sent from the Russian state to the Chinese state they will be given to the Chinese tribunal in charge of external provinces secured with the seal of the Senate or of the Russian tribunal and [with the seal] of the governor of the town of Tobolsk. And likewise, when letters are sent from the Chinese state to the Russian state, from the tribunal in charge of external provinces, they will be sent sealed to the Senate or to the Russian tribunal and to the governor of the town of Tobolsk. If letters are sent from the frontiers or from frontier places about deserters, thefts and other similar matters, then the heads of the towns on the Russian frontiers and those on the Chinese frontiers, Tushetu-khan, Ovan dzhan torzhi, and Ovan tanzhin torzhi, will mutually exchange such letters signed with their own hands and secured with a seal for attestation. And when the Russians will write to Tushetu-khan, Ovan dzhan torzhi and Ovan tanzhin torzhi, they, likewise, will write to the above-mentioned in turn. All couriers who will carry such letters will have to go by the Kyakhta road exclusively. But if some important and great affair occurs, then it is permissible to take the nearest route. If anyone should willfully take a short[er] route (because the Kyakhta route is far away), then the Russian town authorities and commandants and the Chinese frontier khans are to exchange letters among themselves, and each will punish his own in accord with the explanation of the affair.

VII

Concerning the river Ud and places around it, the Russian ambassador Fedor Alekseevich [Golovin] and Samgutu, a dignitary of the Internal Chamber of the Chinese Empire, agreeing together, said: this point will remain unsettled for now, but it will be settled in the future, either through letters or through envoys, and thus it was written in the protocols. Therefore, the dignitaries of the Chinese Empire said to the Russian Ambassador, the Illyrian Count Sava Vladislavich: because you were sent from the Empress with full power to settle all affairs, we can negotiate about this point too, for your people ceaselessly cross the frontiers into our place called Khimkon Tugurik. If this point is not settled now, it [the situation] will be very dangerous, for the subjects of both Empires who live along the frontiers may provoke quarrels and disagreements among themselves. And since this is extremely detrimental to peace and unity, it must be settled now.

The Russian Ambassador, the Illyrian Count Sava Vladislavich, answered: as for this eastern land, not only did I receive no instructions from the Empress concerning it, but even I have no authentic information about that land. Let it remain still, as was decided before. And if any of our people shall cross the frontier, I shall stop and forbid it.

The Chinese dignitaries answered to this: if the Empress did not authorize you to negotiate about the eastern side, we shall no longer insist, and so we are compelled to leave it for the present. But upon your return, strictly forbid your people [to cross the frontier], for if some of your people come across the frontier and are caught, they will undoubtedly have to be punished by us. And then you cannot say that we have broken the peace. And if any of our people cross your frontier, you punish them likewise.

Therefore, because negotiations about the river Ud or other local rivers cannot take place now, they shall remain as before, but your people can no longer be allowed to take possession [of our lands] for settlement.

When the Russian Ambassador, the Illyrian Count Sava Vladislavich, returns, he should clearly report all this to the Empress and explain in what manner it is necessary to send together there people informed about those lands, who could together inspect and decide something, and this would be [a] good [course to follow]. But if this small matter remains [unsettled], it will speak poorly for the peace of both states. A letter was written about this point to the Russian Senate.

VIII

The frontier authorities of both Empires will have to decide quickly and in fairness each matter under their jurisdiction. And if there is a delay for selfish interests, then each State shall punish its own according to its own laws.

IX

If a low or high envoy is sent from one Empire to the other for official business, when he arrives at the frontier and announces his business and [his] status, he will wait for a short time at the frontier until someone is sent out to meet and accompany him. And then he will be given fast carts and provisions and will be guided [to his destination] with diligence. Upon his arrival he will be given lodging and provisions. And if an envoy arrives in a year in which trade is not permitted, merchandise will not be admitted with him. And if one or two couriers arrive for some important matter, then, having shown sealed passports, the frontier mandarins will give them carts, provisions, and guides immediately and without quibbling, as the Russian Ambassador, the Illyrian Count Sava Vladislavich, decided, and as it was confirmed.

And since communications between both Empires through letters or through people is very necessary, it is not to be delayed for any reason. And if in the future letters or messengers are delayed and no rebuke is given, or if they procrastinate with loss of time, since such acts are not in accord with peace, envoys and merchants will not be admitted but for a time both envoys and merchants will be detained until the matter is explained, and upon clarification they will be admitted as before.

X

In the future, if any one of the subjects of either State deserts, he shall be executed on that spot where he is caught. If armed men cross the frontier plundering and killing, they too shall be punished by death. If someone armed likewise crosses the frontier without a sealed passport, although he may not have killed or robbed, still he shall be punished adequately. If one of the serving people [i.e., soldiers] or anyone else, having robbed his master, flees, if he is Russian, he will be hanged, and if he is Chinese, he will be executed on that spot where he is caught, and the stolen things will be returned to his master.

If someone crosses the frontier and steals beasts or cattle, he shall be given over for judgment to his chief, who shall fine him ten times [the amount stolen] for the first theft, for the second twice as much, and for the third he will be given [the] death [sentence]. If someone hunts not far from the frontier on the other side of the frontier for his own profit, his produce will be confiscated for the Sovereign, and that hunter will be [further] punished after a judge's inquiry. Common people who cross the frontier without a passport shall also have to be punished, as the Russian Ambassador, the Illyrian Count Sava Vladislavich, affirmed.

XI

The instrument for the renewal of peace between both Empires was thus exchanged from both sides.

The Russian Ambassador, the Illyrian Count Sava Vladislavich, entrusted for preservation to the dignitaries of the Chinese state [a copy of the treaty] written in the Russian and Latin languages, [signed] by his own hand and secured with a seal. Likewise, the dignitaries of the Chinese state entrusted for preservation to the Russian Ambassador, the Illyrian Count Sava Vladislavich, [a copy of the treaty] written in the Manchu, Russian, and Latin languages, with their own signatures and secured by a seal.

Printed copies of this instrument have been distributed to all frontier inhabitants in order that the matter be known.

In the year of our Lord 1727, the 21st day of the month of October, in the first year of the reign of Peter II, Emperor of All the Russias, etc., etc., etc. Exchanged in Kyakhta on June 14, 1728.

The originals exchanged were signed thus:

[The Russian copy:] (seal) Count Sava Vladislavich
Secretary of the Embassy Ivan Glazunov
[The Chinese copy:] Yung-cheng 5, the 9th month, the 7th day
Chabina, dignitary, Royal Counselor, President of the Mandarin Tribunal and Director of the Chamber of Internal Affairs;
Tegute, dignitary, Royal Counselor, President-Director of the Tribunal of External Provinces, and Lord of the Red Banner;
In the absence of Tuleshin, the Second President of the Military Tribunal, Ashanama Naentai of the Mongolian Tribunal signed for him.

Notes

Abbreviations

Chteniya	*Chteniya v imperatorskom obschestve istorii i drevnostey rossiyskikh pri moskovskom universitete*
DAI	*Dopolneniya k aktam istoricheskim*
PSZ	*Polnoye sobranie zakonov rossiyskoy imperii s 1649 goda*
PTLC	*P'ing-ting Lo-cha fang-lüeh*
SFPS	*Shuo-fang pei-sheng*
SL-CL	*Ta-Ch'ing Kao-tsung Shun Huang-ti shih-lu*
SL-KH	*Ta-Ch'ing Sheng-tsu Jen Huang-ti shih-lu*
SL-SC	*Ta-Ch'ing Shih-tsu Chang Huang-ti shih-lu*
SL-TT	*Ta-Ch'ing T'ai-tsung Wen Huang-ti shih-lu*
SL-YC	*Ta-Ch'ing Shih-tsung Hsien Huang-ti shih-lu*
ZhMNP	*Zhurnal Ministerstva narodnago prosvescheniya*

Introduction

1. See, e.g., John King Fairbank, *Trade and Diplomacy on the China Coast,* 2 vols. (Cambridge: Harvard University Press, 1953).

2. Vadime Elisséeff, "The Middle Empire, a Distant Empire, an Empire without Neighbors," *Diogenes,* 42:60-64 (Summer 1963).

3. Professor John K. Fairbank summarized the ceremonies and forms operative during the Ch'ing dynasty as follows:

"(a) Non-Chinese rulers were given a patent of appointment and an official seal for use in correspondence.

"(b) They were given a noble rank in the Ch'ing hierarchy.

"(c) They dated their communications by the Ch'ing calendar, i.e., by the Ta Ch'ing dynastic reign-title.

"(d) They presented tribute memorials of various sorts on appropriate occasions.

"(e) They also presented a symbolic tribute (*kung*) of local products.

"(f) They or their envoys were escorted to court by the imperial post.

"(g) They performed the appropriate ceremonies of the Ch'ing court, notably the kowtow [three bows and nine prostrations].

"(h) The received imperial gifts in return.

"(i) They were granted certain privileges of trade at the frontier and at the capital."

See John K. Fairbank, "China's World Order: The Tradition of Chinese Foreign Relations," *Encounter* (December 1966), pp. 1-7, esp. 5. See also John King Fairbank and Ssu-yu Teng, *Ch'ing Administration: Three Studies* (Cambridge: Harvard University Press, 1960).

4. *Ibid.,* p. 149.

5. For the regulations governing relations with Mongolia, Sinkiang, and Tibet, see *Ch'in-ting Ta-Ch'ing hui-tien shih-li* (Kuang-hsü 25 edition, reprinted in Taipei by the Taiwan Chung-wen shu-chü, n.d.), chüan 963-997.

Chapter I—The First Sino-Russian Conflict

1. See, for instance, George Alexander Lensen, ed., *Russia's Eastward Expansion* (Englewood Cliffs, 1964), pp. 1-2.

2. Herbert Eugene Bolton, "Fray Juan Crespi with the Portola Expedition," in John Francis Bannon, ed., *Bolton and the Spanish Borderlands* (Norman, 1964), pp. 270-280.

3. There are several important studies of Moscow's Siberian expansion and the fur trade. See particularly Raymond H. Fisher, *The Russian Fur Trade, 1550-1700* (Berkeley, 1943); Robert J. Kerner, *The Urge to the Sea: the Course of Russian History* (Berkeley, 1946). On the fluctuation of the percentage of state income in furs, see Fisher, pp. 119-120.

4. A number of public institutions developed in Moscow itself to serve the state's fur trade, and a group of "treasury merchants" sold or exchanged pelts in markets outside Moscow, particularly abroad. See Fisher, pp. 125-127, 210-211.

5. See, for instance, *Russko-Indiyskie otnosheniya v XVII v.: sbornik dokumentov* (Moscow, 1958), pp. 70-71, 147-148. See also *Pamyatniki diplomaticheskikh i torgovykh snosheny moskovskoy Rusi s Persiey,* comp., Nikolay I. Veselovsky, in *Trudy vostochnago otdeleniya imperatorskago russkago arkheologicheskago obschestva,* vols. 20-22 (St. Petersburg, 1890-1898), esp. I, 311-312, 341 ff.; III, 157, 655-656, citing regulations.

6. The "Bukharans" were allowed to purchase forbidden or restricted goods inside Siberia but could not export them, being required instead to exchange them for Siberian or Russian goods inside Siberia, which were not prohibited for export. See, for instance, DAI., IV, 355, 361. On the Bukharans themselves, see especially Fisher, p. 219; Gaston Cahen, *Histoire des relations de la Russie avec la Chine sous Pierre le Grand, 1698-1730,*

(Paris, 1911), p. 71; Kh. Trusevich, *Posolskiya i torgovyya snosheniya Rossii s Kitayem, do XIX v.* (Moscow, 1882), pp. 12-13, 159. On trade with Persia and India, see Veselovsky, *Pamyatniki, passim*; see also *Russko-Indiyskie otnosheniya v XVII v., passim.* On trade with the Greeks, see Fisher, pp. 217-218. On the Central Asian khanates in general, see V.A. Ulyanitsky, "Snosheniya Rossii s sredniu Azieyu i Indieyu v XVI-XVII vv.," *Chteniya v imperatorskom obschestve istorii i drevnostey rossiyskikh pri moskovskom universitete,* 3.2: 5-6, 12-13, 41 (July-September, 1888).

7. For a thorough study of the Siberian colonial administration, see George V. Lantzeff, *Siberia in the Seventeenth Century: a Study of the Colonial Administration* (Berkeley, 1943).

8. The word *yasak* derives from the Mongolian-Old Turkish word *JasaX**, meaning "government," from *jasa-*, meaning "to govern," hence "law, regulation." See David Miller Farquhar, "The Ch'ing Administration of Mongolia up to the Nineteenth Century," Ph.D. Thesis, cited with permission of the author (Harvard University, 1960), pp. 115, 167. For a full discussion of yasak in Siberia, see S.V. Bakhrushin, "Yasak v Sibiri v XVII v.," in his *Nauchnye trudy* (Moscow, 1955), Vol. 3, Pt. 2, pp. 49-85; see also S.V. Bakhrushin, "Ocherki po kolonizatsii Sibiri," in his *Nauchnye trudy,* Vol. 3, Pt. 2, pp. 15-160, *passim;* Fisher, pp. 49-61; Lantzeff, pp. 123-132.

9. For a discussion of the tithe, see Fisher, pp. 61-65.

10. S.V. Bakhrushin, "Torgi gostya Nikitina v Sibiri i Kitaye," in his *Nauchnye trudy,* Vol. 3, Pt. 1, p. 239 (Moscow, 1955).

11. Serafim Aleksandrovich Pokrovsky, *Vneshnyaya torgovlya i vneshnyaya torgovaya politika Rossii* (Moscow, 1947), pp. 59-60.

12. For information on the indigenous population of the Amur region, see *Narody Sibiri,* ed. M.G. Levin and L.P. Potapov (Moscow, 1956), in the series *Narody Mira: Etnograficheskie ocherki,* esp. (for Daurs) pp. 217, 705-706, 785; (for Solons) pp. 217, 702, 705-706, 721; (for Duchers) p. 785. For a Manchu view of the Amur population, see "So-lun chu-pu nei-shu shu-lüeh," *chüan* 2 of *SFPS,* ed. Ho Ch'iu-t'ao (1881 ed.).

13. F. A. Golder, *Russian Expansion on the Pacific, 1641-1850,* 2nd ed. (Gloucester, England, 1960), pp. 33-34; Fisher, p. 44; Peter P. Golovin, "Instruktsiya pismyanovu golove Poyarkov," *Chteniya,* No. 1, Pt. 5, pp. 1-14 *passim* (January-March 1961). On Bakhteyarov, see *DAI,* II, 240-241, 260-261, 265, 276-279.

14. On Poyarkov's early life, see *DAI,* II, 239, 242, 265, 279. For the official reports of Poyarkov's expedition, see *DAI,* III, 50-60, 102-104. For his later life, see *DAI,* III, 138-139; IV, 283, 292, 293. See also Golovin, *passim,* for the instructions given Poyarkov.

15. *DAI,* III, 102-104, 173-174.

16. For the official reports of Khabarov's first expedition, see *DAI,* III, 258-261. For official documents and reports relating to Khabarov's second Amur expedition, see *DAI,* III, 345-371.

17. *DAI,* III, 360. For the Russian discovery of Manchu suzerainty over the Amur indigenes, see *DAI,* III, 260.

18. *PLTC, (SFPS), chüan shou,* sec. 5-8. See esp. *PTLC,* 1(5): 2b. The *PTLC* is divided into four *chüan,* numbered 1-4 and corresponding to sections 5-8 of the introductory *chüan* of the *SFPS.* Hereafter, all references will indicate the *chüan* of the *PTLC.* Hai-se is called Prince Izinei in the Russian sources. For Khabarov's description of the battle, see Vladimir (pseud. Zenone Volpicelli), *Russia on the Pacific and the Siberian Railway* (London, 1889), p. 120.

19. *DAI,* III, 524; IV, 28, 30, 35, 94, 95, 144-147, 175.

20. For official reports of Stepanov's activities along the Amur, see *DAI,* III, 523-528; IV, 27-31, 35-37, 80-83.

21. *PTLC,* 1:2b-3 and *SFPS,* 2:24b. For a biography of Ming-an-ta-li (Minggadari), see Arthur W. Hummel, *Eminent Chinese of the Ch'ing Period, 1644-1912* (Washington, 1943), I, 576.

22. "So-lun chu-pu nei-shu shu-lüeh," *SFPS,* 2:24a-b. These tribes moved to the Nun-chiang (Lun-chiang, Nonni, in various versions) in Manchuria. According to Chinese sources, a military encounter also took place in 1657 in the region of the Shang-chien-wu River (see *PTLC,* 1:3), but Russian sources make no mention of any such battle. A Manchu force besieged Albazin in 1657, however, and the Cossacks were forced to abandon the site due to lack of provisions; it is possible that this was the encounter referred to.

23. E. G. Ravenstein, *The Russians on the Amur* (London, 1861), p. 33; Golder, pp. 53-54.

24. *SL-SC,* 138:16; see also *PTLC,* 1:3, which states: "in the 17th year of Shun-chih (1660) Pa-hai won a great victory at Ku-fa-t'an village. However, we withdrew at the halfway point and did not annihilate them; therefore, they still kept on appearing and disappearing intermittently."

25. *DAI,* IV, 278-279.

26. *DAI,* IV, 85, 278-279; VI, 44, 45, 153. See "Ya-k'o-sa-ch'eng k'ao," *SFPS,* 14:6-20b; Vladimir, pp. 132-133, n.2.; Ravenstein, pp. 38-39. On Albazi, see *SL-KH,* 143:14b, where Albazi is referred to as A-er-pa-hsi. The Chinese sources, evidently unaware of Chernigovsky's family difficulties, explained the founding of Albazin in slightly different terms: "In the fourth year of K'ang-hsi, the O-lo-ssu, leading more than eighty men, entered the territory of the Solon tribes to collect sable skins and debauch their women and girls. While they were still sleeping, the General of Ninguta, Pa-hai, commanding light cavalry, attacked and annihilated them. Of the whole army only four men escaped. Thereupon, they built a city at Ya-k'o-sa [Albazin] and disturbed our frontier for more than twenty years." See Yang Pin, "Liu-p'ien chi-lüeh," in Chin Yü-fu, *Liao-hai ts'ung-shu* (Dairen, 1934), 1st collection, *ts'e* 8, 1:12. This battle is not reported by the Russian sources, perhaps because the men involved were followers of Chernigovsky and therefore outlaws. One of the men, however, may have been a Russian named I-fan (Ivan), who "reformed himself" and surrendered to the Manchus. He later became famous in negotiations between China and Russia,

but his surname is lost to history. See "So-lun chu-pu nei-shu shu-lüeh," 2:25; Michel N. Pavlovsky, *Chinese-Russian Relations* (New York, 1949), pp. 154, 178, n. 249.

27. Wu Chen-ch'en, *Ning-ku-t'a chi-lüeh* (first published about 1721), in Cheng Kuang-tsu, *Chou-ch'e so-chih, ts'e* 1:2b-4; Chang Yü-shu, *Wai-kuo-chi,* in *Chao-tai ts'ung-shu,* supplement to collection VIII, *ts'e* 104, *chüan* 6:7. It is not likely that this passage refers to activity by Russians from Nerchinsk, as definite plans were made to attack Nerchinsk before the discovery that Nerchinsk was occupied by official, not outlaw, Russians. See also *SL-KH,* 37: 3-3b; Pavlovsky, pp. 134-136.

28. Yang Pin, 2:5. The combined garrisons of Ninguta and Wu-la were at a later period about 3,900 men. Kao Shih-ch'i, *Hu-tsung Tung-hsün jih-lu,* in Chin Yü-fu, *ts'e* 7, 2:6, gives the size of the garrison at Wu-la as about 2,000 men. Therefore, it seems improbable that Ninguta had more than 2,000 men at this early period when the Manchus were suffering from a manpower shortage. See also Golder, p. 54, note 93.

29. Chang Yü-shu, *Wai-kuo chi* 6:7. Chang was mistaken about Korean participation in the first Sino-Russian conflict. Actually, the Koreans on two occasions contributed men and supplies to support the Ch'ing campaign against the Russian outlaws in the Amur basin. For a thoroughly documented account of the Korean role in this first conflict, including a detailed analysis of the debate at the Korean court concerning the advisability of supporting the Ch'ing against the Russians, see Inaba Iwakichi, "Chōsen Kōsōshō ni okeru ryōji no Manshū shūppei ni tsuite (Shin-Rō Kankei chūki no shiryō)," *Seikyū gakusō,* Pt. 1, 15:1-26 (February 1934); *ibid.,* Pt. 2, 16:47-60 (March 1934). For a biography of Chang Yü-shu, see Hummel, I, 65-66.

30. Wu Chen-ch'en, *ts'e* 1:2.

Chapter II—The Beginnings of Sino-Russian Diplomacy

1. Wu Chen-ch'en, *ts'e* 1:2b-4, esp. 3-3b.

2. Plano Carpini speaks of one Kuzma, a Russian goldsmith in the khan's employ at Karakorum. See V. Bartold, *Istoriya izucheniya vostoka v Evrope i Rossii* (Leningrad, 1925), p. 117. See also George Vernadsky, *The Mongols and Russia* (New Haven, 1953), pp. 63, 123-124, 339.

3. Vernadsky, pp. 87-88; V.G. Schebenkov, *Russko-kitayskie otnosheniya v XVII v.* (Moscow, 1960), p. 99; E. Bretschneider, *Mediaeval Researches from East-Asiatic Sources* (London, 1888), p. 73.

4. Schebenkov, p. 99. For a slightly different version, see John F. Baddeley, *Russia, Mongolia, China,* 2 vols. (London, 1919), I, lxi-lxv.

5. Schebenkov, p. 100.

6. N.I. Aristov, *Promyshlennost drevney rusi* (St. Petersburg, 1866), p. 194, n. 601.

7. *Khozhenie za tri morya Afanasiya Nikitina: 1466-1472 gg.* (Moscow, 1958), pp. 20, 22, 41, 43, 60, 61, 80-82, 198, 202, 227-229, 231, 232, 238, for references to China.

8. Anthony Jenkinson et al, *Early Voyages and Travels to Russia and Persia* (London, 1886). This work is #72 of the publications of the Hakluyt Society. See especially pp. 107-108.

9. Schebenkov, 102.

10. The title *altyn-khan* (in Russian transliteration) is a Turkish form of the original Mongol title, *altan-khan* (golden khan). The Mongols used this appellation to refer to the emperors of the Juchen Chin dynasty. The title probably had its origin in the meaning of the Chinese word *chin,* or gold. It was first used by the Tümet khans during the life of the grandson of Dayan-khan, who ruled the Tümets some time during 1507-1583. The form *altyn-khan* came into Russian from the nomadic, Turkish-speaking tribes south of Tomsk and along the upper reaches of the Enisei. See N. P. Shastina, *Russko-Mongolskie posolskie otnosheniya XVII veka* (Moscow, 1958), p. 19, n.1, and pp. 21-22. See also Baddeley, II, 30-36; *Russko-Mongolskie otnosheniya, 1607-1636: sbornik dokumentov,* ed. I. Ya. Zlatkin and N.V. Ustyugov (Moscow, 1959), pp. 31-32.

11. For the text of the deposition, see Baddeley, II, 37-40. For other documents concerning this mission, see Zlatkin and Ustyugov, pp. 45-50, 50-54. It was the custom for travelers from Siberia to appear before the various government departments to make depositions, whereby the state obtained additional information about Siberia and had to some extent an independent source of data outside official reports of the Siberian bureaucracy.

12. Schebenkov, p. 104; Baddeley, II, 51. Evidently Kurakin's dispatch of the Petrov-Kunitsin mission to the Kalmuks was an independent act. For materials on the Petrov-Tyumenets mission, see Baddeley, II, 46-62; Zlatkin and Ustyugov, pp. 55-58, 59-66; Shastina, pp. 22-26.

13. Schebenkov, p. 107, stated categorically, "It is extremely important that this data was given to him by the very representatives of the Ming government, who at that time were on a diplomatic mission to the Altyn-khan." He did not, however, cite any sources for this statement, nor have any been found in Chinese materials to indicate that there was such a Chinese mission at the time of the Russians' visit.

14. Shastina, p. 26, gave the names of the first envoy as Daya and of the second as Kicheng, but inasmuch as the original Russian draft of a letter from the tsar to the Altyn-khan gave the names as Shayan and Kichen, I have used these forms, though Shastina may be phonetically correct. See Zlatkin and Ustyugov, pp. 11, 67, 68, 79, 308 (Shayan); pp. 11, 68, 79, 308 (Kichen). They told the Russians, "And weapons in the Chinese state are the best . . . the Chinese state is great." Schebenkov, p. 108.

15. Baddeley, II, 51-52, n. 3.

16. Until 1914 the very existence of the Petlin mission to Peking was

questioned by some Russian scholars. Nikolay M. Karamzin, *Istoriya gosudarstva rossiyskago,* 12 vols. (St. Petersburg, 1892), IX, 234, wrote that Ivan the Terrible, "wanting to find out about distant countries, for that purpose in 1567 sent two atamans [Cossack chieftains], Ivan Petrov and Burnasha Yalychev, through Siberia on the south." Upon their return to Moscow the two Cossacks are supposed to have presented a description of all the countries through which they passed, including China. Karamzin's statement was generally accepted by Russian historians, though there were dissenters. Trusevich wrote in 1882, for instance, that he doubted the very existence of the Petrov-Yalychev mission, pointing out that their *stateyny spisok* (see n. 56 below) was remarkably the same as Petlin's, "a resemblance not only in its beginning, not only in the description of the peoples, countries, and cities, but even in its names." Reigning monarchs, such as "Manchika in Mongolia and Taibun in China," were mentioned in both. Even tales about *propusknye gramoty* (letter of safe conduct) were identical. Trusevich, in contrast to Karamzin, argued with cogency that Petlin had been in China but that Petrov's embassy had never taken place. No mention was made of Petrov in the archives of the Ministry of Foreign Affairs (which included the archives of the old Ambassadorial Department). Furthermore, both Petrov and Petlin began their descriptions of their travels with Zabaikalia. Since Siberia was almost completely unknown in Petrov's time, he should rationally have described it, whereas it was already well-known in Petlin's time, so he felt no need to describe it and began with the unknown Zabaikalia. Trusevich, pp. 1-3. In 1882, V.M. Florinsky, in notes to N. Bantysh-Kamensky, *Diplomaticheskoe sobranie del mezhdu rossiyskim i kitayskim gosudarstvami s 1619 po 1792 god; sostavlennoe po dokumentam, khranyaschimsya v Moskovskom Arkhive Gosudarstvennoy Kollegy Inostrannykh del. v 1792-1803 godu,* ed. V.M. Florinsky (Kazan, 1882), pp. 514-515, also argued that Petrov and Yalychev had never made such a journey. Nevertheless, as late as 1910 reputable scholars such as Kiuner continued to support the thesis that Petrov and Yalychev were the first Russians to make a trip to China since the disappearance of the Mongol Empire. See N.B. Kyuner, *Noveyshaya istoriya stran dalnago vostoka* (Vladivostok, 1910), Pt. 2, Sec. 3, p. 2. The issue was not resolved until 1914, when F.I. Pokrovsky convincingly summarized all the arguments to prove Petlin's primary claim. See F.I. Pokrovsky, "Puteshestvie v Mongoliyu i Kitay sibirskago kazaka Ivana Petlina v 1618 godu (mnimoye puteshestvie atamanov Ivana Petrova i Burnasha Yalycheva v 1567 g.)," *Izvestiya russkago yazyka i slovesnosti imperatorskago akademii nauk,* 18.4:258-260. Concerning the historical evidence of the very existence of Ivan Petrov and Burnash Yalychev, the already noted fact that one Ivan Petrov accompanied Vasily Tyumenets on the embassy to the Altyn-khan in 1616 would have made it extraordinary had he been old enough in 1567 to accompany Yalychev to Peking, or, conversely, young enough in 1616 to accompany Tyumenets. Bartold suggested, however, that Yalychev did not exist at all. The envoys of the Altyn-khan who returned to Moscow as a result of Petlin's visit were accompanied by one Burnash Nikonov, and Petlin's deposition was copied down by the clerk Ivan Bulychev. Bartold therefore suggested, "It is possible that from these two persons there was formed one name, 'Burnash Yalychev.' " See Bartold, p. 187. For further evidence of the veracity of Petlin's journey, see Zlatkin and Ustyugov, pp. 81-86, 88-91. For a Soviet view of this problem, see Schebenkov, pp. 109-199.

17. See Galeatius Butrigarius, *Of the Northeast Frostie Seas, and Kyngdoms Lying That Way, Declared by the Duke of Muscouia, to a Learned Gentleman of Italie named Galeatius Butrigarius,* in Richarde Eden and Richarde Willes, *The History of Trauayle* (London, 1577), pp. 261-320 (these pages are misnumbered 254-400). The translation of Butrigarius' work was originally published in 1555 (see p. 320). On China, see especially pp. 265-266.

18. On Mericke, see Baddeley, II, 66, 68.

19. Baddeley, II, 69-70, stated that this letter was lost but that its contents were preserved in the acknowledgement of its receipt written by the Tomsk voevoda to Kurakin. For the Russian text, see *ibid.,* I, ccxix, and for a translation, see *ibid.,* II, 69-70.

20. Baddeley, II, 70-71.

21. Baddeley, II, 71, 79, 82. A *stateyny spisok* is a written document or report in which the contents are divided into articles, paragraphs, or some other form by subject. See D.N. Ushakov, *Tolkovy slovar russkago yazyka,* 4 vols. (Moscow, 1940), IV, 494. Baddeley's work is valuable as a source book for the texts of the various stateyny spisoks now unavailable to non-Soviet scholars. For the text of Petlin's stateyny spisok, see Baddeley, II, 70-85. Petlin's stateyny spisok was taken down by the Tobolsk voevodas in the form of a deposition on September 25, 1619. Petlin identified the city with high towers as Shiro-Kalga. For a discussion of this place name, see Baddeley, II, 71, n. 5.

22. Baddeley, II, 82. The "Great Embassy Courtyard" may have been the court of the Li-pu (The Board of Rites), where tribute missions were traditionally lodged.

23. Baddeley, II, 72.

24. This letter with three others was given Milescu to take back to China for translation. Of the four letters, two were in Chinese, which he was able to have translated at Tobolsk, while the other two, in Manchu, remained untranslated until he arrived at Peking. Baddeley, II, 285. For an English translation, see *ibid.,* II, 72.

25. Baddeley, II, 103. Tangut is Tibet, the center of the Lamaist faith of the Altyn-khans. On the Central Asian political situation at the time, see I. Ya. Zlatkin, *Istoriya dzhungarskogo khanstva, 1635-1758* (Moscow, 1964), Chaps. 2 and 3.

26. On a Russian attempt to find silver in northern Mongolia that led

to information concerning the Manchu conquest of China, see Shastina, pp. 61 ff. The Russian historian P. Shumakher suggested in the last century that as early as 1649 Moscow had sent representatives to the frontier to make a trade agreement with the Ch'ing dynasty, but there is no evidence to support his assertion. See P. Shumakher, "Nashi snosheniya s Kitayem [s 1567 do 1805]," *Russky Arkhiv*, 6:145 (St. Petersburg, 1879).

27. See, for instance, Baddeley, II, 133. The expression *Bogdykhan Tsar* is redundant. *Bogdoi* (*bogd* in modern Khalkha Mongolian) means "holy, saintly," but it has a second meaning, "high, most august." See *Mongol Oros Tol* ed. A. Lubsandendeb (Moscow, 1957), p. 71. *Bogdykhan* means, therefore, "most august khan," and the entire title, as it appears in Russian documents, might be translated "the Tsar the most August Khan," but the expression *Bogdykhan* came eventually to stand by itself as the Russian customary appellation for the Manchu emperors. For further examples of this usage, see Baddeley, II, *passim*. Schebenkov, p. 104, incorrectly used this appellation for the Ming emperors.

28. Arsenev suggested that an immediate cause of the dispatch of the Baykov embassy was a letter from the Manchu emperor to Russia in 1649. See Yu. V. Arsenev, "Puteshestvie chrez Sibir ot Tobolska do Nerchinska i granits Kitaya russkago poslannika Nikolaya Spafariya v 1675 godu: dorozhnyi dnevnik Spafariya s vvedeniem i primechaniyami," *Zapiski imperatorskago russkago obschestva po otdeleniyu etnografy*, 10.1:18 (St. Petersburg, 1882). However, in neither Russian nor Chinese sources is any mention found of this incident, nor is there any evidence of it in the USSR's Central State Archives of Ancient Acts. See Schebenkov, 136. Nevertheless, one of the letters Milescu had translated during his 1675 mission has raised serious questions as to its origins and meaning in terms of Baykov's embassy. For a translation of this letter, see Baddeley, II, 72-73. Milescu claimed, "This letter was written twenty-six years ago," which would place it in 1649. The letter contains serious internal textual contradictions that would discount it as an immediate source of the Baykov embassy; moreover, its contents were not known until 1675. Quite possibly it was a letter to some local Amur chieftain that somehow fell into Russian hands. See also A. Lyubimov, "Nekotorye manchzhuriskie dokumenty iz istorii russko-kitayskikh otnosheny v XVII veke," *Zapiski vostochnago otdedleniya imperatorskago arkheologicheskago obschestva*, vol. 21.2 (St. Petersburg, 1912).

29. Bantysh-Kamensky, p. 8. Baddeley, II, 132, suggested that five thousand was a more likely figure, but the commercial aspects and expense of the embassy tend to support Bantysh-Kamensky's statement.

30. Bantysh-Kamensky, pp. 8-9. Baddeley, II, 133, reported, "there are fragments of a transcription of this letter," and provided a translation. Schebenkov, 140, who evidently had access to the original or at least to a copy of the letter of which Baddeley could find only fragments, gave a more detailed description of its contents, which varied somewhat from Baddeley's.

31. Bantysh-Kamensky, pp. 9-10.
32. *Akty istoricheskie,* IV, 202.
33. Bantysh-Kamensky, p. 10.
34. *SL-CL,* 135:2a-b.
35. Baddeley, II, 142-143. Baykov claimed that the Manchu frontier officials "refused both food and transport; [saying] 'we have no order from the Tsar, and without the Tsar's order we cannot give food and transport.' "
36. Baddeley, II, 144. Baykov described the place: "and in that courtyard, where they lodged Fedor Isakovich Baikoff, there were only two stone halls; and in the halls ceilings, and on the benches coverings—plaited grass mats."
37. Baddeley, II, 144-145.
38. Baddeley, II, 144-145. "In this courtyard there were four great stone pavillions; and the ties in them were of wood; and the cornice painted in various colours."
39. Baddeley, II, 145-146. The Ch'ing officials cited precedent and custom in support of their statement: "Yet, before you, there came from your great sovereign, an ambassador, Peter Yarishkin, his great master's principal servant, and he fulfilled all the commands of our Tsar: he came to the Ministry [the Li-fan yuan], to the State Officials; and falling on his knees, bowed down; and from whatever countries ambassadors come to our Tsar, they none of them have sight of him; we ourselves do not see him, but only the intimate people and the Uvans, [which are] in Russian boyars." The term *uvan* is undoubtedly the Chinese *wang,* "king," Chinese "w" being commonly transliterated "v" in Russian. I cannot identify Peter Yarishkin.
40. Baddeley, II, 151. Baykov's failure in Peking and his proposed abject surrender require further explication than he himself saw fit to offer in his *stateynyi spisok.* Schebenkov's explanation of the failure, pp. 144-145, in terms of the hostility of the Ch'ing court toward Russia, is not very constructive. An account of the Dutch embassy to Peking in 1656, which was at the capital at the same time as Baykov, suggests that the Russians, in addition to refusing to comply with the customary ceremonies, misbehaved publicly to such an extent that the Manchu authorities were forced to confine them to their quarters. See John Nieuhoff, *An Embassy from the East-India Company of the United Provinces to the Grand Tartar Cham, emperor of China* (London, 1669), Pt. II, pp. 7, 10. See also Melchisedic Thevenot's account as quoted in Baddeley, II, 151. In view of the evidence, Baykov's own statements concerning his dismissal from Peking must be considered inadequate and self-justificatory at best, and Schebenkov's apologia for the embassy an unwarranted interpretation of the historical record for other than scholarly reasons. Baykov also curiously remarked that "he, Fedor, had sent that [messenger] to Kanbalik unknown to all the militiamen and the traders; and he remained at this place seven days." Braddeley, II, 151-152. Why he should have offered his surrender in secret is not clear.
41. Bantysh-Kamensky, p. 11.

42. For the text of Baykov's stateyny spisok, from which all the quotes in the text are taken, see Baddeley, II, 135-153. Nikolay Bantysh-Kamensky, the great Russian historian of early Sino-Russian relations (he wrote his magistral work between 1792 and 1803), claimed that Baykov was unable on his return to Moscow to give a report of China's political and economic conditions to the Ambassadorial Department, "being himself illiterate and not having with him scribes." Bantysh-Kamensky, p. 11. The charge of illiteracy cannot be substantiated or disproved, but the existence of Baykov's stateyny spisok is sufficient evidence that the ambassador did make a full report upon his return to Moscow. It is quite possible that he dictated it. His stateyny spisok contains a great deal of valuable information about China as seen through the eyes of the first Russian envoy.

43. Bantysh-Kamensky, p. 12. If Bantysh-Kamensky is correct in his summary of the letter, it was the first recognition by Moscow that the Amur stood in a special relationship to Peking that it did not have to Moscow. The letter also stands as evidence of China's sovereignty over the region at least as early as 1658.

44. Baddeley, II, 167; Bantysh-Kamensky, p. 12.

45. Baddeley, II, 167-168.

46. Schebenkov, p. 158. See also Bantysh-Kamensky, p. 13; Baddeley, II, 168.

47. *SL-SC* 135:2-3. Bantysh-Kamensky, 13, stated, "There is no information extant as to what reception these *gontsi* [messengers] met with in Peking," but Schebenkov claimed, "The Ch'ing government met the Russian embassy of Iv. Perfilev in a hostile manner. He, just as Baykov, did not succeed in fulfilling his diplomatic mission." Schebenkov, p. 159. Both, of course, were in error. The Chinese term for "tsar" was *Ch'a-han han,* adopted from the Mongol *Chakhan khan,* meaning "white khan," an obvious reference.

48. Bantysh-Kamensky, p. 13. A pud equals 36 pounds.

49. Schebenkov, p. 159. It must be remembered that Russian accounting procedures of that period based calculation of profits and income from the sale of goods over the original cost of the goods to the merchant without including overhead costs such as transportation. Furthermore, when no plundering occurred, profits could naturally be expected to be even larger.

50. Praskovya Tikhorovna Yakovleva, *Pervy russko-kitaysky dogovor 1689 goda* (Moscow, 1958), pp. 101-102. Bantysh-Kamensky, p. 14, reported about this mission, "There is not to be found even the smallest information as to what he took to China and with what he returned from there. It seems that aside from trade and reconnoitering the condition of Chinese affairs, both Ablin . . . and others sent after [him] did not have [any] other important commissions." Yakovleva's account was the first one in which this second trip was studied and documented using available archival sources. She correctly remarked, "up to the present time the history of this journey has not received consideration in historical literature," and maintained that

one of the reasons was that there was no information about it in the archives of the Ambassadorial Department. "But in the files of the Siberian Department there is detailed and very interesting data, which witnesses to the mutual interest of the Russian state and the Ch'ing government in the adjustment and broadening of mutual trade." Furthermore, "the results of the journey of Ablin were one of the most important causes of sending to China the embassy of Spatharii [Milescu]." Note that her attitude is generally contrary to Schebenkov's, which continually followed an anti-Ch'ing line.

51. Yakovleva, pp. 102-103.

52. Yakovleva, p. 105.

53. *SL-KH,* 31:13.

54. Yakovleva, pp. 106-107. Ablin had sold the tea given him as a gift on the Peking market rather than carry it back to Russia. Tea was not yet an item of import from China, nor would it become so for another hundred years.

55. For a biography of Gantimur, see "Ghantimur," Hummel, I, 269. Schebenkov's evaluation of Gantimur was that he was "one of the retainers of the emperor, but nevertheless he was extremely dissatisfied with the high yasak payments and especially with the policy of the government—the removal of the local peoples from their normal places of habitation and hunting advantages." Claiming that in the person of Gantimur the Ch'ing lost one of the greatest payers of yasak, he also suggested that Peking was fearful lest Gantimur give intelligence to the Russians. Schebenkov, 162-163.

56. *PTLC,* 1:4.

57. Baddeley, II, 428; see also *DAI,* VI, 41, 42, 44, 45. The letter that Arshinsky reported had been brought in the name of the emperor has not come to light. Schebenkov stated, "In it the Bogdykhan expressed his grief on account of the continuing advance of the Russians and the imposition of yasak on the local tribes," but whether his statement was fact or conjecture is not clear. Schebenkov, p. 163.

58. For materials on the Milovanov mission, see Baddeley, II, 195-203. Schebenkov chose to ignore completely the problem of Arshinsky's letter to the emperor (see Schebenkov, pp. 163-164), while Yakovleva, pp. 107-109, suggested that it was the translators who kept the real contents from the knowledge of the Ch'ing court.

59. For the text of the offending letter (which may have been meant simply as a guide to the speech Milovanov was expected to make upon his presentation to the emperor), see Bantysh-Kamensky, pp. 18-20. For the text of a cover letter, see Wang Chih-hsiang and Liu Che-jung, *Ku-kung O-wen Shih-liao* (Peking, 1936), pp. 121-123.

60. *SFPS,* 61:13b. Schebenkov misunderstood this as a reference to Setkul Ablin, who carried no letters and, as a common merchant, was in no position to present anything so formal as a piao to the emperor. Schebenkov, p. 160. Furthermore, Ablin had left Peking before Milovanov's arrival.

61. Baddeley, II, 197. Michel N. Pavlovsky discussed in detail the prob-

lem of the origin of Arshinsky's suggestion and the apparent fact that Peking either did not or refused to understand the proposal, but he came to no conclusions. The only solution to the puzzle lies in the assumption that Milovanov need not have been literate to make a speech; very probably he simply made up his speech as he went along. Pavlovsky was correct in assuming that it must have been a translator who deleted the offending request from the documents so as not to jar the delicate sensibilities of the Manchu court, since the document was written in Russian and, as far as we know, there was only one translator, named Fedorov, in Peking at the time.

62. At a later date Mala, the vice-president (*shih-lang*) of the Board of Rites (Li-pu), who had conducted Milovanov to Peking and was afterward charged as a "Russian expert" with the negotiations with Milescu, explained the problem of identification to Ferdinand Verbiest, S.J., then resident at Peking. See Pavlovsky, p. 134.

63. Arshinsky transmitted the letter to Moscow in a translated and inoffensive form in a letter to the tsar dated August 26, 1671—one year after Milovanov's return to Nerchinsk on August 11, 1670. For text, see Baddeley, II, 196-197.

64. Baddeley, II, 200-202.

65. Baddeley, II, 196-197.

Chapter III—Milescu and Mala

1. In 1675, at the same time that Milescu was on his way to China, Moscow dispatched an embassy to India under the leadership of the Astrakhan merchant Mukhammed-Iusuf Kiasimov. For documents concerning this embassy, see *Russko-indiyskie otnosheniya,* pp. 9, 17-20, 90, 91, 189, 191-194, 196-199, 201, 204-206, 209-225, 227-236, 358-360.

2. Donald F. Lach, *The Preface to Leibniz' Novissima Sinica* (Honolulu, 1957), pp. 8-9.

3. For a review of Rinhuber's life, see A. G. Brikner, "Lavrenty Rinhuber," *ZhMNP,* 231.2:396-421 (February 1884). See also Rinhuber's letter to the elector of Saxony, dated Hamburg, August 29, 1674, in Laurent Rinhuber, *Relation du voyage en Russie* (Berlin, 1883), pp. 78-85, especially pp. 79-80. This volume contains letters by Rinhuber and other documents concerning his Russian activities.

4. Brikner, pp. 406-408; Bantysh-Kamenskii, p. 23. After the event Rinhuber wrote, "I certainly would have participated in the journey of Spathari; but at that time I was in Vienna." Brikner, p. 410.

5. One of Milescu's biographers described him as "a Romanian boyar of the XVII century, traveler in the Occident, author of historical and theological writings in Greek, Latin, Russian, and Romanian, diplomat and politician, high official in the service of the Tsars of Russia and their ambassador in China, a curious combination of Byzantine and western culture." P. P.

Panaitescu, "Nicolas Spathar Milescu," *Melanges de l'ecole roumaine en France,* Pt. I (Paris, 1925), pp. 35-39.

6. There is some confusion about the exact date of Milescu's birth. In 1676, during an audience with the K'ang-hsi emperor in Peking, Milescu stated that he was forty years of age, which would place the year of his birth at 1636. The Romanian chronicler Neculcea placed the year of his birth around 1625, but his chronicle, written during the first part of the eighteenth century, is often inaccurate. Milescu finished his education by 1653, which would have made him very young if he were indeed born in 1636. Emile Picot, *Notice biographique et bibliographique sur Nicolas Spatar Milescu* (Paris, 1883), p. 2. Panaitescu, writing about 1925, accepted the 1636 date. Panaitescu, p. 41. The latest Romanian scholarship on Milescu supports this contention. Nicolaie Milescu, *Jurnal de calatorie in China,* ed. Corneliu Barbulescu (Bucharest, 1958), especially editor's preface, p. 7.

7. The diplomat Alexander Mavrocordato was one of Milescu's fellow students. For a discussion of Milescu's education, see Panaitescu, pp. 41-44.

8. *Hospodar* was the title given the rulers of Moldavia and Wallachia. These two Romanian principalities were part of the Ottoman Empire, and the tenure of the *hospodar* depended on the will of the Sublime Porte. An important study of Milescu's early life is Yu. B. Arsenev, "Nikolay Spafary i ego vremya," *Russky Arkhiv,* 2.7:349-360 (St. Petersburg, 1895).

9. Nikolai Gavrilovich Spathari Milescu has usually been known in the literature of Sino-Russian relations as Spathari, Spafari, or Spathar. This is a misnomer. The word *spathari,* in its various corruptions, is the Romanian word *spatar,* meaning, in Milescu's Wallachian dialect, "commander of cavalry." It also signified "the dignitary who carried the sword of the prince" and was used as a noble rank. See Frederic Dame, *Nouveau dictionnaire roumain-francais,* 4 vols. (Bucharest, 1895), IV, 90. The word *spatar* ultimately derived from the Greek *spatharios,* meaning "sword-bearer," which was the title of an official Byzantine rank and came into Romanian from Byzantium. For various uses of the Greek *spatharios,* see Carolo du Fresne du Cange, *Glossarium ad scriptores mediae et infimae Graectatis,* 2 vols. in 1, reprint (Graz, 1958), p. 1415.

10. Milescu, *Jurnal,* p. 9; Panaitescu, p. 45.

11. A Greek observer of the Romanian scene remarked in 1720, "Milescu's translation is found in all the churches of the Romanians," referring undoubtedly to the Bucharest edition of 1688. For a discussion of the first period of Milescu's literary career and his translation of the Bible, see Panaitescu, pp. 47-52.

12. Milescu, *Jurnal,* pp. 11-13. The reasons for Milescu's quick departure from Berlin are unclear. It has been suggested that the king of Poland denounced him to the elector as a traitor. See Foy de la Neuville, *Relation curieuse et nouvelle de Moscovie* (Paris, 1698), p. 220, also cited in Panaitescu, p. 53.

13. On Sundays and holidays Milescu attended mass with Pomponne. A. Arnauld and P. Nicole, *Perpetuite de la Foy de l'eglise catholique* (Paris, 1841), I, 544. Pomponne was a friend of the Jansenists Arnauld and Nicole, who at that time were preparing their elaborate defense of the Catholic doctrine of transubstantiation, published under the above title. For it Pomponne obtained from Milescu a short statement of the Orthodox position, entitled *Enchiridon, sive Stella orientalis; id est sensus Ecclesiae orientalis, scilicet graecae, de transubstatione corporis Domini aliisque, controversiis, a Nicolau Spatario, Moldavocone, barone et olim generali Wallachiae, conscriptum, Homiae, anno 1677, mens. febr.*, which occupied four pages of the second edition of Paris, 1704. Panaitescu, pp. 55-56, 60-63, 170.

14. Panaitescu, p. 56.

15. Panaitescu, pp. 56-57. For additional information on Milescu's treason and different dates for it, see Picot, p. 7; I. N. Mikhaylovsky, *Ocherk zhizni i sluzhby Nikolaya Spafariya v Rossii* (Kiev, 1896), p. 4.

16. Yu. B. Arsenev, "Nikolai Spafary i ego vremya," pp. 353, 359.

17. N.F. Kapterev, *Kharakter otnosheny Rossii k pravoslavnomu vostoku* (Moscow, 1914), p. 286.

18. Panaitescu, pp. 58-60. The voevoda of Smolensk reported that the "Greek, Nikolai Spathari, a noble of Moldavia" had passed the frontier and demanded to be received in Moscow, as he was carrying secret letters to the tsar.

19. The letter of recommendation was quite effusive, saying in part: "The fingers of hands are not all of the same length, and God has made the stars in the sky of different sizes; thus each merits consideration equal to the talents which God has given him. We beg you therefore to honor him as a zealous man, learned and wise. You can consider him as your slave and command him to translate and to write historical works, in any language you desire." See Panaitescu, pp. 66-67, for excerpts from this document.

20. Mikhaylovsky, p. 5.

21. Matveev was married to a Scots woman and belonged to the party of innovators devoted to the introduction of Western culture into Russia. S. A. Belokurov, *O posolskom prikaze* (Moscow, 1906), p. 45. Under Matveev's predecessor, Ordin-Nashchokin, the Ambassadorial Department had begun to collect European books. Sergey M. Solovev, *Istoriya Rossii s drevneyshikh vremen,* 7 vols. (St. Petersburg, 1894-1895), III, 181. Matveev carried the process further, appointing translators and clerks for the "building" (*stroyenie*) of books. One of his first products was the *Great State Book,* which described the origins of all the great princes and tsars of Russia. Solovev called these early products of Matveev's inspiration "the first incoherent, infantile babblings of Russian historiography." Solovev, III, 185.

22. Panaitescu, pp. 68-69. On Milescu's close relationship to Matveev, see "Pismo Nikolaya Spafariya k boyarinu Artemonu Sergeevichu Matveevu," *Russky Arkhiv,* 1.1:52-58 (1881).

23. For a discussion of Milescu's literary output at the Ambassadorial

Department, see Panaitescu, pp. 72-79. He suggested that Matveev's reforms were inspired in part by Milescu, because almost all the works "published" by the Ambassadorial Department were from his pen. On specific works, see N. Kedrov, "Nikolay Spafary i ego Arifmology (Materialy dlya istorii kontsa XVII veka)," *ZhMNP,* 183:1-31 (January, 1876); V. Fursenko, "Spafary Milescu," *Russky Geografichesky slovar,* 18:183-190, esp. 189-190.

24. Panaitescu, pp. 70-72. Ligarides was a scholar who had studied in Italy and "was all his life a secret agent for the Catholic Propaganda among the Orthodox." He had been a professor in Moldavia and Wallachia as well as in Russia and occupied a privileged position with the tsar. He played a decisive role in the deposition of Patriarch Nikon, and there was even a question of appointing him Patriarch of All Russia. Dositheos and the Greek community in Constantinople attacked him as a Catholic agent, however, and though the tsar defended him for a while, Dositheos' influence was sufficiently strong to have Ligarides exiled to Kiev, where he died.

25. For the text of the preamble, see Arsenev, *Puteshestvie,* p. 151. For the text of the instructions issued to Milescu, see Bantysh-Kamensky, pp. 25-26. Arsenev, *Puteshestvie,* pp. 151-153, gave a different version of Milescu's instructions, in an unnumbered form. It is possible, of course, that Arsenev's document was a different set of instructions from the one cited by Bantysh-Kamensky. Arsenev's appears to be a list of desiderata for a report. At any rate, the tsar's commercial interests were quite as apparent in the one as in the other.

26. Bantysh-Kamensky, pp. 24-25, 416-417.

27. Bantysh-Kamensky, p. 24, n. 1.

28. Arsenev, *Puteshestvie,* p. 25; Baddeley, II, 244-245; *DAI,* VII, 322.

29. For studies of Krizhanich, particularly with reference to his intellectual achievements, see H.J.A. van Son, *Autour de Krizanic: etude historique et linguistique* (n.p., 1934); Paulin-Gerard Scolardi, *Krijanich, messager de l'unite des cretiens et pere du panslavisme: au service de Rome et de Moscou au XVII siecle* (Paris, 1947); Sergei A. Belokurov, *Iz dukhovnoy zhizni moskovskago obschestva XVII v.* (Moscow, 1902). Belokurov's magnificent work is divided into two sections, the basic text, paginated 1-294, and *prilozheniya* (appendices), paginated 1-302. On Krizhanich, see pp. 85-294 and all appendices.

30. Belokurov, *Iz dukhovnoy zhizni,* p. 226. Little is known about the nature of the conversations between Milescu and Krizhanich, though the latter left a short description in his *Historia de Sibiria,* quoted in A. A. Titov, *ed., Sibir v XVII veke: sbornik starinnykh russkikh statey o Sibiri i prilezhaschikh k ney zemlyakh* (Moscow, 1890), pp. 212-213. On *Historia de Sibiria,* see Belokurov, *Iz dukhovnoy zhizni,* p. 226.

31. P.A. Bezsonov in Belokurov, *Iz dukhovnoy zhizni,* pp. 5-6. Bezsonov claimed that *Description of Siberia* was written during the "bitter hours and days" of Krizhanich's exile in Tobolsk, and suggested that Milescu's embassy resulted from the smaller work, *About the Chinese Trade.* Belokurov, *Iz*

dukhovnoy zhizni, prilozheniya, 6. Belokurov (p. 224), however, pointed out that there is no record of the book. Furthermore, he noted that Milescu's instructions were dated February 25, 1675, and that if Krizhanich's book had any influence on them, the book would have had to be known in Moscow not later than 1674. Yet Bantysh-Kamensky showed that the decision to send Milescu to China was made on July 13, 1674, which would tend to support Bezsonov's position. Belokurov (p. 225) admitted that he "cannot support or deny the word of Krizhanich." Upon Milescu's return from China he had no chance to meet Krizhanich, who had left Tobolsk in March 1676, and Milescu arrived there only at the end of 1677. Nowhere in his known writings did Milescu mention the aid Krizhanich gave him in Tobolsk, but this may be explained by a defect in Milescu's character, which was manifest in the lack of mention of other aid he received in his other works as well. Baddeley (II, 208-214) suggested that at least two chapters of Milescu's *Opisanie Kitaya* were plagiarized. After Milescu left Tobolsk, Krizhanich wrote in his notebook, "I pray God and hope that he will return, having accomplished what will prove to be a good business and to the advantage of the whole nation." Baddeley, II, 213.

32. O. Dapper, *Gedenkwaerdig bedryf d. Nederl. Oost-Ind. Maetschappye op de Kuste en i het Keizerrijk van Taising of Sina* (Amsterdam, 1670).

33. Krizhanich also claimed to have influenced Milescu's choice of the Nerchinsk-Amur route to Peking. To what degree this claim was accurate cannot be determined, though Krizhanich was doubtless among the Tobolsk residents who attended Saltykov's conference. Krizhanich reported his own argument in the matter, which reflected his interest in the development of Russia. See Belokurov, 227. In any event, Krizhanich wrote down all his knowledge "and all that was necessary for Siberia and China, in two manuscripts, and he took it with him . . . and he knows from it everything which he needs, as if he were born there himself." Baddeley, II, 213.

34. Baddeley, II, 245-246. Milescu evidently also had some initial difficulty in providing a priest for the spiritual needs of his mission.

35. Baddeley, II, 257. For details of the trip from Tobolsk to Eniseisk, see Baddeley, II, 246-256; Milescu, *Jurnal,* pp. 11-30; Arsenev, *Puteshestvie,* pp. 50-87.

36. For text of letter, see Baddeley, II, 256-257.

37. Baddeley, II, 257, 259.

38. Baddeley, II, 275-276. For details of the trip from Eniseisk to Nerchinsk, see Baddeley, II, 260-277; Milescu, *Jurnal,* 36-66; Arsenev, *Puteshestvie,* 87-139. When Milescu reached Selenginsk on October 2, he prophetically recorded, "Better here than elsewhere can a great trade be established, for the Chinese Empire is not far off, as we prove below; and the Mongols wander round in great numbers, and trade with the cossacks, selling horses and camels and cattle; as likewise all kinds of Chinese merchandise, buying, in return, sables and many other Russian articles. But there are not many Russians in the fort itself, and no one to do business with." Baddeley,

II, 269. Milescu evidently had difficulty with the natives all along. At one point he recorded, "As we rode along, the cossacks fired off their guns frequently and they [the Mongols] came, many of them, and begged us not to fire any more, because it frightened their women, children, and cattle." Baddeley, II, 272-273.

39. On Milescu's interview with Gantimur, see Bantysh-Kamensky, p. 27.

40. For a description of the encounter, see Baddeley, II, 279-281.

41. Baddeley, II, 281. The speech was made January 3, 1676.

42. Picot, p. 3. By January 5, 1676, the ambassador had still received no word from Milovanov, whom he had sent ahead from Eniseisk to Peking to announce the embassy's approach to the Manchu authorities. Milovanov had left Nerchinsk for the first settlements across the frontier in China as early as November 18, 1675. He took the Albazin route and on December 14 arrived on the Nun-chiang (a river known in Russian documents and translations therefrom as the Naun or the Nonni). After a week's delay, he was permitted to proceed to Peking accompanied by Mangutei, the same Manchu official who had taken him back to Nerchinsk after the conclusion of his 1670 mission. In Peking, Milovanov's movements were restricted. Detained a full month, he was questioned closely but denied any knowledge concerning the purpose of the embassy, insisting that his only task was to announce its arrival. Baddeley, II, 286, 311-312. See Milescu's letter to the tsar, dated the Nun-chiang, April 17, 1676, and delivered to Nerchinsk by Milovanov himself. Baddeley, II, 286. For a description of Milescu's first encounter with Manchu officials, see Baddeley, II, 286-287.

43. The memorial noted that the embassy had come in response "to our edict, which we sent to the Solun elders for handing over to the chiefs of the cities under [Russian] control, Albazin and Nerchinsk." A. Ivanovsky, "Posolstvo Spafarya," *Zapiski vostochnago otdeleniya imperatorskago Russkago arkheologicheskago obschestva,* 2:195-226 (1887), especially p. 202. This is a translation of the original Manchu language documents, also published by Ivanovsky, *ibid.,* 2:81-124. All references to these documents will be to the Russian translation. For a description of the original manuscript from which the documents were published, see *ibid.,* 2:81-82.

44. Baddeley, II, 287-289, 293. That the court reacted immediately is shown by the speed with which the courier returned from Peking. A fast trip between Peking and the Nun-chiang took twelve days. The total time elapsed between the dispatch of the messenger and the arrival of the courier was only twenty-five days, or one day longer than the required travel time. See also Fairbank and Teng, *Ch'ing Administration,* pp. 12-17, especially 15. Note that Fairbank and Teng give the time for dispatches carried by horse from Kirin to Peking as twelve days and from Tsitsikar to Peking as eighteen days; the fact that an answer was received within twenty-five days would indicate that Milescu's encampment was somewhere on the Nun-chiang in the vicinity of, but not at, its confluence with the Sungari. Note

also that Milescu used the Manchu title *askaniama,* the equivalent of the Chinese *shih-lang* or vice-president of a board, in referring to Mala.

45. For the most extensive biography of Mala, see *Kuo-ch'ao ch'i-hsien lei-cheng ch'u-pien,* ed. Li Huan (n.p., ca. 1890), 275:23-25. Note that Chao-ying Fang gives a variant form of the characters used to transliterate this Manchu name into Chinese. Hummel, II, 665. For a biography of Nikan, see Hummel, I, 591.

46. Hummel, I, 4-5.

47. See the biography of the empress Hsiao-tuan, Hummel, I, 304-305, esp. 305.

48. The day of the announcement of Mala's appointment to the Board of Rites was the fourteenth day of the first month of the fifteenth year of K'ang-hsi's reign, or February 27, which corresponds to February 17 in the Old Style calendar used throughout this chapter. Mala arrived at the Nun-chiang on February 26 O.S. He continued in the Ch'ing bureaucracy after Milescu's departure, specializing in Russian affairs when the occasion arose. In K'ang-hsi 16 (1677-1678) he was promoted to the position of president (*shang-shu*) of the Board of Works (Kung-pu). In K'ang-hsi 17 (1678-1679), together with a grand secretary, he was sent to make an imperial pronouncement to the Mongols. In K'ang-hsi 19 (1680-1681), while still president of the Board of Works, he failed to carry out an imperial order to increase the wages of the men working on the imperial mausoleum and was degraded one rank. His reply to the emperor's edict was considered insincere and slightly jocular, as a result of which he was demoted another five ranks but retained in office. In K'ang-hsi 20 (1681-1682) he was accused of carelessness in the repair of the imperial sacrificial ceremonial vessels and was removed from office, though he retained his ancestor's ranks. After the fourth month of K'ang-hsi 22 (1683-1684), when preparations began for the anti-Russian campaign along the Amur, Mala was sent to the Soluns to prepare provisions and accumulate troops, for which he was granted four thousand *liang* (ounces) of silver. He was also responsible for proposing and carrying out the policy whereby the Soluns and other indigenous tribes were removed from the Amur to the Nun-chiang in order to depopulate the area around Albazin. In K'ang-hsi 23 (1684-1685) he conducted extensive investigations of the situation in and around Albazin and Nerchinsk and memorialized his findings to the throne. He also proposed the policy whereby the Khalkha Mongols were forbidden to trade with the Russians. From K'ang-hsi 24 (1685-1686) to about the beginning of K'ang-hsi 29 (1690-1691) Mala participated in the anti-Russian campaigns and consequent negotiations in various administrative and military capacities; he was one of the negotiators and signatories of the Treaty of Nerchinsk; and he was apparently in charge of the military administration of the area after the end of the campaign and the signing of the treaty. From K'ang-hsi 29 (1690-1691) to K'ang-hsi 31 (1692-1693) he participated in the campaign

against Galdan and in resettlement projects for the victims of the war. He died in the ninth month of K'ang-hsi 31, while still in office. Mala's life, therefore, was largely spent at the vortex of the triangular struggle between Russian, Manchu, and Jungar.

49. For a record of the conversations and negotiations, which took place February 26-March 2, see Baddeley, II, 293-295.

50. Ivanovsky, p. 203. The problem of examination of the documents had actually been raised before Mala's arrival at the Nun-chiang, shortly after Milescu crossed the Chinese frontier. As early as January 23 the local officials on the Nun-chiang had asked the ambassador if he brought letters and gifts from the tsar to the emperor. Milescu refused to answer on the grounds that the tsar's affairs were not "any business of theirs." Similar inquiries were made again on January 26, and while Milescu still refused to divulge the contents of the letter from the tsar, he displayed to the local officials one of the Chinese letters he was returning for translation. This letter was in a box covered with imperial yellow satin, the emperor's own color, and when the Manchus saw it, "all who were present fell on their knees, in great fear." Baddeley, II, 287-289. Although this dramatic display impressed the local bureaucrats, it was insufficient to impress Mala after his arrival. Unless otherwise specified, the discussion of the Milescu embassy hereafter is based on Baddeley, II, 295-420.

51. Baddeley, II, 299. Italics added.

52. Ivanovsky, p. 202. For Milescu's discussion with Mala, see Baddeley, II, 297 ff.

53. For conflicting views of the second Albazin raid, see Baddeley, II, 292 and 300.

54. Baddeley, II, 310. Milescu's prohibition against sending a tribute-collecting mission down the Amur was reported in a letter to the tsar, also carried by Milovanov to Nerchinsk.

55. This memorial was sent to the emperor under the signature of the president of the Board of Rites. For the Russian translation of the Manchu text, see Ivanovsky, pp. 202-207.

56. For the text of the memorial, see Ivanovsky, pp. 207-208.

57. Baddeley, II, 305-306, 308-309.

58. For examples, see Baddeley, II, 288, 293, 302, 308, 312, 322, 326. The "Hollanders" evidently refers to de Keyser's embassy of 1656, although the passage contains a reference to the embassy of 1666 as well.

59. For material on the compromise attempts, see Baddeley, II, 337, 340-341, 345-346, 348-349.

60. For a description of the ceremony, see Baddeley, II, 351-352. Note that there is an occasional slight discrepancy between Grimaldi's and Milescu's description of the event.

61. *SL-KH,* 61:3b-4. Note that this is dated June 15, but a ten-day correction must be made since this chapter uses the Old-Style calendar. Therefore, the date June 15 in the *Shih-lu* and Milescu's June 5 are the same day.

62. Baddeley, II, 360. The K'ang-hsi *Shih-lu* noted that the audience took place on the occasion of the presentation of newly promoted civil and military officials. The performance of the kowtow was also recorded: "The tributary ambassador of the Ch'a-han Han of O-lo-ssu performed the audience ceremony." *SL-KH,* 61:6b.

63. Baddeley, II, 384, 392, 393. Milescu protested that the misconduct of his men resulted from their confinement.

64. Baddeley, II, 331-332. There is no evidence that Mala really did have such instructions.

65. Baddeley, II, 383. Milescu was convinced that the restrictions on trade, in addition to serving as a form of political pressure, were meant to reserve the trade to the court officials. When Mala informed Milescu the day after his first audience that free trade would begin, Milescu immediately asked that the embassy be provided with "an honest man" who knew the value of silver, "for we have heard that, here in your capital, the silver is very bad, mixed with copper and tin; there being no Imperial regulation to follow as in other countries." Mala summoned one Solom, who, together with his partners, had served Baikov in a similar capacity. These men were essentially interpreters of Chinese and Mongolian, resembling the compradores who were to appear at a later date along the coast in the Anglo-Chinese trade. Their task was to sell the Russian goods for silver, which they in turn used to purchase Chinese goods for the Russians. For their services they expected 20 percent of the value of each transaction. Baddley, II, 363-364. Mala warned the ambassador that these interpreters were thieves, not to be trusted, but Solom informed Milescu that Mala had sought to prevent the opening of public trade and had wanted his own men used as intermediaries. Milescu believed that in fact Mala and the interpreters were working together.

66. For an example of a restriction on items to be sold to foreigners, see *Ch'ing-shih-lu ching-chi tzu-liao chi-yao* (Peking, 1959), p. 455; see also Baddeley, II, 394.

67. On Milescu's other explanations for the failure to open trade, see Baddeley, II, 346, 369, 374, 381-383, 393.

68. Baddeley, II, 370, 383-384. The superiority of Russian over Chinese products was obvious upon simple inspection, according to Milescu.

69. For a survey of the Jesuits at Peking, see Arnold H. Rowbatham, *Missionary and Mandarin: The Jesuits at the Court of China.* The Soviet scholar V. G. Schebenkov stated doctrinairely and categorically that the Jesuits were the agents of the western European powers in Peking. As such, they strove to prevent the establishment of good relations between the Russian and Manchu Empires and to prevent the spread of Russian influence inside China. See Schebenkov, pp. 177-178, especially 177, where he wrote, "The Jesuits were agents, scouts of the colonial policies of the Western European states in China."

70. Baddeley, II, 336-337. On Verbiest, see Ferdinand Verbiest, *Cor-*

respondence de Ferdinand Verbiest de la Compagnie de Jesus, ed. H. Josson, S.J., and L. Willaert, S.J. (Brussels, 1938). For a Jesuit study of his relations with Moscow, see H. Bosmans, S.J., *Le problème des relations de Verbiest avec la cour de Russie* (Bruges, 1913). See also Pavlovsky, p. 112-126.

71. Baddeley, II, 337, 345. Milescu also reported to the tsar that Verbiest had suggested the use of bribery in negotiations with the Manchus. According to the *stateyny spisok,* Verbiest carried a bribe for Milescu to one of the Grand Secretaries, who promised his services to Russia for the future. Baddeley, II, 356. The bribe consisted of "ten poor-quality sables."

72. For the record of this conversation, see Baddeley, II, 366-368.

73. For the record of this interview, see Baddeley, II, 394-396.

74. Baddeley, II, 395-396. Pavlovsky, 118, who called the results of Verbiest's interview with Milescu "important advice," pointed out correctly that in addition to this particular strategic information, Milescu, "during his stay in Peking, thanks to the Jesuits . . . collected data about China—her condition, military forces, etc.—and that on departing he had left behind a number of Fathers who had become discreet and useful friends, his mission cannot be regarded as having ended in complete failure." For Milescu's description of China, see N.G. Spafary, *Opisanie pervye chasti vselennyya imenuyemoy Azii, v ney zhe sostoit Kitayskoe gosudarstvo s prochimi ego gorody i provintsii,* ed. F.T. Vasilev, A.I. Yatsimirsky, A.A. Aleksandrov, N.F. Katanov (Kazan, 1910). See also Nicolaie Milescu, *Descrierea Chinei,* ed. Corneliu Barbulescu (Bucharest, 1958). For a discussion of the parts of this book plagiarized by Milescu from Martinius Martini, see Baddeley, II, 219-222; Milescu, *Descrierea Chinei,* V-XXVII; Panaitescu, pp. 113-118. For an English translation of Chapters IV and V of Milescu's work, describing the route he took to China, see Baddeley, II, 223-230.

75. For text, see Baddeley, II, 352-353. See also Baddeley, II, 362.

76. For texts of the memorials, see Baddeley, 195-202.

77. For records of these unsuccessful discussions, see Baddeley, 375-378, 396-397, 401.

78. Baddeley, II, 394, 396, 401-403.

79. *SL-KH,* 62:3.

80. For Milescu's description of the events of August 29, see Baddeley, II, 403-407.

81. Baddeley, II, 406. This extraordinary session was painful not only diplomatically but physically. Milescu reported, "It was with difficulty that some could rise from their knees; for they had been kneeling for more than two hours, on stones, in the rain."

82. Baddeley, II, 407.

83. For a record of the discussion of August 30, see Baddeley, II, 407-410.

84. Baddeley, II, 409. For confirmation of this attitude at a later date, see "Ting-k'ao I-yü-lu," *SFPS,* 43:37b.

85. Baddeley, II, 410.
86. Baddeley, II, 411.
87. Baddeley, II, 420. For a record of the embassy's return journey, see Baddeley, II, 415-422.

Chapter IV—War Along the Amur

1. On Wu San-kuei, the Manchu invasion of China, and the Rebellion of the Three Feudatories, see Hummel, I, 195-196, 215-219, 491-493; II, 635-636, 679, 877-880. On Cheng Ch'eng-kung (Koxinga), see *ibid.,* I, 108-109.
2. If it is assumed that Cheng Ch'eng-kung and the Manchu forces faced each other at Nanking in September 1659 in a ratio of one to one, somewhere between 100,000 and 170,000 Manchu troops must have taken the field in that battle. *Ibid.,* I, 109. Actually, the more the ratio favored the Manchus, the higher their percentage of involvement. In the years of struggle against Wu San-kuei, Fang Chao-ying estimated that between 160,000 and 200,000 men fought on the various fronts. Chaoying Fang, "A Technique for Estimating the Numerical Strength of the Early Manchu Military Forces," *Harvard Journal of Asiatic Studies,* 13.1-2: 192-215 (June 1950), esp. pp. 201-202. These figures are presumably for actual participants in the fighting forces as opposed to potential fighting strength. If one further assumes 300 men per company (*niru* in Manchu; see Edwin O. Reischauer and John K. Fairbank, *East Asia: the Great Tradition* (Boston, 1960), 351), potential Manchu fighting strength can be estimated on the basis of the number of companies in the Banner Forces as determined by Fang Chaoying. Accordingly, one may surmise that 54 to 92 percent of the potential Manchu military manpower was engaged in the struggle with Cheng Ch'eng-kung at one time or another, and somewhere between 71 percent and 89 percent was engaged against Wu-San-kuei. For the data and method of these calculations, see Fang Chaoying, *passim.,* esp. pp. 208-209. Although these figures must be considered only as indications of a probable commitment of manpower to the struggle, it is obvious that the overwhelming involvement of the Manchus in the effort against Wu and Cheng could easily have prevented them from diverting even the minimum financial and military resources to build up an offensive force on the Amur, as they were to do in the eighties of the seventeenth century.
3. For a record of the progress, see Kao Shih-ch'i, *passim.* During it the emperor probably made basic military decisions about the Russians.
4. See also Golder, pp. 51, 53; "So-lun chu-pu nei-shu shu-lüeh," p. 24b. Until his meeting with the officials of the Nun-chiang settlements, Milescu met hardly a soul in the frontier region.
5. Wu Chen-ch'en, *ts'e* 1, p. 2. On Bahai, see Hummel, I, 14-15; Kao Shih-ch'i, 2:6; "Kuo-ch'ao pei-chia yung-ping chiang-shuai chüan," in *SFPS,* 36:11-14. A ch'ih equals 0.3518 meters, or 14.1 inches.

6. Wu Chen-ch'en, 1:6. A shih equals 133.33 lbs. The character for *shih* can also be read *tan.* A chin equals 16 ounces.

7. *SL-KH,* 131:16b-17.

8. For a biography of Langtan, see Hummel, I, 442-443. For a biography of Pengcun, see Hummel, II, 621. On Singde, who accompanied them, see Hummel, II, 662-663; Hsü Ch'ien-hsüeh, *Tan-yüan chi* (1694), ch. 8, *passim.*

9. *PTLC,* 1:2b.

10. *SL-KH,* 104:8b-9; "Lang-t'an chuan," in *Pa-ch'i t'ung-chih* (1739), *chuan* 153, esp. 153:13; *PTLC,* 1:3b.

11. *PTLC,* 1:4; *SL-KH,* 104:8b-9; "Lang-t'an chuan," 153:13; *SFPC,* 36:5b-6. In order not to alarm the Russians, the reconnaissance expedition was to send messengers to Nerchinsk to tell the Russians about the deer hunt. Furthermore, everything was to be done to maintain the pretense of good relations. If the Russians sent a gift of food, the food was to be accepted and appropriate gifts given in return. If the Russians wished to fight, however, the Manchus were to retreat, for K'ang-hsi said, "We have other plans to deal with them." *Ibid.; SL-KH, ibid.; PTLC,* 1:4b. Basically K'ang-hsi seemed to believe at this period that "the Lo-ch'a dare not face us." After receiving their instructions, Langtan and Pengcun were given presents of imperial clothes, bows, and arrows from the hands of K'ang-hsi himself. All the other members of the expedition were also given gifts of encouragement before their departure.

12. *PTLC,* 1:5b-6; *SL-KH,* 106:23b-24. On Sabsu, see Hummel, II, 630-631.

13. The emperor's edict was discussed by the council of princes and other ministers. On the council of princes (*i-cheng-wang*), see Hsiao I-shan, *Ch'ing-tai t'ung-shih,* 2 vols. (Shanghai, 1927), I, 453-454. Their reply not only supported the emperor's recommendations but indicated a certain degree of impatience on the part of the court to have done with the matter by a quick blow. They recommended that as soon as the warships were built and the provisions sufficient to the purpose, the attack should begin. They further noted that the supply of food at Wu-la (Kirin) was low and that both the Board of Revenue and the Li-fan yuan should arrange for the purchase of food at Hsi-po-kua-erh-ch'a for the soldiers stationed at Wu-la.

14. The conceptions of priority and planning behind the precise Ch'ing approach to northern Manchuria's logistic problems, as well as the meticulous attention to detail that characterized K'ang-hsi's direction of the entire anti-Russian campaign, were graphically illustrated in an edict dated April 4, 1683. Ordering Grand Secretary Ledehun to send food supplies to the army at Wu-la, the emperor described each step carefully and often explained specific decisions. For a comment on Ledehun, see Hummel, II, 683; see also *Ch'ing-shih,* 8 vols. (Taipei, 1961), IV, 2456. For text of the edict, see *PTLC,* 1:6b-8. The emperor ordered food taken from central Manchurian *t'un-chuang* (military grain colonies) and transported to the

Liao River by the *t'un-chuang* laborers themselves, together with tools such as wooden stakes and poles. The food was to be transported to Teng-szu-tun on the Liao River, where granaries were to be constructed for storage. Mongols would transport the stored grain through the portage to I-tun-men at the mouth of the I-tun River, where other granaries were to be prepared. From I-tun-men the grain would again be loaded on boats for the trip along the Sung-hua River to the front area. Within firmly controlled Manchu territory, Manchu soldiers were to be used for escort, but outside those areas Mongols were to be employed. In order to speed deliveries, amounts of grain loaded on each boat were to be decreased and more men used to pull the boats along the rivers where the current was too weak. The wooden stakes and poles brought from the t'un-chuang were for use in shallow waters. Wagons were to be prepared at all portages to transport grain along clearly marked paths. The transport ships were to be constructed "in proportion to the size of the river." The *fu-tu-t'ung* of Wu-la was placed in charge of the operation and ordered to investigate the details and memorialize.

K'ang-hsi followed developments closely. Ledehun memorialized that along the Chü-liu River sixty boats should be constructed, each thirty feet in length and ten feet wide. Each boat could carry 100 shih of grain with a six-man crew, recruited from the local population and specially trained. The crew would receive, per person, one liang of silver from the day the actual transportation began. He recommended that the direction of the project be placed under the supervision of the general at Mukden and the ministers at Peking. Officers and men from Mukden would escort the supplies to the Teng-szu-tun portage, and the fu-tu-t'ung at Wu-la would be charged with the construction of the I-tun-men granaries and transportation along the Sung-hua. In other words, administration of the project would be geographically divided at the portage. K'ang-hsi, dissatisfied with Ledehun's proposals, ordered Fo-pao, a *lang-chung* of the Construction Department of the Nei-fu, and I-ch'ang-a, a vice-president of the Hu-pu, to test the validity of Ledehun's proposals by experimentally carrying grain along the rivers in boats. He also ordered the vice-president of the Hsing-pu in Mukden, Ka-erh-t'u, to measure the depth of the Liao River between its confluence with the Chü-liu, and the portage that began at Teng-szu-tun. Measurements were made on the other side of the portage as well. Ka-erh-t'u's report supported Ledehun's recommendations, but Wa-li-hu, the fu-tu-t'ung at Ninguta who had carried out the other measurements, discovered that the I-tun River could accommodate boats thirty-five feet long. He recommended that wood cut in Kirin be used to construct 100 boats on the I-tun side of the portage. With this evidence in hand, the emperor accepted Ledehun's modified proposals and divided the transportation system into two parts, connected at the I-tun-men granaries. Grain could be carried up to I-tun-men by river and portage through the first system, stored there, and moved along the second system when conditions were appropriate. The independence of the two systems distributed the responsibility more evenly over the limited available managerial resources and thus increased efficiency. As the Manchus established more forward positions, the transportation network expanded to include new regions. Wu-la, for instance, took over from I-tun-men as the major depot for goods en route to Aigun on the Amur itself. *PTLC,* 1:16a-b and 18. Concerned lest the burden of actual transportation fall too heavily on the shoulders of any one group and endanger morale, the emperor took measures to distribute the responsibility for providing labor among various groups along the supply network.

The actual storage of grain in the area of contact was only one aspect of the supply problem. Another aspect was transportation in a situation of scarcity of manpower. In April 1683 this problem became acute when the emperor ordered that in addition to a six-month ration of grain per soldier to be carried along with the troops, further rations be transported to the portage between the Sung-hua River and the Amur. *PTLC,* 1:8b-9. Sabsu had stored grain at Meng-ku-hsi-po, and this stock, together with the amount of grain issued by the authorities at Sheng-ching and based on the number of soldiers, was to be transported on fifty boats constructed at Wu-la. The personnel problem was raised for consideration. The emperor, interested in the morale of his soldiers as well as their physical condition, pointed out that the soldiers from Wu-la and Ninguta were generally quite poor. At least half of them were already involved in arduous transportation duties, and if the others were used for the transport of the new grains, it would be too much of a burden for them to carry. Instead, therefore, he ordered that eight hunting household groups who were under the jurisdiction of Hsi-t'e-k'u of Wu-la should stop hunting for a year and be assigned to transportation, so that the soldiers involved in that activity could be released. The hunting households were instructed to proceed to the portage, where they would be met by Sabsu. By the use of the hunters to transport the grain to the portage and Sabsu's men to transport it in boats beyond the portage, the burden would be equalized.

The establishment of postal stations to improve communications was another Manchu logistic problem. The Board of Revenue recommended that, with Wu-la as a base, ten stations be set up between Wu-la and Aigun, which was the main center of concentration and staging in preparation for the siege of Albazin. On December 14, 1683, the emperor decided to send in the following spring officials from the Board of Revenue, the Board of War, and the Li-fan yuan (the three agencies most concerned with preparations for the anti-Russian campaign), together with scouts chosen from the Khorchin and Durbet Mongol banners, to survey the land and determine the best locations for proposed stations. *PTLC,* 1:15b. When in 1685 the decision was made to lay siege to Albazin, the need for speedy communications dictated the creation of a new network of stations between Aigun and the Russian settlement. Ordinarily reports from Albazin and its environs were routed through E-su-li to Aigun, but the emperor complained that it was "a crooked way and it is feared that they might be delayed." Consequently, he ordered Ming-ai, a vice-president of the Li-fan yuan, to send 500 men to establish a communications network between Aigun and Albazin via Mo-erh-hun, "for the transmission of military reports, so that nothing may be delayed." Ming-ai himself was ordered to travel the station route to inspect the supply situation and ensure that each station's workers had sufficient food. If he discovered any shortages, he was to correct them personally. The personnel to man the communications stations were supplied by Manchu soldiers from Aigun and by Mongol bannermen. Originally twenty workers were assigned to each station in the Aigun region, but K'ang-hsi, seeking to economize on the use of resources, halved the figure and sent the remaining men to the new stations. Most of the Manchu station workers were "New Manchu" Solun tribesmen, and the emperor, recognizing that the Solun tribes were themselves subject to Russian penetration, declared, "The Solun people have rendered hard services. They should be notified that in the future favors will be granted them as tokens of encouragement." *PTLC,* 1:14a-b.

15. *PLTC,* 1:9, 2:2b.

16. *PTLC,* 1:9b-11b.

17. The exact cause of the ill will between Sabsu and Bahai is unclear. However, in January 1684 Sabsu, who had been a vice-lieutenant general at Ninguta, was promoted to general of Heilungchiang, with headquarters at Aigun. Originally, Heilungchiang (the Amur River) had been under the control of Bahai and his father Sarhuda. On Sarhuda, see Hummel, II, 632. Their failure to contain the Russians resulted in the forfeiture of Bahai's position at Ninguta and his transfer to Wu-la. In Sabsu's new capacity he was ordered to command 1,500 men from Ninguta and Wu-la at Aigun, which was to become a permanent settlement and staging ground for future action against the Russians.

18. *PTLC,* 1:11.

19. *PTLC,* 1:13a-15b, esp. 13b.

20. *PTLC,* 1:14b.

21. *PTLC,* 1:15b, 17.

22. *PTLC,* 2:2b-4.

23. *PTLC,* 2:7-8. In this debate with Sabsu, K'ang-hsi tried to understand why "Sabsu in his memorials and reports has made many excuses to delay action, and [why] he says that if we advance our army in the 4th month, we can only reap their harvests but cannot accomplish anything finally." *Ibid.,* 2:8b. He suggested that the relationship between Sabsu and his advisors caused his hesitancy. Since Sabsu was of humble origin, "he looks highly" at the Heilungchiang officials, who were "haughty and violent people" and tried to obstruct the entire operation. Sabsu respected them and "dared not do anything against them." *Ibid.,* 8b-9.

24. *PTLC,* 2:8. This proposal was recommended for approval by the council of princes, who also suggested that 250 soldiers skilled in the use

of rifles should be dispatched from Chih-li, Shantung, Shansi, and Honan, together with good and able officers, four from each province, to reinforce Sabsu's army for the attack. They were to foregather in Peking, whence they would be dispatched in time to join the attack on Albazin. The emperor, however, did not approve the suggestions of the council, pointing out that while there was no suggestion to send the imperial army, which was in good training, the Green Standard soldiers in Chih-li and the other provinces "are not experienced on the battlefield. Furthermore, there are many fire-weapons in Heilungchiang, and we do not need to send more there." He recommended sending, instead, surrendered officers and soldiers from Fukien, who were skilled in the use of rattan shields and were now settled in the eight banners in such places as Shantung, Shansi, and Honan. Five hundred of these had already been sent under the command of the recently surrendered Ho Yu and others. *Ibid.,* 2:8b. It is obvious that a long and costly debate was taking place between the emperor in Peking and his officers at the front, covering every manner of military problem.

25. *PTLC,* 2:9.

26. *PTLC,* 2:11b-12.

27. *PTLC,* 1:12.

28. *PTLC,* 2:15.

29. *SL-KH,* 119:5b-6, 8. Supplies were distributed along the front through storage depots. At the beginning of 1684 Sabsu requested that the number of officers and men assigned to the Amur region be fixed so that food allowances could be established more precisely. The Board of Revenue memorialized that an estimated 4,870 shih of grain were needed in the front region for a two-year period; 4,570 shih were already on hand, and an additional amount could be obtained from the Dahur people. The emperor ordered that 970 shih be taken from the Teng-szu-tun granaries, and 1,500 shih from the granaries at I-tun-men, all to be transported by boat as soon as the spring thaw. Rice was drawn as needed from several granaries and other sources. *PTLC,* 2:6.

30. *PTLC,* 1:9-9b.

31. See, for instance, *PTLC,* 2:4-5b, 2:14b-15b, 1:12b-13; 1:17a-b, 2:1b-2, 2:1a-b.

32. *PTLC,* 2:10a-b.

33. *PTLC,* 2:10b-11, italics added. See also *SL-KH,* 111:16b-17, 112:4-5, 119:6-7b for similar policy statements. For comments on Manchu military preparations, see Golder, 56.

34. For source of my discussion of the Russian delegation, see Yakovleva, pp. 111, 115-122. This remains the best account available. Yakovleva used archival materials extensively, and until those same materials become available to the scholarly public outside the USSR, her description must remain standard.

35. In order to clarify the situation further, Voeikov sent to inquire from the Albazinian *prikazchik,* Yakov Evsevev, by what order he had sent the

Albazinian Cossack, Grigory Mylnik, and fifteen other Cossacks in 1680 to establish the ostrog at the confluence of the Zeya and the Selimba rivers. Was it done, he asked, "by the tsar's gramota, or by an official memoir from Eniseisk . . . or by petition of the Albazinian Cossacks?" Evsevev tried to side-step the issue of responsibility by declaring that the ostrog had been constructed on petition from Mylnik and his comrades, not by the decision of all the Albazinian Cossacks nor by the tsar's gramota. Yakovleva, p. 118.

36. The figure 15,000 for the size of the Manchu forces in that year is probably an exaggeration.

37. Yakovleva, pp. 120-121. During 1683 the Siberian Department undertook a survey of armaments and military supplies in Siberia, based on information in the reports of the various voevodas. In all Dahuria there were about 2,000 serving people, armed with 21 cannon, 485 harquebuses, 182 puds of powder, and 143 puds of lead. At Tobolsk there were 1,719 serving-people, armed with 46 cannon, 4,139 rounds of ammunition, 244 berdysh (?), 926 puds of powder, 3,451 puds of lead. In Verkhoturye, Tiumen, Pelym, Turinsk, and Tar there were an additional 1,600 men. In other words, Moscow had at its disposal in Siberia military forces numbering between 4,000 and 5,000 men. In the Cadasters compiled by L'ev Poskochin, the Siberian Department also listed possible military reserves to be drawn from the peasants, their children, and their grandchildren. In 1683 there were 8,203 of these in Tobolsk and 5,102 in Verkhoturye, making a possible reserve force of 13,417 men. Apparently no information was available in Moscow concerning possible reserves in other places.

38. On Manchu reports of reinforcements at Albazin, see *SL-KH,* 120:20.

39. *SL-KH,* 119:8b. Yakovleva claims that in 1684 Manchu forces came right up to the gates of Albazin and captured all Russians outside the settlement. The attack included a siege of several months' duration. There is no evidence in the Chinese sources to support this claim, nor does Yakovleva, who is usually precise in her citations, give any sources for the assertion. Yakovleva, p. 121.

40. *PTLC,* 2:11; Hummel, II, 665. Lieutenant-general Pengcun was appointed to lead the army, and the captain-general (*hu-chün-t'ung-ling*) Tung-pao was deputy lieutenant-general. Bandarša was councillor (*ts'an-tsan*), and Sahai, a vice-president of the Board of Revenue, was named supervisor of land cultivation.

41. Liu Hsien-t'ing, *Kuang-yang tsa-chi* (Shanghai, 1957), p. 85.

42. *SL-KH,* 121:11b-12.

43. Liu Hsien-t'ing, p. 86.

44. For accounts of the battle, see *PTLC,* 2:15b-16; SL-KH, 119:4b; "Lang-t'an chüan," 135:16b-17.

45. On the Albazinian Cossacks who settled in Peking and came to be known in Russian history as the "Albazintsy," see Pavlovsky, pp. 145-164.

46. See *Ch'ing-shih,* IV, 2565. A-erh-ni's name was sometimes written A-la-ni. K'ang-hsi wrote: "As for the pacification of the Lo-ch'a people, all

thought that it was too far away to be easily done. I alone made the decision to send an expeditionary force, and now by the Heavenly Favor, we have taken over the place. I am much delighted. You should notify this good news to all princes and ministers." *PTLC,* 2:16b.

47. For these exchanges, see *PTLC,* 2:16b-20.

48. On September 15 the emperor also decreed awards for various officers and groups of men, by name. *PTLC,* 2:21-21b.

49. For details, see *PTLC,* 2:20a-b. For the long debate on this subject. see *PTLC,* 2:22a-24b.

50. *DAI,* X, 257-258.

51. Cahen, *Histoire,* pp. 33-35.

52. *DAI,* X, 252-254. Vlasov evidently had some doubts about Tolbuzin himself returning to Albazin, for he claimed that it was only at the demand of the Albazinians that he allowed Tolbuzin to return with the newly conscripted soldiers.

53. Tolbuzin, however, was not to expect aid in the provision of farming implements from Nerchinsk. He was also informed by Vlasov that reinforcements had reached the Eravinsk ostrog but had not yet arrived at Nerchinsk. *DAI,* X, 253-254. Godoveika is not a Chinese name; perhaps he was an indigene.

54. *DAI,* X, 255.

55. *PTLC,* 3:1b; SL-KH, 124:4, 15.

56. "It is not proper to resort to force immediately," K'ang-hsi declared. *PTLC,* 3:1b. See *PTLC,* 3:2-3, for text of the instructions of March 3, and the appointments made at the end of April 1686. See also "Lang-t'an chuan," 153:18.

57. "Lang-t'an chuan," 153:18-19; Golder, p. 61; see also *DAI,* X, 257, where Tolbuzin, writing on July 12 to Vlasov about the siege, suggested that the siege began on July 7, earlier than the Chinese sources state. He wrote to Vlasov that between July 7 and July 12 the Manchu forces had built up their siege weapons both above and below the city, as well as on the river.

58. *DAI,* X, 260. A funt equals 1 pound.

59. *DAI,* X, 263-265. Note that Golder's citations from this document are inaccurate. Chinese sources say only twenty remained alive. "Lang-t'an chuan," 153:20. See also Ravenstein, p. 52.

60. *PTLC,* 3:3a-4b, 6a-7a. In his decree K'ang-hsi declared: "I did not intend to slaughter the city and intended to treat them with toleration. Sabsu and others are therefore ordered to evacuate their forces from Albazin and gather them in one place near the warships. Moreover, the Lo-ch'a in the city are to be notified that they are free to go in and out of the city, but should not make any seizures. We wait for the Russian envoys to arrive in order to reach an agreement." *Ibid.,* 3:7a-b. The Russian messengers actually carried two letters to the tsar from the emperor, presumably identical in content, one in Latin and one in Mongol. They also carried a private

letter from the Jesuit Verbiest to Milescu, in which he attested to his devotion to the Russian cause and stated that another Jesuit, Pereyra, concurred in this devotion. Verbiest complained that since neither Venyukov nor Favorov spoke Latin, he could not communicate with them. Therefore, the next ambassador, or at least one of his suite, should speak Latin. Cahen, *Histoire,* p. 38.

61. *SL-KH,* 127:23b-24; "Lang-t'an chuan," 153:20; Golder, p. 63.

62. "Lang-t'an-chuan," 153:20. Golder, p. 63, apparently in error states that the supplies were sent in 1688.

63. *PTLC,* 3:7b. Ravenstein claims that Baiton declined the gracious Chinese offer of medical aid and, in order to convince the Manchus that everything was well within his walls, ordered a large pie made, weighing 40 puds, to be sent to the Manchu headquarters. Ravenstein, p. 52-53.

64. *PTLC,* 3:8a.

65. Cahen, *Histoire,* p. 41; *DAI,* X, 273.

Chapter V—The Treaty of Nerchinsk

1. There are three primary sources for the Nerchinsk negotiations. Two are the diaries of the Jesuits, Gerbillon and Pereyra, who served the Manchu envoys as Latin translators. See F. Gerbillon, *The Second Journey of PP. Gerbillon and Pereyra in Tartary, in 1689,* in Jean Baptiste du Halde, *A Description of the Empire of China and Chinese-Tartary,* vol. 2 (London, 1741), pp. 301-333; Joseph Sebes, *The Jesuits and the Sino-Russian Treaty of Nerchinsk (1689): The Diary of Thomas Pereira, S.J.* (Rome, 1961), pp. 169-303. Of the two diaries, Gerbillon's gives every impression of having been compiled from notes made on the spot during the negotiations: it is a day-by-day account, paying close attention to geographical and climatic detail. Pereyra's diary appears rather to be a recollection written in Peking: he pays less attention to detail and dating and concludes with the following significant statement: "Finally, I ask all to forgive me if in some matter or circumstance I have omitted anything out of forgetfulness, and I offer myself to all as one desirous of acting, as I am, a slave in Peking, 10 January [1]690, All to all in the Lord." The third source is the stateynyi spisok of the Russian envoy, Fedor Alekseevich Golovin. This unpublished, 1261-page record of the negotiations at Nerchinsk is in the Soviet Union's Tsentralny Gosudarstvenny Arkhiv Drevnykh Aktov (f. 63, op. 1, stlb. 10). Shastina, p. 119, n. 48. It remains unavailable to non-Soviet scholars. P.T. Yakovleva used this document and quoted from it fairly extensively in her study of the Treaty of Nerchinsk. Although her work is so marred by inconsistencies in interpretation and by an all-pervading, corrosive anti-Manchu Russian chauvinism as to make her citations from the document unreliable, they nevertheless do raise strong doubts about the accuracy or honesty of the diaries regarding the events at Nerchinsk in August and September 1689.

They may also lead to the conclusion that Gerbillon and Pereyra were more interested in the defense of their own conduct than in giving their society an understanding, accurate report of the negotiations.

2. Yakovleva, pp. 128-129; V.S. Mamyshev, *General-feldmarshal i general-admiral graf Fedor Alekseevich Golovin* (St. Petersburg, 1910), p. 5; S.K. Bogoyavlensky, *Prikaznye sudyi XVII v.* (Moscow, 1946), pp. 226, 228; Yakovleva, 129.

3. Yakovleva, pp. 128-129; Bantysh-Kameneky, p. 52. Pereyra characterized Vlasov's obstructionist tactics in the negotiations over the demarcation of the frontier as follows: "The reason for this resolute and short answer, as later we found out from a truthful and reliable source, was that the governor of these territories, a Moscovite and extremely selfish adventurer, who together with some others, when he saw that his district was being diminished, persuaded the ambassador not to concede anything, but to fish around a little, as they say, to see whether he could catch anything." Evidently Golovin was later forced to take matters into his own hands and to curb Vlasov: "The reason for the delay of the Moscovite answer was a difference of opinions among them and the fact that they had persuaded their Ambassador [Golovin], as I mentioned before, to deny everything to see what we would do—a great mistake when negotiating with a nation one does not know. The Moscovite ambassador, realizing in what kind of a situation he was, which his prudence would have avoided had he on this occasion acted as plenipotentiary and not listened to the Governor [Vlasov] and to the many prejudiced opinions which resulted in a confusion like Babylon, and realizing that he was misled by his own people, decided to do now that he should have done before, and taking the whole thing in his own hands as plenipotentiary, reprehended the Governor for being the cause of the earlier resolution and showed him the error he had made." Sebes, pp. 247-249, 252-255. Pereyra and Gerbillon suspected Belobotsky of being a Roman Catholic. Pereyra wrote about him, "I was overcome with joy, first in seeing how well founded my hopes were, and second because he spoke as a Roman Catholic, for until then he had not declared himself and if he were a shismatic [sic] he would not have honored us in such a way." Sebes, p. 251.

4. Yakovleva, p. 139; Bantysh-Kamensky, pp. 54, 56; du Halde, II, 273. For a discussion of this first embassy and for Gerbillon's diary of it, see du Halde, II, 273-301. In the Jesuit's report of this first attempt to reach Selenginsk, he discusses the Khalkha-Jungar wars fairly extensively. Golovin and his embassy left Moscow on January 26 and arrived in Tobolsk on March 24. Having completed their preparations, they left Tobolsk on May 29 and arrived on September 3 at Rybny, an ostrog on the Angara River, where they spent the winter of 1686-1687. With the arrival of spring, Golovin left Rybny on May 15, arriving on September 11 at Udinsk (the present Ulan-Ude), the gateway to the Amur and Nerchinsk. For details of Golovin's journey, see du Halde, pp. 52-53; Yakovleva, pp. 135-136.

5. For the text of the first set of instructions, see Bantysh-Kamensky, pp. 49-52.

6. Golovin received his second set of instructions on September 30, 1689. For the text of the second set of instructions, see Bantysh-Kamensky, pp. 53-54. See also Schebenkov, p. 204. It is interesting to note that this second set of instructions was issued not by the Ambassadorial Department, as would normally have been the case, but by the court directly, which perhaps indicates a disagreement in Moscow. Bantysh-Kamenskii, 53.

7. For the text of the third set of instructions, a description of the contents of the three treaties, and Loginov's Peking sojourn, see Bantysh-Kamensky, pp. 56-57, 60-61.

8. For a thorough account of the development of Russian-Mongol relations in the seventeenth century, see Shastina, *passim*. For the original documents of this relationship up to 1636, see I. Ya. Zlatkin and N.V. Ustyugov, eds., *Russko-Mongolskie otnosheniya 1607-1636: sbornik dokumentov*.

9. Selenginsk was established in 1667. See Kerner, p. 187.

10. Shastina, pp. 108-111. Partly in response to this embassy, the Eniseisk boyar son Ivan Perfilev was sent on a mission to the Tushetu-khan. He used much the same type of historical analysis against the Mongols that the Russians used on the Amur, he claiming that those natives now paying tribute to the Russians had done so from ancient times and were not vassals of the Mongols. Shastina, p. 110.

11. Shastina, pp. 117-118. This envoy went to Selenginsk.

12. Bantysh-Kamensky, pp. 51-52.

13. Throughout 1687 Golovin continued to receive numerous embassies from the Mongol khans. In July at Irkutsk he received the envoys of the Tsetsen-noin khan, whose major purpose was to determine the reasons for the large military support accompanying Golovin's embassy. Golovin maintained that the military force in his entourage was a strictly logistic unit, not meant to conduct war. In an obvious effort to cut the ground from under the Mongol assertions of Russian aggression, Golovin complained about Mongol attacks on Russian subjects. Repeating the traditional Mongol complaints about the Russians, the Mongol envoy proposed that an agreement be drawn up whereby the Mongols and the Russians would live "in advice" with each other and would conduct trade. In the autumn of that year a joint embassy from the Undur-gegen, the Tushetu-khan, and the Shidishiri-bagatur-khuntaiju arrived at Udinsk. These most important Khalkha princes made the same complaints, inquiries, and proposals as the Tsetsen-noin khan, insisting once again on the return of the Buryats. They also complained that the Tushetu-khan had sent many letters to Moscow about the Buryat problem, without any answer. Shastina, 122-123. For the early history of Buryatya, see E.M. Zalkind, et al., *Istoriya Buryat-Mongolskoi ASSR*, vol. I (Ulan-Ude, 1954). For corrections to this text, see Shastina, pp. 139 ff.

14. Shastina, pp. 123-124.

15. Immediately after the departure of the Mongol embassy of November 1687, Golovin sent Korovin to Peking to announce the embassy's arrival at the frontier. Korovin was accompanied by a special envoy, Ivan Kachanov, who was to visit the Undurgegen. Yakovleva, p. 139. Kachanov's instructions were specific: he was to (1) collect information about the situation in Mongolia; (2) establish good relations with the Undurgegen, emphasizing that Golovin did not want to pass through Mongolia to meet the Manchus; (3) convince the Undurgegen that the military forces at Selenginsk were not a threat to the Mongols; (4) explain that the sending of messengers through the Undurgegen's lands to Peking should cause no inconvenience or uneasiness to the Mongols, as the Russians were interested only in peace; (5) present a bill of complaints against the Mongols and emphasize that the Russians, or the Cossacks, would not commit aggressions against them; and (6) discuss free trade. The Undurgegen kept Kachanov and Korovin at his court for two months, but Kachanov's mission was a total failure, for almost precisely the same reasons that had caused the failure of the earlier Russian missions to Peking. It proved impossible to solve the ceremonial difficulties attendant upon contact between such varying cultural traditions, in this case the Russian and the Mongol. Perfilev, who had earlier carried the tsar's gramota and Golovin's gifts to the Undurgegen, had been forced to deliver his message and gifts not to the Undurgegen directly but to the *shangdzoba* (a kind of clerical minister with civil duties) because he had refused to kneel to receive the Undurgegen's benediction, as was the custom at the court. Kachanov for precisely the same reason was not even granted an audience. This ceremonial problem arose only at the moment when an effort was made to establish contact between the sovereign himself and a western ambassador or envoy (Russian, in this case). In cases where a Mongol (or Manchu, as at Nerchinsk and later in the thirties of the eighteenth century) met with a Russian embassy on socially neutral territory, or even journeyed to the Russian capital, such problems did not arise. Golovin was therefore instructed not to journey into China; by holding the conference in the area of frontier contact, they could avoid ceremonial problems. See Shastina, pp. 122-123, 128-132. For a discussion of this siege, see Shastina, pp. 134-142. See also Yakovleva, p. 141.

16. Yakovleva, p. 142. Shastina, p. 149, gave the date of notification as July 30. See also Shastina, p. 152. For a biography of Galdan, see Hummel, I, 265-268. For a history of the Manchu campaigns against Galdan, see Chang Yü-shu, *P'ing-ting shuo-mo fang-lüeh* (1708).

17. Hummel, I, 267.

18. Shastina, p. 162.

19. Korovin's arrival in Peking was mentioned in the edict appointing the members of the embassy. *SL-KH,* 134; 3a-b. For a biography of Songgotu, known in the Jesuit accounts as Sosan La-oyeh, see Hummel, II, 663-666. On T'ung Kuo-kang, known in Jesuit accounts as Kiou-kieou,

from the Chinese *chiu-chiu* or maternal uncle, see Hummel, II, 794-795.

20. *Ch'ing-shih,* IX, 2569. A-erh-ni, a Manchu, is sometimes written A-la-ni.

21. *SL-KH,* 134:3a-b. Maci had been a reader in the Grand Secretariat in 1684, financial commissioner of Shansi in 1685. For his biography, see Hummel, I, 560-561. Chang P'eng-ko left one of the two important Chinese records of the first unsuccessful embassy. On Chang P'eng-ko, see Hummel, I, 49. See also *Feng-shih O-lo-ssu hsing-ch'eng-lu,* in the collectanea *I-hai chu-ch'en;* this diary has sometimes been published, with minor textual differences, under the title *Feng-shih O-lo-ssu jih-chi.*

22. Du Halde, II, 273. In the *Ch'ing shih-lu* these instructions were given as a decree from the emperor. *SL-KH,* 135:14b-16. The *P'ing-ting Lo-ch'a fang-lüeh* gave them in the form of a memorial from the ambassadors, Songgotu and others, which the emperor approved. It is highly likely that this version is the more accurate and that the man chiefly responsible for formulating the policy to be followed at the negotiations was Mala, as suggested by the preliminary instructions given Songgotu by the emperor. The day the emperor approved the memorial, the delegation left the capital; it can therefore be assumed that this policy was officially promulgated on May 30, 1688, probably at a dawn audience. *PTLC,* 4:1b-3.

23. One may speculate whether mention of the fact that the Amur provided access to the sea indicated a concern in the Manchu mind that such access would put Russia in a position not too dissimilar to Japan's in terms of piratical raids along the China coast.

24. Gerbillon recorded the return in his diary. See du Halde, 285. Yakovleva (p. 156) maintained that the embassy's return on the emperor's orders indicated that "in the spring of 1688, K'ang-hsi was not in a hurry to enter into negotiations with Russia." This conclusion was totally unsupported by evidence. Note that Gerbillon left diaries of both embassies, Pereyra of the second only. For the text of the Ch'ing letter to Golovin, see du Halde, 286. Gerbillon prefaced his text of the letter with the following remark: "Our Ambassadors, before they set out on their Return, wrote a long letter to the Russian Ambassadors, which they made us translate into Latin."

25. *PTLC,* 4:3b-4. In Gerbillon's entry concerning the embassy's arrival at Nerchinsk itself, he gave the following description of its size: "We arrived at length over against Nipchu, where we found the Barks, which brought the Soldiers and Provisions from Ula [Wu-la] and Aygu [Aigun], lying in a Row along the Southern Bank. The Tents of the Soldiers were also disposed in Order, according to their Standards by the River-side. The Barks had hung out their Streamers and Flags in Honour to the Chiefs of the Embassy, and near them were 100 others, of a middle Rate, built like Galleys, which went both with Sails and Oars, but were usually hall'd along with Ropes by Men who marched on the Bank. Fifteen Hundred Soldiers arrived in these Barks, who with the Crews made at least 3000; to which

adding the 1400 Soldiers who came by land with us, the Mandarins, the Ambassadors' Guards, their numerous Domesticks, and Servants, who composed the Equipage, the whole might amount to 9 or 10,000 men. There were 3 or 4,000 Camels and at least 15,000 Horses. So San Lau ye [Songgotu] alone had above 300 of the first, and 1500 of the latter besides 100 Domesticks to attend him. Kiw Kyew [T'ung Kuo-kang] had no less than 300 Horses and 130 Camels, with 80 Servants, and the other Mandarins in proportion. We understood that the Governor of Nipchu [Vlasov] was surprised at the Arrival of the Soldiers in the Barks, because he had no notice given him." Du Halde, 308. Vlasov was undoubtedly equally surprised at the embassy's size.

26. Du Halde, 309-310.

27. For a full and colorful description of the event, see du Halde, 310-311.

28. For the records of this conference, see du Halde, pp. 311-316; Yakovleva, p. 168. On the siege, see *ibid.*, 171 ff.

29. Sebes, pp. 233-235. The treaty stated explicitly: "All the differences [quarrels] which may have occurred between the subjects [of each nation] on the frontier up to the date of this Treaty will be forgotten and [claims arising out of them will] not be entertained." See Walter Fuchs, "Der russisch-chinesische Vertrag von Jahre 1698," *Monumenta Serica* 412:546-591 (1939-1940), esp. p. 591, which is a masterful study of the various texts of the Treaty of Nerchinsk. A careful examination of the Chinese texts (pp. 582-585) supports the opinion that the treaty itself contained no linguistic indications of Manchu superiority to the Russians.

30. Sebes, pp. 583, 590. This lack of geographical information was particularly true of the region of the Ud River Valley, which remained undemarcated until the middle of the nineteenth century. Sebes, p. 590.

31. For the text of the article on fugitives and crimes, see Sebes p. 591.

32. For the negotiations on this point, see du Halde, 313.

33. Yakovleva, pp. 293-294.

34. Shastina, pp. 164, 167; du Halde, p. 330.

35. *PTLC.*, 4:4b-5; *SL-KH,* 143:14b-15a.

36. *PTLC,* 4:5-6.

37. Pavlovsky, p. 152.

38. *PTLC,* 4:7b-8, 8b.

Chapter VI—The Sino-Russian Treaty System

1. On the trade at Kyakhta-Maimaichen after 1727, see E. P. Silin, *Kyakhta v XVIII veke: iz istory russko-kitayskoi torgovli* (Irkutsk, 1947). The Selenginsk-Urga route served such settlements as Selenginsk, Irkutsk, Krasnoyarsk, Eniseisk, and Tomsk. The important Irbit market must be included in both the first and second routes because it could be reached by river from either the western or the central Siberian region.

2. After the fall of Kuchum's khanate at Sibir, the Russians found themselves at the end of a long trade route that went to China through Bukhara. Both archeological and documentary evidence suggest that Chinese goods were known at Kuchum's court. Vasili Pignaty's excavations at Sibir in 1915 uncovered shards of porcelain dishes with the typical blue-and-white patterns of the Ming dynasty. *Ezhegodnik Tobolskago muzeya,* 25:26 (Tobolsk, 1915). A letter from Abdullah, khan of Bukhara, to Kuchum, dated sometime in 1595 or 1596, offered to exchange Chinese for Siberian products. *Materialy po istory Uzbekskoy, Tadzhikskoy i Turkmenskoy SSSR,* Vol. 3, Pt. 1, p. 109 (Leningrad, 1932).

3. Kuchum, in an effort to save his khanate, sought to prevent the development of contact between the Russians and the Bukharans. See, for instance, *Sibirskiya letopisi* (St. Petersburg, 1907), p. 37; *Sobranie gosudarstvennykh gramot i dogovoroy khranyaschikhsya v gosudarstvennoy kollegii inostrannykh del,* ed. N.N. Bantysh-Kamensky, A.F. Malinovsky, et al., 5 vols. (Moscow, 1813-1894), II, 129.

4. On February 10, 1595, for instance, an edict was sent to Fedor Eletsky, the second voevoda of Tarsk, ordering him to do everything possible to encourage commerce with the Bukharans. G. Müller, *Istoriya Sibiri* (Moscow, 1937), I, 363. This is a revised edition of Müller's (Mueller) *Opisanie Sibirskago tsarstva i vsekh proisshedskikh v nem del ot nachala a osoblivo ot pokoreniya ego rossiyskoi derzhave po sii vremena,* 2nd ed. (St. Petersburg, 1787). A gramota on August 31, 1596, permitted the Bukharans and Nogais to trade duty-free "wherever suitable" with the single provision that they not trade knives, axes, and similar implements to the native population. *Materialy po istorii Uzbekskoy,* I, 296. On the supply difficulties of the early Siberian colonizers, see V.I. Shunkov, *Ocherki po istorii kolonizatsii Sibiri v XVII—nachale XVIII v.* (Moscow, 1946), pp. 97-109.

5. Shortly after the beginning of the seventeenth century the tithe duty was imposed on the Bukharans in such cities as Tobolsk and Tyumen. This was an irregularly collected impost, however, the decision when to make the collection being left up to the local authorities. Shunkov, I, 109. In Turinsk, for instance, where Bukharan strength was particularly evident, the tithe was collected rarely.

6. In 1622, for instance, tithe collections from Bukharan merchants trading between Siberia and Central Asia were halved. O.N. Vilkov, "Kitayskie tovary na Tobolskom rynke v XVII v.," *Istoriya SSSR* 1:105-124 (January-February, 1958), p. 107. See, for instance, *Akty istoricheskie,* II, 337, on the atrophy of communications.

7. Yu. V. Gote, *Angliyskie puteshestvenniki v Moskovskom gosudarstve v XVI v.* (Moscow, 1937), pp. 189-190; *Materialy po istorii Uzbekskoy,* I, 336-338.

8. Different goods dominated the Jungarian route at different times. Between 1639 and 1649, silk cloth was the largest item of import, whereas nankeens and rhubarb predominated between 1649 and 1659. In 1656 the

state monopolized the rhubarb trade; as a result, rhubarb disappeared completely from the route after 1659. Nankeens then became almost the sole item of import until 1695, when this particular route practically disappeared from sight. Vilkov, pp. 110-111.

9. On the relative importance of Siberian, Russian, and Bukharan merchants to the Jungarian route and on its decline, see Vilkov, p. 111, esp. table 1 on p. 111. The decline of the route was linked directly to the development of alternative routes rather than to any decline in pre-Nerchinsk Sino-Russian trade. Whereas in the years 1639-1658 almost 100 percent of the goods carried directly from China to Tobolsk went along this route through Suchow and Jungaria, from 1658 to 1703 the value of goods along the same route never rose higher than 2.1 percent of the total value of Chinese goods delivered at Tobolsk.

10. For a detailed description of the Yamysh route, see G. Potanin, "O Karavannoy torgovle s Dzhungarskoy Bukhariey v XVIII stoletii", in *Chteniya v imperatorskom obschestve istorii i drevnostey Rossiyskikh pri Moskovskom universitete,* 2:21-113 (April-June 1868), pp. 38-43.

11. On the relationship between the market and the salt industry and on the growth of the latter, see Arsenev, pp. 43-44; Vilkov, p. 108.

12. V.A. Aleksandrov, "Iz istorii russko-kitayshikh ekonomicheskikh svyazey pered Nerchinskim mirom 1689 g.," *Istoriya SSSR,* 5:203-208 (November-December 1957), pp. 204-205. Both state and private merchants participated in the trade. In 1685, for instance, the gost I. Chirev, acting on behalf of the state treasury, exchanged government sables for more than 1,700 puds of saltpeter. In 1689 state-owned goods were brought from Tobolsk and exchanged for 3,000 rubles' worth of Chinese cloth. For a list of goods exchanged at the Yamysh market, see Vilkov, 108.

13. For Russians who traded directly between Yamysh and China, see Aleksandrov, "Iz istorii," p. 205.

14. In 1703, for instance, Central Asian merchants delivered only 90 rubles' worth of Chinese goods to Tobolsk, while Russians delivered 627 rubles' worth, although 19,043 rubles' worth of Chinese goods were available at the Yamysh market. Aleksandrov, "Iz istorii," pp. 114-115, and table 2, pp. 122-123.

15. Aleksandrov, "Iz istorii," p. 109. The statistics quoted by Vilkov are summarized in the following table:

Year	*Chinese goods (in rubles)*	*% of total value of imports*	*Jungarian, Bukharan, Kalmuk goods (in rubles)*	*% of total value of imports*
1668	358	79.8	90.8	20.2
1683	1913	51.8	1789	48.2
1686	1775	76.8	547	23.2
1703	628	94.1	39	5.9

16. Leather, not fur, was the most important Russian export to Lake Yamysh during 1640-1655 (30.7 percent of total value), followed by broadcloth (25.8 percent) and metal objects (18.4 percent). Furs came only in fourth place at 16.6 percent. Unfortunately there is no data about Russian exports for 1655-1675, but it is obvious from the data available for 1675-1691 that a definite shift in favor of leather took place. By the eighties leather made up 75.9 percent of the total export value. Fur also increased slightly to 19.3 percent. This pattern resembled that of exports through Astrakhan, which is not surprising since merchants at both places were purchasing for similar markets. Vilkov, 108-109, n. 27. For a report that goods remained unsold because the Jungar wars interfered with trade, see *DAI*, X, 369.

17. In 1703, although only 628 rubles' worth of Chinese goods were imported into Tobolsk itself, Russians, on the one hand, and Kalmuk and Bukharan merchants, on the other, exchanged a total of 58,000-62,000 rubles' worth of goods at Yamysh, including 20,000 rubles' worth of Chinese goods, or approximately one-third of the total. Vilkov, 109-110. This was a peculiarly good trading season, however, resembling a heavy downpour after a drought, and thereafter the supply of Chinese goods almost disappeared from the market.

18. Aleksandrov, "Iz istorii," pp. 206-207; Bakhrushin, "Torgi," p. 228; K.V. Bazilevich, *V Gostyakh v bogdykhana* (Leningrad, 1927), p. 10. Urging that Selenginsk be developed as a trading center, Milescu wrote: "The Chinese kingdom is not far . . . and the Mongols migrate everywhere and trade with the cossacks: they sell horses and camels and cattle and also all kinds of Chinese goods, and buy from them sables and numerous other Russian goods." Spafary, pp. 17-23. Whether his statement was made from personal observation or hearsay, Milescu was obviously well aware that central Siberia was trading with China along this route, using the Mongols as middlemen. At Eniseisk in 1675 Milescu encountered some Russian merchants recently returned from China, who told him that "their trade had been very unprofitable, owing to the fact that a war had begun between the Chinese [Manchu] and the Nikan [Han Chinese] kingdom." See M.P. Alekseev, *Sibir v isvestiakh inostrannykh puteshestvennikov i pisateley*, Vol. 1, Pt. 2 (Irkutsk, 1936), p. 73. These merchants probably arrived at Eniseisk through the Khalkha Steppe.

19. Aleksandrov, "Iz istorii," p. 207; *SFPS*, 37:9b-13. During the trading season 1687-1688, when Russians and Mongols were in conflict in Transbaikalia, customs tithes collected from Chinese goods at Selenginsk and Udinsk amounted to 1,361 rubles, indicating that at least ten times that amount in value was available on the local market. Chinese goods flowed into Eniseisk from Transbaikalia, Irkutsk, and Krasnoyarsk, and from Eniseisk they were transported into central Russia. The flow of these goods, especially cloth, increased to such an extent that prices on Chinese cloth at Eniseisk during 1649-1687 dropped 25-62 percent from the 1649 price. Aleksandrov, "Iz istorii," p. 207.

20. Aleksandrov, "Iz istorii, p. 208.

21. *PSZ,* IX, 643.

22. Cited in Florinsky, I, 392. The only exception was men under arms. For an interesting discussion of Peter's trade and financial policies, see E.V. Spiridonova, *Ekonomicheskaya politika i ekonomicheskie vzglyady Petra I* (Moscow, 1952), pp. 211-276.

23. *PSZ,* IV, 279.

24. *Pisma i bumagi imperatora Petra Velikago,* 11 vols. (St. Petersburg and Moscow, 1887-1910, 1964), I, 227-228; *PSZ,* III, 410; Spiridonova, p. 222.

25. P.J. Strahlenberg, *An Historico-Geographical Description of the North and Eastern Parts of Europe and Asia; But More Particularly, of Russia, Siberia, and Great Tartary* (London, 1738), pp. 428-429.

26. One observer claimed that at the beginning of the twentieth century Chinese goods on the Irbit market differed little from those available almost three centuries earlier. *The Russian Year-Book for 1912,* H. P. Kennard, ed. (New York, 1912), p. 404.

27. On postal services, see N.N. Ogloblin, *Obozrenie stolbtsov i knig Sibirskago prikaza, 1592-1768 g.g.,* 4 vols. (Moscow, 1895-1900), appendix CXCVI; V.K. Andrievich, *Istoriya Sibiri,* 5 vols. in 2 (St. Petersburg, 1887-1889), II, 244. On Siberian fairs, see M. Chulkov, *Istoricheskoye opisanie rossiyskoi komertsii pri vsekh portakh i granitsakh ot drevnikh vremen do nyne nastoyaschego,* 21 vols. (St. Petersburg and Moscow, 1781-1788), esp. vol. 6 (in Book IV), *passim.* On the Irbit market, see especially S. Udintsev, *Vtoraya irbitskaya sovetskaya yarmarka* (Ekaterinaburg, 1923), Pt. 2, *passim.* On passports, which cost one ruble, see *PSZ,* III, 278, 429; Ogloblin, II, 52. On passport checks and the confiscation of unlisted or prohibited goods, see, for example, *PSZ,* III, 216.

28. For text of regulations, see *PSZ,* III, 160-167. They were drawn up by Andrei Vinius, a Dutchman.

29. *PSZ,* III, 491-517.

30. *PSZ,* IV, 336.

31. *PSZ,* III, 164, 502, 509. Moscow did continue, however, to extend commercial privileges to the Bukharans, who acted as commercial agents for the Jungars.

32. *PSZ,* III, 189-190, 410-411. The decree explained the rationale for the new regulation. First, the customs heads were accepting poor goods in payment of duties. Second, the rise in the supply of Chinese goods on the Moscow market had led to a decline in prices, and the treasury could no longer keep goods received in payment of customs without danger of spoilage and loss. Precious stones were exempted from the new regulation because their prices could not be fairly determined in Nerchinsk. Consequently, the owner of precious stones was to present them to the Nerchinsk customs, which would inform the Siberian Department in Moscow of their nature. They were to be valued, and customs levied, only at the capital.

33. Cahen, *Histoire,* p. 62. According to G. Potanin, the Russians knew quite early that rhubarb grew near Lake Kokonor in the vicinity of Hsining city, "which, even up to the present time [1868] is known as the primary market of this item." Potanin, p. 53. Note that this journal is paginated erratically; the article appears in section V, entitled *Smes* (Miscellany). Evidently rhubarb was sold along caravan routes to the west and northwest and was thus available on the local market at Lake Yamysh. Potanin suggested that "probably in the seventeenth century, and earlier, it was only by this route that it arrived in Siberia." As early as 1653 a Bukharan merchant, Sharip Yariov, brought forty-one puds of rhubarb from Yamysh to Tomsk. Without citing source, Potanin states: "In 1657 an edict was issued, forbidding private persons to trade in this root under pain of death. From that time it became an article of exclusive state trade and is known in Russian acts as "the secret root Rhubarb." With the establishment of trade at Kyakhta and with the wars of the Chinese in Bukharia [i.e., Sinkiang], Kyakhta became the chief market through which Rhubarb went to Europe."

34. *Acty istoricheskie,* V, 444-445.

35. *PSZ,* III, 373. This edict demanded the death penalty for anyone trading illegally in rhubarb.

36. *PSZ,* IV, 245-246.

37. On Martyn Bogdanov's tobacco monopoly, see *PSZ,* III, 301-303, esp. 301, 329, 411-412. For details of the Anglo-Russian tobacco arrangement, see *PSZ,* III, 447-450, 457. Concerning the end of the English company's contract, see P. Milyukov, *Gosudarstvennoe khozyaystvo Rossii v pervoy chetverti XVIII stoletiya i reforma Petra Velikago* (St. Petersburg, 1905), pp. 163-164 and notes; *PSZ,* IV, 302-304.

38. *Pamyatniki sibirskoy istorii XVIII v.,* I, 88-89, 120-128. *Ibid.,* I, 303-306. The order extending the monopoly to Chinese tobacco was contained in a gramota dated Dec. 18, 1706. It is doubtful that the monopoly was fully effective, though Tulishen, the Manchu ambassador to the Torguts in 1712-1714 who on his way to the Volga paused in Kazan, wrote, "Those [Russians] who sell wine or tobacco without licenses are severely beaten, and then banished with their families." [Tulishen], *Narrative of the Chinese embassy to the Khan of the Tourgouth Tartars in the years 1712, 13, 14, & 15,* tr. George Thomas Staunton ([London], 1821; reprinted 1939), p. 127. For a biography of Tulishen, see Hummel, II, 784-787.

39. For documents on the development of the state fur monopoly in the China trade, see *PSZ,* III, 130-141, 164-165, 282-283, 284, 640.

40. For the text of the two edicts, see *PSZ,* III, 282, 402-403.

41. On the local Nerchinsk population, see V.A. Aleksandrov, "Russko-kitayskaya torgovlya i Nerchinsky torg v kontse XVII v., *K voprosu o pervonachalnom nakoplenii v Rossii (XVII-XVIII vv.): sbornik statey* (Moscow, 1958), pp. 422-464, esp. 425.

42. *Ibid.,* p. 426.

43. *Ibid.,* p. 430. The participants in the caravan of 1696 received their

documents at Moscow January-March 1695. By the time they had hired their workers, arrived at Nerchinsk, set out for Peking, and returned again to Nerchinsk, it was November 1697, and winter travel between Nerchinsk and Moscow across Siberia was not the easiest. Ides later indicated that under the best of circumstances the trip from the Amur to Peking and back took about eight months, not including unexpected delays or detentions. E. Isbrants Ides, *Three Years Travels from Moscow Overland to China: Thro' Great Ustiga, Siriania, Permia, Siberia, Daour, Great Tartary, &c. to Peking* (London, 1706), *passim.*

44. Aleksandrov, "Russko-kitayskaya torgovlya," p. 430.

45. F. Tumansky, *Sobranie raznykh zapisok i sochineny, sluzhaschickh k dostavleniyu polnago svedeniya o zhizni i deyaniyakh gosudariya imperatora Petra Velikago,* 10 vols., (St. Petersburg, 1787), I, 106-107.

46. For Ides' remarks on the Argun to Nun-chiang part of the route, see Ides, pp. 83-87.

47. The conditions of trade in Manchuria and Peking were known to the Russians as early as 1669. *The Register about the Chinese Land and Deep India,* compiled no later than that year, explained: "The Manchus do not collect duty from trading [and other] arriving people and give the trading and arriving people provisions; but more than two months they do not give them to reside [in Peking]." S. O. Dolgov, "Vedemost o kitayskoy zemle i glubokoy Indii," *Pamyatniki dreveney pismennosti i iskusstva,* 133:14-35 (St. Petersburg, 1899), esp. p. 19.

48. For data on the social composition of the caravans, see Aleksandrov, "Russko-kitayskaya torgovlya," p. 427. On local workers and their wages, see Aleksandrov, p. 461-462.

49. Bazilevich's statement concerning Russian-Siberian trade in the first half of the seventeenth century could be validly applied to the China trade at the end of the same century: "only great merchant capital was able to utilize to the full extent the advantages which were to be gained in Siberian operations, which called forth considerable expenditures of capital and demanded great periods of time." K.V. Bazilevich, *Krupnoye torgovoye predpriyatie v Moskovskom gosudarstve v pervoy polovine XVII v.* (Leningrad, 1933), p. 25.

50. Aside from the four families mentioned, the names of other gosts do not appear in the records, and members of the *gostinaya sotnya* participated only episodically and usually on a small investment level.

51. The Filatev family had a long and sustained interest in the fur trade. As early as 1635 they appeared on the fur market at Solvychegodsk. In the second half of the seventeenth century their participation in that local market did not as a rule fall below 25 percent of the total market; normally it fluctuated between 42 and 100 percent. I.S. Makarov, "Pushnoy rynok Soli-Vychegodskoy v XVII v.," *Istoricheskie zapiski,* 14:156-168 (1945). Furthermore, they controlled a commercial network that included most of the major Siberian cities. Filatev agents in the two-year period 1687-1689 traded

in Tobolsk, Yakutsk, Eniseisk, Tomsk, Ilimsk, Surgut, and other Siberian settlements. Their activities had a strong family continuity. Bogdan Filatev, who founded the trading house, passed the business on to his son, Ostafy. The names of Ostafy and his sons, Vasily and Aleksey, appear constantly in the Nerchinsk customs books during the last decade of the seventeenth century. Aleksandrov, "Russko-kitayskaya torgovlya," p. 433. The capital that the Filatevs invested in the China trade came not only from furs. In 1672, for instance, Ostafy Filatev began to buy land in Vymsk for the production of salt. His agents participated in the sable trade in Siberia; they bought or hunted sable in Pribaikalaya, and in 1693 alone eleven of his men delivered ten forties of sables to Nerchinsk. *Ocherki po istorii Komi ASSR,* (Syktvykar, 1955), I, 123-124; N.K. Auerbakh, "Zimove v bukhte Promyslovoi Eniseiskogo zaliva," *Severnaya Aziya,* Nos. 5-6:138 (1928).

52. On Nikitin's career, see Bakhrushin, "Torgi," *passim.* Bakhrushin claimed: "After the audience, they were permitted to trade freely in the course of seven weeks, but the market was bad in view of the war with the Nikan Kingdom [i.e., southern China, the Rebellion of the Three Feudatories]." Bakhrushin, "Torgi," p. 228.

53. On the Ushakovs, see Aleksandrov, "Russko-kitayskaya torgovlya," pp. 434-435. The Filatev and Ushakov brothers, the Luzins, and Nikitin were the only great wholesalers on the eastern Siberian market. Although no data exist to show the size of their interests and holdings, in 1690 the Great Treasury listed their holdings and trade interests as follows: the Filatevs—16,000 rubles; the Luzins—8,400 rubles; Nikitin and the Ushakov brothers—1,000 rubles each. Since these figures represented declared value on the basis of which the tithe tax was collected, it must be assumed, particularly in the case of the Ushakov brothers, that they are gross underestimations for the sake of avoiding taxation. *Ibid.,* p. 436.

54. On petty merchant participation in Nerchinsk's China trade, see S.V. Bakhrushin, *Nauchnye trudy* (Moscow, 1954), II, 126-127; *Ocherki po istorii Komi ASSR,* I, 113-115; Aleksandrov, "Russko-kitayskaya torgovlya," pp. 436-438.

55. For some reason the Luzins and the Ushakovs did not participate in the caravan of 1697. Petty merchant capital made up 51.5 percent of the 1696 caravan. For details on petty merchant participation in this caravan, see Aleksandrov, "Russko-kitayskaya torgovlya," pp. 438-441, especially tables 1 and 2 on pp. 438 and 439, and p. 455. For a study of the problem of credit, see S. Ya. Borovoy, "Voprosy kreditovaniya torgovli i promyshlennosti v ekonomicheskoy politike Rossii XVIII, v., *Istoricheskie zapiski,* 33:92-122 (1950), pp. 96 ff.

56. Between June 1691 and June 1692, 7,452 rubles' worth of fur arrived in Nerchinsk in thirty-seven deliveries. Fifteen deliveries came through Yakutsk (valued at 3,455 rubles), and nine from Irkutsk (2,551 rubles). By the end of the 1693 trading season the annual import of fur into Nerchinsk had jumped to 18,882 rubles. The furs were brought to Nerchinsk

along the trade routes by the network of agents for the commercial houses. Aleksandrov, p. 441. On the export of pelts to China through Nerchinsk, see Aleksandrov, "Russko-kitaiskaya torgovlya," p. 442, table 3. See also *PSZ,* III, 491-517; Makarov, "Pushnoy rynok," p. 162; I.S. Makarov, "Volostnye torzhki v Sol-Vychegodskom uyezde v pervoy polovine XVIII v.," *Istoricheskie zapiski,* 1:193-219 (1937), pp. 210, 212. Furs were rather consistently attracted more to Nerchinsk and the China trade than to Moscow or Arkhangelsk for export to western Europe. For a comparison of Nerchinsk and Arkhangelsk exports of fur, see Aleksandrov, "Russko-kitayskaya torgovlya," pp. 444-445, table 4. Those furs that commanded a particularly high demand on the China market began to disappear from Moscow altogether. For a list of such furs, see p. 446. As early as 1670 Kilburger noted that the best Siberian ermine pelts were in such demand among merchants for export to the rest of Asia that they had disappeared from Moscow, and the better quality squirrel skins from Siberia also grew rarer on the Moscow market. B.G. Kurts, *Sochinenie Kilburgera o russkoy torgovle v tsarstvovanie Alekseya Mikhaylovicha* (Kiev, 1915), pp. 96-97.

57. On the pattern of local sales, see Aleksandrov, "Russko-kitayskaya torgovlya," p. 446. One hundred manufactured items were listed in the Nerchinsk customs books by 1696. For a partial list, see p. 447. The purchasing power of the local population was limited, however, and as Bakhrushin pointed out, "This was a peddlers' system, but on a large scale." Bakhrushin, "Torgi," p. 245. For a complete list of articles imported into Siberia from European Russia, see pp. 243-245. Ides observed that there was a slight demand for pocket or small table clocks. For a typical list of such items given as gifts in Peking, see Adam Brand, *A Journal of the Embassy from Their Majesties John and Peter Alexievitz, Emperors of Muscovy &c. Over Land into China through Ustiugha, Siberia, Dauri, and the Great Tartary to Peking, the Capital City of the Chinese Empire. By Everard Isbrand, their ambassador in the years 1963, 1694, and 1695* (London, 1698), p. 83. The growth of Nerchinsk as part of the larger Siberian trade network and as a significant local market, in addition to being a transit point for the China trade, depended in large part on this trade in goods other than fur. Whereas in the fur trade the only function of Nerchinsk was as an export point, the flow of manufactures into Nerchinsk made it perhaps *the* economic center of eastern Siberia. Hops and cattle were imported for distribution to the ostrogs and other settlements in the region. The import of cattle brought Nerchinsk into close relation with the region around Lake Baikal, and the importation of fish tied Nerchinsk into eastern Siberia's lake and river systems. The cattle were used for transportation in the caravan trade as well as for food. See Aleksandrov, "Russko-kitayskaya torgovlya," pp. 447-449.

58. The wide variety of items imported into Nerchinsk from China can be seen in Aleksandrov, "Russko-kitayskaya torgovlya," pp. 450-451, table 5. On regulations concerning imported items, see *PSZ,* III, 410-411;

Bakhrushin, "Torgi," p. 242; Aleksandrov, "Russko-kitayskaya torgovlya," pp. 454-456. For a thorough discussion of Russian weights and measures in the China trade, see Gaston Cahen, *Le livre de comptes de la caravane russe a Pekin en 1727-1728* (Paris, 1911), pp. 111-123. In Russia, damasks were distinguished according to their cost in China, such as *semilanny* (seven liangs) or *piatilanny* (five liangs). These two types differed in both width and quality and were of the most varied colors. Not unnaturally, the value of Chinese damasks on the Russian market at seven rubles in 1692 fell to two rubles in 1697, and middle width damask fell from six rubles in 1690 to three rubles in 1697. Consequently, the names of the different types of damasks had little relation to their cost in Russia. See Aleksandrov, "Russko-kitayskaya torgovlya," p. 452. Silk cloth was measured in units called *postav,* while some specific items, such as velvet, were measured in *portischa.* A postav consisted of two portischa and equaled approximately 16-18 *arshins.* An arshin equaled 28 inches. For disagreements on the exact measurements involved, see *ibid.,* p. 453; N. Kostomarov, p. 289; A.I. Nikitsky, 160; Trusevich, p. 169. Cotton cloth—the nankeens of the Canton trade—was imported in a wide variety of colors and qualities, but all were measured in "ends," which equaled 8.3 arshins or 6.46 yards. One type of nankeen (*kitayka* in Russian), called *tyumovaya kitayka* or bailed nankeen, was measured in larger units called *tyum* or *tyun,* which consisted of ten ends (one bail). The nankeens commanding the greatest demand on the Russian market were called *kitayki tyumovyei odnoportschnye,* or bailed nankeens approximately eight or nine yards in length. Nankeens were transported in *shih* or widths of ten *tyums* each. In addition to cloth, cloth products were imported. Window and bed curtains of various materials and colors, with or without embroidery, belts and girdles of silk, sash girdles of silk and cotton, were all imported into Nerchinsk from China.

59. Aleksandrov, "Russko-kitayskaya torgovlya," pp. 453-454; Bakhrushin, "Torgi," p. 242. A pud of tea or saffron cost about twenty rubles at Nerchinsk. Bakhrushin, "Torgi," 454. Kilburger claimed that tea was already widely distributed in Moscow, where he had bought it at thirty kopeks a *funt* (equal to a pound). Kurts, *Sochinenie Kilburgera,* p. 113. The validity of this statement is highly doubtful, as tea did not overtake cloth in importance among imports from China until the end of the eighteenth century, by which time it had become especially popular in Siberia and in Moscow court circles. Cloth, not tea, was the chief object of Russian commerce between 1689 and 1727.

60. Aleksandrov, "Russko-kitayskaya torgovlya," p. 451; Pokrovsky, p. 67; *Akty istoricheskie,* V, 519-520; *DAI,* X, 293. The differential fluctuated but was always significant. Thus, in 1706 sable was two to three times as valuable in Peking as in Siberia; squirrel, five to seven and a half times; red fox, three and a half to six times. Trusevich, pp. 199, 290-291.

61. Aleksandrov, "Russko-kitayskaya torgovlya," p. 463. The actual difference between the Nerchinsk and Moscow prices was probably greater than

these figures indicate because Moscow prices were set by the Siberian Department, which purchased goods for the state at prices usually lower than the going market rate.

62. For a discussion of profits, see Aleksandrov, "Russko-kitayskaya torgovlya," pp. 459-460. According to his calculations, Izbrant's embassy made 48.1 percent profit on initial total investments, Nikitin 48.6 percent, and Lyangusov only 15.7 percent.

63. Ides, pp. 1-2.

64. Cahen, *Histoire,* pp. 81-82, n. 4. Ides is a German name, although Adam Brand, who was a member of Ides' suite and himself left a detailed description of the embassy, claimed that Ides was "German, but born at Glückstadt in the duchy of Holstein." Cahen, *Histoire,* p. 81, n. 3. The 1699 French edition of Brand's work, published at Amsterdam, read," *Evert Isbrand,* Alleman, & natif de *Gluckstadt.*" (Italics in original.) Adam Brand, *Relation du voyage de Mr. Evert Isbrand envoye de sa Majeste Czarienne a l'empereur de la Chine en 1692, 93 & 94* (Amsterdam, 1699), p. 1. Note incorrect title referring to a tsarina in Russia. According to one source, Ides' parents were Dutch, and he himself had relations with the burgomaster of Amsterdam, the great geographer N. Witsen. Cahen, *Histoire,* p. 81. Ides' memoirs also appeared first in Dutch. However, he himself stated in official Russian documents that he was born in Denmark. Cahen, *Histoire,* p. 82, esp. nn. 1-5. For the text of Ides' petition, see *ibid.,* XXVI-XXVIII.

65. The *nakaz* (instruction) was issued to Ides sometime between January 29, 1692, when his petition was turned into a state appointment, and March 14, 1692, when he left Moscow. For the contents and texts of Ides' instructions, see Cahen, *Histoire,* XVII-XXXI; Bantysh-Kamensky, pp. 67-68.

66. Brand remarked, for instance, "It ought to be remembered here, to the great honour of the Chineses, that they treat Strangers with a great deal of civility." For a description of the journey, see Brand, *A Journal,* pp. 3-83.

67. Cahen, *Histoire,* p. 84. Ides gave the date as November 13. See his description of the event, which evidently did not impress him, in Ides, 68-69. Brand supported the November 14 date and gave a longer description of the ceremony. See Brand, *A Journal,* pp. 83-84.

68. The letters were returned the very next day. Cahen, *Histoire,* p. 84. Neither Ides nor Brand mentions the return of the documents.

69. The dates of the receptions were November 14, 15, 17, December 12, 1693, and February 16, 1694. Descriptions may be found in Ides and Brand. As with all Russian envoys before him, Ides also had dealings with the Jesuits. See, for instance, Ides, pp. 79-81.

70. The *K'ang-hsi shih-lu* for November 24, 1693 (K'ang-hsi 32:X:27), stated the problem in a combination of court vocabulary and political realism upon the occasion of Ides' arrival in Peking and his first audience with the emperor: "The Ch'a-han han of Russia has sent an ambassador to present tribute. The Grand Secretaries had the Russian memorial of tribute-presentation translated and handed it in. The emperor said, 'The nation of

Russia has many able men, but their character is narrow and obstinate, and their argument is persistent and slow. From ancient times she has not communicated with China. The country is very far from our capital, but we can reach their territory directly by the land route . . . Beyond T'u-lu-fan [Turfan] is Russia. We hear that the extent of the country is more than 20,000 li . . . although to have a vassal state come to do homage and present tribute is a glorious thing, we fear, however, that after we have passed through several generations, probably she might cause some troubles in the future. In short, as long as China is at peace [and strong], foreign disturbances will not arise. Therefore, we shall build our own strength. This is a matter of fundamental importance.' " *SL-KH,* 160:26b-27.

71. *SL-KH,* 161:7, 162:1b. See also Cahen, *Histoire,* pp. 83-87.

72. Brand, *A Journal,* pp. 91-92; Ides, p. 69; *SL-KH,* 162:11. For details of the Manchu response, contained in a letter handed Ides at his leave-taking audience, see Cahen, *Histoire,* p. 86, n. 1. For the text of the Russian paraphrase, see Cahen, *Histoire,* p. XXXI-XXXIII; for a French translation of the Russian paraphrase, see Cahen, *Histoire,* p. XXXIII-XXXVI. Concerning the address of the letter, see first line of the paraphrase, *ibid.,* p. XXXI.

73. For the regulations, see *Chia-ch'ing hui-tien shih-li* (comp. 1818), 746:3b-4b.

74. On the Manchu embassies to Russia, see Mark Mancall, "China's First Missions to Russia, 1729-1731," *Papers on China,* 9:75-110 (August 1955).

75. *Chia-ch'ing hui-tien shih-li,* 746:4a-b. Adam Brand admitted in his journal that even while the embassy was at Peking, some 350 Cossacks of "Nertsinskoy" had attacked Ch'ing subjects. Brand, *A Journal,* pp. 111-112.

76. Cahen, *Histoire,* p. 87, n. 1, and p. XXXIV. It is evident that Verbiest's promise to Milescu to serve Moscow's interests in Peking was operative at least as late as Ides' mission.

77. Ides' information mostly concerned the Peking market, and his recommendations reflected the existing trade. Ides, pp. 75-76. He recommended the following items as most suitable for export to China: sables of various qualities in undressed condition, underskins of sables of medium and superior quality, ermines, squirrels, lynx, polar fox paws, and hares. He recommended that Moscow import precious stones, damask, and nankeens. Cahen, *Histoire,* p. XXXVI, and pp. 87-88. On Peking's refusal to permit Chinese to go to Moscow, see Cahen, *Histoire,* p. XXXV.

78. Ides supported his argument in favor of state participation in the trade by referring to the large profits made by indigenes in the border trade alone. Ides, p. 103.

79. The nine state caravans between 1696 and 1719 were as follows, with the first and last dates of the caravan's activities in parentheses: Lyangusov (1695-1701), Bokov (1698-1703), Savateev (1702-1795). Oskolkov (1703-1707), Khudyakov (1705-1709), Savateev (1707-1712), Khudyakov (1709-1713), Oskolkov (1711-1716), and Gusyatnikov (1714-1719).

80. Cahen, *Histoire,* p. 96. Kurts suggested that the state only recom-

mended the creation of an official caravan in 1696, and that Liangusov was appointed in 1697 on the strength of the general decision of the year before. B.G. Kurts, "Yak povstala derzhavna karavanna (valkova) torgovlya Rosii s Kitayem u XVII vitsi," *Zapiski istorichno-filologichnogo viddilu, Vseukrainskoi Akademii Nauk,* 21-22: 249-296 (1928), 270-201 (sic).

81. The letter permitting Lyangusov and his tselovalniks to pass through Siberia was ordered January 13, 1697, and the letter itself was dated January 25. Other pertinent diplomatic documents, such as passports and letters of recommendation, were dated in the early days of February 1697. Cahen, *Histoire,* p. 97.

82. For the texts of these two aides-memoire, see *DAI,* X, 285-286; *Akty istoricheskie,* V, 470, 491.

83. For documents pertaining to the Lyangusov caravan, see *DAI,* X, 293-294, 297-298; *Akty istoricheskie,* V, 537-538.

84. *PSZ,* III, 596-597; IV, 95-129, especially paragraphs 7 (pp. 98-101) and 35-37 (pp. 115-116); *Akty istoricheskie,* V, 519-520.

85. B.G. Kurts, "Gosudarstvennaya monopoliya v torgovle Rossii s Kitayem v pervoy pol. XVIII st.," *Naukovi zapiski kiivskogo institutu narodnogo gospodarstva,* 9:59-134 (1928), pp. 60, 62, 65, 70-71, 74-75; Kurts, "Yak povstala," p. 286. Personnel were subject to sudden change due to death, replacement, etc. See, for instance, Kurts, "Gosudarstvennaya monopoliya," pp. 60, 65, 67-68; see also Bantysh-Kamensky, p. 75. Lyangusov had been a leading merchant at Astrakhan, and his tselovalniks, Glukhikh and Nechayevsky, were from Vyatka and Vazhenin, respectively. Savateev included staff members from Ustyug and Vyatka. On the geographic origins of these and other participants in the trade, see Kurts, "Yak Povstala," pp. 271, 286.

86. Cahen, *Histoire,* p. 100, n. 6. For extracts from the Latin texts (the complete letters have never been published), see Cahen, *Histoire,* pp. XXXIX-XL.

87. Kurts, "Gosudarstvennaya monopoliya," p. 60. The difference between the size of the caravan when it left Nerchinsk and size permitted by Manchu regulation to go to Peking may be explained by the fact that all personnel in excess of the two hundred men allowed were left on the Nunchiang. Kurts, "Yak povstala," p. 295.

88. Cahen, *Histoire,* p. 101, n. 2. A letter dated June 13, 1704 (K'ang-hsi 43:V:12), confirmed the decision to authorize the new route, justifying it on the ground that there had been numerous disorders in Peking during Savateev's last caravan, which had been over-large owing to the need for extra porters on the inconvenient Manchurian route. Cahen, *Histoire,* pp. 101, and 101, n. 3. See also Kurts, "Gosudarstvennaya monopoliya," pp. 61, and 61, n. 2.

89. Cahen, *Histoire,* p. 102, esp. n. 3, and 103. The opening of the new Mongolian route marked the beginning of the end of Nerchinsk's importance as an entrepôt in the Sino-Russian trade system. The Nerchinsk voevoda

tried to persuade the Li-fan yuan to withdraw its approval of the new route, but to no avail. The Li-fan yuan itself informed Moscow that Nerchinsk had lodged a formal complaint, whereupon the Nerchinsk voevoda was severely reprimanded for representing his own personal interests at Peking. See *ibid.*, pp. 103, 104, n. 4; Kurts, "Gosudarstvennaya monopoliya," p. 64.

90. Kurts, "Gosudarstvennaya monopoliya," p. 60; *Pamyatniki sibirskoy istorii XVIII v.*, I, 278-279. See also Trusevich, p. 151; Kurts, "Gosudarstvennaya monopoliya," p. 70.

91. Kurts, "Gosudarstvennaya monopoliya," p. 74.

92. *Pamyatniki sibirskoy istorii XVIII* v., II, 34-35.

93. Kurts, "Gosudarstvennaya monopoliya," pp. 78-79, esp. table and n. 1 on pp. 79, 81-82.

94. Cahen, *Histoire,* pp. 107-109. See also Lange's remarks in Friedrich Christian Weber, *The Present State of Russia,* 2 vols. (London, 1722), II, 34. On the Bukharans, see *Pamyatniki siberskoy istorii XVIII* v., I, 288. A Sino-Russian market had developed at Urga, where prices were lower than in Peking owing to lower transportation costs. On this market, see *Ibid.*, II, 367-368.

95. For texts, see Cahen, *Histoire,* pp. XXXVI-XXXIX, XLI-XLII. See also Bantysh-Kamensky, p. 512.

96. The Li-fan yuan itself was aware that most of the caravans coming from Siberia had not been official and had contributed to the glut on the market. See Kurts, "Gosudarstvennaya monopoliya," pp. 76-77.

97. On the contents of the letter, see Kurts, "Gosudarstvennaya monopoliya," pp. 76-77, 83-84; see also Cahen, *Histoire,* p. 111.

98. For comparisons of profits and other factors in the various caravans, see Kurts, "Gosudarstvennaya monopoliya," pp. 72, 133.

99. In 1727 another institution, the O-lo-ssu hsüeh or Chinese-Manchu school of Russian students in Peking, was founded on the grounds of the O-lo-ssu nan kuan. For an excellent study of these institutions, to which I am indebted for much of the material presented here, see Meng Ssu-ming, "The E-lo-ssu-kuan (Russian Hostel) in Peking," *Harvard Journal of Asiatic Studies* (1961).

100. Cahen, discussing Lange's early life, remarked, "One would like to know the life of this personage whom Russia continually used in her relations with China beginning in 1715; unfortunately, Russian archives and works are some of the poorest in biographical information on this subject, and one is forced to await studies based on perhaps more explicit Swedish documents." Such documents, however, do not appear to exist. Aside from the fact that Lange took part in the wars of Charles XII with Peter the Great, which supports the theory that he was a prisoner of war, nothing is known of his life in Sweden. Sven Åstrand of the Swedish State Archives stated in a letter to me dated June 14, 1962, "Any document about Lange's activities in Sweden have not been found in the National Archives." A similar reply was received in response to inquiries at the Swedish Military

Archives in Stockholm. Three works from Lange's own pen have been published. The first, referred to in note 94 above, is the diary of his journey to Peking in Gusyatnikov's caravan in the company of the English physician Thomas Carwin. The second is the diary of his sojourn in Peking as Russian consul in 1721-1722. See Lorents Lange, *Journal of the Residence of Mr. De Lange, Agent of His Imperial Majesty of All the Russias, Peter the First, at the Court of Pekin, during the Years 1721 and 1722*. This work has been published in English in John Bell of Antermony, *Travels from St. Petersburg in Russia, to Various Parts of Asia,* 2 vols. (Edinburgh, 1788), vol. 2, pp. 221-423. The third work is the diary of Lange's sojourn in Peking, 1727-1728, where he had led the first Russian caravan after the negotiation of the Treaty of Kyakhta in 1727. See John Dudgeon, *Historical Sketch of the ecclesiastical, political, and commercial relations of Russia with China* (Peking, 1872; reprinted in an Anastatic Edition, 1940), pp. 3-18 of the appendix, which Dudgeon, p. 3, claims is a translation of the Russian. The diary was not known to Cahen, nor has it been published in any other language, including Russian, as far as I can determine. It can only be assumed that Dudgeon had access to a Russian manuscript which may have been in the Russian Ecclesiastical Mission in Peking. A fourth work bearing Lange' signature, though not necessarily written by him, is the account book of the Russian caravan of 1727-1728. See Cahen, *Le livre de comptes.*

101. For a discussion of Carwin's name, which Cahen suggested might be Harwing, see Cahen, *Histoire,* pp. 107-108, n. 3.

102. Weber, II, 3, 25, 28. For a description of the journey and crossing the frontier, see *ibid.,* II, 4-20, 22. For the full text of Lange's description of K'ang-hsi, see *ibid.*, II, 33-34.

103. George Timkowski, *Travels of the Russian Mission through Mongolia to China and residence in Peking in the years 1820-1821,* 2 vols. (London, 1827), vol. I, p. 318. It was located just west of the Yü-he Bridge. See Yü Cheng-hsieh, *Kuei-ssu lei-kao* (Shanghai, 1957), 336. *Hsiang* means "street, alley."

104. *K'ang-hsi hui-tien* (1690), 73:15. *Ch'ien-lung hui-tien* (1763), 56: 8b; *Ch'ien-lung hui-tien tse-li* (1763), 95:1b. *Jih-hsia chiu-wen k'ao* (1781), 63:15a-b.

105. *Yung-cheng hui-tien* (1733), 105:16.

106. Bell, I, 429, II, 291-292; *Ch'ien-lung hui-tien tse-li,* 95:1-2.

107. *Jih-hsia chou-wen k'ao,* 63:15b.

108. John Bell of Antemony, *Travels from St. Petersburg in Russia to Various Parts of Asia.* (Edinburgh, 1788), I, 439-440.

109. Dudgeon, Appendix 5.

110. *SL-KH,* 240:19b; *Ch'ien-lung hui-tien tse-li,* 142:40b. Bell, I, 439, II, 274, 332, 342; Timkowski, II, 46; Dudgeon, p. 20, note; *Hsien-feng ch'ao ch'ou-pan i-wu shih-mo* (Peking, 1930), 15:12b-13; *Ch'ing-ch'ao wen-hsien t'ung k'ao* (Shanghai, 1936), p. 7485; *SFPS,* 9:9-21; *Chia-ch'ing hui-tien* (1818), 69:15b-16.

111. Bell, II, 23-24. On the organization of the Albanzinians in Peking, see Yü Cheng-hsieh, *Kuei-ssu lei-kao,* pp. 332-333; *Ch'ien-lung hui-tien tse-li,* 171:8a-b, 9b-10. *Chia-ch'ing hui-tien shih-li,* 837:8a-b. See also Pavlovsky, pp. 145-164; I.I. Serebrennikov, *Albazintsy* (Peking, 1922).

112. Bell, II, 25; C. de Sabir, *Le fleuver Amour* (Paris, 1861), p. 20; Dudgeon, pp. 40, 42; Cahen, *Histoire,* pp. 247-248; J.N. L'Isle and A.G. Pingre, *Description de la Ville de Peking* (Paris, 1765), p. 24; Tulishen, *Narrative of the Chinese Embassy to the Khan of the Tourgouth Tartars in the Years 1712, 13, 14, & 15,* tr. George Thomas Staunton (London, 1821; reprinted 1939), p. 87.

113. It has been commonly but mistakenly asserted that the school was established in 1757 (Ch'ien-lung 22). See, for instance, *Calendar of the Tungwen College* (Peking, 1879), pp. 29, 58. W.A.P. Martin, at one time head of the Tungwen College faculty, wrote, "It [the College] had a record as an existing institution dating back to the middle of the eighteenth century, having been created to meet the exigencies of intercourse with Russia in the reign of Kienlung." W.A.P. Martin, *A Cycle of Cathay,* 2nd ed. (New York, 1897), p. 295. This view was also supported by Biggerstaff's study of the Tunkwen College. Knight Biggerstaff, "The T'ung Wen Kuan," *The Chinese Social and Political Science Review,* 18.3 (October, 1934), p. 309 and n.6. He relied for his information on the *Ch'ou-pan i-wu shih-mo* but was unable to confirm this date in the *Tung-hua lu,* the *Ch'ing-shih kao,* or the *Ta-ch'ing hui-tien.* Although it is quite true that a set of rules governing the school was promulgated in the twenty-second year of Ch'ien-lung's reign, there is no evidence to support the contention that the school was only founded in that year. *T'ung-chih ch'ao ch'ou-pan i-wu shih-mo* (Peking, 1930), 8.33b. Furthermore, the memorial proposing the rules for the school, which were then adopted, stated definitely that the school had been established during the K'ang-hsi reign. *SL-CL,* 539:23-a-b; *SL-KH,* 160:26; Timkowski, I, 369.

114. *Jih-hsi chiu-wen k'ao,* 62:20a. As late as 1871, Dudgeon reported that the school's building was still recognizable and that a tablet over the outside door of the building could still be read: Nei-ko O-lo-ssu wen-kuan, or the Russian Language School of the Grand Secretariat. Dudgeon, p. 26. See also *SL-CL,* 539:23a-b; *Chia-ch'ing hui-tien shih-li,* 12:21-22a, 829: 16b-17a; *T'ung chih i-wu shih-mo,* 8: 32b-35; Timkowski, I, 369.

115. *SL-CL,* 539:23; *Chia-ch'ing hui-tien shih-li,* 12:22b. Dudgeon suggested that each banner probably supplied three candidates to make up the total. Dudgeon, 26. However, the full contingent was not always available. In 1820, according to Timkowski, there were only twenty students in the school. Timkowski, I, 369. When in 1862 the school was incorporated into the newly established T'ung-wen kuan, the number of students had dropped to sixteen. *T'ung-chih i-wu shih-mo,* 8:35.

116: *Hsien-feng i-wu shih-mo,* 8:33; *T'ung-chih i-wu shih-mo,* 8:34b; Timkowski, I, 369; *SL-CL,* 539:23. According to the regulations promulgated in 1757, students who received a first on the general examinations were to be appointed to the eighth official rank and given the title of *chu-shih* or second-class secretary of a board. They took up their appointments as their turns came up or vacancies appeared. *SL-CL,* 539:23a-b.

117. Yü cheng-hsieh, *Kuei-ssu ts'un-k'ao* (1848), 6:13a-b. See also Dudgeon, p. 26; *T'ung-chih i-wu shih-mo,* 8:34b-35. The success or failure of the school's program of instruction cannot be determined for its early years, but by the beginning of the nineteenth century it was a total failure. See, for instance, Timkowski, I, 368-370.

Chapter VII—Trade and Diplomacy

1. On Galdan, see Hummel, I, 265-268.
2. On Tsewang Araptan, see Hummel, II, 757-759.
3. On Galdan Tseren see Hummel, II, 759. On Furdan, see Hummel, I, 264-265.
4. Instructions to the chiefs of customs on August 30, 1963, forbade the export of firearms to the Jungars but at the same time provided that Bukharan and Russian merchants should be treated equally, without any discrimination against the Bukharans. Articles of instructions to the Nerchinsk voevodas on February 18, 1696, dictated that Jungar envoys be received hospitably, though they were not to be entertained so long as to become a burden on the treasury. On September 1, 1697, the new voevodas of Tobolsk were given precise instructions to govern their relations with Bukharans and Jungars: they were to be neither molested nor baptized against their will, and private merchants were not to sell them as slaves—a privilege reserved to the state. *PSZ,* III, 164-165, 249-251, 351-352.
5. For instance, the tax imposed on Bukharan residents in the regulations of March 22, 1698, was the same as that imposed on the Russians. *PSZ,* III, 446-447.
6. *PSZ,* III, 508-510. On January 16, 1699, these instructions were confirmed in correspondence with the voevoda of Tiumen, who was requested to show the utmost goodwill toward the Jungars. *PSZ,* III, 541.
7. *Akty istoricheskie,* V, 520-532.
8. Cahen, *Histoire,* p. 142. The agent was in the employ of Matvey Poppa, who formerly held the rhubarb monopoly. See also Cheredov's *stateyny spisok* in *Pamyatniki sibirskoy istorii XVIII v.,* I, 515-527.
9. G. Müller, *Eröffnung eines Vorschlages zu Verbesserung der Russischen Histoire durch den Druck einer Stückweise herauszugebenden Sammlung von allerley zu den Umständen und Begenbenheiten dieses Reichs gehörigen Nachrichten,* 10 vols. (St. Petersburg, 1732-1764; vol. 10, Dorpat, 1816), esp. IV, 183-274. Müller's account is complete, based on his study of the Tobolsk archives and eye-witness reports gathered by him in 1734

See also *Pamyatniki sibirskoy istorii XVIII v.*, II, 35, 37, 138-144. "Erket" may have been Darya; "Selim" and "Daba" are probably Sining and Ta-pa in Kansu Province. Gagarin wrote the tsar that according to his information one could reach "Erket" in a few weeks along the Irtysh River, and that such a move should be supported by the construction of fortified places. Gagarin wrote the kontaisha on February 17, 1715, rebutting the Jungar claims brought back by Cheredov and contesting Jungar rights on the upper Enisei, Ob, and Lena, all of which he claimed were entirely within Russian territory. In reciprocity for favors shown Bukharan merchants in Siberia, he claimed full commercial liberty for Russians in Jungaria. In a second letter he informed the kontaisha of Bukholtz's expedition and attempted to reassure him as to its aims, promising the Jungar aid and assistance if he would refrain from interfering with Russian forces. This letter was carried to the kontaisha in February 1716 by the Tara centurian B.B. Cherendov and the Tobolsk boyar T. I. Etiger. Peter's personal interest in the affair is indicated by the fact that on August 7, 1716, he addressed an order to Bukhholtz from his ship, the *Ingermoland,* which was then in Copenhagen, telling the lieutenant colonel that Gagarin had been instructed concerning the augmentation of Bukhholtz's forces. On December 18, 1716, Peter addressed a letter from Amsterdam to the kontaisha himself. *Pamyatniki sibirskoy istorii XVIII v.*, II, 66-68, 85-87, 126; Cahen, *Histoire*, p. 144.

10. *Pamyatniki sibirskoy istorii XVIII v.*, II, 151-152; Cahen, *Histoire,* p. 144, n. 4.

11. Cahen, *Histoire,* p. 145-146; *Pamyatniki sibirskoy istorii XVIII v.,* II, 138-149. Bukhholtz's own deposition was given in St. Petersburg on January 22, 1719. For a letter written to Bukhholtz by Cheren Donduk, one of Tsewang Araptan's generals, threatening attack, see *ibid.,* II, 150-151. Gagarin himself attempted to repair the disaster by sending a messenger to Tsewang Araptan with the tsar's gramota of December 18, 1716, but the Jungar imprisoned the messenger until February 28, 1718, and wrote Gagarin threatening letters. See *ibid.,* II, 171-174.

12. *PSZ,* V, 616-617, 622-623.

13. Cahen, *Histoire,* p. 147. For materials concerning Likharev's activities, see *Pamyatniki sibirskoy istorii XVIII v.,* II, 182-209.

14. Cahen, pp. 148-149. For a thorough study of Unkovsky's embassy, see N.I. Veselovsky, "Posolstvo k zyungarskomu khun-taichzhi Tsevan Rabtanu kapitana ot artillerii Ivana Unkovskago i putevoy zhurnal ego za 1722-1724 godu: dokumenty, izdannye s predisloviem i primechanyami," *Zapiski imperatorskago russkago geograficheskago obschestva,* Vol. 10, pt. 2 (1887).

15. Veselovsky, pp. VIII-XIX, XXII-XXVI, 1, 3, 10, 13-18, 21, 31, 34, 145-152, 156-162, 215. For a summary of Unkovsky's route, see Cahen, *Histoire,* p. 150, n. 2. In order to prepare the ground for the mission, the new governor general of Siberia, Prince M. Cherkasky, wrote Tsewang Araptan on June 26, 1722, that Jungar and Bukharan prisoners were to be

returned, that his envoy had been well received, and that he looked forward to a situation of reciprocity and the amicable settlement of all outstanding differences. Veselovsky, pp. 216-217.

16. Veselovsky, pp. 105, 107-109, 119. Note that *ibid.*, pp. 34-145 is the text of Unkovsky's journal.

17. On the Istopnikov caravan, see Kurts, "Gosudarstvennaya monopoliya," pp. 83-90.

18. For the text of this letter, see Bantysh-Kamensky, pp. 83-84. The Ch'ing agreed to permit border tribes to trade at Selenginsk if they wished.

19. Cahen, *Histoire,* pp. 154-155. Izmailov himself in his official report dated his Commission from June 4, 1719. His nomination as *chrezvychainy poslannik* or envoy extraordinary was contained in an edict dated May 10, 1719.

20. Bantysh-Kamensky, p. 421. "Bodgy" here means "holy."

21. Bantysh-Kamensky, pp. 155-156. From the historian's point of view, John Bell of Antermony was the most interesting and important member of the embassy. Bell was a keen observer with a commanding literary style, who left a detailed account of the embassy, including many perceptive remarks. As a Scotsman, he was not as deeply committed to Russian attitudes as were his companions. For his travel account, see Bell, I, 183-442; II, 1-220. Note that Vol. II also includes the journal written by Lange during his seventeen-month stay in Peking.

22. For the text of Izmailov's instructions, see Bantysh-Kamensky, pp. 425-432. For a note on the signatures on the document, see Cahen, *Histoire,* p. 156, n. 3.

23. For the text of the commercial instructions, see Bantysh-Kamensky, 432-433. For the date on which they were issued, see Cahen, *Histoire,* p. 157, n. 7. For the full text of Lange's instructions, see Bantysh-Kamensky, pp. 508-511. Note that Bantysh-Kamensky dated these instructions from August 1725. However, both internal evidence and documentation indicate that they were issued to Lange for his participation in the Izmailov embassy and then reissued to him *in toto,* in 1725, for his participation in the Vladislavich embassy. See, for instance, the aide-memoire sent from the College of Commerce to the College of Foreign Affairs, Bantysh-Kamensky, pp. 507-508. For a list of the gifts, see Cahen, *Histoire,* p. 159, n. 1.

24. *Ibid.,* pp. 159-160. Cahen gave this date on the basis of Izmailov's stateyny spisok. *Ibid.,* p. 160, n. 1. Bell, I, 187, stated that he "set out from St. Petersburg the 14th of July, 1719."

25. For a description of the embassy's entry into Peking, see Bell, I, 436-439. All ceremonial differences had been resolved when K'ang-hsi received Izmailov the first time. Bell described in detail the negotiations before the first audience. Bell, II, 3-5.

26. Bell, II, 7-9. This quotation is an interesting testimonial to the effect that Manchu was used in court ceremonials at least until the end of K'ang-hsi's reign.

27. Cahen, *Histoire,* p. 165; Bantysh-Kamensky, pp. 94-95.

28. For a description of Izmailov's negotiations in Peking, see Bantysh-Kamensky, 95-98.

29. Despite the protracted negotiations between Izmailov and the Li-fan yuan, the only mention of this embassy in the *Ch'ing Shih-lu* is the statement: "This year [K'ang-hsi 60:3:1] the Russian envoy came to do homage and presented us with a map of his country. We inquired about their people and climate. They replied that some areas of their country were above the 20th degree of north latitude and is called the ice-sea, where the strong ice is so solidly condensed that people cannot approach." *SL-KH,* 291:19b-20.

30. The only important and available source for the day-to-day details of Lange's consulship in Peking is his own diary. For text, see Bell, II, 221-423.

31. Bell, II, 253, 266-267.

32. Bell, II, 253-254.

33. No mention of Lange is found in the *Ch'ing Shih-lu.* Presumably, had he been considered by the court as a tribute envoy, his arrival, presence, and audience with the emperor would have been recorded in official court documents.

34. For details of the provisions, see Bell, II, 239-241. Lange's *fun* should be read *fen,* or 1/100 of a tael or an ounce. He himself noted, "By ... *gin* ... you are to understand pounds."

35. Bell, II, 236-237, 239, 280, 355.

36. See, for instance, Bell, II, 367.

37. Bell, II, 245-246, 276-279, 285, 287. The theory of collective debt responsibility that Lange put forth in conversations with his debtors was in no way supported by organizational fact in the Peking trade. In contrast to the Canton trade, where the Chinese merchants were officially organized in groups and a strong element of mutual responsibility was present, there is no evidence that the merchants with whom the Russians traded at Peking were organized in any way beyond their normal commercial ties. Although a strong element of official organization was to be introduced into the Chinese participation in the frontier trade after 1728, the purely barter nature of that market precluded the need to develop articulated collective responsibility in matters of debt.

38. Bell, II, 314-315, 320-321, 326. On Yin-t'ang and Yin-t'i, see Hummel, II, 927-931. An equally possible explanation of this incident is that the 10,000 liang came from Jesuit funds and Mourao simply used Yin-t'ang's name to give weight to the proposition. Yin-t'ang may have known nothing of the suggestion. A third possibility is that Mourao wished to influence Lange in the hope that he would use his influence at the Russian court to favor Jesuit propositions, such as the use of the Siberian overland route for Jesuit communication between Rome and Peking. However, since Lange was a Protestant, this explanation is unlikely.

39. On Lange's performance as a commercial representative, see Bell, II, 254, 257-258, 262-263.

40. Bell, 315, 318-319; Cahen, *Histoire,* p. L. It is curious that Lange, who was much concerned with official recognition of his status as Russian consul or agent, did not interpret the court's request for passports as recognition of his status in the light of his own concepts of international legality.

41. For Lange's commercial report, see Bell, II, 287-300. His remarks on Sino-Japanese trade are particularly interesting. See *ibid.,* 300-301.

42. See Lange's letter to the tsar of October 21, 1721, in Cahen, *Histoire,* p. LI.

43. Bell, II, 242-243, 249, 270-273. Lange was painfully aware of the difficulty involved in making contact with Westerners and Chinese in Manchu-held Peking. He remarks in his journal that taking advantage "of the opportunity the sickness of one of my Mandarins gave me, to make some visits to merchants . . . and to the Father Jesuits, hoping thereby to induce them to return my visits," he found them all receiving him "with very forced civilities, and with great reserve." *Ibid.,* II, 249-251. On another occasion a German Jesuit informed Lange that he had often sent his servant to the consul's gate "with his compliments," but the servant had always been turned back by the guards "as a person who had no business" with Lange. *Ibid.,* II, 269-270.

44. Bell, II, 316-317, 319, 329-332, 335-337, 347-352, 359-360. The court's demands appear to be an intrusion of the tribute system into the commercial caravan system. In other words, the court, accustomed to receiving luxury goods in the form of tribute, expected to receive goods from Istopnikov's caravan under favorable conditions, if not completely gratis. The "accounting and description" of goods—one of the court's demands—was itself a tribute practice. In his accounts of the Istopnikov caravan, Lange discussed the relative value of the ruble and the tael, or liang (ounce of silver). See Cahen, *Le livre de comptes,* pp. 120-123. According to Cahen, Lange estimated that at the time of the caravan of 1727-1728, the tael was worth 1.40 rubles. Finally, Lange suggested that the sables put on sale by the court to press its demands against the caravan did not come from Siberia but had been presented as tribute by the Solons on the Manchu side of the Amur. Bell, II, 350-351. If true, this substantiates the Manchu use of the commercial process for political ends.

45. Bell, II, 307-310, 312-313, 361-366.

46. Bell, II, 264, 361-364, 375-377. For the record of Lange's midnight interview, see *ibid.,* II, 367-375.

47. Bell, II, 378-379.

48. Bell, II, 379-382. In Lange's account, the title *allegamba* is the same as Milescu's *alikhamba* or president of the Li-fan yuan. See, for instance, Baddeley, I, cclxviii, column 3.

49. For the record of this interview, see *ibid.,* II, 387-399. Lange did not identify the "first minister."

50. *Ibid.,* II, 405-406, 422-423. Lange presumably performed the kowtow at his final audience with the emperor, because he remarked, "The

17th, I had my audience of leave of the Bogdoi-Chan, *with the ceremonies usual at this court* [italics added]."

51. Cahen, *Histoire,* p. 182; p. 182, n. 1.
52. Lange referred to the mission of Likharev and Unkovsky.
53. Cahen, *Histoire,* pp. 182-185. Fefilov was appointed by decree on December 11, 1722.
54. *Ibid.,* 185-186; *PSZ,* VII, 208-209.
55. Cahen, *Histoire,* 186-188.

Chapter VIII—Sava Vladislavich and the Search for Stability

1. See the biography of Yung-cheng in Hummel, II, 915-920. Unofficial accounts claimed that Yin-t'i was designated K'ang-hsi's successor and that the emperor's will was changed by Lungkodo, who, as commandant of the Peking Gendarmerie, controlled the capital when the old emperor died. Yin-t'i and Yin-t'ang were both eventually imprisoned, where they died.
2. Cahen, *Histoire,* p. 197.
3. Cahen, *Histoire,* pp. 197-198.
4. Cahen, *Histoire,* pp. 193-194; *PSZ,* IV, 222-223, 301-302; Milyukov, pp. 388-389.
5. *Ibid.,* pp. 195, 198-199. Petr Vlasov, who was probably the son of Ivan Vlasov, Golovin's associate, and therefore acquainted with the region to be demarcated, was appointed second frontier commissioner, but he died in Moscow in January 1726. Mikhail Krenitsyn, a former counselor of the College of Justice, was nominated to his place but died en route in September 1727, and Kolychov alone assumed the responsibility for the task.
6. Cahen, *Histoire,* pp. 199, and 199, n. 4 and n. 5, and p. 200, and p. 200, n. 2. See also *Polnoye sobranie postanovleny i rasporiazheny po vedomstvu pravoslavnago ispovedaniya Rossiyskoi Imperii,* 99 vols. (St. Petersburg, 1872-1905), V. 157-158. Kulchitsky's appointment was made official on August 4, 1725.
7. For details on the salaries paid to members of the embassy and a full list of the gifts and values thereof, see Cahen, *Histoire,* p. 201-202 and notes.
8. Cahen, *Histoire,* p. 203.
9. For complete text of these instructions, see Bantysh-Kamensky, pp. 434-455. The instructions generally covered all aspects of the embassy's proposed activities: a general description of the Sino-Russian crisis and the structure of the embassy (paragraphs 1-8); the conduct of the embassy up to its entry into China, including notification to the Manchus of its arrival (9-12); rules for the presentation of the embassy's official documents and the ceremonial of the imperial audience in Peking (13-17); commerce caravans, and a consular agent to be established at Peking (8-21); fugitives

(22-25); the frontier (26-36); miscellaneous items on trade, the Jesuits, gifts, and the use of a code (37-42); the question of the introduction of an Orthodox bishop into China (43-44); and the State Secrets Act (45).

10. This caravan was led by S.M. Tretyakov, who upon his death was replaced by D. Molokov. For details, see Kurts, "Gosudarstvennaya monopoliya," pp. 90-111. Cahen's *Le livre de comptes* is the official commercial record of this caravan.

11. Bantysh-Kamensky, pp. 438-441. In case of difficulty, Vladislavich was instructed to appeal to the Jesuits, promising in return for their aid free transport for their letters through Siberia and the tsarina's favor to their society.

12. Bantysh-Kamensky, pp. 450-451, 453-455. The instructions about the frontier concluded with an article demonstrating the fear in the College of Foreign Affairs over pressures that might be brought to bear on the Russian envoy. The College assumed that the Manchus might cleverly admit the caravan to Peking and then detain it until a frontier agreement had been reached. Such a situation would bring tremendous pressure on Vladislavich, who would have to carry the ultimate responsibility for the safety of the caravan's personnel, not to speak of the financial investment in it. In view of this possibility, Vladislavich was instructed to carry on discussions with the Manchus concerning areas of comparatively little dispute until the caravan had returned. Vladislavich was to communicate with St. Petersburg, Lange, and Bukhholtz in cipher only and to obey the State Secrets Act of January 13, 1724.

13. For the text of the two secret instructions, see Bantysh-Kamensky, p. 456.

14. For the text of Vladislavich's questions and the answers from the College of Foreign Affairs, see Bantysh-Kamensky, pp. 457-468.

15. For full text of the instructions, Vladislavich's remarks or questions, and the College of Commerce's replies, in parallel columns, see Bantysh-Kamensky, pp. 469-483. These instructions concerned three distinct subjects: establishment of a consulate at Peking (paragraphs 1-3, 20); the conditions of Sino-Russian trade (4-13); and information that the College wished Vladislavich to collect (14-19).

16. Bantysh-Kamensky, pp. 471-472. For details on the kind of information Vladislavich was instructed to collect, see *ibid.*, pp. 477-482.

17. Cahen, *Histoire,* p. 206. For a detailed itinerary of the embassy's journey, see *ibid.*, p. 206, n. 6.

18. In a letter dated August 31, 1726, the ambassador described his impressions of Siberia to the College of Foreign Affairs: "I am not neglecting to report, as is my duty, that Siberia—as far as I can see and hear, is not a *guberniya* [province], but an empire, ornamented with all kinds of lands and fruits in abundance, more than forty rivers bigger than the Danube and more than one hundred bigger than the Neva . . . a land well suited to grain culture, to fishing, hunting, and to ores of various metals and

various marbles, forests in abundance, and so gloriously pleasing as I think exists nowhere else in the world.

"But Siberia is quite empty for a variety of reasons, particularly the enormous distances, the few habitations, the stupidities of former administrators, and the frontier disorders." See Cahen, *Histoire,* LXVII.

19. Cahen, *Histoire,* pp. 207, and 207, n. 4.

20. For Vladislavich's comments on Lange, see Cahen, *Histoire,* LXVI-LXVII.

21. Lange's secretary was David Grave, probably a German. See Cahen, *Histoire,* pp. 208, and 208, n. 4 and 5.

22. Cahen, *Histoire,* pp. 209-210, esp. 210, n. 1, n. 2. On Lungkodo, see Hummel, I, 552-554.

23. Bantysh-Kamensky, p. 128; *Ch'ing-shih* IV, 2612-2613; V, 4105-4106. Note that Bantysh-Kamensky, p. 129, evidently unsure of Chabina's name and positions, referred to him simply as "Ta."

24. On the negotiations, see Bantysh-Kamensky, pp. 129-131, 134-136.

25. Bantysh-Kamensky, pp. 131-132, 137; Cahen, *Histoire,* p. 213. On Vladislavich's correspondence with Petersburg from Peking, see Cahen, *Histoire,* pp. 214-215. Cahen also suggested that Vladislavich and his staff were ill not for the reasons given but owing to their misbehavior. On the role played by the Jesuits in the Peking negotiations, see Vladislavich's own testimony in *ibid.,* LX-LXV. Note that the ambassador corresponded in code with Parrenin, the French Jesuit, who served as go-between in establishing relations with Maci (Vladislavich's Masi, whom he identified as "the great counselor of the khan, first minister, called Allegoda Masi"). On Maci, who was a Grand Secretary, see Hummel, I, 560-561. Vladislavich informed Moscow that Maci had promised to serve Russia's interests in return for the ambassador's promise to send him two thousand rubles from the frontier.

26. On Lungkodo Tsereng, see Hummel, I, 552-554; II, 756-757.

27. Cahen, *Histoire,* p. 218 and notes. The Russian commission, headed by Vladislavich, included Kolychov, Lange, Glazunov, Kireev (Kolychev's secretary), and Ivan Pavlov, a sublieutenant. The Manchu commission, headed by Lungkodo, included Tseren, Tulishen, and Ssu-ko. On Ssu-ko, see Hummel, I, 553. For the text of the Treaty of the Bura, see *Russko-Kitayskie otnosheniya, 1689-1916: ofitsialnye dokumenty,* ed. L. I. Duman (Moscow, 1958), pp. 11-12. See also Bantysh-Kamensky, pp. 341-343.

28. Galdan, not to be confused with the Jungar leader, was evidently in the train of the Manchu delegation. For Vladislavich's comments, see Cahen, *Histoire,* LXV-LXVI. For the contents of the report, see *ibid.,* pp. 218-219. For a transcript of Lange's statement to Vladislavich concerning details of the frontier agreements incorporated into the Treaty of the Bura, see Bantysh-Kamensky, pp. 343-346.

29. For this document, see Bantysh-Kamensky, pp. 347-352. See also *PSZ,* VII, 876-882. For a discussion of this document, see M. Venyukov,

Ocherk starykh i novykh dogovorov Rossii s Kitayem (St. Petersburg, 1861), p. 13. Glazunov signed the protocol for Russia; Khubitu and Nayantai, representing the Li-fan yuan, for the Manchus.

30. For the text of this document, see Bantysh-Kamensky, pp. 358-360. See also *PSZ,* VII, 887-890. Ssu-ko led the Manchu commission for this document. Note that Cahen, *Histoire,* p. 219, n. 3., incorrectly gave Ssu-ko's name, in French transcription, as Po-sseu-ko. *Po* was simply Ssu-ko's title and meant "earl."

31. See Bantysh-Kamensky, pp. 352-353, 360-363.

32. F.A. Kudryavtsev, *Istoriya Buryat-Mongolskogo naroda* (Moscow, 1940), p. 871.

33. N. Semivsky, *Noveyshie, lyubopytnye i dostovernye povestvovaniya o Vostochnoy Sibiri* (St. Petersburg, 1817), p. 136 (*pribavleniya*). A *sagene* is 2.13 meters.

34. It became Article III of the treaty. See, for instance *Russko-Kitayskie otnosheniya, 1689-1916,* pp. 18-19.

35. Cahen, *Histoire,* pp. 219-220, and 220, n. 1.

36. Bantysh-Kamensky, pp. 372-373. The date of the second draft was October 21, 1727.

37. For the text of the Treaty of Kyakhta, see *Russko-Kitayskie otnosheniya, 1689-1916,* p. 17-22. For a French translation, see Godfrey E. P. Hertslet, *Treaties, &c., between Great Britain and China; and between China and Foreign Powers; and Orders in Council, Rules, Regulations, Acts of Parliament, Decrees, &c., Affecting British Interests in China,* 2 vols. (London, 1908), I, 439-446. See also Bantysh-Kamensky, pp. 365-373.

38. The preamble read: "Now, upon the establishment of the frontiers of both empires, fugitives from either one side or the other will not be retained; and as a consequence of this, for the reestablishment of peace, as has been decided with the Russian envoy, the Illirian Count, Savva Vladislavich, there will be free commerce between both empires." Bantysh-Kamensky, p. 367. Note that Hertslet's wording of this article differed slightly from Bantysh-Kamensky's. Note, too, that the relationship between the problems of the frontier and fugitives, on the one hand, and commerce, on the other, was emphasized by the order in which the articles came in the treaty itself, the articles on fugitives and boundaries preceding the articles on commerce.

39. Bantysh-Kamensky, p. 364.

40. Bantysh-Kamensky, p. 369. For a history of the Russian Ecclesiastical Mission in Peking, see Albert Parry, "Russian (Greek Orthodox) Missionaries in China, 1689-1917: Their Cultural, Political and Economic Role (Chicago, 1938), an unpublished doctoral dissertation. For a good discussion of early Sino-Russian religious contacts, see Cahen, *Histoire,* pp. 245-267.

41. This version of the punishments was given by Bantysh-Kamensky, p. 372, and supported by Duman, in *Russko-Kitayskie otnosheniya,* p. 21.

Hertslet, I, 445, however, incorrectly gave the prescribed punishments as beheading for the Chinese and strangling for the Russians.

42. Cahen, *Histoire,* LXIX-LXX. This work was completed on June 30, 1728, by a series of detailed instructions from Vladislavich to Bukhholtz; Captain Knyaginkin, charged with Kyakhta's construction; Aleksey Tretyakov, in charge of frontier control at Kyakhta; and Captain Firsov and Anisim Mikhalev, inspectors at the frontier. On the new frontier regime, see *ibid.,* pp. 221-222.

43. Cahen, *Histoire,* pp. 222-223.

44. For the text of this document, see Bantysh-Kamensky, pp. 483-503.

45. For the text of this memorial, see Bantysh-Kamensky, pp. 373-375.

46. For the original Russian text and a French translation of Vladislavich's report, see Cahen, *Histoire,* LXXIII-LXXX.

47. For Vladislavich's reference, see Cahen, *Histoire,* LXXVI. I have been unable to identify this edict.

48. For the text of Dolgorukov's critique of Vladislavich's recommendations, see Cahen, *Histoire,* LXXX-LXXXIV.

49. For the text of Lange's critique of Vladislavich's recommendations and Dolgorukov's comments see Cahen, *Histoire,* LXXXV-XCVI. For Lange's figures, see *ibid.,* XCIII-XCIV.

50. The Tsurukhaitu emporium never became a successful commercial center, perhaps because Kyakhta was more easily accessible to various North China markets, whereas Tsurukhaitu was accessible only to Peking.

51. Kurts, "Gosudarstvennaya monopoliya," 99. The passport of Tretyakov, commissar of the caravan, was dated July 20, 1722. See Cahen, *Histoire,* pp. 228-229.

52. Cahen, *Histoire,* pp. 231-232.

53. Cahen, *Histoire,* p. 236. For details of the caravan's business, see Cahen, *Le livre de comptes.*

54. Kurts, "Gosudarstvennaya monopoliya," pp. 111, 133.

55. *SFPS.,* 37:18b-19.

56. *Baikal,* No. 10:3 (Aug. 3, 1897). This was a weekly newspaper published at Kyakhta from June 1897, edited by I.V. Boganov. I have been unable to determine when it ceased publication.

57. D. Johann Georg Gmelin, *Reise durch Sibirien, vom den Jahr 1733 bis 1743* (Gottingen, 1751), pt. 1, p. 445. Pallas wrote: "Kyakhta is not as poor in anything as it is in water. A small river of the same name flowing to the north, passes by the fortress and the settlement. Besides, the water in it is putrid and cannot be used by people. Therefore, wells are always dug in the fortress as well as in the settlement. But in these wells the water is either bitter because of salts or smells of lime, and it spoils and thickens the best sort of tea." P. S. Pallas, *Puteshestvie po raznym provintisiyam rossiyskago gosudarstva* (St. Petersburg 1788), Sec. 3, pt. 1, p. 150. Pallas was wrong in that the river actually flows from north to south.

58. Glavnoye upravlenie geodezii i kartografii MVD SSSR, *Atlas mira* (Moscow, 1954), p. 73.

59. V.N. Basin, *ed., Istoricheskaya zapiska o kitayskoi granitse, sostavlennaya sovetnikom Troytsko-savskago pogranichnago pravleniya Sychevskim v 1846* (Moscow, 1875), p. 224.

60. Kurts, "Gosudarstvennaya monopoliya," pp. 103, 106.

61. A.P. Vasilev, *Zabaykalskie kazaki,* (Chita, 1916), II, p. 26.

62. V.K. Andrievich, *Kratky ocherk istorii Zabaikalya ot drevneyshikh vremen do 1762 goda* (St. Petersburg, 1887), p. 148. See also Gmelin, Pt. 1, p. 449.

63. Trusevich, p. 272.

64. For the texts of these agreements, see Hertslet, pp. 446-445; *Russko-Kitayskie otnosheniya, 1689-1916,* pp. 22-29.

An Hypothesis as Epilogue

1. Roscoe Pound, "Toward a new jus gentium," in F.S.C. Northrop, *Ideological Differences and World Order: Studies in the Philosophy and Science of the World's Cultures* (New Haven, 1949), pp. 1-17, esp. 4. For other studies of the development of international law, see, for instance, J. L. Brierly, *The Law of Nations: An Introduction to the International Law of Peace* (Oxford, 1955); Arthur Nussbaum, *A Concise History of the Law of Nations* (New York, 1955).

2. C. H. Alexandrowicz, "Doctrinal Aspects of the Universality of the Law of Nations," *The British Year Book of International Law: 1961* (London, 1962), pp. 506-515, esp. 507.

3. Johann Christian Lünig, *Theatrum Ceremoniale Historico-Politicum,* 2 vols. (Leipzig, 1719), numbered variously. On Asia, see II, 1461-1472, esp. 1465-1467 on China.

4. Alexandrowicz, "Doctrinal Aspects," p. 515.

5. C. H. Alexandrowicz, "Le droit des nations aux Indes Orientales aux XVI, XVII, XVIII siecles," *Annales* 5:869-884, Esp. 872 (September-October, 1964).

Bibliography

The documentary sources on early Sino-Russian relations are voluminous, but a word is necessary to clarify the definition of "documentary" as used in this study. While the student of Sino-Russian relations who is neither Chinese nor Russian can approach his subject in the midtwentieth century with a greater degree of dispassion than the exigencies of contemporary politics permit his Soviet or Chinese (Communist or Nationalist) counterparts, he is, thus far, denied access to what by all accounts are the great archival treasures in the Soviet Union and China and must rely, instead, almost wholly on published documents. Soviet archives dealing with Sino-Russian relations are, at this date, still closed to Western scholars; the Chinese Communists have yet to begin publication of the mass of documents issued from the various Ch'ing government departments that might have been concerned with relations with Russia. Nevertheless, the available evidence in Soviet studies of early Sino-Russian relations, particularly of the period dealt with in this book, indicates that while the unavailable documentation would add detail to my narrative, it would not seriously modify the interpretations and conclusions.

On the Russian side, this study has relied heavily on certain standard documentary collections. Among these, three are especially important. The *Polnoye sobranie zakonov rossiyskoi imperii* is the official collection of the most significant laws and edicts issued by the Tsar's government after 1649. The first series, in forty-four volumes, which was compiled under the editorship of M. M. Speransky, has been particularly relevant to this study. It includes documents collected from registers of laws in outlying areas as well as from the various archives in Moscow and St. Petersburg. The collection of materials was intiated in 1826 and continued uninterruptedly until March 1, 1830. Some 30,920 documents are included in the first series, and the texts are said to be exact copies of the originals; the only additions have been short introductory sentences indicating the date of issue and summarizing the contents of each document. That the collection is not complete is indicated by the fact that while the *Polnoye sobranie zakonov* includes 42,860 documents for the years 1649–1865 (in the first and second series), the archives of the Senate alone contained 124,177 documents for the years 1704–1865. The second and third series contain valuable materials for the study of later periods of Sino-Russian relations.

The two other vital Russian collections are *Akty istoricheskie*, published in five volumes in 1841 and 1842, and the supplementary *Dopolneniya k aktam istoricheskim*, published in twelve volumes between 1846 and 1872. Both have separately published indexes. Volumes 4 and 5 of the *Akty istoricheskie* contain documents with numerous references to the development of political and commercial contacts with China. The *Dopolneniya k aktam istoricheskim* is a rich collection of the business papers of the Moscow *prikazes* and the chancelleries of the *voevodas*. Readers desiring detailed descriptions of the genesis and contents of these collections may consult the appropriate entries in *Entsiklopedichesky slovar* (St. Petersburg: F. A. Brokgauz and I. A. Efron, 1890–1907).

John F. Baddeley's *Russia, Mongolia, China*, published in two volumes in London in 1919, is another extraordinarily important collection of source materials for the early period of Russia's relations with China, as well as with Central Asia. It is also a monument to the bookmaker's art. Baddeley, who died in 1940 at the age of 85, was led to his work by a spirit of high adventure and historical romanticism. After graduating from Wellington College, where he was a diligent student and outstanding athlete, he went in 1871 to western South America, where he spent more than a year. Upon his return to London he was introduced to the Russian ambassador to the Court of St. James; the two became fast friends, and the ambassador took Baddeley back to Russia, where he sponsored the Englishman's entry into Russian society. "After some months spent acquiring Russian and in Sport," Baddeley was appointed, through the ambassador's intercession, the St. Petersburg correspondent of the *Standard.* Because of his labors, that paper became noted for its reporting of Russian affairs. Baddeley traveled widely in Russia, the Caucasus, and "the Farther East," visiting the Amur in 1900, 1907, and again in 1909. Becoming fascinated with the distant marches where Europe met Asia, he began to collect the documents pertinent to the early history of Sino-Russian relations, and through his Russian connections obtained access to the archives of the Russian Ministry of Foreign Affairs. "It was," he wrote, "with Spathary's account of his journey from the Chinese frontier to Peking and sojourn there that, in May 1912, I began my work of translation." Over the next few years he collected, transcribed, translated, and painstakingly annotated the most important documents in Russia, Sweden, and England, many now available to western scholars in no other form. This work is particularly valuable because Baddeley published along with his translations the original Russian texts of the documents. For additional biographical information, see Baddeley's obituary in *The Times* (London), February 21, 1940, page 11, column 6, as well as his introduction to *Russia, Mongolia, China.*

Nikolay Nikolayevich Bantysh-Kamensky's *Diplomaticheskoye sobranie del mezhdu rossiyskim i kitayskim gosudarstvami s 1619 po 1792 god: sostavlennoye po dokumentam, khranyaschimsya v Moskovskom Arkhive Gosudarstvennoy Kollegii Inostrannykh del, v 1792–1803 godu* is another vital collection of quotations from, and paraphrases of, archival materials and other types of information available in Russian archives. Although this work was edited and published at Kazan only in 1882 by V. M. Florinsky on the occasion of the three hundredth anniversary of the Russian conquest of Siberia, Bantysh-Kamensky had completed it in 1803. The author of many collections and studies, he stands out as one of the earliest and greatest of Russian archivists. Born in 1737 in Chernigovskaya *guberniya*, he entered the Kiev Academy in 1745, and when the University of Moscow was established in 1755 he enrolled as a student of mathematics, physics, and history. A student of languages as well, he was proficient in Hebrew, Greek, French, German, and Italian, in addition to his native Russian. Refusing a diplomatic appointment to the College of Foreign Affairs proffered him by M. I. Vorontsov, he chose instead to become an archivist in the college's archives, and in 1800 he was appointed its chief archivist. For a full biobibliography, see S. A. Vengerov, *Kritiko-biografichesky slovar russkikh pisateley i uchenykh ot nachala russkoy obrazovannosti do nashikh dney*, 5 vols. (St. Petersburg, 1889–1897), v. 2, pp. 94–100.

The best and most complete available collection of documents pertaining to Sino-Russian relations before the Treaty of Nerchinsk is *Russko-Kitayskie otnosheniya v XVII veke: materialy i dokumenty, 1608–1683*, ed. L. I. Duman (Moscow, 1969). Unfortunately, this volume, the first of a projected two-volume work, was published after the completion of my own study. However, while the documents add a wealth of detail not previously available to students of the early period of Sino-Russian relations, they do not change my own conclusions. The important work by V. A. Aleksandrov, *Rossiya na dalnevostochnykh rubezhakh* (*vtoraya polovina XVII veke v.*) (Moscow, 1969), also did not become available before my volume went into production.

The two works by the French historian of Sino-Russian relations, Gaston Cahen, *Histoire des relations de la Russie avec la Chine sous Pierrre le Grand* (1689–*1730*) and *Le livre de comptes de la caravane russe a Pekin en 1727–1728*, both published at Paris in 1911, are invaluable sources because they, too, are based on currently unavailable archival materials. In the former, a standard study based wholly on Russian sources, Cahen generously published extracts from many of the documents he himself used. The latter is the only account book of a Russian caravan to Peking now available to Western scholars, though others doubtless exist in Soviet archives. The works of certain Soviet scholars as well, such as Shastina and Schebenkov, have been useful for their indications of the contents of various Soviet archives and for their extensive quotations from the documents.

Another important source for this study has been the diaries of the various Western participants in Russian missions to Peking, long available in published form. The diaries of John Bell, Adam Brand, Isbrants Ides, and Lorents Lange, together with the reports of the various Russian missions to Peking published by Baddeley, provide interesting insights into the situation at Peking as well as into the course of Sino-Russian relations.

Finally, the reader's attention must be drawn to the invaluable research of

American scholars into the history of Russian expansion to the east, without which my own work could not have been accomplished. Particularly outstanding are the monographs by Robert J. Kerner, Raymond H. Fisher, and George V. Lantzeff, published by the University of California at Berkeley between 1943 and 1946. Much of the Russian background for my study has been drawn from their work.

On the Chinese side, two sets of documents were central to this study and deserve special notice. The *Shih-lu* is the primary source for the history of Ch'ing dynastic policy, since in theory it is a daily record of all edicts issued by the emperor on any matter coming to his attention. Moreover, the practice of including in the edicts extensive quotations from the memorials to the throne that occasioned specific policy decisions provides partial access to the thinking and at times even the politics of the imperial bureaucracy. The *Ch'ing shih-lu ching-chi tzu-liao chi-yao*, or "A compendium of economic materials in the *Ch'ing shih-lu*," published in Peking in 1959, is a useful guide to documents in the *Shih-lu* concerning economic and commercial policy and history. However, care must be taken to check its excerpts against the original *Shih-lu* documents, because minor editing and deletions appear to have been made by the editors.

The most significant collection of Chinese source materials concerning the early history of Sino-Russian relations is the *Shuo-fang pei-sheng*, or "Historical source-book of the Northern Regions," which is a Ch'ing compendium in 80 *chüan*, or sections, of official documents and other materials pertaining directly or tangentially to the subject. Among the selections in the collection, the *P'ing-ting Lo-ch'a fang-lüeh*, or "The official account of the plans for the pacification of the Russians," in four sections, is a rich source for the study of the campaigns along the Amur in the 1680's, the negotiations at Nerchinsk, and the preparations for them. This and other items in the *Shuo-fang pei-sheng* that were most important for my study are listed separately in the bibliography below. The complex history of the *Shuo-fang pei-sheng* is described in the biography of its original editor, Ho Ch'iu-t'ao, in Arthur W. Hummel's *Eminent Chinese of the Ch'ing Period* (*1644–1912*), 2 vols. (Washington, 1943).

Extensive use has also been made of the diaries of the various Ch'ing envoys to the Russians—Chinese, Manchu, and Western alike. With the exception of the diary of Thomas Pereira, S. J., published by Father Sebes in 1961, all have long been available to both Chinese and Western scholars. Father Gerbillon's diaries have been used in the English translation published in the London edition (1741) of Father Jean Baptiste du Halde's *A Description of the Empire of China and Chinese-Tartary*. It may be noted that although the official Russian report of the Nerchinsk negotiations, written by the Russian ambassador, Fedor Golovin, has been used extensively by Russian students, particularly Schebenkov, it has never been published in toto. A request to Soviet authorities for access to it was refused because of their plans to publish it in the future.

Chinese and Japanese names are given throughout in their normal Sino-Japanese order: family name followed by personal name.

Akty istoricheskie, 5 vols. St. Petersburg, 1841–1842; Index, 1843.

Aleksandrov, V. A. "Iz istorii russko-kitayskikh ekonomicheskikh svyazey pered Nerchinskim miron 1689 g." *Istroiya SSSR*, 5: 203–208 (November-December 1957).

———. "Russko-kitayskaya torgovlya i Nerchinsky torg v kontse XVII v."; in *K voprosu o pervonachalnom nakoplenii v Rossii (XVII–XVIII vv.): sbornik statey*. Moscow, 1958.

Alekseev, M. P. *Sibir v izvestiyakh inostrannykh puteshestvennikov i pisateley*. Irkutsk, 1936.

Alexandrowicz, C. H. "Doctrinal Aspects of the Universality of the Law of Nations," *The British Year Book of International Law: 1961* (London, 1962).

———. "Le droit des nations aux Indes Orientales aux XVI, XVII, XVIII siècles," *Annales* 5: 869–884 (September-October 1964).

Andrievich, Vladimir K. *Kratky ocherk istorii Zabaikalya ot drevneyshikh vremen do 1762 goda*. St. Petersburg, 1887.

———. *Istoriya Sibiri*, 5 vols. in 2. St. Petersburg, 1889.

Aristov, N. I. *Promyshlennost drevney rusi*. St. Petersburg, 1866.

Arnauld, A. and P. Nicole. *Perpetuite de la Foy de l'église catholique*. 2 vols.; Paris, 1841.

Arsenev, Yu. B. "Puteshestvie chrez Sibir ot Tobolska do Nerchinska i granits Kitaya russkago poslannika Nikolaya Spafariya v 1675 godu: dorozhny dnevnik Spafariya s vvedeniem i primechaniyami"; in *Zapiski imperatorskago russkago obschestva po otdeleniyu etnografii*, 10.1: 1–215. St. Petersburg, 1882.

———. "Nikolay Spafary i ego vremya"; *Russky Arkhiv* 2.7: 349–360 (1895).

Auerbakh, N. K. "Zimove v bukhte Promyslovoy Eniseyskogo zaliva"; *Severnaya Aziya*, Nos. 5–6 (1928).

Baddeley, John F. *Russia, Mongolia, China*. 2 vols.; London, 1919.

Baikal, No. 10 (Aug. 3, 1897).

Bakhrushin, S. V. *Nauchnye trudy*. 3 vols. in 4; Moscow, 1954.

———. "Ocherki po kolonizatsii Sibiri"; in *Nauchnye trudy*, Vol. 3, Pt. 2 (Moscow, 1955).

———. "Torgi gostya Nikitina v Sibiri i Kitaye"; in *Nauchnye trudy*, Vol. 3, Pt. 1 (Moscow, 1955).

———. "Yasak v Sibiri v XVIII v."; in *Nauchnye trudy*, Vol. 3, Pt. 2 (Moscow, 1955).

Bantysh-Kamensky, N. *Diplomaticheskoye sobranie del mezhdu rossiyskim i kitayskim gosudarstvami s 1619 po 1792 god: sostavlennoye po dokumentam, khranyaschimsya v Moskovskom Arkhive Gosudarstvennoy Kollegy Inostrannykh del, v 1792–1803 godu*, ed. V. M. Florinsky. Kazan, 1882.

Bartold, B. *Istoriya izucheniya vostoka v Evrope i Rossii*. Leningrad, 1925.

Basin, V. N., ed. *Istoricheskaya zapiska o kitayskoy granitse, sostavlennaya sovetnikom Troytsko-savskago pogranichnago pravleniya Sychevskim v 1846*. Moscow, 1875.

Bazilevich, K. V. *V gostyakh u bogdykhana*. Leningrad, 1927.

———. *Krupnoye torgovoye predpriyatie v Moskovskom gosudarstve v pervoy polovine XVII v.* Leningrad, 1933.

Bell, John, of Antemony. *Travels from St. Petersburg in Russia to Various Parts of Asia.* 2 vols.; Edinburgh, 1788.

Belokurov, S. A. *Iz dukhovnoy zhizni moskovskago obschestva XVII v.* Moscow, 1902.

———. *O posolskom prikaze.* Moscow, 1906.

Biggerstaff, Knight. "The T'ung Wen Kuan," *The Chinese Social and Political Science Review.* 18.3: 307–340 (October 1934).

Bogyavlensky, S. K. *Prikaznye sudyi XVII v.* Moscow, 1946.

Bolton, Herbert Eugene. "Fray Juan Crespi with the Portola Expedition," in *Bolton and the Spanish Borderlands.* John Francis Bannon, ed., pp. 270–280. Norman, 1964.

Borovoy, S. Ya. "Voprosy kreditovaniya torgovli i promyshlennosti v ekonomicheskoy politike Rossii XVIII v."; *Istoricheskie zapiski*, 33: 92–122 (1950).

Bosmans, H., S. J. *Le problème des relations de Verbiest avec la cour de Russie.* Bruges, 1913.

Brand, Adam. *A Journal of the Embassy from Their Majesties John and Peter Alexievitz, Emperors of Muscovy &c. Over land into China through Ustiugha, Siberia, Dauri, and the Great Tartary to Peking, the capital city of the Chinese Empire. By Everard Isbrand, their Ambassador in the years 1693, 1694, and 1695.* London, 1698.

———. *Relation du voyage de Mr. Evert Isbrand envoye de sa Majesté Czarienne à l'empereur de la Chine en 1692, 93, & 94.* Amsterdam, 1699.

Bretschneider, E. *Mediaeval Researches from East-Asiatic Sources.* London, 1888.

Brierly, J. L. *The Law of Nations: An Introduction to the International Law of Peace.* Oxford, 1955.

Brikner, A. G. "Lavrenty Rinhuber"; *Zhurnal Ministerstva narodnago prosvescheniya*, 231.2: 396–421 (February 1884).

Butrigarius, Galeatius. *Of the Northeast Frostie Seas, and Kyngdoms Lying That Way, Declared by the Duke of Muscouia, to a Learned Gentleman of Italie named Galeatius Butrigarius;* in Richarde Eden and Richard Willes, *The History of Trauayle*, pp. 261–320 (note that these pages are misnumbered 254–400). London, 1577.

Cahen, Gaston. *Histoire des relations de la Russie avec la Chine sous Pierre le Grand* (1689–1730). Paris, 1911.

———. *Le livre de comptes de la caravane russe à Pekin en 1727–1728.* Paris, 1911.

Calendar of the Tungwen College. Peking, 1879.

du Cange, Carolo du Fresne. *Glossarium ad scriptores mediae et infimae Graectatis.* 2 vols. in 1; reprint. Gras, 1958.

Chang P'eng-ko 張鵬翮. *Feng-shih O-lo-ssu hsing-ch'eng-lu* 奉使俄羅斯行程錄 (An account of the journey of the mission to Russia); in the collectanea *I-hai chu-ch'en* 藝海珠塵. See also *chüan* 42 of the *Shuo-fang pei-sheng.*

Chang Yü-shu 張玉書. *P'ing-ting shuo-mo fang-lüeh* 平定朔漠方略 (The official

account of the pacification of the northern deserts; completed in 1708).
———. *Wai-kuo chi* 外國記 (An account of foreign countries); in *Ch'ao-tai ts'-ung-shu* 朝代叢書, supplement to collection VIII, *ts'e* 106.
Ch'en, Agnes Fang-chih. "Chinese Frontier Diplomacy: The Coming of the Russians and the Treaty of Nertchinsk," *The Yenching Journal of Social Studies*, 4.2: 99–149 (February 1949).
———. "Chinese Frontier Diplomacy: Kiakhta Boundary Treaties and Agreements," *The Yenching Journal of Social Studies*, 4.2: 151–205 (February 1949).
Chia-ch'ing hui-tien: Ta-Ch'ing hui-tien 嘉慶會典：大清會典 (Collected statutes of the Ch'ing dynasty, of the Chia-ch'ing period). 80 *chüan;* 1818.
Chia-ch'ing hui-tien shih-li: Ta-ch'ing hui-tien shih-li 嘉慶會典事例：大清會典事例 (Cases and precedents of the collected statutes of the Ch'ing dynasty, of the Chia-ch'ing period). 920 *chüan;* 1818.
Ch'ien-lung hui-tien: Ta-Ch'ing hui-tien 乾隆會典：大清會典 (Collected statutes of the Ch'ing dynasty, of the Ch'ien-lung period). 100 *chüan;* 1763.
Chin Yü-fu 金毓黻. *Liao-hai ts'ung-shu* 遼海叢書. Dairen, 1934.
Ch'ing-ch'ao wen-hsien t'ung-k'ao 清朝文獻通考 (Encyclopedia of the historical records of the Ch'ing dynasty). 400 *chüan;* Shanghai, 1936.
Ch'ing-shih 清史 (The history of the Ch'ing dynasty). 8 vols.; Taipei, 1961.
Ch'ing shih-lu ching-chi tzu-liao chi-yao 清實錄經濟資料輯要 (A compendium of economic materials in the *Ch'ing shih-lu*). Peking, 1959.
Ch'in-ting Ta-Ch'ing hui-tien shih-li 欽定大清會典事例. Kuang-hsü 25 edition, reprinted in Taipei by the Taiwan chung-wen shu-chü, n.d.
Chulkov, M. *Istoricheskoye opisanie rossiyskoi komertsii pri vsekh portakh i granitsakh ot drevnikh vremen do nyne nastoyaschego*. 21 vols.; St. Petersburg and Moscow, 1781–1788.
DAI: Dopolneniya k aktam istoricheskim. 12 vols.; St. Petersburg, 1846–1872; Index, 1875.
Dame, Frederic. *Nouveau dictionnaire roumain-français*. 4 vols.; Bucharest, 1895.
Dapper, O. *Gedenkwaerdig bedryf d. Nederl. Oost-Ind. Maetschappye op de Kuste en i het Keizerrijk van Taising of Sina*. Amsterdam, 1670.
A Documentary Chronicle of Sino-Western Relations (*1644–1820*), comp., trans., and annot. by Lo-shu Fu. 2 vols.; Tucson, 1966.
Dolgov, S. O. "Vedemost o kitayskoy zemle i glubokoy Indii" (The register concerning the Chinese land and deep India); *Pamyatniki drevney pismennosti i iskusstva*, 133: 14–35 (St. Petersburg, 1899).
Dopolneniya k aktam istoricheskim, see *DAI*.
Dudgeon, John. *Historical Sketch of the Ecclesiastical, Political, and Commercial Relations of Russia with China*. Peking, 1872, reprinted in an anastatic edition, 1940.
Elisséeff, Vadime. "The Middle Empire, a Distant Empire, an Empire without Neighbors," *Diogenes*, 42: 60–64 (Summer 1963).
Ezhegodnik Tobolskago muzeya (The annual of the Tobolsk museum), Vol. 25. Tobolsk, 1915.
Fairbank, John King. *Trade and Diplomacy on the China Coast: The Opening of*

The Treaty Ports, 1842–1854. 2 vols.; Cambridge, Mass., 1953.

Fairbank, John K. and Ssu-yü Teng. *Ch'ing Administration: Three Studies*. Cambridge, Mass., 1960.

Fang Chaoying. "A Technique for Estimating the Numerical Strength of the Early Manchu Military Forces," *Harvard Journal of Asiatic Studies*, 13.1–2: 192–215 (June 1950).

Farquhar, David Miller. "The Ch'ing Administration of Mongolia up to the Nineteenth Century." Ph. D. thesis; Harvard University, 1960.

Fisher, Raymond H. *The Russian Fur Trade, 1550–1700*. Berkeley, 1943.

Foust, Clifford M. *Muscovite and Mandarin: Russia's Trade with China and Its Setting, 1727–1805*. Chapel Hill, 1969.

Fuchs, Walter. "Der Russisch-Chinesische Vertrag von Nertschinsk von Jahre 1689," *Monumenta Serica*, 4.2: 546–591 (1939–1940).

Fursenko, V. "Spafari Milesku"; *Russkiy Geograficheskiy slovar*, 18: 183–190.

"Glavnoye upravlenie geodezii i kartografii MVD SSSR," *Atlas mira* (Moscow, 1954).

Gmelin, D. Johann Georg. *Reise durch Sibirien, vom den Jahr 1733 bis 1743*. Gottingen, 1751.

Golder, F. A. *Russian Expansion on the Pacific, 1641–1850*. 2nd ed.; Gloucester, Mass., 1960.

Golovin, Petr, P. "Instruktsiya pismyanovu golove Poyarkov." *Chteniya v imperatorskom obschestve istorii i drevnostey rossiyskikh pri moskovskom universitete*, 1.5: 1–14 (January-March 1861).

Gote, Yu. V. *Angliyskie puteshestvenniki v Moskovskom gosudarstve v XVI v*. Moscow, 1937.

Halde, Jean Baptiste du. *A Description of the Empire of China and Chinese-Tartary*. 2 vols.; London, 1741.

Herberstein, Sigismund von, et al. *Notes upon Russia: Being a Translation of the Earliest Account of That Country, Entitled Rerum Moscovitarum Commentarii, by the Baron Sigismund von Herberstein*, tr. and ed. by R. H. Major. 2 vols. (Hakluyt Society Works, Vols. 10 and 30); London, 1851–1852.

Hertslet, Godfrey E. P. *Treaties &c. between Great Britain and China; and between China and Foreign Powers; and Orders in Council, Rules, Regulations, Acts of Parliament, Decrees, &c., Affecting British Interests in China*. 2 vols.; London, 1908.

Hsiao I-shan 蕭一山. *Ch'ing-tai t'ung-shih* 淸代通史 (A comprehensive history of the Ch'ing period). 2 vols.; Shanghai, 1927.

Hsien-feng ch'ao ch'ou-pan i-wu shih-mo 咸豐朝籌辦夷務始末 (The complete account of our management of barbarian affairs in the Hsien-feng period). 80 *chüan;* Peking, 1930.

Hsü Ch'ien-hsüeh 徐乾學. *Tan-yüan chi* 憺園集 (The collectanea of the tranquil garden). 36 *chüan;* 1694.

Hummel, Arthur W. *Eminent Chinese of the Ch'ing Period, 1644–1912*. 2 vols.; Washington, 1943.

Ides, E. Isbrants. *Three Years Travels from Moscow Overland to China: Thru'*

Great Ustiga, Siriania, Permia, Siberia, Daour, Great Tartary, &c. to Peking. London, 1706.

Inaba Iwakichi. "Chōsen Kōsōshō ni okeru ryōji no Manshū shuppei ni tsuite (Shin-Rō Kankei chūki no shiryō)"; *Seikyū gakusō*, 15: 1–26 (February 1934); 16: 47–60 (March 1934).

Istoriya Buryat-Mongol'skoy ASSR, ed. E. M. Zalkind, et al. 2 vols.; Ulan-Ude, 1954.

Ivanovsky, A. "Posolstvo Spafariya"; *Zapiski vostochnago otdeleniya imperatorskago Russkago arkheologicheskago obschestva*, 2: 195–226 (1887).

Jenkenson, Anthony, et al. *Early Voyages and Travels to Russia and Persia.* Vol. 72 of the Hakluyt Society publications. London, 1886.

Jih-hsia chiu-wen k'ao 日下舊聞考 (An examination of old things in Peking). 1781.

K'ang-hsi hui-tien: Ta-Ch'ing hui-tien 康熙會典：大清會典 (Collected statutes of the Ch'ing dynasty, of the K'ang-hsi period). 162 *chüan;* 1690.

Kao Shih-ch'i 高士奇. *Hu-ts'ung tung-hsün jih-lu* 扈從東巡日錄 (Diary of a follower of the imperial progress in the Eastern provinces). 2 *chüan;* in *Liao-hai ts'ung-shu*. Ser. I, *ts'e* 7.

Kapterev, N. F. *Kharakter otnoshenyi Rossii k pravoslavnomu vostoku.* Moscow, 1914.

Karamzin, Nikolay M. *Istoriya gosudarstva rossiyskago.* 12 vols.; St. Petersburg, 1892.

Kedrov, N. "Nikolay Spafary i ego Arifmologiya (Materialy dlya istorii kontsa XVII veka)"; *Zhurnal Ministerstva narodnago prosvescheniya*, 183: 1–31 (January 1876).

Kerner, Robert J. *The Urge to the Sea: The Course of Russian History.* Berkeley, 1946.

Khozhenie za tri morya Afanasiya Nikitina: 1466–1472 gg. Moscow, 1958.

Kudryavtsev, F. A. *Istoriya Buryat-Montolskogo naroda.* Moscow, 1940.

Kuo-ch'ao ch'i-hsien lei-cheng ch'u-pien 國朝耆獻類徵初編 (Classified biographies of famous men of the Ch'ing period), ed. Li Huan 李桓. 720 *chüan;* c. 1884.

Kurts, B. G. *Sochinenie Kilburgera o russkoy torgovle v tsarstvovanie Alekseya Mikhaylovicha.* Kiev, 1915.

———. "Gosudarstvennaya monopoliya v torgovle Rossii s Kitayem v pervoy pol. XVIII st."; *Naukovi zapiski Kiivskogo institutu narodnogo gospodarstva*, 9: 59–134 (1928).

———. "Yak povstala derzhavna karavanna (valkova) torgovlia Rossii z Kitaem u XVII vitsi"; *Zapiski istorichno-filologichnogo viddilu Vseukrainskoi Akademii Nauk*, 21–22: 249–296 (1928).

Kyuner, N. B. *Noveyshaya istoriya stran dalnago vostoka.* Vladivostok, 1910.

Lach, Donald F. *The Preface to Leibniz' Novissima Sinica.* Honolulu, 1957.

Lange, Lorents. *Laurence Lange's Journey from Petersbourg to Peking in China;* in Friedrich Christian Weber, *The Present State of Russia.* 2 vols.; London, 1722, II, 3–36.

———. *Journal of the Residence of Mr. De Lange, Agent of His Imperial Majesty of All the Russias, Peter the First, at the Court of Pekin, during the years 1721 and 1722*; in John Bell of Antermony, *Travels from St. Petersburg in Russia, to Various Parts of Asia*. 2 vols.; Edinburgh, 1788.

"Lang-t'an chuan" 良坦傳 (The biography of Lang-t'an); in *Pa-ch'i t'ung-chih* 八旗通志 (Comprehensive gazetteer of the eight banners), *chüan* 153.

Lantzeff, George V. *Siberia in the Seventeenth Century: A Study of the Colonial Administration*. Berkeley, 1943.

Lensen, George Alexander, ed. *Russia's Eastward Expansion*. Englewood Cliffs, 1964.

L'Isle, J. N., and A. G. Pingre. *Description de la Ville de Peking*. Paris, 1765.

Liu Hsien-t'ing 劉獻廷. *Kuang-yang tsa-chi* 廣陽雜記 (Notes of Liu Hsien-t'ing). Shanghai, 1957.

Lünig, Johann Christian. *Theatrum ceremoniale historico-politicum*. 2 vols.; Leipzig, 1719.

Lyubimov, A. "Nekotorye manchzhurskie dokumenty iz istorii russko-kitayskikh otnosheny v XVII veke" (Some Manchu documents on the history of Russo-Chinese relations in the seventeenth century); *Zapiski vostochnago otdeleniya imperatorskago arkheologicheskago obschestva*, 21.2–3: 65–94.

Makarov, I. S. "Pushnoy rynok Soli-Vychegodskoy v XVII v."; *Istoricheskie zapiski*, 14: 156–168 (1945).

———. "Volostnye torzhki v Sol-Vychegodskom uyezde v pervoy polovine XVIII v."; *Istoricheskie zapiski*, 1: 193–219 (1937).

Mamyshev, V. S. *General-feldmarshal i general-admiral graf Fedor Alekseevich Golovin*. St. Petersburg, 1910.

Mancall, Mark. "China's First Missions to Russia, 1729–1731," *Papers on China*, Vol. 9 (August 1955).

Martin, W. A. P. *A Cycle of Cathay*. 2nd ed.; New York, 1897.

Materialy po istorii Uzbekskoy, Tadzhikskoy i Turkmenskoy SSSR. Leningrad, 1932.

Meng Ssu-ming, "The E-lo-ssu Kuan (Russian hostel) in Peking," *Harvard Journal of Asiatic Studies*, 23: 19–46 (1960–1961).

Mikhaylovsky, I. N. *Ocherk zhizni i sluzhby Nikolaya Spafariya v Rossii*. Kiev, 1896.

Milescu, Nicolaie. *Descrierea Chinei*, ed. Corneliu Barbulescu. Bucharest, 1958.

———. *Jurnal de calatorie in China*, ed. Corneliu Barbulescu. Bucharest, 1958.

Milyukov, P. *Gosudarstvennoe khozyaystvo Rossii v pervoy chetverti XVIII stoletiya i reforma Petra Velikago*. St. Petersburg, 1905.

Mongol Oros Tol. ed. A. Lubsandendeb. Moscow, 1957.

Müller, G. (G. F. Mueller, G. F. Miller). *Eröffnung eines Vorschlages zu Verbesserung der Russischen Historie durch den Druck einer Stückweise herauszugebenden Sammlung von allerley zu den Umständen und Begenbenheiten dieses Reichs gehörigen Nachrichten*. 10 vols.; St. Petersburg, 1732–1764.

———. *Opisanie Sibirskago tsarstva i vsekh proisshedshikh v nem del ot nachala a osoblivo ot pokoreniya ego rossiyskoi. derzhav po sii vremena*. 2nd ed.; St. Petersburg, 1787.

———. *Istoriya Sibiri*. Moscow, 1937.

Narody Sibiri, ed. M. G. Levin and L. P. Potapov. Moscow, 1956; in the series *Narody Mira: etnograficheskie ocherki.*

Neuville, Foy de la. *Relation curieuse et nouvelle de Moscovie*. Paris, 1698.

Nieuhoff, John. *An Embassy from the East-India Company of the United Provinces, to the Grand Tartar Cham, Emperor of China*. London, 1669.

Nussbaum, Arthur. *A Concise History of the Law of Nations*. New York, 1955.

Ocherki po istorii Komi ASSR. 2 vols.; Syktyvkar, 1955–1962.

Ogloblin, N. N. *Obozrenie stolbtsov i knig Sibirskago prikaza, 1592–1768 g. g.* 4 vols.; Moscow, 1895–1900.

Pallas, P. S. *Puteshestvie po raznym provintsiyam rossiyskago gosudarstva*. St. Petersburg, 1788.

Pamyatniki diplomaticheskikh i torgovykh snosheny moskovskoy Rusi s Persiey. comp. Nikolay I. Veselovsky; Vols. 20–22 in *Trudy vostochnago otdeleniya imperatorskago russkago arkheologicheskago obschestva*. St. Petersburg, 1890–1893.

Pamyatniki sibirskoy istorii XVIII v. 2 vols.; St. Petersburg, 1882–1885.

Panaitescu, P. P. "Nicholas Spathar Milescu," *Mélanges de l'école roumaine en France*, Pt. 1 (Paris, 1925).

Parry, Albert. "Russian (Greek Orthodox) Missionaries in China, 1689–1917: Their Cultural, Political, and Economic Role," Ph. D. thesis; University of Chicago, 1938.

Pavlovsky, Michel N. *Chinese-Russian Relations*. New York, 1949.

Picot, Emile. *Notice biographique et bibliographique sur Nicolas Spatar Milescu*. Paris, 1883.

P'ing-ting Lo-ch'a fang-lüeh, see *PTLC*.

Pisma i bumagi imperatora Petra Velikago. 11 vols.; St. Petersburg and Moscow, 1887–1910, 1964.

"Pismo Nikolaya Spafariya k boyarinu Artemonu Sergeevichu Matveevu," *Russky Arkhiv*, I. 1.52–58 (1881).

Pokrovsky, F. I. "Puteshestvie v Mongoliyu i Kitay Sibirskago kazaka Ivana Petlina v 1618 godu [mnimoye puteshestvie atamanov Ivana Petrova i Burnasha Yalycheva v 1567 g.]" (The journey to Mongolia and China of the Siberian Cossack Ivan Petlin in 1618 [and the imaginary trip of the hetmans Ivan Petrov and Burnash Yalychev in 1567]); *Izvestiya russkago yazyka i slovesnosti imperatorskago akademii nauk*, 18.4: 257–304 (1913).

Pokrovsky, Serafim Aleksandrovich. *Vneshnyaya torgovlya i vneshnyaya torgovaya politika Rossii*. Moscow, 1947.

Polnoye sobranie postanovleny i rasporiazheny po vedomstvu pravoslavnago ispovedaniya Rossiyskoi Imperii. 9 vols.; St. Petersburg, 1872–1905.

Polnoye sobranie zakonov rossiyskoi imperii s 1649 goda, see *PSZ*.

Potanin, G. "O karavannoy torgovle s Dzhungarskoy Bukhariey v XVIII stoletii"; *Chteniya v imperatorskom obschestve istorii i drevnostey Rossiyskikh pri Moskovskom universitete*, 2: 21–113 (April-June 1868).

Pound, Roscoe. "Toward a new jus gentium"; in F. S. C. Northrop, *Ideological Differences and World Order: Studies in the Philosophy and Science of the World's Cultures*. New Haven, 1949.

PSZ: Polnoye sobranie zakonov rossiyskoy imperii s 1649 goda. Ser. 1. 44 vols.; St. Petersburg, 1830.

PTLC: P'ing-ting Lo-ch'a fang-lüeh 平定羅刹方略 (The official account of the plans for the pacification of the Russians); in the *chüan-shou* section of the *Shuo-fang pei-sheng, chüan* 5–8.

Ravenstein, E. G. *The Russians on the Amur*. London, 1861.

Reischauer, Edwin O. and John K. Fairbank. *East Asia: The Great Tradition*. Boston, 1960.

Rinhuber, Laurent. *Relation du voyage en Russie*. Berlin, 1883.

Rowbotham, Arnold H. *Missionary and Mandarin: The Jesuits at the Court of China*. Berkeley, 1942.

Russian Year-book for 1912, The, ed. H. P. Kennard. New York, 1912.

Russko-Indiyskie otnosheniya v XVII v.: sbornik dokumentov. Moscow, 1958.

Russko-Kitayskie otnosheniya v XVII veke: materialy i dokumenty, 1608–1683, ed. L. I. Duman. Moscow, 1969.

Russko-Kitayskie otnosheniya, 1689–1916: ofitsialnye dokumenty, ed. L. I. Duman. Moscow, 1958.

Russko-Mongolskie otnosheniya, 1607–1636: sbornik dokumentov, ed. I. Ya. Zlatkin and N. V. Ustyugov. Moscow, 1959.

Sabir, C. de. *Le fleuver Amour*. Paris, 1861.

Schebenkov, V. G. *Russko-Kitayskie otnosheniya v XVII v*. Moscow, 1960.

Scolardi, Paulin-Gerard. *Krijanich, messager de l'unité des crétiens et père du panslavisme: au service de Rome et de Moscou au XVII siècle*. Paris, 1947.

Sebes, Joseph. *The Jesuits and the Sino-Russian Treaty of Nerchinsk (1689): The Diary of Thomas Pereira, S. J.* Rome, 1961.

Semivsky, N. *Noveyshie, lyubopytnye i dostovernye povestvovaniya o Vostochnoy Sibiri*. St. Petersburg, 1817.

Serebrennikov, I. I. *Albazintsy*. Peking, 1922.

SFPS: Shuo-fang pei-sheng 朔方備乘 (An historical source book of the northern regions), comp. Ho Ch'iu-t'ao 何秋濤. Compiled about 1860; published 1881.

Shastina, N. P. *Russko-Mongolskie posolskie otnosheniya XVII veka*. Moscow, 1958.

Shumakher, P. "Nashi snosheniya s Kitayem [s 1567 do 1805]"; *Russky arkhiv*, 6: 145–183 (1879).

Shunkov, V. I. *Ocherki po istorii kolonizatsii Sibiri v XVII—nachale XVIII v*. Moscow, 1946.

Shuo-fang pei-sheng, see *SFPS*.

Sibirskiya letopisi. St. Petersburg, 1907.

Silin, E. P. *Kyakhta v XVIII veke: iz istorii russko-kitayskoi torgovli*. Irkutsk, 1947.

SL: Ta-Ch'ing li-ch'ao shih-lu 大清歷朝實錄 (The veritable records of the Ch'ing dynasty). Mukden, 1938. The *Shih-lu* for Abahai's reign is properly entitled

Ta-Ch'ing T'ai-tsung Wen-huang-ti shih-lu 大清太宗文皇帝實錄. 65 *chüan*.
The *Shih-lu* for the Shun-chih reign is properly entitled *Ta-Ch'ing Shih-tsu Chang-huang-ti shih-lu* 大清世祖章皇帝實錄, 147 *chüan*. The *Shih-lu* for the K'ang-hsi reign is properly entitled *Ta-Ch'ing Sheng-tsu Jen-huang-ti shih-lu* 大清聖祖仁皇帝實錄, 303 *chüan*. The *Shih-lu* for the Yung-cheng reign is properly entitled *Ta-Ch'ing Shih-tsung Hsien-huang-ti shih-lu* 大清世宗憲皇帝實錄.

Sobranie gosudarstvennykh gramot i dogovoroy khranyaschikhsya v gosudarstvennoy kollegii inostrannykh del, ed. N. N. Bantysh-Kamensky, A. F. Malinovsky, et al. 5 vols.; 1813–1894.

Solovev, Sergey M. *Istoriya Rossii s drevneyshikh vremen*. 7 vols.; St. Petersburg, 1894–1895.

"So-lun chu-pu nei-shu shu-lüeh" 索倫諸部內屬述略 (A brief account of the subjugation of the Solun tribes); *chüan* 2 of *Shuo-fang pei-sheng*.

Son, H. J. A. van. *Autour de Krizanic: étude historique et linguistique*. N. p., 1934.

Spafary, N. G. *Opisanie pervye chasti vselennyya imenuyemoy Azii, v ney zhe sostoit Kitayskoe gosudarstvo s prochimi ego gorody i provintsii*, ed. F. T. Vasilev et al. Kazan, 1910.

Spiridonova, E. V. *Ekonomicheskaya politika i ekonomicheskie vzglyady Petra I*. Moscow, 1952.

Strahlenberg, P. J. *An Historico-Geographical Description of the North and Eastern Parts of Europe and Asia; But More Particularly, of Russia, Siberia, and Great Tartary*. London, 1738.

Ta-Ch'ing hui-tien, see K'ang-hsi, Yung-cheng, Ch'ien-lung, Chia-ch'ing for editions.

Ta-Ch'ing li-ch'ao shih-lu, see *SL*.

Ta-Ch'ing Man-chou shih-lu 大清滿州實錄 (The Manchu veritable records of the Great Ch'ing). Taipei, 1964.

Timkowski, George. *Travels of the Russian Mission through Mongolia to China, and Residence in Peking in the Years 1820–1821*. 2 vols.; London, 1827.

Titov, A. A., ed. *Sibir v XVII veke: sbornik starinnykh russkikh statey o Sibiri i prilezhaschikh k ney zemlyakh*. Moscow, 1890.

Treaties, Conventions, etc., between China and Foreign States, 2nd ed.; 2 vols.; Shanghai, 1917.

Trusevich, Kh. *Posolskiya i torgovyya snosheniya Rossii s Kitayem* (*do XIX v.*). Moscow, 1882.

Tulishen. *Narrative of the Chinese embassy to the Khan of the Tourgouth Tartars in the years 1712, 13, 14, & 15*, tr. George Thomas Staunton. London, 1831; reprinted 1939.

Tumansky, F. *Sobranie raznykh zapisok i sochineny, sluzhaschikh k dostavleniyu polnago svedeniya o zhizni i deyaniyakh gosudariya imperatora Petra Velikago*. St. Petersburg, 1787.

T'ung-chih ch'ao ch'ou-pan i-wu shih-mo 同治朝籌辦夷務始末 (The complete account of our management of barbarian affairs in the T'ung-chih period). 100 *chüan*; Peking, 1930.

Udintsev, S. *Vtoraya irbitskaya sovetskaya yarmarka*. Ekaterinberg, 1923.

Ulyanitsky, V. A. "Snosheniya Rossii s srednieu Azieyu i Indieyu v XVI–XVII vv."; *Chteniya v imperatorskom obschestve istorii i drevnostey rossiyskikh pri moskovskom universitete*, 3.2: 1–62 (July-September, 1888).

Ushakov, D. N. *Tolkovy slovar russkago yazyka*. 4 vols.; Moscow, 1940.

Vasilev, A. P. *Zabaykalskie kazaki*. 2 vols.; Chita, 1916.

Venyukov, M. *Ocherk starykh i novykh dogovorov Rossii s Kitayem*. St. Petersburg, 1861.

Verbiest, Ferdinand. *Correspondance de Ferdinand Veribest de la Compagnie de Jesus*, ed. H. Josson, S. J. and L. Willaert, S. J. Brussels, 1938.

Vernadsky, George. *The Mongols and Russia*. New Haven, 1953.

Veselovsky, N. I. "Posolstvo k zyungarskomu khun-taichzhi Tsevan Rabtanu kapitana ot artillerii Ivana Unkovskago i putevoy zhurnal ego za 1722–1724 godu: dokumenty, izdannye s predisloviem i primechaniami"; *Zapiski imperatorskago russkago geograficheskago obschestva*, Vol. 10, Pt. 2 (1887).

Vilkov, O. N. "Kitayskie tovary na Tobolskom rynke v XVII v." *Istoriya SSSR*, 1: 105–124 (January–February 1958).

Vladimir (Zenone Volpicelli). *Russia on the Pacific and the Siberian Railway*. London, 1889.

Wang Chih-hsiang 王之相 and Liu Che-jung 劉澤榮. *Ku-kung O-wen shih-liao* 故宮俄文史料 (Documents in Russian, preserved in the National Palace Museum of Peiping). Peking, 1936.

Weber, Friedrich Christian. *The Present State of Russia*. 2 vols.; London, 1722.

Wu Chen-ch'en 吳振臣. *Ning-ku-t'a chi-lüeh* 寧古塔紀略 (A brief account of Ninguta); in Cheng Kuang-tsu 鄭光祖, *Chou-ch'e so-chih* 舟車所至, *ts'e* 1.

"Ya-k'o-sa-ch'eng k'ao" 雅克薩城考, in *Shuo-fang pei-sheng*, *chüan* 14.

Yakovleva, Praskovia Tikhonovna. *Pervy russko-kitaysky dogovor 1689 goda*. Moscow, 1958.

Yang Pin 楊琳. "Liu-pien chi-lüeh" 柳邊記略 (A short account of the region beyond the Willow Frontier). 5 *chüan;* in Chin Yü-fu, *Liao-hai ts'ung-shu*, Collection I, *ts'e* 8.

Yung-cheng hui-tien: Ta-Ch'ing hui-tien 雍正會典：大清會典 (Collected statutes of the Ch'ing dynasty, of the Yung-cheng period). 250 *chüan;* 1733.

Yü Cheng-hsieh 俞正燮. *Kuei-ssu ts'un-kao* 癸巳存稿 (Personal drafts of the year Kuei-ssu [thirteenth year of Tao-kuang, 1833]). 15 *chüan;* 1848.

———. *Kuei-ssu lei-kao* 癸巳類稿 (Miscellaneous articles of the year Kuei-ssu [thirteenth year of Tao-kuang 1833]). Shanghai, 1957.

ZhMNP: *Zhurnal Ministerstva narodnago prosvescheniya*.

Zhurnal Ministerstva narodnago Prosvescheniya, see ZhMNP.

Zlatkin, I. Ya. *Istoriya dzhungarskogo khanstva* (*1635–1758*). Moscow, 1964.

———. and N. V. Ustyugov, eds. *Russko-Mongolskie otnosheniya, 1607–1636: sbornik dokumentov*. Moscow, 1959.

Glossary

A-erh-ni 阿爾尼
A-erh-pa-hsi 阿爾巴西
Aigun 愛琿
A-la-ni 阿喇尼
A-mu-hu-lang 阿穆瑚瑯
Ayuki [A-yü-ch'i] 阿玉奇

Bahai [Pa-hai] 巴海
Bandarša [Pan-ta-erh-sha] 班達爾沙

Chabina [Ch'a-pi-na] 察畢那
Ch'a-han han 察罕汗
Chang P'eng-ko 張鵬翮
Chang Yü-shu 張玉書
Chao-tai ts'ung-shu 昭代叢書
Cheng Ch-eng-kung [Koxinga] 鄭成功
Ch'eng-ch'ing-fang-ta-chieh 澄清坊大街
Ch'en Shih-an 陳世安
chiang-chün 將軍
Ch'ien-lung 乾隆
chien-tu 監督
ch'ih 尺
Ch'in 秦
chin 斤
Ch'ing 清
ch'ing-ch'e-tu-yu 輕車都尉
chu-chiao 助教
Chü-liu 巨流

Dahur 達呼爾

E-erh-sa 額爾塞
E-lo-ch'un 俄樂春
E-su-li 額蘇哩

Fei-yao-to-lo-e-li-k'e-hsieh 費要多羅額禮克謝
Fo-pao 佛保
fu-chiao-hsi 副教習
Fu-ch'üan 福全
fu-li-shih-kuan 副理事官
fu-tu-t'ung 副都統

Gantimur [Ken-t'e-mu] 根特木

Haise [Hai-se] 海色
Hei-lung-chiang 黑龍江
Ho-ch'ing 赫慶
Ho Yu 何佑(祐)
hsi-kua-p'ao 西瓜砲
Hsi-po-kua-erh-ch'a 錫伯瓜爾察
Hsi-po-wu-la 錫伯烏拉
Hsi-t'e-k'u 席特庫
Hsin Man-chou 新滿州
Hsing-pu 刑部
hu-chün-t'ung-ling 護軍統領
Hu-pu 戶部
huang-ti 皇帝
Hui-t'ung-kuan 會同館

I-ch'ang-a 宜昌阿
I-cheng-wang 議政王

I-fan [Ivan] 伊番
I-tun-men 伊屯門

Ka-erh-t'u 噶爾圖
K'ang-hsi 康熙
kuan-chuang 官庄
Kuan-pao 關保
kuan-tun 官屯
Ku-fa-t'an 古法壇
kung 貢
Kuo-p'i 果丕
Kyakhta [Ch'ia-k'o-t'u] 恰克圖

lang-chung 郎中
Langtan 郎坦
Lao-ch'iang 老羌
Ledehun 勒德洪
Li-fan yuan 理藩院
Li-k'e-ting-ko 立克頂格
Li-pu 禮部
liang 兩
Liao (river) 遼
Lo-ch'a 羅刹
Lo-ch'a-miao 羅刹廟
Lo-ch'e 羅車
Lungkodo 隆科多

Maci 馬齊
Maimaichen [Mai-mai-ch'eng] 買賣城
Mala 瑪喇
Man-p'i 滿丕
Mao-ming-an 茂明安
Meng-ku-hsi-po 蒙古錫伯
Ming 明
Ming-ai 明愛
Minggadari [Ming-an-ta-li] 明安達禮
Mi-ti-li [Dmitri] 米提理
Mo-erh-hun 漠爾渾
Mo-le-ken 墨勒根

Nan hui-t'ang 南會堂
Nayentai 納延泰
Nei-fu 內府
Nei-ko 內閣
Nei-ko O-lo-ssu wen-kuan 內閣俄羅斯文館
nei-ta-ch'en 內大臣
Ni-kuo-lai [Nikolay Milescu] 尼果賴
Ninguta 甯古塔
Ni-p'u-ch'u [Nerchinsk] 尼布楚
Niu-man (river) 牛滿
Nun-chiang 嫩江

O-lo-ssu [Russia] 俄羅斯
O-lo-ssu hsüeh 俄羅斯學
O-lo-ssu nan kuan 俄羅斯南館
O-lo-ssu pei kuan 俄羅斯北館
O-lo-ssu wen kuan 俄羅斯文館

Pei-ch'ih chieh 北池街
Pei hui-t'ang 北會堂
Pei-le-erh 倍勒兒
Pengcun [P'eng-ch'un] 朋春
piao 表
P'ing-ting Lo-ch'a fang-lüeh 平定羅刹方略
pi-t'ieh-shih 筆帖式

Sabsu [Sa-pu-su] 薩布素
Sahai [Sa-hai] 薩海
Sarhuda [Sha-erh-hu-ta] 沙爾虎達
Shang-ssu yuan 上駟院
Sheng-ching 盛京
shih 石
shih-lang 侍郎
shih-wei 侍衛
Shun-chih 順治
Solun 索倫
Songgotu 索額圖
Sung-hua (river) 松花

T'e-ku-t'e 特古忑
Teng-szu-tun 等色屯
t'ien-tzu 天子
t'i-t'iao 提調
ts'an-ling 參領
ts'an-tsan 參贊
Tsereng 策棱
Tsung-li O-lo-ssu shih-wu 總理俄羅斯事務

Tulishen 圖理琛
Tushetu-khan 土謝圖汗
tun-chuang 屯莊
Tung Chiang-mi hsiang 東江米巷
Tung Chiao-min hsiang 東交民巷
Tung-hua-men 東華門
T'ung Kuo-kang 佟國綱
T'ung Kuo-wei 佟國維
T'ung-pao 佟寶
T'ung-wen kuan 同文館
tu-t'ung 都統

Wa-li-hu 瓦里虎
Wasan 瓦山(三)

Wen Ta 文達
Wu-cha-la 烏札拉
Wu-chu-mu-ch'ing 烏朱穆秦
Wu-la 烏喇
Wu San-kuei 吳三桂

Ya-k'e-sa [Albazin] 雅克薩
Yin-ssu 胤禩
Yin-t'ang 胤禟
Yin-t'i 胤禵
Yuan 元
Yung-cheng 雍正
yü-shih 御史
yu-shih-lang 右侍郎

Index